IDOLIZED

IDOLIZED

MUSIC,
MEDIA,
AND
IDENTITY IN
AMERICAN IDOL

KATHERINE MEIZEL

INDIANA UNIVERSITY PRESS

Bloomington & Indianapolis

This book is a publication of

Indiana University Press
601 North Morton Street
Bloomington, IN 47404-3797 USA

www.iupress.indiana.edu

Telephone orders   800-842-6796
Fax orders   812-855-7931
Orders by e-mail   iuporder@indiana.edu

∞The paper used in this publication
meets the minimum requirements of
the American National Standard for
Information Sciences—Permanence
of Paper for Printed Library Materials,
ANSI Z39.48-1992.

Manufactured in the United States of
America

Library of Congress Cataloging-in-
Publication Data

Meizel, Katherine.
  Idolized : music, media, and identity
in American idol / Katherine Meizel.
    p. cm.
  Includes bibliographical references
and index.
  ISBN 978-0-253-35571-3 (cl : alk.
paper) — ISBN 978-0-253-22271-8
(pb : alk. paper) 1. American idol
(Television program) 2. Popular
music—Competitions—United
States. 3. Music—Social aspects—
United States. 4. Music and television.
5. Popular culture—United States.
I. Title.
  ML76.A54M45 2010
  791.45'72—dc22

                                    2010034622

1 2 3 4 5 16 15 14 13 12 11

This book is lovingly dedicated to my family:
Janet and Stanley Meizel
and
Laura, Marc, and Sadie Reeve.

"My political ideal is that of democracy.
Let every man be respected as an
individual and no man idolized."

ALBERT EINSTEIN,
The World As I See It

"Every one of us is, even from
his mother's womb, a master
craftsman of idols."

JOHN CALVIN

CONTENTS

ACKNOWLEDGMENTS

Writing this document, I have been constantly aware of just how much I owe to others. My work for this project was inspired, encouraged, supported, and shaped by my friends, colleagues, and advisers, and I am truly grateful to all of them.

To my advisers at the University of California, Santa Barbara (UCSB)—Timothy Cooley, Jon Cruz, Sonia Seeman, and Scott Marcus—I extend my sincerest thanks for the mentorship, guidance, and unwavering encouragement that helped me to shape the early stages of this book. I do not have the words to say how deeply I appreciate their generosity of time, and their knowledge, kindness, and respect; I can only offer them my eternal gratitude. Cornelia Fales, who left UCSB just after I began this study, was also an invaluable source of advice and support in its infancy, and I am very grateful to her as well. Special acknowledgments to Stewart Hoover, Lynn Schofield-Clark, and Rhys Williams, who, in conjunction with a grant from the Media, Religion, and Culture project at the University of Colorado, Boulder, greatly influenced my research into the relationship of popular music to sacral and civil religion.

I am profoundly indebted to those who participated in my research. I was particularly fortunate to have opportunities to interview *American Idol*'s associate music director, Michael Orland, and vocal coach, Debra Byrd. They generously spent much time talking with me, and not only provided me with inestimably important information but also showed me that those who work behind the *Idol* scenes are extraordinary musicians who love their jobs and the vision of the show, and do much to contribute to its indefinably genuine character. Thanks also to Byrd's publicist, Deborah Mellman, at Lip Service PR, for so kindly helping to arrange our interview. I was privileged to speak with *Idol* celebrity William Hung, and with former contestants Charly Lowry and Bao Viet Nguyen, whose detailed descriptions of their *Idol* experiences were central to my research. I am extremely grateful to them, and it was an absolute joy to talk with all three. Thanks also to Henry Hung, William's father and agent. Several other wonderful young singers were instrumental to my project, including Gisela (Kati) Roberts and Rhiannon Giddens, with whom I attended my first *Idol* auditions; then UCSB students Celina Lima, Matthew Maimoni, and Alexandra Rajaofera, with whom I attended further auditions; and Rocío Torres and Grover Anderson, who also recounted their experiences for me. At the 2004 auditions in San Francisco I coincidentally encountered Branden James, with whom I had attended the San Francisco Conservatory of Music some years before, and he was also kind enough to talk with me about his *Idol* audition. Standing in line at *Idol* auditions and dress rehearsals, I was also pleased to meet and talk with Aleks Will; *Idol* hopeful Jessika Murphy and her supporters, Andrew, TJ, and Glenna Marie; and later April DuPlantier, Christopher Allen, the Riccios, Pritesh Shah, and Dalak Kotnari, and many others, including the dozens who completed my surveys. My project additionally owes much to fans who posted on the *American Idol* electronic message board, and to the forum moderator, who answered my questions. Thanks also to Chris Rainey, Vice President of Marketing at the Christian apparel company Kerusso, and to Allie Vered, who generously sent me a copy of her article about Elliott Yamin in the *Virginia Jewish News*. For their help and hospitality at the Village Idiot in Maumee, many thanks to Nikki and John Schafer, Nathan Woodward, Ed Lopez, and Jason and Jodi Szczublewski, and for her interview at Bowerstock, Shelley Crossley of the Juvenile Diabetes Research Foundation.

Additional gratitude goes to other *Idol* scholars who have shared their work with me, including Matthew Stahl, who also provided brilliant suggestions as a reader for my manuscript, Andrea Warren, Aswin Punathambekar, and Samuel van Straaten. And for his perceptive and sensitive reading of my manuscript, I extend many thanks to Chris McDonald as well. I thank Jane Behnken and the editors at Indiana University Press for their faith in this project and for their help in bringing it to fruition.

My interest in *American Idol* was first piqued by an editorial that Jody Rosen published in the *New York Times* in 2003. I thank him sincerely for that essential inspiration, and for the many kindnesses he has shown me since then. Additional thanks to Jody, Michael Agger, and the folks at *Slate* for the invaluable opportunity to work out my ideas without using words like "postmodern" and "teleological." That connection came about through my participation in the always dazzling Pop Conference, and I also thank Eric Weisbard, Ann Powers, and all involved for the annual infusion of pop passion. I owe gratitude to Revell Carr, who brought Jody's editorial to my attention, and who took the time to document Jasmine Trias's Honolulu visit and to tape local television programs for me, all while conducting his own dissertation research in Hawai'i. He and many other colleagues have been immeasurably important to me as friends, role models, editors, critics, and teachers. They have also kept a weather eye out for information, called me and e-mailed me when they encountered *American Idol*–related topics in the media, given me newspaper clippings, and even brought me recordings from other shows in the *Idols* franchise, from the countries of their own fieldwork. Special thanks to my colleagues at Bowling Green State University, Jeremy Wallach and Esther Clinton, for their invaluable experience and input in the later phases of the book, and again to them and to David Harnish, Mary Natvig, Eftychia Papanikolaou, Joshua Duchan, and Amanda Villepastour for listening to me talk about *Idol* endlessly. And nothing would have been possible without my California compatriots, including Sonja Downing, Kara Attrep, Rob Wallace, Amy Cyr, Matthew Dorman, Eric Ederer, Elizabeth Freudenthal, Denise Gill, Mina Girgis, Lillie Gordon, Ken Habib, Max Katz, Alan Kirk, Temmo Korisheli, Karen Liu, Ralph Lowi, Anthony McCann, Eve McPherson, Justin Scarimbolo, Gibb Schreffler, Barbara Taylor, Masen Uliss, and ethnomusicologist Juan Zaragoza, who offered me his insight into the success of *Idol* contestant and former fellow postal worker Vonzell Solomon. Further thanks to Rev, Kara, and Sonja for being my early *Idol* companions in front of the television and at dress rehearsals in Los Angeles. Finally, many thanks to my dear friends, my Girls— Nichole Dechaine, Charlene Chi, Cara Iverson, and Christine Hollinger—whose beautiful voices continue to be my voices of reason.

IDOLIZED

INTRODUCTION · NO BOUNDARIES

On May 20, 2009, Kris Allen took his musical victory lap on the stage of the Nokia Theater in Los Angeles. Clutching his microphone like the trophy he had just won, he proclaimed his triumphant message: "There are no boundaries," he sang, over and over, "there are no boundaries." The song itself—Allen's acceptance address as the eighth winner of the televised singing competition *American Idol*—was heavily criticized in the press, not least for its lyrical clichés. But the refrain embodies something more than a sentimental celebration of achievement. Instead, it articulates a crucial and persistent feature of postmodern discourse. Since Fredric Jameson observed a complicated postmodernism in part characterized by "the effacement of some key boundaries and separations," wall after discursive wall has grown transparent and permeable. Still, many remain standing. A recurrent trope of Lévi-Strauss's work theorized that cultural codes are reified through the imagination of their transgression—any movement across a line signifies as much avowal as contravention, and the crossing of boundaries always at once attenuates their power and reminds us they are there.[1]

American Idol capitalizes upon this kind of paradoxical mapping, working with a cartography of geographical, cultural, and ideological boundaries that blur toward dialecticism while at the same time supporting the clear delineation of contemporary American identities. The barriers have slipped that formerly held apart production and consumption, performer and audience, public and private, reified musical genres, even politics and entertainment. The simultaneous reinforcement and collapse of divisions that marks turn-of-the-millennium popular culture becomes part of *American Idol*'s marketing strategy, resulting in a wider audience, more profitable advertising spots, and impressive revenue. But it also contributes to the equation of identity with brand, and to the imagination of the U.S. itself at a historical moment when Americans are struggling with identity on multiple levels—being *American* in an ever more identity-conscious nation, and being *America* in a global context with its own blurring borders, that increasingly relies upon transnational economic, political, social, and cultural structures.

This concurrent erasure and drawing of boundaries also relates to a fundamental tension in *American Idol,* and in current national politics at large, between multiculturalist and assimilationist understandings of American identity. The reality-show diversity among contestants, reflecting the demographics necessary to draw a massive audience, at once supports the multiculturalist tenet that the maintenance of discrete ethnic identity is essential to the American citizen's well-being[2] and the older, conflicting belief that cultural assimilation (the "melting pot" model introduced by Israel Zangwill in the early twentieth century) is a required step on the road to the American Dream, everyone singing the same songs along the way. The fraught continuum between the postmodern celebration of difference and the deeply ingrained impulse toward nationalized identity complements another set of competing/interdependent American values: individualism and community. On *American Idol,* where viewers vote to determine a new pop star, a contestant is a candidate for election, and the successful singer typically performs both a clear individual identity and some kind of familiar ethnic, racial, religious, or regional identity, and demonstrates a relationship with larger narratives of Americanness.

With its audience vote, *American Idol* narrows the psychological distance between electoral politics and pop culture politics. It reflects and factors in the accelerated overlap of these spheres, at a time when presidential candidates are vetted on comedy talk shows and every online opinion poll is called "voting." *American Idol* both is and is not like an election. It represents the pinnacle of consumer choice camouflaged in the familiar trappings of democratic process. Its interactively engaged audience, with universal suffrage in the U.S., is offered a compelling sense of agency, both in the narrative of the televised program and in the selection of the end product. The votes of *Idol* fans influence the way each broadcast season plays out, and viewers may also be transformed into performers themselves through the nationwide open-audition process. Producers, performers, and the audience all fulfill triple duties: collaboratively manipulating the narrative of the show, maintaining a presence on camera, and watching each season unfold. Together they weave a traditional set of American identities, reiterated through music and image and rhetoric.

Culture in the United States is created in the continuous negotiation and renegotiation of these identities—of personal, community, and national identities, informed by ideas about race and ethnicity, religion, place, gender, and what it means to be American. "Our America is an identity culture," observes the University of Chicago's Bill Brown, "definable not by *an* identity but by the fixation *on* identity." There are, however, no fixed qualities or criteria of Americanness, of American identity. As Akhil Gupta and James Ferguson write, although studies of "Americans" and "American culture" often rely upon a set of "ethnological and . . . national naturalisms" that presume as given certain kinds of relationships between people and place, such relationships are always "in fact contested, uncertain, and in flux." The dynamic nature of American identity construction is reflected and reinforced in popular culture, through a network of visual and aural cues that call on the historical past to express the experiences of the cultural present.[3]

Popular music is a key source of these identity markers, which help to shape understandings of Americanness. "I Hear America Singing," Walt Whitman wrote in 1860, and as Josh Kun argues in his 2005 book, *Audiotopia*, Whitman's poem suggests a kind of aural nationalism, in which the acts of performing and listening to the "sounds Americans make" are part of the construction of national identity. The words imply, Kun suggests, that "political and cultural citizenship is configured through the performance of popular music and its reception, via acts of listening, by the people."[4] This book examines the relationship between such acts of performance and acts of listening in relation to *American Idol*.

While *American Idol* purposely clouds some kinds of identity for the sake of marketing, others are carefully constructed and outlined for similar reasons. As Henry Jenkins points out, *American Idol* walks a fine line between representation and exploitation, offering Americans a chance to see themselves (literally or figuratively) on television but at the same time supporting a reduced, commodified, and easily saleable account of their identities. Identity, however, is not all about maintaining boundaries and borders—national or otherwise—but rather involves complex networks of relational interaction, and is, as Sara Cohen describes it, "always in the process of being achieved, negotiated, invented, symbolised, of becoming." The interactive structure of the program makes it a site, or constellation of sites, in which the negotiation of American identities is played out in a number of strategic ways.[5]

AMERICAN IDOL AND THE IDOLS FORMAT

American Idol debuted, as *American Idol: The Search for a Superstar*, on June 11, 2002, on the FOX Network. Its premiere advanced the 2001 success of the hit British reality series *Pop Idol*, and since its introduction the *Idols*[6] franchise has grown to include forty programs past and present, worldwide. Each version of *Idols* around the globe follows the same format: a viewership delimited by national or regional borders votes to (s)elect a new singing sensation. Singers compete to win a recording contract and the "Idol" title, narrowed down over the broadcast weeks from initial open auditions across a nation, region, or even diaspora.

For each of the recent seasons of *American Idol*, around 100,000 have attended those first cattle-call auditions in selected U.S. cities.[7] Producers screen these thousands, and at every audition location a few hundred are selected to sing for a second group of producers. Next, a smaller group of those fortunate singers perform before the panel of three judges who appear on the broadcast show. The numbers sent on from this round to California vary each season—120 in Season 1, 240 in Season 2, 117 in Season 3, 193 in Season 4, 175 in Season 5, 172 in Season 6, 164 in Season 7, 147 in Season 8, and 181 in Season 9. They travel to Hollywood (or Pasadena, where some of the next rounds have taken place), where they audition again alone, then in small groups, and then alone once more. The initial Hollywood numbers are narrowed down several times, until a set of semifinalists[8] (30 in Season 1, 32 in Seasons 2 and 3, 24 thereafter until Season 8, when there were 36, and 24 again in Season 9) is chosen by the judges and producers. Approximately a dozen finalists (the number was 10 in Season 1 and 13 in Season 8) are selected by the voting audience, from among semifinalists presented as soloists performing in sets of 10 (Season 1), 8 (Seasons 2 and 3), or 12 (Seasons 4, 5, 6, 7, 8, and 9) per episode. In Season 1 producers and judges contributed the tenth finalist in a "wild-card" round, which brought back five singers who had been cut in the previous rounds.[9] The following two seasons held wild-card rounds for the last four places in the finalists' roster; the judges selected three and the voting audience selected one. After 2004 the wild-card round did not appear again until Season 8, when the judges were responsible for choosing all four from a set of eight candidates.

The viewing audience at large sees only certain edited footage from the early Hollywood rounds, and the live (Eastern Time) broadcasts only begin with the semifinals, as do the live audience and the voting process. From Season 4 through Season 7, the finalists were divided equally by gender;[10] in Season 8 there were eight men and five women, but Season 9 returned to the equal division. Sometimes the semifinal performances are also segregated by gender; in Season 8, in every semifinal round, the top male and female voice advanced to the finals, as did whichever contestant had the third-highest number of votes. In Season 9, two men and two women were eliminated after every vote until the 24 had been reduced to 12. All this takes place over eighteen or nineteen weeks from January through May, with the exception of the first season's shorter span of thirteen summer weeks.

Singers perform live before a studio audience, accompanied in the semifinals and finals by a house band (since 2005), and are critiqued by a panel of judges. The panel has most famously comprised Simon

Cowell, a recording executive; Randy Jackson, an A&R executive, music director, and bass player known for his work with Journey and Mariah Carey; and Paula Abdul, a pop star/choreographer whose career as a solo artist peaked in the late 1980s and early 1990s. The 2009 season added a fourth judge, singer-songwriter and producer Kara DioGuardi, and in 2010 comedienne Ellen DeGeneres joined the panel after Paula Abdul announced her departure. During the completion of this volume, Simon Cowell also declared his intentions to leave after Season 9, in order to produce a U.S. version of his U.K.-based format *The X Factor*. Although Season 7 mostly eschewed them, other seasons have offered a series of guest judges or coaches as well—usually important figures in the history of American popular music from the 1960s on—such as the songwriting team Ashford and Simpson of Motown or singers like Gladys Knight and Diana Ross. Occasionally someone outside the music industry has filled this role, as film director Quentin Tarantino did in Seasons 3 and 8. Well-known artists have also appeared as mentors and performers.

At least two broadcasts are televised each week, and during some semifinal rounds there have been three, in order to fit in a male-performance episode, a female-performance episode, and a "results" episode. Other extra episodes throughout the season have included retrospectives, compilations of the previously aired audition broadcasts, or special events. Once the finalists are chosen, an *Idol* viewing week typically includes a Tuesday episode in which each singer performs for the judges and for "America," and a Wednesday episode featuring a group performance, a musical Ford commercial filmed and recorded with the finalists, and the results of Tuesday night's audience vote.

Viewers vote by dialing designated numbers on home phones or cell phones, or by text messaging through their unlimited plans with AT&T (at first called AT&T Wireless, later branded "Cingular Wireless," then re-branded "AT&T Mobility").[11] An unlimited number of votes may be placed, although the use of enhanced technology that allows an individual to produce thousands of votes at a time is not permitted. Until 2007 the show's popularity grew steadily for a few years, from its weekly average of 9.8 million viewers for the premiere of Season 1 to a peak of 37.3 million viewers for the premiere episode of Season 6.[12] Telescope Creative Interactive Solutions, the company that manages *American Idol* voting, reported that a total of 110 million votes were placed throughout the first season, and those numbers have risen steadily so that during the eighth season's finale, host Ryan Seacrest announced the totals for 2009 at approximately 624 million votes.[13] In just the final week of the first season, the 15 million votes logged made Kelly Clarkson the winner; for the final week of the eighth season, "just under 100 million" votes were counted (see Table 0.1).[14]

A drop to 33 million viewers for the premiere of Season 7 attracted a great deal of press attention, as well as many subsequent predictions of the show's imminent demise. But however great the decline in season-premiere viewership may seem, *American Idol* still won the ratings for that night and continued to overshadow all other network programming through its next season.[15] A few million viewers have not yet made a life-or-death difference to *American Idol*—still consistently at the top of the ratings as I finish this volume—and the decrease in those numbers has been offset by the increased activity of the mass of viewers remaining, measured in votes placed and by the increasing advertising revenue the show takes in.[16] Further, more than 49 million Google hits as of October 2010 (up from 28 million at the end of 2008, and in the off-season to boot) indicate that I am not the only one talking about *American Idol* all the time. Its name is on the lips, not to mention the televisions, computer screens, cellular phones, and front pages of millions of Americans, and it has played to more than half the countries in the world.

That sustained popularity is based on more than just clever financing. The *Idols* franchise has created a set of studio stages across the world, a set of forums where politics of national, regional, ethnic, and religious identities are performed. And when a riot breaks out in the Middle East over an *Idol* show, when violence erupts between Nepalese and Bengali locals over the results of *Indian Idol,* or when the U.S. military adapts the format for a psy-ops effort in Mosul, it is clear that this *Idol* business is deadly serious.[17] The narrative of each show in each of its regional variants represents real life, and real politics, renegotiated in song.

Within the global array of more than forty *Idols* programs, *American Idol* is one of only a handful whose titles specify place, identify-

Table 1. Viewing and Voting Statistics

| Sources: | Season 1 (June 11–September 4, 2002) |

Sources:

(a) Telescope Creative Interactive Solutions 2003a

(b) Telescope Creative Interactive Solutions 2003b

(c) Nielsen Media Research 2003b

(d) Nielsen Media Research 2003a

(e) Nielsen Media Research 2005

(f) Telescope Creative Interactive Solutions 2004

(g) Telescope Creative Interactive Solutions 2006

(h) Gough 2007

(i) de Moraes 2005a

(j) MSNBC.com 2005

(k) La Monica 2006a

(l) La Monica 2006b

(m) *American Idol*, FOX Network, May 25, 2005

(n) RTL Group 2006

(o) MSNBC.com 2006b

(p) Today at MSNBC.com 2007

Season 1 (June 11–September 4, 2002)

- Viewers avg. for premiere: 9.8 million (e)
- Viewers weekly avg.: > 12.6 million (c)
- Viewers avg. for finale: > 23 million (c)
- Votes during final week: 15.5 million (a)
- Total votes during season: 110 million (a)

Season 2 (January 21–May 21, 2003)

- Viewers avg. for premiere: 26.5 million (e)
- Viewers weekly Tues. avg.: 21.6 million (e)
- Viewers weekly Wed. avg.: 21.9 million (e)
- Viewers avg. for finale: > 38 million (e)
- Votes during final week: 24 million (b)
- Total votes during season: 240 million (b)

Season 3 (January 19–May 26, 2004)

- Viewers avg. for premiere: 28.6 million (e)
- Viewers weekly Tues. avg.: 25.7 million (e)
- Viewers weekly Wed. avg.: 24.3 million (e)
- Viewers avg. for finale: 28.8 million (e)
- Votes during final week: 65 million (f)
- Total votes during season: 360 million (f)

Season 4 (January 18–May 25, 2005)

- Viewers avg. for premiere: 33.6 million (i)
- Viewers weekly Tues. avg.: 27.3 million (j)
- Viewers weekly Wed. avg.: 25 million (k, l)
- Viewers avg. for finale: 29.4 million (j)
- Votes during final week: n/a
- Total votes during season: 500 million (m,n)

Season 5 (January 17–May 24, 2006)

- Viewers avg. for premiere: 35.5 million (n)
- Viewers weekly Tues. avg.: 31.3 million (k)
- Viewers weekly Wed. avg.: 29.4 million (k)
- Viewers avg. for finale: 35.4 million (o)
- Votes during final week: 63.5 million (g)
- Total votes during season: 580 million (g)

Table 1. Viewing and Voting Statistics (*cont.*)

	Season 6 (January 16–May 23, 2007)
(q) *American Idol,* FOX Network, May 23, 2007	· Viewers avg. for premiere: 37.3 million (h)
	· Viewers avg. for finale: 29.5 million (p)
(r) Nielsen 2008	· Votes during final week: 74 million (q)
	· Total votes during season: > 609 million (q)
(s) CNN.com 2008	
	Season 7 (January 15, 2008–May 21, 2008)
(t) *American Idol,* FOX Network, May 21, 2008	· Viewers avg. for premiere: 33 million (r)
	· Viewers avg. for finale: 31.7 million (s)
	· Votes during final week: 97.5 million (t)
(u) Collins 2009	· Total votes during season: n/a
	Season 8 (January 13, 2009–May 20, 2009)
(v) Ryan 2009	· Viewers avg. for premiere: 30.1 million (u)
	· Viewers avg. for finale: 28.84 million (v)
(w) *American Idol,* FOX Network, May 20, 2009	· Votes during final week: "just under" 100 million (w)
(x) Toff and Itzkoff 2010	· Total votes during season: 624 million (w)
(y) Steller 2010	
	Season 9 (January 12, 2010–May 26, 2010)
	· Viewers avg. for premiere: 29.8 million (x)
	· Viewers avg. for finale: 24.2 million (y)

ing the nation where a show is filmed. In this way its very brand name offers a declaration that *American Idol,* while part of an increasingly transnationalized popular culture, is designed and constructed as explicitly American. The show reflects a range of socioculturally significant concerns at this critical point in the nation's history. In the wake of September 11, 2001, and the subsequent conflicts in Afghanistan and Iraq, interest in the redefinition and reaffirmation of American culture has been very much at the forefront of public attention. This is not to say that such concerns did not exist prior to the events of 9/11—the matters at stake are rooted in historically familiar anxieties about faith, patriotism, the future and nature of democracy, narratives of the "American Dream," and even about consumer choice.

Still, *American Idol,* born nine months to the day after 9/11, offers a microcosmic arena where discourses of American music and correlating, intertwined narratives of American identity are belted into a microphone and judged by millions. It is my hope that this book will support the fast-accelerating ethnomusicological interest in mainstream commercial music, and the understanding that mainstream pop music in the U.S. can be as exquisitely meaningful as any other ethnomusicological object.

RESEARCH METHODOLOGY: MAPPING THE *IDOL* FIELD

The sounds Americans make sound and re-sound across a constellation of sites.[18] *American Idol* and its identity politics play out across multiple places and in multiple spaces—onstage, onscreen, online, and in line waiting for *Idol* events. The show's omnipresence in American culture and its interactive structure demand a special methodology when it comes to ethnomusicological research. In 1995 George E. Marcus described a developing, interdisciplinary ethnography that replaced location-restrictive, in-depth study with a multisite approach. Marcus observed that this kind of approach was especially appropriate for objects of study that must be investigated "in diffuse time-space," particularly those involving identities and cultural meanings (Marcus 1995:96). As a mediated cultural product, *American Idol* itself inhabits such an insubstantive realm, and is inscribed with ideologies and identities generated beyond geographically mappable places, in televisual signals and across cyber-spaces. Multisite research is also, as Christine Hine writes, less suitable for the examination of an entire way of life than for learning about people as they live specific *aspects* of that life—for example, how they live as television viewers or music consumers.[19]

American Idol is a transnational phenomenon. It is also an American phenomenon and, telescoped further, a localized phenomenon in places across the U.S. Finally, it represents a spatially dispersed technological experience, sounded through ringing mobile phones and hypertextual gossip at the internet's abundant cyber-watercoolers. A research object like *American Idol,* extending across physical and virtual space, offers an imprecisely defined field for ethnographic study. But as Timothy Rice has written about locating fieldwork in general, "there is no field there; the field is the metaphorical creation of the researcher."[20]

The field I have created, then, takes into account *American Idol*'s polylocal and multisite structure, and my research was necessarily conducted in several different ways. Because of the exceptionally cross-mediated nature of the *American Idol* enterprise, and the discourse surrounding it, research in this project required not only ethnographic research but also the study of multiple *Idol* texts. The five main components of research material included: (1) ethnographic research conducted through interviews and participant observation; (2) analysis of televised *American Idol* footage; (3) commercial recordings affiliated with the show and its contestants; (4) critical discourse in print and online periodicals, regarding the show and its performance styles; and (5) internet literature officially associated with the show, including FOX's website and its message board.

Born of the postmodern role of anthropological methodologies in other humanistic disciplines, including media studies and cultural studies, multisite ethnographic research is "designed around chains, paths, threads, conjunctions, or juxtapositions of locations in which the ethnographer establishes some form of literal, physical presence."[21] For the present volume, this form of presence involved my attendance of auditions and public rehearsals for the broadcast show, and at an "Idols Live" tour concert in Anaheim in 2004. I had the opportunity to accompany several acquaintances to the open auditions in San Francisco for Seasons 4 and 5, where, although my age exceeded the limit for performers, I was allowed, according to the official rules, to be a member of the large crowd and participate in all activities other than the actual audition. These I was able to observe from the stands, at San Francisco's Cow Palace stadium. The first time I attended the auditions, I went with two young women whose studies in vocal performance at my undergraduate institution had overlapped with my own, and one of them had also attended the conservatory where I received a graduate degree. At the Cow Palace we were surprised to meet several undergraduate students from the University of California, Santa Barbara (UCSB) and, also unexpectedly, another alumnus of my graduate conservatory. I attended the Season 5 auditions with one of my own former singing students, later a voice major at another California university, and, by chance, we met one of the same undergraduate students with whom we had sat the

FIGURE 0.1. Long line outside the Cow Palace just after dawn, August 17, 2005. *All photographs by author.*

previous year. These singers were all invaluable consultants for this book. While waiting in line before the 2004 auditions, I also collected survey data from the young men and women who planned to audition. Both years my consultants and I arrived at the Cow Palace in the wee hours of the morning before auditions began (Figure 0.1)—before 2 AM in 2004 and around 5 AM in 2005—as my first experience had taught me that camping out all night in the parking lot did little to guarantee any particular order when the lineup began. These hours spent among the thousands huddled under blankets and in camping chairs (and later the hours waiting in our stadium seats) allowed me prime opportunity to hear the enthusiastic warming up and group sing-a-longs, to conduct my survey up and down the rows of those who seemed awake, and to talk with many around me, both those auditioning and those who came to support them.

Similarly, time spent waiting in additional lines—a sign of *American Idol*'s location firmly within consumer culture—at show rehearsals later in the season provided occasions to interview fans. I placed my name on the eternally long waiting list (a *virtual* line) to attend the filming of an episode of *American Idol* in Los Angeles, and I managed to attend two dress rehearsals. One took place at CBS Television City, where the bulk of the season was being filmed, and one at the larger Kodak Theater in the final week of the season. The latter is located, appropriately, within a large commercial shopping mall (or, more accurately, the mall is part of the Kodak Theater) and immediately adjacent to the Walk of Fame on Hollywood Boulevard—conveniently placed between icons of American consumerism and the fame-oriented version of the American Dream. During my field research I learned from many voices at different levels of participation in *American Idol:* auditioning singers, fans, former contestants featured on the television broadcasts, and the show's important behind-the-scenes figures (occasionally seen onscreen as well). Although my efforts to request an interview elicited no response from *Idols* franchise co-creator Simon Fuller's office at 19 Entertainment, and though I joined the millions of Americans rejected by the other co-creator and *American Idol* judge Simon Cowell (or, in my case, by his personal assistant), I am grateful to others involved with production who generously gave their time to share their experiences with me.

Because *American Idol* comprises a network of cultural products, the participatory aspect of my research took shape in ways for which my understanding of ethnomusicological methodology had not prepared me. And I had to consider new questions about my relationship with the object of my study. Did watching season after season of *American Idol* position me as part of an audience, even if I did not think of myself as a "fan"? At first, unnerved by this thought, I attempted to maintain a certain amount of critical detachment, not supporting any specific contestants. However, by the end of the fifth season, I had voted during the final week for my favorite singer, participating in the *Idol* electoral process.

When I later attended *Idol* dress rehearsals, it was as a member of the studio audience. In the crowd, in both the auditions and dress rehearsals, I was still a participant but at a minimally involved level.

The audience was filmed in both situations (footage from the dress rehearsals is used to wrap up at the ends of performance episodes), but I never saw myself on any broadcasts. I did, however, briefly see on-screen one of the students I had talked with at the auditions in 2004, as well as a featured audition segment focusing on a young woman whose group of supporters had sat behind me in the Cow Palace. We had all chatted extensively, and they allowed me to photograph them holding a homemade sign in support of Jessika, the singer. I felt great regret to learn later that the *Idol* broadcast about San Francisco mocked her, not for her singing but for what was cast as youthful arrogance. Even though my companions and I had no screen time, we became composite viewer-characters of a sort. The surprising amount of direction given the crowd at the auditions and at the dress rehearsals made it feel like we were onstage, though at the same time we were "backstage" surrounded by cameras and their teleprompters, watching the production process.

The degree of my participation was a subject my consultants sometimes broached. While in line for a May 2005 *Idol* public dress rehearsal, a young man I was interviewing asked with concern whether I was, in fact, planning on attending the rehearsal or just using the queue outside to collect information. He seemed to be reassured when I introduced him to the friend holding my place in line, verifying that I was not a complete outsider but someone who habitually watched and liked the show. (Admitting to myself that I was, in fact, a fan, took about three seasons.) This young man's readiness to share his *American Idol* experiences depended upon my own participation as an *Idol* viewer. That incident was not the only hitch I encountered in my fieldwork. In order to attend the 2004 auditions in San Francisco I was required to accompany someone actually auditioning, but I knew of no one who was planning to do so. A friend of mine recommended that I contact a mutual acquaintance who might agree to audition, and this singer later invited a close friend along. Both women have successful singing careers at the time of this writing, but neither one made it past the first round of auditions. And even though, before setting out, we had agreed on the unlikely odds that either of them would be cast in *American Idol,* one of them wept as we exited the auditorium. I spent some time considering my own part in her distress: she had only been involved in the auditions, after all, because I needed to tag along with someone auditioning, which had meant a cold night outdoors in the Cow Palace parking lot, the stress of a cattle-call audition, and the disappointment of being rejected, not to mention other pressures added by my own documentarian presence. For the first time I understood that, even in my local research in mainstream American music, among consultants who had been student colleagues of mine, I was still "casting shadows in the field."[22] This was also my first inkling that even in a research field where imbalances of power and the perception of Otherness are not as obvious as they might be in decolonizing nations, or in situations comprising clear and deep class divisions, field-workers still bear a responsibility to reflect upon their consultants' experience in relation to the complications and impositions of music research.

I also encountered difficulties with the online portion of my research; I have detailed elsewhere[23] my experiences with the use of internet forums and the citation problems I encountered in earlier versions of this book, but it is important to note that in this volume quotations from idolonfox.com, the official show website until 2006, are not identified because they—and their authors—ceased to be accessible when the platform changed, before I could make contact. For documentation, however, I retain printouts of all posts reproduced here. Despite these complications, I believe that the interactive structure of *American Idol* offers more opportunity for participant observation than other music-television programs, and thus provides an especially fertile field for ethnomusicology.

OVERVIEW OF THE CHAPTERS

Each of the seven chapters in the book centers on the concurrent erosion and articulation of particular discursive boundaries performed on *American Idol*, and explores how they impact the imagining of American identities. Another overarching theme is the national (and nationalist) values, myths, and narratives that make up the American Dream—the story *American Idol* tells every season—and that inform the construction of Americanness. Chapter 1, "Facing Reality," concerns the transgression of boundaries between production and consumption in the entertainment industries. *American Idol* is not a wholly novel phenomenon; it represents an escalation of this dialecticism and the continuing relevance of the sociocultural themes at work there. It definitively shatters a fourth wall already weakened by the largely actor-less nature of reality television, illuminating the power struggle between producers and viewers, and between belief and skepticism, that marks the twenty-first-century television experience so far.

Chapter 2, "Facing the Music," examines *Idol* play involving genre boundaries in popular music and how they relate to the voicing of American identity in contestants' performance practices. Among the "effaced" boundaries that Jameson held up as exemplary of postmodernism, he reiterated the discursive collapse of high and low culture.[24] Popular music has had its own high/low discourses, and *American Idol* bends and intertwines them so that their boundaries, too, are both confounded and reinforced, a business strategy to reach as wide an audience, and as wide a market, as possible.

The third chapter, "Win or Lose," illustrates the ill-defined boundaries between success and failure, focusing on two cases in Season 3 that highlight the importance of both outcomes in the concept of the American Dream. The first section describes a success story, with the Dream itself used as a political tool, a way to conduct an audition campaign; the second holds up the public failure of William Hung as a paradoxical means of fulfilling the Dream. The exploitation of American ideologies strengthens every well-planned *Idol* campaign.

Chapter 4, "Idol Worship," discusses the ways in which American religious, political, and moral codes intersect on the show, softening the lines between civil and sacral religious discourses. *American Idol* highlights the significance of religion in the musical life of the nation, and illuminates the ways in which religious faith, politics, and the American Dream converge in popular culture.

Pursuing the Dream is a way of establishing a nationalized American identity, of becoming American. It is a process of leaving one place, one identity, and arriving at another, but this process does not require the crossing of national borders: class boundaries and regional borders within the United States will do just as well on *American Idol*. Further, racially and ethnically marginalized Americans enact onscreen the constant struggle to prove their Americanness, always treading a discursive boundary that is undeniable if unacknowledged in mainstream media. The fifth and sixth chapters of the book, "Going Places" and "Politics as Usual," consider the intertwined identities of place and race—at once components of, and separate from, Americanness—that figure in the performing, viewing, and hearing of *American Idol*. These chapters center on weakened boundaries between politics and entertainment.

Chapter 7, "The United Nations of Pop," examines the broader effects of this changing relationship. The overlap between politics and entertainment in the *Idols* franchise extends far beyond U.S. borders. Though the format originated in the United Kingdom, the reality-TV manufacture of the pop star is intricately linked with the worldwide discourse and commodification of democratic ideals. Perhaps even more significant, the viewer voting process also becomes a saleable metonym for democracy itself. At a time when promoting democracy is a chief preoccupation of American foreign policy and the global gaze, it may serve us well to ask *what*, exactly, in terms of images, ideals, and ideologies, is being exported to such a large percentage of the world. Chapter 7 explores the role of the *Idols* format as an indicator and factor in the configuration of post-9/11 geopolitics, as the democratic process and the American Dream are simultaneously glorified and naturalized, and transmitted by satellite into living rooms worldwide.

This book investigates how *American Idol* teaches Americans to listen, and with what kind of voice—to paraphrase *Idol* sponsor Coca-Cola—it teaches the world to sing. The extraordinary success of the *Idol* phenomenon hangs not only on innovative marketing strategies but also on the way the show utilizes and reinforces certain narratives of Americanness. It is not only a talent contest but a five-month-long advertisement and a didactic demonstration of responsible capitalism, an exhibition of the risks and benefits of the American Dream, and an exercise in the values of democratic citizenship. It also represents the peak of what Jameson saw occurring in 1991, a situation in which the market and the media are so interdependent that the "products sold on the market become the very content of the media image." Here the audience can no longer feel certain of "when the narrative segment has ended and the commercial has begun," when, in the media, one finds "free programs in whose content and assortment the consumer has no choice whatsoever but whose selection is then rebaptized 'free choice.'" Jameson goes on to point out the de-differentiation of the commodity and its image, brand name, or logo. Strangely fitting is that, upon proclaiming "no boundaries," Kris Allen received a new winner's statuette, designed in the shape of a microphone—an Idol's idol, in the image of opportunity and the chance to make one's voice heard. It is this image, as an artifact of agency, and the concomitant ideologies underlying the construction of American identities, that become both the merchandise and the content of *American Idol*. If popular music is, as Reebee Garofalo suggests, "a social and political indicator that mirrors and influences the society we all live in," then the show offers invaluable reflections of twenty-first-century America.[25]

FACING REALITY ·
AMERICAN IDOL AS REALITY
TELEVISION

THE REAL THING

In February 2006 a report began circulating that several fans of Season 2 runner-up Clay Aiken had filed a complaint with the Federal Trade Commission (FTC). Unsettled by a tabloid piece claiming that Aiken had engaged in a same-sex liaison, nine women had voiced their displeasure in legal terms, and were considering a class-action suit against RCA (at the time, Aiken's label) and parent company Sony/ BMG. Newspapers and online news sites widely quoted a press release from the women:

> As consumers, we feel ripped off. It is obvious now that the private Clay is very different from the manufactured, packaged Clay that was marketed to us . . . This is tantamount to a manufacturer concealing information about a defective product. Therefore these actions were unfair and deceptive to consumers.[1]

Rumors of homosexuality had dogged Aiken since his time on *American Idol*; he often sidestepped the issue when journalists broached it, insisted in *Rolling Stone* in 2003 that he was not gay, was resigned in 2006 that "people are going to believe what they want," and came out publicly in the fall of 2008.[2] The veracity of the FTC story was heavily questioned when it broke, but later CNN's Brooke Anderson reported that the FTC had confirmed the existence of the complaint.[3] In March 2006 a BBC website discussed another statement, issued in response to comments made by Simon Cowell on *Larry King Live,* where the *Idol* judge had described the situation as "crazy":

> We have been dismayed to see our complaint characterized in the media as homophobic. That is not our intention and while central to our complaint it is regrettable that Mr. Aiken's sexuality has come under scrutiny. Our complaint is not about defaming Mr. Aiken or his sexual preferences. It is directed towards the deceptive practices of the record companies.[4]

This declaration first clarifies that Aiken's sexuality was indeed the locus of the alleged deception, and then, in contradiction, denies that the former fans take issue with his sexuality (despite having compared Aiken to a "defective product" in the earlier press release), and casts the blame not on the singer but on his management. In a sense, the statement's authors are correct in maintaining that Aiken and his sexuality are not the chief focus of their objections. The core of the grievance, beyond its oblique bigotry, virtually ignores him. It assigns enormous power to producers, made liable here for Aiken's supposed image transgression, and consumers, who can take the music industry to task and to court, but it entirely denies the possibility of the star's agency in the construction of his own commodified identity.

This situation not only marks the continuing difficulties American singers face when it comes to challenging the hegemony of heteronormativity but also highlights three elemental issues that make *American Idol* emblematic of early-twenty-first-century television: the important position of belief within the complex producer-star-consumer triangle, the growing overlap of those discrete roles in the entertainment marketplace as production and consumption engage in more dialectic ways, and the heightened sense of empowerment— even entitlement—consumers have consequently attained, complicating the perception of who is running the show.

The FTC plaintiffs speak clinically of manufacture, of packaging and marketing, but the upshot of their protestations is that they initially felt convinced of one text and later believed a different one—a shift enabled by the seemingly infinite number of *American Idol*–related texts available through diverse media. These are conditions omnipresent in late-twentieth- and early-twenty-first-century entertainment, resulting in what Joshua Gamson understands as "production awareness and the problem of authenticity." Gamson offers a detailed model of strategies through which audiences interpret stories of celebrity; overall they demonstrate an inverse relationship between consciousness of manufacture (e.g., the process through which a celebrity is made) and belief in the truth of a given text (e.g., the idea that a celebrity has earned that status through natural merit). He connects the strongest awareness of production to the weakest level of belief, and assigns this equation to an audience type he labels "postmodernist."[5]

American Idol's audience negotiates the product/text puzzle in a scenario where awareness of manufacture, as a central theme of the show, is high, but somehow belief remains strong as well. It is one of *American Idol*'s most intriguing properties that viewers can maintain a skeptical attitude about the show and its processes, and yet still sit down in front of the television every Tuesday with their AT&T phones at the ready to log their votes. The voting system and the intimidating odds at work in the nationwide open auditions become primary sites of this contradiction. One young man, Matthew Maimoni, had auditioned four times over two years by the time I interviewed him. He wanted to be on the show, but he did not believe that it worked the way it claimed to. For him, audience voting was not the true determinant of the winner: "People think it's like, oh, America chooses the American Idol, but that's not really how it goes, you know? So I don't think it's really a reality show—I mean, like all the reality shows, I don't think they're really real at all." If he did not believe that the premise was honest, what kept him going back? Social bonds, it seems, and a resilient self-confidence:

> *Well, this year I wasn't going to audition, but I met a friend who wanted to go, and she was like, "Oh, you gotta come with me," and so I went with [her]. But I don't know if I'm going to audition again. I might. . . . Right now I'll say I won't, and then I'll watch all the people*

on American Idol, and I'll be like, "Oh, I'm so much better than all
these people," and I'll go audition again, and I won't make it anyway,
and it's a vicious cycle![6]

He tried for a fifth time the following year. The contradictory attitudes
experienced by viewer/participants like Mr. Maimoni express the layered juxtaposition of a practiced postmodern cynicism and anxieties about the entertainment industry with faith in something even
more powerful: the self and the possibilities outlined in the American
Dream. Viewers may be suspicious of Hollywood machinations, but
when handed the prospect of becoming part of the Dream machine,
the opportunity is hard to turn down. The *Idol* audience seizes the
power it is given and is anything but idle, not only witnessing but
actively contributing to the creation of stars and their stories. By voting, joining fan communities, and auditioning to become part of the
cast, viewers are granted the potential to author, even become, the
text they are asked to believe—and perhaps it is difficult to disavow
something you feel you've had a hand in making. Participation potentially mitigates distrust in the industry and keeps the television
experience feeling like, as *American Idol* sponsor Coca-Cola touts,
"the real thing."

THE SEARCH FOR THE REAL

American Idol has garnered dozens of Emmy nominations,[7] including
an annual presence in the "Outstanding Reality-Competition" category established in 2003. Simon Fuller, co-creator of the *Idols* franchise, had long experience selling a cross-media, behind-the-scenes
view of the music industry. He is responsible for the groups the Spice
Girls and S Club (S Club 7), both of them successful on either side
of the Atlantic and promoted through television or film. The Spice
Girls starred in a *Hard Day's Night*–style movie fantasy, *Spice World*,[8]
about their experience as stars, and S Club appeared in the United
States (1999–2001) in two fictional television series modeled on *The
Monkees*, on the new FOX Family Television channel. Both groups
were assembled in open-audition processes as occurs in the *Idols* franchise;[9] in a kind of study for the *Idols* format, the auditions for S Club

screened ten thousand aspiring singers. It is this process that has been expanded and displayed in the *Idols* series.[10] *Spice World* and S Club's television programs were all premised on the public disclosure of the (fictional) thrills and trials that pop stars undergo. From these projects it was only a very small step for Fuller to enter the world of reality television, and to *Idol,* where the entire process of becoming a star is ostensibly exposed.

Although "reality television" is a fin-de-millennium moniker, the relevant formats have abundant precedents from the earliest days of television as a medium—and in the case of *Candid Camera,* even to the radio days before. Anna McCarthy and Bradley D. Clissold each trace its roots back to that show, first introduced in its televised form in 1948. McCarthy situates this "first wave" of reality programming within a postwar climate of realism in visual culture and, in the devastating wake of the Second World War and the Holocaust, new thinking about "the unthinkable." For Clissold, too, *Candid Camera* is a postwar phenomenon, offering a release from cold war–era anxieties concerning surveillance. Such programs effected, writes Clissold, a naturalization of surveillance itself but at the same time provided a form of symbolic resistance to it.[11]

Philip Auslander pinpoints a similar era of worry in the early 1990s—immediately after the end of the cold war, so perhaps more of an extension of it—this time amid fears about authenticity that reified live and mediated performance. Auslander concludes that the live and the mediated are, in fact, mutually dependent and overlapping, a relationship that *American Idol,* filmed live before a studio audience, underlines. Auslander discusses the 1990 scandal in which the two members of the group Milli Vanilli were stripped of their Grammy award, after it was revealed that they consistently lip-synched to recordings of voices other than their own. He identifies a morally centered panic following this event that incited a new search for authenticity in the music industry and led to, among other things, MTV's acoustic performance series *Unplugged.*[12] Twenty-first-century consumers retain these anxieties. Those who filed the complaint about Clay Aiken referenced Milli Vanilli in their response to *Larry King Live,*[13] and in 2009 lip-synching became a topic of minor *Idol* scandal when Season 1 runner-up Justin Guarini, co-hosting *Idol Wrap* on the

TV Guide Network, observed that the Wednesday group numbers were now being performed to prerecorded vocal tracks. A Fremantle-Media spokesman first refuted the allegation but then admitted that, during the choreographed ensemble performances, the finalists were singing along with their own voices over the live band.[14] While this means that they were not silently mouthing the words, not precisely "lip-synching," the music was not completely live in the television studio either. The story notably came to light in the month following similar reports about former *Idol* finalist Jennifer Hudson, who delivered the national anthem to a recording of her own voice at the Super Bowl. Rickey Minor, the music director for both the Super Bowl and *American Idol*, claimed responsibility for that decision, explaining that "there were too many variables to go live . . . the slightest glitch would devastate the performance."[15]

Lip-synching need not always symbolize inauthenticity; it can mean the opposite in certain circumstances. In 2005 I spoke with Grover Anderson, a young man who auditioned for Season 5 in San Francisco, about the organized crowd-focused moments staged for the cameras during the first round of auditions. When all attendees throughout the Cow Palace were asked to sing and dance together along with a recording of "It's Raining Men," I saw across the auditorium that Mr. Anderson remained in his seat. Later I asked him what he thought of these engineered vignettes, and he replied, "I was not the most enthusiastic person about doing the little things for TV, I just kind of—I mouthed everything . . . I'm not the kind of person who will go crazy and join the crowd. I just like to do my thing."[16] In this instance lip-synching, or "faking," became a statement of personal authenticity and individuality, with Mr. Anderson withholding his voice as an act of resistance and a rejection of the manufacturing process in which he had nevertheless willingly involved himself.

The Milli Vanilli incident in 1990 occurred just prior to a new wave of reality television, launched with the 1992 premiere of *The Real World* on MTV. The First Gulf War began around the same time, in 1991. Adding further to the confluence of national anxieties and reality programming, in 1990 *Candid Camera* also returned to television for the first time since 1967. The search for authenticity in the 1990s, the search for the "real" in popular culture, resulted in a proliferation of writing about what critical theorists like Jean Baudrillard named the *hyperreal* and the *simulacrum*—"the truth which conceals that there is none," an image that replaces reality. The early years of the decade also raised concerns that Americans (literally) viewed the Gulf War as a kind of ultimate reality program. Baudrillard famously took on the topic of the Gulf War in *La Guerre du Golfe n'a pas eu lieu*. He proposed that the war was not real in the ways that war is generally understood, but that instead it primarily took place on the television screen. Baudrillard wrote, "We are no longer in a logic of the passage from virtual to actual but in a hyperrealist logic of the deterrence of the real by the virtual." 9/11 and the following military conflict(s) were similarly broadcast to most of America—with the attacks on the World Trade Center replayed relentlessly on television, and with shocked bystanders or viewers telling journalists, "It was like a movie."[17]

From its origins during the coincidence of television's popularization, the psychosocial effects of the Second World War, and the initiation of the cold war, reality television has been fundamentally linked to social and political anxieties. Periods of crisis on the national, even global, scale have exacerbated such articulations of distress—in the early cold war, McCarthyism, and the attendant public alarm about surveillance; the televised character of the Gulf War from a living-room perspective in the U.S.; the TV reality of 9/11. Concerns regarding the nature and understanding of "reality" in the context of late capitalism by no means constitute only a contemporary phenomenon; they are detailed throughout the long history of twentieth-century critical theory. But such uneasiness has been especially apparent when national trauma dominates media discourse, and it was in these conditions that *American Idol* debuted. This is not to suggest a cause-and-effect relationship between incidents of foreign conflict and reality television in the U.S.; my intention here is merely to underline certain trends interwoven between the mutual histories of American politics and American media.

The broadcast of talent competitions, another major format that *American Idol* builds on, also began in radio, with programming like *Major Bowes' Amateur Hour* in the 1930s. That show continued on television with a new host in the 1950s, providing a partial prototype for the competition formats that followed. Winners of *Amateur Hour* rounds returned to compete with new talent, a feature picked up by *Star Search* in the 1980s. And as in the *Idols* series, listeners and, later, viewers voted by telephone or mail for favorite contestants, who could win a performance contract in the subsequent touring show. The *Idols* design also applies lessons learned from the Eurovision Song Contest, which in the late 1990s had implemented its own international popular vote submitted by telephone.

As Henry Jenkins points out, late in the twentieth century reality television became a strategic and cost-effective development for network television to ward off the encroachment of cable programming, with the advantages of dramatically lower production costs and an "amateur" cast that does not demand millions of dollars per episode. Adding original reality shows in the summer decelerated "viewer erosion" from the broadcast networks, and *American Idol*, combining two successful programming genres, arrived just in time to compensate for an increased market loss in 2002. From an array of reality and competition formats, *American Idol* followed proven models. It also capitalized on the popularity of recent serialized competitions in music television programming.[18] These included *Making the Band*, which debuted on MTV in 1999, and The WB's 2001 *Popstars*, the immediate predecessor of the *Idols* format in both the U.K. and the U.S.[19] It is not an entirely new animal, though it is an especially profitable one. For James Friedman of the University of California, Los Angeles (UCLA) Film and Television Archive, the millennial domination of reality programming does not indicate a sea change but a marketing strategy; rather than a new product, it is a new (and wildly successful) sales technique. Friedman proposes that "what separates the spate of contemporary reality-based television from its predecessors is not the form or content of these programs . . . but the open and explicit sale of television programming as a representation of reality."[20]

DEFINING *AMERICAN IDOL* AS REALITY TELEVISION

It is difficult to characterize reality television as a unified genre. The term, ubiquitous in media discourse since the 1990s, has referred to a proliferating series of programming formats, from confessional talk shows (*Jerry Springer*) to crime documentaries (*Cops*) to social-experiment game shows (*Survivor*) and the globally distributed music-based competitions that have flourished since the turn of the twenty-first century, including the *Idols* format and the earlier *Popstars*.[21] However, certain themes link many types of reality programming, hallmarks that are firmly rooted in earlier precedents but clearly outlined in *American Idol*.

First, reality television is essentially "television about making television."[22] *American Idol* lets its viewers in on the casting process, and allows them, to a degree, to steer the narrative. It also shows production seams so that viewers cannot help but be aware of them; for example, cameras and prompters are often visible in the wide angles over the studio, the studio audience is given screen time, and musical coaches appear rehearsing the contestants in brief prerecorded clips. It is in part a voyeuristic appetite, long a prominent feature of reality TV (from hidden-camera pranks to tabloid talk shows) that makes the nation privy to these *American Idol* processes. Viewers witness the construction of fame and infamy, successes and failures, and the public humiliation that is intrinsic to that scopophilia.

Another tried and true feature of reality television is a high visibility of sponsorship. The *Idols* franchise, like most television, collects much of its financial gain through the sale of advertising opportunities. Henry Jenkins reports that television viewers are "more accepting of product placements in reality programming than in any other genre," and product placement on *American Idol* is so heavy as to be reminiscent of early television advertising practices. Weekly Ford commercials featuring the *Idol* finalists and aired during the Wednesday "results" episodes harken back to the 1950s, when Milton Berle drove a Buick accompanied by choirs singing its praises on the frankly titled *Milton Berle's Buick Hour*.[23] In several seasons *Idol* contestants have been interviewed pre- and post-performance in a "green room" that is in fact red, in homage to its major sponsor, Coca-Cola, and for some time displayed a sofa in a design strikingly like the swirl adorning recent Coca-Cola logos. Coca-Cola bottles have also appeared in the room, and glasses with the logo have consistently graced the judges' desk in front of the stage. (In the first episodes of Season 9, those glasses were briefly replaced with a set advertising Vitaminwater, a brand acquired by Coca-Cola in 2007.) The sofa, in Season 6, was upholstered in a fabric displaying Coca-Cola bottles, and the wheel of an automobile (a tribute to Ford?) was embedded in the top of a nearby coffee table. Text-messaged votes are linked exclusively to sponsor AT&T (briefly Cingular Wireless owing to temporary corporate mergers). And although it may be a coincidence that the blue and white oval *American Idol* logo strongly resembles the logos of sponsors Ford and Old Navy, it is surely a convenient one.

Every season of *American Idol* functions as a long advertisement for the albums to be released, for the new Idol, and for the products offered by major sponsors. *American Idol* has been said to earn up to $500 million each year in advertising, and FOX sold thirty-second advertising spots during the 2006 finale for a reported $1.3 million each.[24] In service of its promotional designs, the show not only sells advertising time but sells its viewers on ideas, too. The pursuit of fame is a well-worn trope in reality television, which produces numerous celebrities "famous for being famous." As Catharine Lumby sees it, fame is central to the reality genre, specifically the appealing notion that anyone at all might be made famous simply by appearing on television. That fame might result from even the tiniest deviation from conformity is something that rankled Baudrillard in his critique *America*. But the impact of this possibility is perhaps most evident in the statistics for *American Idol*'s preliminary audition rounds, which take place in several selected cities each year. The numbers of hopefuls for *American Idol* increased over its nine seasons to date from the "around ten thousand" for the first season to the more than one hundred thousand claimed in each of the opening broadcasts of Seasons 4 through 9. The overwhelming emphasis placed on the acquisition of fame was perfectly encapsulated during one audition segment in Season 6. The mother of a teenager tried in vain to comfort her son after the judges turned him away, reassuring him that he was only sixteen and would still have time to prove himself. Sobbing inconsolably, he said, "I wanted to start out famous!"[25]

Reality television also illuminates the complicated discursive relationship and messy boundaries—smudged by twenty-first-century meanings of fame—between "amateur" and "professional." Robert Stebbins points out that characteristics associated with amateurs and professionals are sometimes not too far removed, and are often largely distinguished by degree—how much time a person spends on a pursuit, how much of his or her income is earned in that pursuit, how much specialized knowledge he or she has gathered.[26] In *American Idol* and similar competitive reality television programming, that narrow distance is the basis of numerous success stories. For these shows, the goal is to find performers without current professional contracts (*Idol* contestants cannot be signed to any other management or recording contracts at the time they appear on the show) and bestow one upon them, thus effecting a change in their social— and economic—status from amateur to professional. In *American Idol* this shift, this movement, is tied up in the motion of American Dream narratives, in which someone ordinary is recognized as extraordinary; he or she is still the same person but no longer an amateur. While participating in the show, singers are under contract but are still presented as only potential professionals, setting the *Idol* stage up as a liminal space—and the broadcast season as a transitional time—between statuses. Another facet of American dreaming stresses the maintenance of connections to the geography of amateurness, to the farm town or ghetto that nurtured or inspired a potential star to move on in the first place. That movement must be tempered. There is no leaving the past behind; instead, a new star must continuously acknowledge in some way where he or she came from (Jennifer Lopez's 2002 "Jenny from the Block" is a textbook example of this theme) and remain anchored in a stationary geography of authenticity.

American Idol is not the only purveyor of amateur stars (an oxymoron?). In 2009 another Simon Cowell venture, *Britain's Got Talent*, yielded Scottish singer Susan Boyle, building on her long amateur experience in karaoke and church performance, and the surprise associated with an image atypical of stardom. She became an international media darling and, like the show's 2007 phenomenon Paul Potts, was touted (and subsequently marketed) as a breakthrough talent, a fortuitously discovered diamond in the rough. Although she came to public attention on a television show, the venue that drew the most interest and gained her fans around the world was the internet. The viewing numbers for Boyle-related videos during the first ten days of her YouTube presence reached more than 85 million—more, the *Washington Post* reported, than videos of President Obama's acceptance speech on election night.[27] As of November 24, 2009, one Boyle clip alone, posted the previous April, had garnered nearly 79,200,000 views.

Scholars, journalists, and the general public have long acknowledged the internet as a potential factor in the breakdown between the concepts of amateur and professional. Andrew Keen, in a 2007 polemic titled *The Cult of the Amateur: How Today's Internet is Killing Our Culture,* asserts that the nonprofessional, glorified by tales of technological democratization, is essentially a "noble amateur," representing "the triumph of innocence over experience, of romanticism over the commonsense wisdom of the Enlightenment." Certainly, like the construct known as the "noble savage," amateur singing stars occupy a discursive space closer to the wild realm of the instinctual ("untrained" or perhaps merely the less feral "un-represented") than to the perils and benefits of civilization in the entertainment industry. Press about Boyle and other TV-competition sensations tends toward praise of *natural* talent—even her own proclaimed idol Elaine Page extolled her "natural voice" on *Good Morning America.* Boyle's village background, her self-described virginity, and the mild brain damage she suffered at birth are frequently invoked, all characteristics that leave her an icon of innocence.[28] *Idol* contestants offer American versions of this amateur archetype, often regionalized and, as discussed in chapters 5 and 6, sometimes troublingly racialized.

Stebbins also notes that many professional events attract amateurs, so that an audience at a baseball game—like the viewing audience of *American Idol*—may include dedicated amateurs who might aspire toward professionalism themselves. What *Idol* presents is a glossy view of the transformative process from amateur to professional, from consumer to commodity, and the proposition that such a change is possible for all. The exposure of process in reality programming contributes to a kind of demystification of television itself. In the *Idols* format, it is the star-making process that is somewhat demystified—now that viewers have some idea of how the recording industry might create a pop star, they can imagine the possibility of their own fame. The "search for a superstar," revealing what is ostensibly inside knowledge about the music industry to viewers, also draws attention to the importance of information as cultural capital, so that the postmodern distancing of Gamson's hyper-aware audience counteracts the stigma of habitually watching low-culture programming like *American Idol*. Furthermore, reality television's "behind-the-scenes" discourse supports what Todd Gitlin calls a "fetishism of means" in entertainment, wherein the privileging of process over purpose distracts consumers "from any desire to control the goals." A sense of do-it-yourself participation in programs like *American Idol* may therefore serve to temper some potential concern about its overtly commercial purposes.[29]

Any demystification involved in reality television is carefully controlled and limited, however. In their study of space and studio discussion shows, Sonia Livingstone and Peter Lunt apply the ideas of Goffman and Giddens about the binary distinctions of *front* and *back* (public and private) in performance, and of *disclosure* and *enclosure*. These concepts address the aspects of the television show and the production mechanism that are, respectively, presented to and hidden from the viewers. The front, as disclosed information, comprises a selected portion of the studio space allowed to the viewing audience, and the back, as enclosed, includes "all the means of production of the image."[30] In *American Idol* the bulk of the program takes place in a television studio, with host Ryan Seacrest sometimes interviewing contestants onstage or in the "green room" before and after each singer performs. Early broadcasts present certain stages of the preliminary audition process in several cities spread across the nation—these broadcasts both stretch and compress the space of the show. Although viewers are allowed to see some auditions filmed in front of the judges, these auditions are by no means comprehensive, are not broadcast live, and do not show the parts of the process that preceded them days before. In fact, audition segments at the beginning of the broadcast season conflate three rounds of mostly unseen auditions, and are constructed to imply a seamless single event encompassing both the interminable convention-center lines and the judges' decisions to send certain contestants to Hollywood. Enclosed in this situation is the mechanism in which the one hundred thousand auditionees are narrowed down to those few hundred who actually

see the judges. The lack of information in this area leads to speculation regarding the quality of the auditions shown on television. If the
judges receive so many of them poorly, viewers wonder, then how and
why did these singers end up in the third round with the judges? Not
only are talented competitors eliminated before they get there, but
the audience only sees certain successful auditions in the early broadcasts of each season. And during the subsequent weeks some entirely
new faces are introduced for the Hollywood rounds. Not having seen
their auditions, viewers might not feel as invested in their *Idol* narratives, and this lack of disclosure can work to the disadvantage of such
contestants when the voting begins.

Narrative uncertainty is another typical component of reality
television. Mary Beth Haralovich and Michael W. Trosset discuss
this element in relation to the show *Survivor,* noting *Survivor's* slogan "Expect the unexpected." For them, uncertainty is defined as
the gap between cause and effect, the unpredictability inherent in
the process of prediction. *American Idol* also makes rhetorical use of
the aforementioned phrase; in the first broadcast of Season 3, Ryan
Seacrest encouraged the viewing audience verbatim to "expect the
unexpected."[31] The outcome of each week's vote on *American Idol* is
always uncertain and sometimes surprising to viewers. But, in the
end, they are told "*you* decide," and viewers are invited to believe in
a sense of their own participation in the *Idol* political process, their
own agency. The opportunity to vote also allows a sense of reactive
control over the very unexpectedness they are warned of, where viewers might rectify a contestant's shocking near-elimination by voting
more often the following week. This perception of control is crucial
in the show's success and in its social context. It may also serve as a
kind of antidote to millennial American feelings of helplessness, expressed succinctly by John McGrath in his study of reality television
and surveillance. About watching the events of 9/11 unfold on television, he laments that upon seeing a victim jump to certain death from
the burning World Trade Center, "There is nothing we can do."[32] But
watching *American Idol,* in perhaps the subtlest and seemingly most
ineffectual of consolations—and unlike previous reality programming or, indeed, unlike reality—there is always something Americans can do.

The impact of national crises, and crisis discourses, regarding class, race, and gender has consistently been reflected, even showcased, in the various reality television formats. Although *American Idol* has not demonstrated any effort to explicitly expose or stir up examples of social conflict among contestants in the manner of flagship reality programs like *The Real World*[33] or *Big Brother,* such issues nevertheless remain ingrained in the singing contest's process. The competition in *American Idol* is the foundational competition of American capitalism—the social, economic, and political pursuit of opportunity, the fabric of the American Dream, through which balances and imbalances of power are relentlessly woven.

Livingstone and Lunt note the significance in audience-discussion talk shows of the "juxtaposition of representatives of established power and the laity."[34] In *American Idol* a similar juxtaposition occurs in the presence of both ordinary contestants and the authoritative A & R executives/former pop stars who make up the judging panel. There is also tension between the voting audience and the judges, regarding, first, to whom the power of choice/election actually belongs and, second, who knows best. During the Wednesday results episodes, host Ryan Seacrest, before revealing how the voting went, recaps the Tuesday comments of the judges. The contestants are told, "America voted and agreed with Simon" or "America disagreed with the judges, and you are safe." America has to be told how it has voted, addressed directly: "America, you chose Kelly Clarkson." These moments simultaneously affirm the power of the judges (and producers) and the power of the viewers to uphold or challenge their evaluations. The reverse has also occurred; on the eighth season of *American Idol,* the balance of power perceptibly shifted for the first time in the direction of the judges (and, again, the producers) when a one-time "judges' save" was added, allowing the judges to overrule the viewers' decision to send a contestant home. This innovation was kept for Season 9.

Finally, implementing a related technique of reality television, *American Idol* capitalizes on the American desire for representation. Previous reality-competition programming set the stage, appealing to the demographic diversity of its audience and the thrill of seeing one's own identity reflected onscreen. In their 2001 study of *Pop-*

stars, L. S. Kim and Gilberto Moisés Blasini link this tendency to the multiculturalist thinking that pervaded television in the 1980s and 1990s. At the turn of the twenty-first century, while scripted television continued to disappoint on this score—just before *Popstars* and three years before *American Idol,* groups including the NAACP and La Raza were protesting the continued omission of leading characters of color—reality television did acknowledge contemporary changes in racial relations and commodified them. Although on the surface the casting of minority participants seems to embrace them as icons of the American Dream, Kim and Blasini caution that it also at once erases and emphasizes difference. Viewers may choose whether to celebrate the attractive picture as "color blind" or to focus on the markers of cultural identity that essentialize the minority cast in the first place. Like the young singers in *Popstars,* those in *American Idol* reflect an array of American identities, including the growing number of Americans who see themselves as part of more than one racial group. Representation on television does not necessarily mean the end of racialized hegemonies, but it can be compelling. It was with my tongue only partly in cheek that upon the 2007 *Idol* victory of Jordin Sparks, whose father is black and mother white, I predicted Barack Obama's election in *Slate Magazine.* Of course, the two events bear no causal relationship, but it is possible that the *Idol* election might have helped to rehearse the nation in affirming already rising trends of social and political thought.[35]

But in spite of all these tropes it is perhaps discourse itself—as Su Holmes and Deborah Jermyn have theorized—rather than a list of unifying features, that actually defines reality television. Echoing James Friedman, Holmes and Jermyn view the "discursive, visual and technological *claim* to 'the real'" as an open mode of marketing that capitalizes on an idealizing desire for truth.[36] FOX News's controversial slogan "Fair and Balanced"[37] might be considered a response to public distrust of mediated information sources, and the concurrent reality television boom answers similar concerns. What is really happening, Americans want to know, that no one is telling us? By taking part in the construction of truth as it is performed on *American Idol,* viewers are perhaps more willing to grant it some degree of legitimacy.

FACING THE AUDIENCE: AT HOME, ONSCREEN, AND ONLINE

American Idol's participatory design goes deeper than voting. It represents the pinnacle of a recent emphasis on interactivity and intertextuality in entertainment, the extension of the televisual experience far beyond watching an hour or two of weekly programming. Viewers of *American Idol* can play their part in a number of ways: by voting, by auditioning, by posting on the official website's forum (and, as of 2007, by posting a blog entry that may be featured on the site), by attending free show rehearsals and tapings, and, in 2007 and 2008, by submitting compositions to be selected for the final performance. The audition structure is especially vital in the establishment of interactivity and, when *American Idol* premiered, was in some ways unique to it. Offering in-person, cattle-call auditions on an enormous scale afforded even those without access to video equipment the opportunity to participate, unlike other contemporary shows, such as *Survivor*, which required a mailed-in recording.[38] Audition sites are a physical place in which the relationships among viewers (and between viewers and future cast members) can begin to develop. Some viewers aspiring to be cast in the show encounter one another in person at the preliminary auditions, where thousands of hopefuls wait together to sing for producers. Many auditions are held at stadiums and sports arenas to accommodate the large turnout. This arrangement means that singers wait their turn in numbered stadium seating, already spatially organized into the shape of an audience.

The formation of identity-based bonds begins early, often on the internet. The *American Idol* message boards and the audition experience are not entirely separate; many viewers discuss the auditions before and after they occur, and some arrange to meet one another at the audition sites. Attending the San Francisco auditions I noticed a group of five or six young women sporting blue feather boas. They had met through the idolonfox.com message board and had agreed to wear the boas together so that they could find one another. Two weeks later one post title on the message board confirmed the women as "Boa Buddies for Life!!!!" In this instance, both the physical place of the audition site and the virtual space of the website contribute to the negotiation of viewership and the creation of the audience.

Since the audition events are filmed for edited broadcast during the televised season, those who braved the lines to try out may search the first episodes for their own faces onscreen so that viewers may be essentially transported into their TV sets. This is not a relocation peculiar to reality television, of course; metaphorical transportations into television shows or sets are a perennial part of news programming, and big-screen entertainments—the 1998 film *Pleasantville,* the 1992 film *Stay Tuned,* and 1982's *Poltergeist* contain notable examples— where it is more clearly stated as a fantasy embodying television-age anxieties about the unclear boundaries between the social world and the virtual world. That blurring is of some consequence in the formation and negotiation of *American Idol*'s audience.

Media theorists have long noted that television audiences do not exist in a vacuum but are formed by the media industry.[39] The continuous introduction of new technologies and new media forms, accompanied by the development of new theoretical approaches, has obliged sociologists to regularly redefine the concept of audience. Audiences and audience members have been studied variously as consumers, as commodities, as sources of ethnographic information, and as cultural agents. In the past several decades theory regarding audience dynamics has gradually shifted from views presuming a reified, passive, and susceptible public influence from "above"—the "effects" model, crucial to the Frankfurt School's notion of the Culture Industry—to models suggesting a more active role,[40] and finally to the concept of the interactive audience.[41] Today academic attention has focused heavily on audiences as dialectically constructed through relationships with the media industry.

But it is not only the audience breaking through the fourth wall of the television screen. Reality television programs *overflow* the boundaries of television, extending the viewers' engagement well into the temporal gap between regular broadcasts. *American Idol* viewers are given two hours after each weekly sing-off to call in or text-message their votes, providing an immediate extension of their engagement with the text of the program. And, as Henry Jenkins notes, because the contestants are "real people whose lives continue beyond the series' borders," unlike the characters in a scripted drama, viewers are interested enough to search for information about them across various available media channels outside the text of the show itself.[42] The audience is itself positioned as an onscreen and offscreen character named "America." It is explicitly referenced on each Wednesday "results" broadcast—each contestant is told that "America voted" and has placed him or her in the group with the highest or lowest number of votes. Viewers are also often spoken to collectively in the second person, advised by host Ryan Seacrest to "take action" and support their favorite contestants (e.g., broadcast of April 28, 2004). The audience is part of the action also, the studio audience working as a kind of visual synecdoche for the invisible, nationwide living-room whole. The viewing audience for *American Idol* not only extends to both sides of the television screen and across America but also beyond national borders to additional countries where the show is broadcast (see chapter 7). Viewers in these locations may watch the broadcasts, purchase *American Idol*–related recordings, and participate in online bulletin boards about the show. They may not vote, however, and so they maintain a somewhat less than completely interactive relationship with the televisual text.

Media Convergence

Though the viewing audience is named a single, generic "America," it is possible to differentiate two *kinds* of audience: those who can claim the ostensibly direct agency afforded by the opportunity to vote, and those who cannot. This distinction not only depends on geographic location, but it also is complicated by problematic technological matters. Viewers may vote for their favorite contestants by telephone, by dialing any wireless phone, or by text-messaging through their AT&T mobile phones. But because of high volumes of voting calls from certain locations (especially in the hometowns or home states of finalists), some viewers have encountered jammed phone lines and have been unable to place their votes. Message board threads expressing outrage over voting difficulties have been common throughout the nine seasons to date. Text-messaging a vote virtually guarantees that it will get through and be counted, but text-messaging is not necessarily free, and for *American Idol* may only be applied through AT&T

plans. It is therefore not as accessible a voting method as the simple telephone call—which more often than not ends in a "busy" signal—and some audience members may thus be considered somewhat "disenfranchised."[43] An economic issue is in play here that highlights the show's ultimately commercial goals and somewhat diminishes any democratic effect in the *Idol* process.

AT&T executives consider the coordination of their text-messaging campaign with *American Idol*'s voting process critical. Andre Dahan, who in 2003 was the president of AT&T Wireless Mobile Multimedia Services, stated then, "Our sponsorship of American Idol has inextricably linked text messaging with American pop-culture . . . We've changed people's behavior, engaging and motivating viewers to use their wireless phones for more than just placing phone calls."[44] Dahan's statement neatly illustrates the current environment of technological and economic synergy tied to the development of new media. Here AT&T is concerned with a specialized market—composed of *viewers,* not just a generalized group of AT&T customers—and is interested in influencing both their conception of wireless phones and their "behavior," their interaction with the show. *American Idol*'s relationship with its audience partially depends, then, upon an inter-reliant relationship between the television industry responsible for *American Idol* (collectively 19 Entertainment, FremantleMedia, and the FOX Network) and AT&T's wireless division.

American Idol supplies its audience with a comprehensive website featuring recaps of each broadcast, biographies and photographs of each finalist, interviews with contestants and judges, and a message board. (Originally at idolonfox.com, the site changed platforms and design in late 2006 and moved to americanidol.com.) This site initially connected viewers to the forums attached to other FOX Network programs, and to *American Idol*'s major sponsors including Coca-Cola, Ford, Old Navy, and AT&T Mobility. Downloads have been available for ring-tones, wallpaper, e-cards, screensavers, and games. In some seasons hypertext links accompanied photos of contestants' onscreen fashions, directing viewers to stores where the outfits may be purchased. During Season 6 the site began to offer downloadable studio recordings ($0.99), as well as video footage ($1.99), of the contestants performing their weekly song selections.[45] For Seasons 7, 8, and 9 the downloads were available through a partnership with iTunes. There have also been links to *American Idol* albums, tour tickets, souvenirs, and even public service organizations. In 2004, for example, the site included a link to an anti–drug-use website sponsored by the National Clearinghouse for Alcohol and Drug Information (of the U.S. Public Health Service), at freevibe.com. And until 2006 other links led viewers to the original FOX web pages for past seasons of *American Idol*, where the audience could transcend temporal as well as spatial limitations.

Some of these connections contribute to the economy of what Henry Jenkins has termed "media convergence," a nexus of synergistic processes fostering "the flow of content across multiple media platforms, the cooperation between multiple media industries, and the migratory behavior of media audiences who will go almost anywhere in search of the kinds of entertainment experiences they want." For Jenkins, *American Idol*, along with *Survivor*, represents the most powerful application of media convergence to date.[46] The combination of the broadcast series, AT&T promotions, tours, CDs, video games, books, films—the beach-blanket musical *From Justin to Kelly* (which failed at the box office), as well as a first-season compilation video and a set of retrospective DVDs, titled *The Best & Worst of American Idol, Seasons 1–4*—and the official website create such a convergence. *American Idol* host Ryan Seacrest even promotes the website and the products available there during *American Idol* broadcasts; in 2007 the website was given its own advertising spots during the show's commercial breaks. The aforementioned link to freevibe. com shows a different type of convergence, in which a popular media product attaches itself to an issue of public health or well-being; the anti-drug message supports *American Idol*'s reputation as family entertainment.

Intertextuality

The website in particular underscores the intertextual nature of reality television programming. In literature Julia Kristeva posits a biaxial structure to texts: a horizontal axis linking the author and the reader of a text, and a vertical axis linking the text to other texts. In reality television, this structure is perhaps even more multilayered.

Will Brooker has written about the ways in which online message boards, among other concepts, extend viewers' engagement with reality programs, overflowing the boundaries of television.[47] This creates multiple texts outside the purely televisual, which may be drawn on to create an increasingly holistic experience of a show. Reality television today involves connections among viewers online and in the press (critics), connections between producers and viewers both through the onscreen text and through reference to the other, and dialogic texts of online viewer interaction. For *American Idol*, technology sometimes provides direct connection between both sides of the screen; Seasons 7 and 8 featured the finalists onstage answering telephoned questions from fans, and contestants have occasionally spoken on air about reading the message boards. And some posters on americanidol.com have expressed a belief that producers read the forums and adjust the show based on viewer comments.

The voyage into cyberspace adds a new element of *hyper*textuality. In their study of the archetypal reality program *Big Brother*, Estella Tincknell and Parvati Raghuram propose a return to "cultural studies' early emphasis on the idea of audience as a set of *relations with a text*." Su Holmes points out that in those authors' analysis, the ideas of active audience and interactive audience are connected by the ways in which the show's metatext may be accessed. *American Idol*'s audience is generated at multiple convergent sites, including websites, on the telephone, and in the popular press, but there is also another important element. As in *Big Brother*, Tincknell and Raghuram point out, viewers are "not only invited to *identify* with the actors; she or he can *become* one of them" and thus are also invited to "be the text."[48] *American Idol* viewers not only vote and become part of the narrative, but they are also solicited as participants like those in *Big Brother*, resulting in the massive attendance at the annual open auditions. It is also telling that 2007 saw the opening of Idol Camp, a two-week sleep-away experience for children ages ten to fifteen interested in the performing arts. There students in several disciplines (including singing) were coached by staff, including former *American Idol* cast members. The camp's age range ended precisely before the minimum audition age for *American Idol* (age sixteen), as if it were a preparatory school for matriculation into the nationwide tryouts.

Like the audition sites, the camp also provided a space for direct social interaction among young fans of the show, and between the children and some of their Idols.

Interactions

The message board at the official *American Idol* website has, nearly every season, been identified by its hyperlink labeled "community."[49] How is this audience community formed, and how does it establish itself as a social agent, or collective of social agents? Denise Bielby and C. Lee Harrington explain the processes through which television viewers may "generate meaning" by creating social bonds—"with each other (viewer-viewer), with television characters (viewer-character), and with producers (viewer-producer)."[50] In *American Idol* the categories of viewer, character, and producer are not mutually exclusive. Viewers act both as audience and onscreen performers, and producers sometimes act as characters in the show's narrative (as in the case of Simon Cowell). The types of bonds described by Bielby and Harrington are all clearly present and integral to the definition of *American Idol*'s audience, but they exist as overlapping, interrelated connections.

The ways in which viewers, characters, and producers relate in the context of a reality television series are not always entirely isolable. Gray Cavender invokes Robert Putnam's theory of social capital in his discussion of community and reality television. In Putnam's model, social capital may involve a process of bonding or bridging. The former is "narrow, inward looking and underpins specific reciprocity among homogenous groups," whereas the latter comprises "networks that cross diverse groups."[51] Posters on the *American Idol* message board construct an audience identity organized on both principles. It is a network of individuals who form a heterogeneous group in terms of age, location, and occupation, and a composite of smaller, more homogeneous subgroups divided by contestant-based solidarity. Supporters of a given contestant may even be so enthusiastic that they create internal competitions among fellow fans of a favorite singer. Particularly common are "color wars," which, despite the potentially sinister title, represent only the friendliest sort of rivalry. Small teams choose a posting color, and simply post the name of their color (blue, pink, etc.) in a font of that color, as many times as possible up to a specified goal, for example, eight hundred thousand posts. I first noticed such competitions during the third season, carried out by supporters of the contestants, particularly those claiming to come from the contestant's hometown or even his or her high school. Derek Foster has written about online fan competition related to the CBS reality show *Survivor*, observing that such activity mimics the competition performed onscreen each week.[52] *American Idol* viewers are in a way mapping the friendly, competitive behavior played out in the television studio onto their own collective relationships.

Producers may also attain indirect acquaintance with the audience through the official online message board (previously at idolon-fox.com, now americanidol.com). The corporate teams behind the show do not ignore the message boards; a warning upon entering the pre-2006 "Community" read:

> By posting your message, you agree that FOX Broadcasting Company, its affiliated companies, and their successors and licensees have the unlimited and irrevocable right, without further consideration, to use any portion of your message and your first name in all media now known or hereafter created, worldwide and in perpetuity in connection with the advertising, promotion and publicity of the series or any of its episodes.[53]

Online, producers have access to the profiles of some members of the audience, and thus to some demographic and personal information. The profiles provide data regarding the age, gender, and social class (occupation) of many viewers. Producers, contestants, and the website moderators—moderators, if not directly overseen by producers, still act as "powers that be"—can also react to the content of the messages. Once a forum post was read on the air by Season 1 co-host Brian Dunkleman, and in the same episode contestant Alexandra Bachelier was shown reading messages posted about her.[54] *Idol* creator and *American Idol* judge Simon Cowell (both a character and a producer) has written about his experience reading website posts early in the series:

I made the mistake of logging on to the *American Idol* website and going to the Judges section, where fans can leave messages for us. I was absolutely horrified. There were hundreds of nasty comments about me. . . . The more I read, the more I began to believe the terrible things that people were saying. . . . The next week on the show, I realized that these comments were starting to influence the way I was behaving. In short, I was observing myself at a distance, trying to be more judicious than usual, even saying kind things that I didn't exactly mean, but that I rationalized as important to building the confidence of these budding young entertainers.[55]

Although Cowell says he eventually returned to his customary mode of behavior, his anecdote shows that the actors—actors in terms of both stagecraft and agency—around whom the narrative flows may be subject to the direction of the invisible audience at home.

The bonds described by Bielby and Harrington are essential in *American Idol*'s construction of Americanness. They are in part created and maintained through the discursive negotiation of a particularly American politics of identity. It is clear from dialogue on electronic message boards that viewers may identify with contestants (characters) not only based on singing talent, appearance, and personality but also on the singers' (professed or presumed) regional, ethnic, and religious affiliations. These elements are also important in the ways that viewers relate to one another, in virtual communities, or even in more physical spaces such as audition sites or tapings of the show. They may coalesce into groups, especially online, that are unified both by loyalty to a particular contestant and by identification with his or her individual sociocultural background. Such associations and the connections formed around them are clearly powerful in the creation of meaning from the intertextual experience of *American Idol*. *American Idol*'s viewers form not only a television audience but also a music fan base unlike most others. It does not revolve around a single performer or band, or even a single genre, but around a media brand encompassing a network of different musical and social identities. As Daragh O'Reilly and Kathy Doherty remind us in their study of the band New Model Army and its web community, the internet message board can play an important role in the construction of "brand communities"—social communities in which "consumption and marketing interests" become a unifying factor in a complex of relationships among producers, consumers, and the product.[56]

In the construction of these relationships, brand communities rely upon several specific modes of communication. Bielby and Harrington describe four principal functions carried out through messages posted to reality television–based electronic bulletin boards: commentary, speculation, request for information, and diffusion of information. Commentary consists of opinions about elements of the televisual product and, the authors propose, reveals much about the interpretations of that product generated by viewers. It also shows how viewers communicate their interpretations to one another. Speculation involves both primary text (the show) and secondary text (outside press covering the show), and contributes to the collective creation of cultural meaning. Tertiary text (external gossip, oral culture, and letters from fans to producers) is also sometimes invoked. Requests for information usually focus on missed episodes, "backstory," and news related to the show, and highlights the importance of intertextuality in the generation of cultural meaning. Responses to these requests, as well as other types of postings, constitute the last functional category, diffusion of information.[57]

Messages posted to the *American Idol* website fulfill all these functions. Forum threads cover topics such as the weekly televised episodes, the *American Idol* auditions, tour concerts, judges, and each finalist, plus a section for "Off-Topic Discussions" not directly germane to *American Idol*. On the original site, idolonfox.com, members of the discussion forum had access to some information about one another; as viewers registered, they were invited to enter information for a "profile" available to others by clicking on a username. Not all members completed all, or any, of the fields presented, including location, gender, age, birthday, astrological sign, occupation, and, perhaps most notable, "personal quote." The gender of each member was automatically given, as it was entered separately, prior to the profile, at the time of registration. The profiles allowed viewers some knowledge about one another, bringing the social world into the virtual (idolonfox.com).

CONCLUSIONS

All this, along with the show's voting procedure, builds on the idea of public agency, and a pseudo-democratic process that echoes the delicate relationship between governmental authority and citizens free to question the decisions of those in power. The idea of democracy is another trademark of competitive reality television, where voting takes many forms—internal systems such as the "tribal" voting in *Survivor* or the house voting in *Big Brother,* or external viewer voting as in the *Idols* format. In offering consumers this enfranchisement *American Idol* combines two attributes of American citizenship that Judith Shklar recognizes as crucial to empowerment, a sense of belonging, and social standing: the right to vote and the opportunity to earn. For Shklar, the locus of modern American citizenship lies not only in the relationship between the citizen and the state but also, significantly, in the marketplace, where the citizen "finds his social place, his standing, the approbation of his fellows, and possibly some of his self-respect." The world of American politics and the world of American commerce are fundamentally different, the former espousing the idea of equality and the latter being "entirely unequal." *American Idol* symbolically bridges the two with an election that suggests both universal "inclusion in the polity" and commercial power—consumer choice. If, as Shklar proposes, Americans are used to thinking about citizenship more in terms of inclusion than deep civic activity, it is an easy bridge to cross, a facile experiential connection between democracy and participatory television.[58]

The fans who complained about Clay Aiken's sexuality inflated this relationship and conflated identity with commodity, consumption with citizenship. It is this collapsing of the political and the commercial that set the stage for the latest reality television boom at the turn of the millennium, and that defines it now. The authority consumers might feel in their interactive television experience is limited. To the best of my knowledge, nothing further ever came of the complaint; nothing really could. But it remains an intriguing strategy at a moment when postmodern television viewers can, to reorder Hannah Arendt's words, at the same time believe nothing and everything, think that nothing is true and that everything is possible.[59]

CODA: YOU CAN ASK, BUT I WON'T TELL

There are, of course, numerous websites dedicated to *American Idol* that are not sanctioned by FOX, and these provide further interaction for viewers, away from any direct connection to *Idol* powers and texts. *American Idol*–related blogs, episode recaps, fan sites, and forums are ubiquitous, and there are even fan fiction communities focusing on specific contestants, for example, a LiveJournal page for original stories featuring as protagonists the Top 2 Season 8 finalists, Kris Allen and Adam Lambert. Much of the writing on that site deals with an imagined sexual relationship between the two, who shared a room in *Idol* housing during the season; while Lambert was widely assumed to be gay but never spoke about sexuality onscreen, Allen was straight and became the first married winner of *American Idol.* Fan-authored fiction about celebrities (rather than scripted television, film, or literary characters), sometimes called "Real Person Fiction," extends the earliest form of fandom, the admiration of the actor instead of the play.[60] According to Francesca Coppa, music and celebrity fan communities began separately from media fandoms, based on the distance between mainstream and subcultural objects of interest. When the two styles of fandom met on the internet, the convergence resulted in a proliferation of what is known as *popslash,* a genre that has primarily, though not exclusively, comprised speculative erotica about boy bands. The popslash phenomenon gathered momentum after a 2001 story that imagined Chris Kirkpatrick of the band 'N Sync experiencing a sudden overnight gender change, and while the moral implications of regarding actors—real people—as characters was initially heavily debated, the genre remains a way to "explore celebrity culture as a metaphor for gender identity and other performances of the self" including sexuality.[61] Fan fiction about *American Idol* contestants allows viewers to tell stories about identity that are never addressed onscreen.

The sexual orientation of semifinalists and finalists has never been discussed openly on *American Idol,* though the Gay and Lesbian Alliance Against Defamation has issued statements rebuking the judges for their disparaging comments about gender expression during preliminary audition episodes, and for onscreen banter that featured Ryan Seacrest and Simon Cowell questioning each other's heterosexuality.[62] Otherwise, sexuality is striking in its absence on *American Idol*; it is one of the only identity markers not plainly exploited for its audience potential. Not only sexual alterity but any kind of sexuality is articulated more subtly here than is typical of the commercial pop world. To a degree, this is because of the way the show privileges the voice, an embodied instrument, over any kinetic use of the body as an instrument of sexuality. Dance is not as important to the *American Idol* singing competition as it otherwise typically is in the pop world; choreography is minimal in the weekly group performances, and solo performances may or may not involve stage movement, but the focus remains centered on the voice.

American Idol's "You can ask, but I won't tell" tone may also be a correlate of its family television standing, although it is not clear who is responsible for the silence. Season 1 finalist R.J. Helton has said that he was advised by assistant producers to keep quiet about his homosexuality while part of the *Idol* cast (though a FOX spokesman denied knowing of any such counsel), but also that, at twenty-one, he wasn't ready to declare it yet, anyway. Adam Lambert was the topic of much journalistic and blogging speculation in 2009 after photographs depicting Lambert kissing another man, and others showing him in female drag, made the internet rounds. Lambert did not satisfy public curiosity until several weeks after Season 8 ended, when he described himself as gay in *Rolling Stone* (and also said that "there's part of me that's almost bi-curious"), but stressed that during his time on *Idol* producers had left the decision to talk about it up to him. He explained that he had been concerned that the issue "would overshadow what I was there to do, which was sing."[63]

Because he did not talk about it then, his audience (and producers) turned to other texts, including the photos and onscreen rhetoric, to piece together an identity. There was almost nothing to go on in terms of the clearly delineated identity markers that usually inform the contestants' *Idol* campaigns. Lambert offered no onstage shout-outs to his hometown, no regional southern accent (he came from San Diego, California), no proclaimed desire to share a marginalized culture with America, and no mention of church or debts to Jesus. (He is Jewish, although this also went unacknowledged onscreen.)

Thus limited, from the beginning of the season Lambert's image was linked with a music genre instead—as it happens, a specific genre that bears connotations of non-heteronormative culture.

Throughout his time on the show, *Idol* talk aligned Lambert with glam rock, though he smoothly adjusted his style to R&B and acoustic rock in addition to Queen. Simon Fuller has described Lambert as "Marc Bolan meets Bowie, with a touch of Freddie Mercury and Prince."[64] His preliminary broadcast audition, with Queen's "Bohemian Rhapsody," was branded "theatrical" by the judging panel. Although this may have alluded in part to an earlier discussion of Lambert's participation in the touring and Los Angeles casts of *Wicked,* the word "theatrical" followed him through the season. It is a term not only associated with musical theater and its attending discourses of sexuality but also with glam, a genre that has historically defined gender and sexual identity as social constructs, flaunted the juxtaposition of the masculine and the feminine, and highlighted "style and pose." The reasons why some fans called themselves "Glamberts" may be less about Lambert's relationship with glam rock as a musical genre—and Philip Auslander writes that glam is more a sociological category than a musicological one—than about his relationship with its iconic accoutrements, including, most notably, androgynous fashion hinting at the possibility of homosexuality or bisexuality, and visible makeup on men. Although he alternated tight leather and large jewelry with classic suits, eye makeup was so closely tied to Lambert's image that Ryan Seacrest announced the last performance episode (May 19, 2009) as a showdown between "the Guy Next Door" and "Guyliner." Makeup also bears general connotations of theater, of the kind of self-aware performance that defines glam. But even though Auslander identifies makeup as part of glam's celebration of inauthentic identity in the 1970s, for Lambert, performance was not the end of the story.[65] Toward the end of the season, he answered persistent press questions about the internet photos with a non-answer as much about authenticity as sexuality: "I know who I am," he told *Entertainment Weekly.*[66]

While such personal authenticity and self-knowledge are recurring themes on *American Idol,* the eighth season's early cast included an unusual contestant. From his televised audition through his elimination from the semifinals, comedian Nick Mitchell sustained a fictional persona named "Norman Gentle."[67] There was no question that Norman, with his terrycloth head-and-wrist-bands, satin print shirt, and flamboyantly dramatic showmanship—kneeling center stage to sing or fondling the letters of the neon "American Idol" sign at the side—was a performance. He was identified in onscreen captions as "Norman Gentle," in quotation marks below his given name. As his first Hollywood moments were introduced, Ryan Seacrest reminded the viewing audience that "Nick used the character named Norman Gentle to make it through the New York auditions" (February 3, 2009) and, as the judging progressed, wondered "which persona would he choose for his final performance?" (February 10, 2009). In a video for *American Idol*'s official website, Mitchell explained his alter ego as an invention that would allow him to be funny, and to sing virtuosic showpieces usually gendered as female: "I'm a sketch comedian, but I also am a singer, and I was like, 'what guy can ever get away with singing a *Dreamgirls* song or a Whitney Houston song,' so I created this character a couple of years ago."[68] Norman Gentle effected this repertoire transvestism with two performances of the *Dreamgirls* show-stopper "And I Am Telling You I'm Not Going" (although certain lyrics which, sung from a male perspective, might imply a same-sex romance were altered to reflect a non-gendered star-fan relationship instead).

As Norman Gentle, Mitchell celebrated "pose" in a way previously discouraged on *American Idol,* which had traditionally rejected auditionees who came to the preliminaries with costumes or routines. Mitchell was performing "camp," what Jack Babuscio defines as not necessarily about the direct expression of homosexuality in itself, "never a thing or person per se, but, rather, a relationship between activities, individuals, situations, *and* gaynesss." Neither Norman Gentle nor Nick Mitchell ever mentioned sexual orientation on the show, but the persona was widely interpreted in camp terms—one reviewer of his Hollywood "And I Am Telling You" encompassed three camp concepts at once, celebrating his "flamboyant diva bad lounge act," where "flamboyant" and "diva" are terms associated with queer theatricality and cross-gender modes of performance, and "bad lounge act" invokes the definition of camp as "bad art or kitsch." As for why

Mitchell made it as far as he did in the competition, the judges commented frequently that he really could sing, but other possible factors were at work as well. In a setting that emphasizes American Dream mythology and values, that encourages its contestants to "be unique" and individual, camp becomes a particularly appropriate aesthetic. "Camp is individualistic," writes Babuscio, and "as such it relishes the uniqueness and the force with which personality is imbued."[69] Mitchell was unique in *American Idol* history, had a striking personality, and expressed an American identity, even if it was openly a pose.

Although *American Idol* has never overtly championed gay culture, the show does maintain a camp kind of relationship with it that might be termed, to borrow a word that emerged in public discourse around the same time as *American Idol,* "gay-adjacent." In the U.K. newspaper *The Guardian,* Oliver Burkeman traces the first published use of this phrase to the American magazine *The Advocate* in 2002, when Chuck Kim applied it to a cast member of another reality television show, *The Real World*; however, as far back as *The Advocate*'s thirtieth anniversary edition in 1997, the magazine included the term in its entertainment section "The Buzz." In applying "gay-adjacent" to *The Real World* character, Kim's implication was that the straight "hunky bartender" for a gay club had been included to draw gay viewers in a season with an atypically "queer-free" cast. But Burkeman notes that, a few years later, "gay-adjacent" meant something more— the adoption of articulations of gay culture in mainstream contexts, without designating it specifically *as* gay: "an attempt to have it both ways . . . to stop commercialised gay culture losing its edge (so that its core audience doesn't desert it) while rendering it more inviting to straight but non-homophobic consumers (who none the less might feel excluded by anything labelled 'gay')."[70] It is a marketing decision that *American Idol* also seems to have made, catering to the maximum potential audience, offering as many American identities as possible, but stopping short of explicitly making "gay" one of them. Amid *Idol*'s heavy reliance on nation, race and ethnicity, region, and religion to make viewers into fans, the omission of gay and other queer identities is a reminder that those fans are consumers, and identity here is principally a device that serves the financial heart of the enterprise.

2

FACING THE MUSIC

IDOL DISCOURSES

Amid the slew of successful Season 3 auditions aired on February 2, 2004, Micah Read's stood out—not for any unusual vocalism or visual gimmick but for the way his broadcast segment located *American Idol* within a crucial discourse of popular music. Read began his broadcast audition with Bob Seger's "Old Time Rock and Roll." Praising the performance, judge Simon Cowell recalled that he had found the "obligatory rocker" in the previous season's cast "fake" but that he heard Read's as a true rock voice. Nevertheless, he warned the singer, "If you're into rock and roll, you have to understand you may have to sell yourself out a bit." He asked to hear a few lines of "A Whole New World," a pop hit from the 1992 Disney film *Aladdin,* and when Read had finished, the panel agreed that the song had made him sound "like a fraud." "You just did the whole Bob Seger throaty rock sound," Paula Abdul explained, "and we thought that was you. And then you sang this . . ." and ". . . it was bad," interjected Randy Jackson. "You've got to stay and remain who you are. You can't change just to please us."[1] To be on the show, Read learned, he would be asked to sell out, but when he did, he'd be seen as an impostor. The judges, contradictorily, admonished Read to stay true to his "real" musical identity as a rock singer but also implied that, if he wanted to be on the show, he couldn't.

In sending Read to Hollywood to ponder that psychological catch-22, Cowell, Abdul, and Jackson outlined a widespread and enduring dichotomy. With their response to Read, the judging panel situated *American Idol* on the "pop" side of a rock/pop binary, perhaps not surprising in a franchise whose first effort was called *Pop Idol*. That name, even, hints at the nature of the discourse; where rock might have its gods, pop has only idols, empty images to be foolishly (if lucratively) deified. As Simon Frith has written, pop is tricky to define: it does not so much comprise a particular style of music as an assemblage of whatever remains when the other genres have been identified. The genre distinction is built more on "sociological difference" than on any characteristic musical features, and its elusive definition is only part of what makes pop an object of disdain. What Frith calls "rock ideology," or what some journalists have self-consciously named "rockism," privileges particular ideations of authenticity as intrinsic to rock while positioning pop musicians as artistically inconsequential, false, and excessively focused on salesmanship. Kelefa Sanneh summarizes it as an attitude that "means idolizing the authentic old legend (or underground hero) while mocking the latest pop star; lionizing punk while barely tolerating disco; loving the live show and hating the music video; extolling the growling performer while hating the lip-syncher."[2]

The generic polarization of rock and pop hinges on a well-documented social politics of aesthetics, taste, and late capitalism—a network of dogmatic historical narratives describing art and commodity as fundamentally opposite, and operating with a gaze prejudiced toward the former. Frith has identified two significant streams of thought in this formulation, one from folk discourse and the other from art discourse. Rock authenticity, for Frith, depends simultaneously on a feeling of community experience and a sense of "truth-to-self"—the musician's honesty to his own experience. Frith's model influences Keir Keightley, who recognizes in rock rhetoric a Romantic sense of tradition, sincerity, and populism complemented by a modernist interest in experimentation and the elite artist.[3] Although rock ideology is by no means confined to the United States, I would additionally propose here that somewhere in the mix lies a particularly American ethos of individualism—a combination of the "rugged" competitive kind to which Herbert Hoover in 1928 famously attributed America's status as "land of [financial] opportunity" and what Michel Foucault terms "the intensity of the relations to self . . . of the forms in which one is called upon to take oneself as an object of knowledge and a field of action, so as to transform, correct, and purify oneself, and find salvation."[4] Such a blend makes self-knowledge at once a moral/spiritual responsibility and a commodifiable quality, and awareness of the market a key quantity in self-knowledge. Knowing "who you are" as an artist is an authenticity that makes you more saleable; that reflexive understanding requires you to know your place in the market and to hold it as your compass as you navigate the music industry.

In reality, the principles outlined above are not the sole province of rock. In spite of the challenging logic issued to Micah Read, *American Idol* makes it clear that they also permeate the realm of commercial pop. Pop, too, demands that its stars demonstrate their own awareness of tradition, a separate brand of creative independence, sense of community, and honesty of self-expression. On *American Idol,* which offers the nation's voting viewers a feeling of cultural agency, pop echoes folk discourse as heartily as rock, and becomes a different kind of American "people's music." The *Idol* judges' circular counsel about selling out is explained by old academic arguments in folklore. Regina Bendix, in her analysis of folklore studies, explains that, in a market-driven setting, cultural products that come to represent folk authenticity quickly lose that connotation. A declaration of authenticity leads to demand and therefore to market value. Then, because folklore discourse sees "ideological and market forces as outside agents that spoil" authenticity, the product's status shifts immediately toward inauthenticity. The opposition of authentic/inauthentic becomes authentic/commercial.[5]

THE SEARCH FOR AUTHENTICITY IN THE SEARCH FOR A SUPERSTAR

Authenticity functions not only as a social, cultural, and political commodity but also as a constructed identity. In Lawrence Grossberg's words, "authenticity itself is a construction, an image, which is no better or worse than any other." In order to approach the kind of value paradox that Bendix details—the inevitable transformation from cultural capital to market capital—Grossberg has introduced the idea of *authentic inauthenticity*. If every identity is equally fake, he suggests, then every identity can be equally—*democratically*—celebrated and sold, in the full awareness of its fakeness: "any pose can gain status by virtue of one's commitment to it."[6] During Micah Read's audition, *American Idol* acknowledged and even embraced such a commitment.

Authenticity is a concern for producers, contestants, and viewers, built into the *Idols* format at several levels. It is an Idol campaign platform, a set of performance practices that demonstrate an authenticity of personal expression, a compact between producers and viewers, and a sales technique. Simon Cowell himself has written about the integration of industry convention and consumer desire for creative authenticity. He uses the short-lived but sensational 1990s girl group the Spice Girls as an example, detailing how his *Idols* partner Simon Fuller, at 19 Entertainment, had packaged the Spice Girls so that artistic control seemed to belong to the singers themselves. As Cowell remarks,

> The one thing people tend to want is authenticity. That can mean many different things, but what made the Spice Girls so successful when they were launched in '94 is that every kid who bought their record believed that the girls had done it all themselves. . . . They didn't look as if they had been put together by a record label, even though Simon Fuller had decided everything.[7]

By distancing the pop group from its corporate management, and imbuing the Spice Girls with the force of their own "girl power," Fuller increased their authenticity quotient in the rock ideology. In the case of *American Idol,* this kind of authenticity is insinuated through the prominence of the do-it-yourself audience vote, and in how the contestants are presented to that audience. It is frequently asserted onscreen, for example, that the contestants choose their own repertoire, as well as their clothing, for each broadcast, and that they develop their own performances of each song. Finalists (generally the Top 12) make their selections each week based on a theme—disco songs, songs by Barry Manilow, film songs, and so on—choosing from a long list of repertoire pre-cleared for copyright. According to *American Idol*'s associate music director, Michael Orland, the list can contain more than one hundred items, and singers are also provided with a CD:

> It's up to them to listen to it, and you know, find four or five songs they respond to, and they come into the session with Debra [Byrd] and myself, and we'll work through all that. So everybody helps, without making that final decision of what they should sing. Because really, that's the biggest part of the contest, is the song selection.[8]

Contestants work with vocal coach Debra Byrd, who is also the vocal coach for *Canadian Idol*. Byrd, as she prefers to be called, corroborates the notion that producers prohibit staff interference with song selection and certain performance choices—though she frames it in the context of protection from emotional liability rather than merely in the interests of authenticity:

> We have to walk very carefully, in terms of information that's given out, because as [executive producer] Nigel [Lythgoe] said, they will blame me. Let me give you a for-instance. There was a young lady who, and it's happened quite a few times, but one young lady chose to sing a song in a certain key—and you know, we have to find keys for these contestants. So I said, "Oh, let's try it a little higher." And, clearly, she sang better in the higher key. It was hands down. But her nervousness would not allow her to sing higher. And when I'm saying higher, I mean a half step. I'm not talking a third, I'm talking about just a half step higher. And so she said, "No, I have to—I'm gonna go down." But her voice, her tonal quality changed, and when it was higher, it just brightened up just enough to go, "Wow, that's a great voice!" Now, Nigel Lythgoe had to call me on the carpet for it, because it was clear to me that this kid sounded magnificent in the higher key, and "ehh" in the lower key. And so I could not say to her, "This is the key you're singing in." She has to decide which key she's singing in. So she chose to sing the lower key, and she was sent home. However, if she had performed in the higher key, she could have said, "Well, it's her [Byrd's] fault, she's the one that told me to sing in that higher key."[9]

By staying out of this decision process, those behind the scenes escape accountability, and both they and the contestants become less vulnerable to accusations of corporate manipulation. And to be accepted as potential Idols, contestants must continually prove and re-prove their authenticity by demonstrating self-knowledge, an awareness of their own voices, and an understanding of the kind of song that will display their talents to the maximum effect.

THE RIGHT SONG

Repertoire decisions provide a key site for the negotiation of *Idol* authenticity. Appropriate song selection is paramount, as the judges often remind the singers and their audience, and weekly successes and failures often seem to hinge upon it. Onscreen, assessment of this choice involves several overlapping modes of thinking about authenticity. To choose the right song, a contestant must consider (1) the authenticity of the song—something that resonates with viewers, preferably a song familiar to many people, associated with a respected artist, maybe evoking a sense of history; (2) personal artistic authenticity—finding the song that is right for *you*, for your vocal capabilities, and your personality, and then, as the judges repeat endlessly, "making it your own"; and (3) musical authenticity—the ability to sing the song convincingly and appropriately for the genre or audience's expectations or both, and the ability to communicate something to your audience.

Songs without history are risky. Ayla Brown of Season 5, upon singing "Unwritten," at the time a very recent vehicle for British singer Natasha Bedingfield, was sent home instead of being voted into the Top 12. As Brown stood onstage after the revelation of her dismissal, judge Simon Cowell reassured her, "Ayla, you know, it was the song. It wasn't you—it was the song."[10] This situation points again to the way the show requires concomitant consciousness of individualism and collective culture. First, although producers want "unique voices"—and at auditions ask the attendees to present "what makes you different from everyone else"—this uniqueness must function within the context of the show's well-known music. Additionally, although the music industry of which *American Idol* is a part moves—and moves on—at a very fast pace, it has often been considered unadvisable on the show to perform an extremely recent work. The same admonition also applies, at least to a degree, to the early rounds of auditions. Associate Music Director Michael Orland, who served as a judge for the Season 5 auditions, suggests that the judges' own acquaintance with the chosen repertoire could be important in the selection process. "Don't sing a song we probably don't know," he advised, "because we're not going to know how great your singing is or not."[11]

The familiarity rule is not set in stone. The 2007–2010 seasons introduced a new *Idol* interest in more recent repertoire. With contestants occasionally allowed to choose their songs in the absence of a predetermined theme, or from a general list of Billboard hits, some more current examples have popped up. When 2008 runner-up-to-be David Archuleta sang Chris Brown's 2006 hit "With You," he was praised by the judges for trying something new, but criticized for choosing the wrong song. In 2009 the semifinals included a "Billboard Hot 100" theme, and later in the season eventual winner Kris Allen successfully performed an arrangement of "Heartless," a Kanye West release from late in the previous year. And later seasons have also seen guest mentors of fairly fresh stardom (Jennifer Lopez and Gwen Stefani, for example, whose careers began to bloom in the late 1990s, and, in 2010, seventeen-year-old *Hannah Montana* star Miley Cyrus).

Even a beloved classic can come with hazards. Describing his experience as a judge for *American Idol*'s preliminary auditions in Season 5, Michael Orland admits, "I don't think I ever need to hear 'At Last' again, by Etta James [as sung by aspiring *Idol* contestants], and . . . I mean, I love the Bonnie Raitt song 'I Can't Make You Love Me,' but so do a lot of other people, evidently." About "At Last," he acknowledges, "there's not much anybody can do to that song for me."[12] During the live (on the East coast) broadcasts that air as the finalists are culled, the situation is equally precarious. The downfall of Season 5's Heather Cox, in the Top 24 (the level at which viewers began voting that season), was her decision to sing Mariah Carey's 1993 single "Hero." The song had been a highlight of Carey's early career and had been re-released as part of a charity single following 9/11. After a brief career slump, Carey had made a dazzling comeback in 2005, and was a very current artist when Cox sang "Hero" at the beginning of 2006. In response to Cox's performance, judge Paula Abdul regretfully told her, "when you sing songs that the great Mariah Carey sings, you run the hugest risk of being compared to icons. And right now there's no one hotter than Mariah Carey, and we're constantly reminded of how brilliant her voice is. It's a big, big, huge risk to take on a song like that."[13] Cox was eliminated from the competition following that performance.

The emphasis on older music is about more than accessibility and licensing fees. Michael Orland partially attributes the prevalence of music from the 1970s and 1980s to producer preference, positing that they "know all that music the best." In turn, he believes, the show may contribute to the perpetuation of interest in these older songs. He continues, "and it's funny, because I have heard, too, that there's been a little resurgence in, you know . . . People are buying Lionel Richie albums and Neil Sedaka albums, and I think *American Idol* had a lot to do with that."[14] It is important to note, however, that any such revivals inspired by *American Idol* have been part of a larger flare of pop nostalgia. CD reissues, the karaoke boom in the 1990s, and the importance of historical awareness in rock ideology are potential contributing factors. And even before *Pop Idol* aired in the U.K., British series such as *The 100 Greatest TV Moments* (Channel 4, 1999) and *I Love the Seventies* (BBC2, 2000) formed a chain of retrospective pop culture programming that in 2002 spread to the music station VH-1 in the U.S. However, it is entirely possible that *American Idol*'s link to the contemporary "retro" movements in music and media has also had an impact on their perpetuation.

American Idol anthologizes American popular music, especially from the 1960s on. Viewers watch performances on the show, then in turn choose these songs for their own auditions, and, if they are lucky, for their own performances onscreen, so that a cycle is set in motion. In this way a kind of *American Idol* canon—a pop canon to rival any rock canon—is established. This is the reason why Michael Orland and other judges must listen to hundreds of versions of "At Last" and "I Can't Make You Love Me" before the broadcast season even begins. People, too, are introduced as symbols of historical authenticity. For the first three seasons, special guest stars appeared to evaluate the finalists or to perform, or both, and later seasons featured occasional guests acting as mentors. Some broadcasts are even structured as outright tributes to these artists. The guests have been drawn from a pool of significant figures in American music history—guest judges and performers have included iconic songwriting teams Nick Ashford and Valerie Simpson, Kenneth Gamble and Leon Huff, and Jerry Lieber and Mike Stoller, as well as individual performers and songwriters such as Gladys Knight, Smokey Robinson, Tony Bennett, Diana Ross, Stevie Wonder, Donna Summer, and Barry Manilow.[15] A period of music history between the 1960s and 1970s was favored for the first several seasons, with the creative teams mentioned above, and the appearance in March 2004 of Motown's historic house band, The Funk Brothers. A genealogical line is being clearly drawn on the show, then, from the golden age of soul to its most recent progeny, the *American Idol* finalists. In one case there is also a direct dynastic link between the legacy of soul and the show: when finalist Elliott Yamin performed Donny Hathaway's "A Song for You," he pointed out that one of the *Idol* backup singers, Kenya C. Hathaway, was Hathaway's daughter.[16]

Under these conditions, and congruent with the features of Frith's rock-folk discourse, nostalgia is implicit. Sociologists Fabio B. DaSilva and Jim Faught have written of nostalgia as involving a "collective emotional reaction toward, if not an identification with, a symbolization of the past." They emphasize the inherent inauthenticity of the nostalgic past, in spite of common associations to the contrary, and suggest that it "becomes, ironically, an ahistorical defense of the status quo."[17] If, in the context of nostalgia, the imagined past lacks a specific historical context, then it may better appeal to an intergenerational market, allowing consumers in diverse age groups, with distinct ways of understanding their own historical experiences, to share one in music. According to *Idol*'s production firm FremantleMedia, the fifth season of *American Idol* ranked number 1 and number 2 (Tuesday and Wednesday broadcasts) among the 18–49, 18–34, and teen demographic age brackets. Additionally, I have encountered many avid pre-teen fans, as well as fans over 49. These viewers may participate through voting, online forums, and attendance at *Idol* events, but an age limit (16–28, formerly 16–24) prevents them from participating as contestants. Both Michael Orland and Debra Byrd emphasize the potential of the show as a family attraction, and in 2003 the Association of National Advertisers honored *American Idol* with a "Family Television Award" for its "cross-generational appeal."[18]

There are also ties between nostalgic repertoire choice and a wistfulness for older production techniques. In rock discourse, technological manipulation can equal an interference with natural sound and, therefore, inauthenticity. Unmediated, live performance, as Philip Auslander observes, has been interpreted as the "true test of musicianship undisguised by studio trickery."[19] Even recordings, if they are produced without extensive (or at least audible) technological treatment, can satisfy those with a disdain for "studio trickery." Top 32 contestant Charly Lowry, who appeared in Season 3 of *American Idol*, alludes to a similar concept in relation to her song choices (most notably, the 1969 Aretha Franklin hit "Chain of Fools"):

> *Well, every one of those songs that I chose to turn in were older songs, from like the fifties and sixties. None of them were contemporary, or songs that you would hear on the Top 40 at the present, at the current moment. They were all older songs. And the reason I did that is because . . . I feel like those were true artists, those were real singers, like there's no synthesizers to their voices, just their pure voices, and I feel like they were the most talented people. And that's what I want to be known for, I want to be known for making quality music instead of having to go into a studio, and have all these effects added to my voice, and, you know, just computer-generated vocals. And so I chose those older artists, and I chose the same songs from the older days because I feel like that's the style of music that I would love to sing—when I make it big.*[20]

In this case a pop singer relied on historical repertoire as if it contained some essence of authenticity now endangered by technological intrusion—as if it were folk music. Mastery of the music made by the first generations of soul singers becomes proof of real ability, real musicianship, and a sign of the authentic singer. But there is more to *Idol* success than proving oneself capable of singing Aretha. Contestants must negotiate the same sort of delicate equilibrium that defines the rock ideology, between tradition and innovation.

MAKING THE SONG YOUR OWN

American Idol performances sometimes provoke unfavorable comparisons to karaoke, even in the judges' comments. When Simon Cowell felt a contestant's performance to be particularly lacking, for example, he often employed such a reference to drive his point home. It is possible that the derogatory tenor of the word is based in the relationship between definitions of "amateur" (as in karaoke) and "professional," a distinction somewhat confounded on *American Idol* (see chapter 1). Are the singers considered to be professionals while they appear on the show? If they made a living singing before they entered the competition, do they revert to amateur status during their time awaiting the judgment of the *Idol* panel and America? The answers to these questions are uncertain, at best, when folk and rock discourse take place along a complex continuum between amateur and professional, art for art's sake and art for sale. Clearly the goal set for the contestants is to somehow be professional at the end of the season, and allusions to karaoke diminish that image. Nevertheless, Mattel's "*American Idol* Barbie" comes with her own karaoke machine, and by the end of 2008 there were three *American Idol* video games in Konami's *Karaoke Revolution* series.

If *American Idol* relies on the new fluid dynamics between production and consumption, the idea of karaoke is particularly powerful. Jacques Attali saw a "subversive practice" in the way that the karaoke-like *Minus One* permitted a person "to insinuate oneself into production."[21] *Idol* contestants (and, to a degree, players of the Konami games) have a similar opportunity to participate in what is happening behind the scenes of the music industry. It has been implied onscreen that some finalists even contribute to the musical arrangements they perform. The comparison to karaoke, however, is imperfect, as it suggests that the singing takes place with a prerecorded soundtrack. With several single-episode exceptions, as in Season 1's Big Band–themed night or Season 3's visit from the Funk Brothers, finalists during the first three seasons indeed sang to prerecorded backing tracks. However, since Season 4 *American Idol* finalists have sung with a live band led by Musical Director (and bassist) Rickey Minor and including three female backup vocalists. But the songs are rarely new;[22] almost always they are arrangements of preexisting, sometimes even iconic, works. They are "cover" songs.

Both George Plasketes and Christine R. Yano note that the cover song can be a pedagogical tool or even an instructional requirement. In *American Idol* it serves this purpose during the sixteen weeks of each season, the equivalent of the finalists' apprenticeship at a School of Pop. When recording their post-season albums, singers typically include several new songs written for them or even "co-written" by them.[23] But on their way to this independence, they must undergo an onstage training course in canonic literature in order to understand their place in music history as it can be imagined on *American Idol*. They also have to add something new, something all their own, to that history. In her study of *enka*, a prevalent genre in Japanese karaoke, Christine R. Yano turns Walter Benjamin's concept of *aura* on its head. She proposes that rather than resulting in a loss of aura, a loss of what is essentially authenticity, the popularity of *enka* in karaoke performance actually allows songs to *accumulate* authenticity with each repetition. Cover versions in fact become "the mark of a song's status."[24] This also happens, to a degree, among American popular music genres, and, as suggested above, songs repeated on *American Idol* contribute to a pop canon. Upping the Baudrillardian ante, there are even covers of covers (like Baudrillard's simulacra, copies of copies that replace the original as truth), as in Chris Daughtry's Season 5 performance of Live's arrangement of Johnny Cash's "I Walk the Line," or, in Season 8 (curiously, also a Johnny Cash song), Adam Lambert's controversial orientalist version of "Ring of Fire," which a singer named Dilana Robichaux had previously sung on another talent-based reality show, *Rock Star: Supernova*.[25] In both cases the singers eschewed the original major modality in favor of a minor one, perhaps in itself a change significant enough to forestall accusations of imitation, and for "Ring of Fire" the house band was supplemented with tabla, zil, and sitar sounds. Songs can gain renewed currency through this kind of performance history, a reinvigoration through replication. But as Yano also points out, Euro-American cover singers are also practically *morally* obligated to deviate from the original in order to earn the inscription of authenticity. This responsibility is a banner taken up by the *American Idol* judges, who continuously enjoin contestants to "make the song your own."

The most fortunate of *American Idol*'s singers will be praised for having satisfied that requirement.; others are chastised for "copycat". With cover songs, as Plasketes writes, artists experience the phenomenon of personalization, of "possession," as an exercise, as a challenge, or, in a more passive process, as a natural "inhabitation" of the song.[26] In *American Idol* the idea of a unique performance becomes a key trope, a duty and goal for contestants trying to reach a precarious balance between two understandings of originality—an originality of *origins,* the need to live up to the work of a song's original artist, and an originality that is seen as an innovative expression of individuality.

Voicing Identity: Melisma

How does a singer stake out his or her claim to someone else's vocal territory? One method frequently used and alluded to on *American Idol* involves melismatic melodic variation, articulated through elements of vocal style that function here as ornamentation. On the show this practice is usually described as "ad libs" or "riffing" (two terms associated with improvisatory performance), "runs," or, when deemed particularly indulgent, "oversinging." In his study of African American musics, Earl L. Stewart refers to it as "Afro-melisma,"[27] and identifies it as a characteristic practice in both African American gospel and secular American popular music. He cites Whitney Houston's 1992 cover of "I Will Always Love You," originally recorded by Dolly Parton in 1973, as an example. That is a significant instance: the story of an iconic African American singer covering a song associated with a white country artist—in a virtual reversal of historical rock 'n' roll appropriations—and laying claim to her fame through the use of melismatic vocalism. It is imperative to note the racializing implications of melisma's omnipresence in contemporary popular music and in the explicitly American context of *American Idol.* There it becomes a vocal, and thus embodied, symbol of blackness, and demonstrates how, as Deborah Wong incisively puts it, "White appropriations of Black authenticities continue to have ideological and commercial force."[28] It polysemically bestows different authenticities to African American and white singers, as well as to singers who fit neither racial categorization. In one deft, quicksilver vocal gesture, we can hear all of America's music history—a performance of the racialization of popular music, a reenactment of the tensions woven throughout the fabric of American culture. Melisma's racialized, nation-specific connotations have even been obliquely acknowledged on *American Idol*. In 2004, during her broadcast audition, eventual finalist Leah Vladowski (in Hollywood, she changed her name to Leah LaBelle) told the judges of her parents' flight from communist Bulgaria, and then sang Whitney Houston's 1996 song "I Believe in You and Me." After her melismatic performance, Randy Jackson appeared startled. "It's weird," he declared, "that kind of, like, gospel thing coming from Bulgaria, dude—that's wild!" This response from Jackson, who is African American, confirmed the interpretation of melisma as both a national American and specifically African American (religious) musical practice.[29] Melisma highlights the importance of vocal expression outside of textuality, exposing the voice as what Aaron A. Fox astutely calls a "summarizing symbol of identity." But whereas Fox's study of country music centers on the voice as a "medium of class-conscious social practice," in pop melisma we can hear the voice as a medium of race-conscious, religion-conscious social practice as well. We hear the love affair with *Love and Theft*—Eric Lott's name for the racial complexities of appropriation in America's early popular culture—and the racialized interchange where the sacred and the secular have crossed.[30] Melisma becomes a kind of shibboleth, a vocal emblem at the nucleus of musical Americanness.

The *Idol* judges' reaction to melisma varies, but both positive and negative responses frequently cite the importance of musical individualization. Early in the first season Randy Jackson critiqued a rendition of Whitney Houston's 1993 hit "Run to You" performed by semifinalist Angela Peel: "I thought there were, like, too many runs going on, but you were trying to make it your own," and the other two judges echoed the latter part of his statement. During the same episode semifinalist Gil Sinuet sang the Stevie Wonder hit "Ribbon in the Sky" and ended with a long melisma. Jackson complimented him on this ornamental figure, telling him: "I like the way you did the little

curl thing at the end, because you kind of tried to make it your own."
A writer at the *Sacramento News and Review* describes a moment on
American Idol in which a judge complained that he could not hear the
melody through a young woman's ornamentation. "I was just making
the song my own," the contestant insisted.[31] Such incidents indicate a
discursive relationship between voice and vocal practice, the mediation of individual identity in reality television, and a double-edged
concept of virtuosity that encompasses competence and excess, replication and creativity.

The idea of virtuosity is complicated by a somewhat convoluted
interpretational history not only involving music but also intertwined
with Roman Catholic, Calvinist, and republican moral and political
ideals. Foreshadows of this story can be found in Niccolò Machiavelli's political conceptualization of *virtù*, laid out in *The Prince*. Machiavelli's definition of political virtuosity—the possession of qualities of
virtù—incorporates, like *American Idol*'s vocal virtuosity, both an assertion of individuality and a mimetic process. Robert Walser has referred to the virtue of individuality in his study of heavy metal guitar
style and the Western classical (musical) model of virtuosity, citing
the interpretation of Machiavelli's use of "*virtù*" in the sense of heroism and will (a meaning that also informs Max Weber's religious virtuoso), of skill, strength and power, of the development of "individual
excellence." This is *virtù* in rock ideology, celebrating individuality.
But Martyn de Bruyn points out in his dissertation on the politics of
virtù that, for Machiavelli, *virtù* is "not acquired through training but
through imitation instead. By imitating the examples of the great in
history some level of *virtù* can be achieved."[32] In Machiavelli's words
(here translated by Harvey C. Mansfield, who chooses to write "*virtù*"
as a polyvalent "virtue"):

> A prudent man should always enter upon the paths beaten by great
> men, and imitate those who have been most excellent, so that if his
> own virtue does not reach that far, it is at least in the odor of it. He
> should do as prudent archers do when the place they plan to hit ap-
> pears too distant, and knowing how far the strength of their bow
> carries, they set their aim much higher than the place intended, not
> to reach such height with their arrow, but to be able with the aid of so
> high an aim to achieve their plan.[33]

Successful virtuosi in *American Idol* must enter upon a similar path, walking a careful line between musical genealogy and the performance of individuality. They display the often overreaching ambition Machiavelli counsels for his Prince in singing the repertoire of American icons, and further it with the incorporation of their own, personalized demonstration of vocal virtuosity. It is also worth noting, as De Bruyn does, that Machiavelli does not position *virtù* as a binary opposite to badness or to vice but to "idleness."[34] In the context of popular music, however, vocal virtuosity has conversely become synonymous with *Idol*-ness, a desired quality in a cultural leader elected by citizens. The Machiavellian in *American Idol*, then, is less associated with the familiar idea of ruthless strategizing than with a combination of individuality, the appreciation of music history, and a keen aptitude for mimesis.

The imitation of historical examples provides a key point of contention for critics of *American Idol*'s contestants. Contrasting the *American Idol* finalists with the artists whose songs they have covered, Jody Rosen tells *New York Times* readers that "the great soul singers of the 70's were distinguished by the grain of their voices . . . rather than by cramming songs with hundreds of gratuitous notes."[35] His choice of words here is significant. Roland Barthes coined the phrase "the grain of the voice" as part of a framework within which he believed "the temptation of ethos" could be avoided. Rosen and other critics are searching for a similar component in the voice, beyond cultural and aesthetic consideration, "the body in the voice" that seems to them obscured by an overuse of melisma. The vocal ornamentation under consideration, then, is based in the world of what Barthes understands, after Julia Kristeva, as *pheno-song*, encompassing taste, expression, and everything that "forms the tissue of cultural values." Within the category of *pheno-song*, Barthes names "the coded form of the melisma."[36] It is also notable that the first definition listed for the term "melisma" in the *New Grove Dictionary of Music and Musicians* (2nd ed.) is given as "a manner of singing" and then as "an *ethos* of singing."[37]

Alternatively some criticism implies that there is *too much* body in the voice, berating *Idol* contestants for their "vocal gymnastics."[38] It is a particularly kinetic way of singing, very often accompanied by a physical gesture, a hand lifted into the air in a way reminiscent of prayerful supplication—although one gospel singer told me that for her the two were very different, one guiding the vocal motion between pitches, the other a sign of submission to God's will.[39] And singers in the first televised rounds of *American Idol*'s auditions present their voices and bodies in a particularly naked way, a cappella and alone on a stage in front of the judges. Without instruments or co-performers, it is very nearly *only* the "body in the voice" and the voice in the body that can be judged. In a striking moment early in Season 8 (2009), the new fourth judge, singer-songwriter Kara DioGuardi, engaged in what might be termed a melisma fight with auditionee Katrina Darrell. Darrell performed her broadcast audition, Mariah Carey's 1990 single "Vision of Love," wearing only a bikini swimsuit and high heels. After Cowell and Jackson approved her for Hollywood, DioGuardi objected to her sartorial decision and critiqued her singing. DioGuardi demonstrated how she would have preferred the song, and Darrell fired back, arguing that her version had been better. The climax of this squabble was the simultaneous utterance of a cadenza-like melisma, two voices in competitive virtuosity. During the season finale in May, Darrell was invited onstage (again, in a bikini) to receive a tongue-in-cheek "Golden Idol" award and, after Ryan Seacrest offered comment on her apparent recent bust enhancement, he asked her to perform "Vision of Love" once more. The performance was interrupted as Kara DioGuardi entered the stage, microphone in hand, took over the song—and tore open her dress to display her own bikini.[40] What had been a battle of vocal gesture was suddenly, literally, revealed to be an (explicitly gendered) contest of bodies.

The general practice of melisma has, in recent years, been widely maligned by music critics. The magazine *Blender* has called it one of the "50 Worst Things to Happen to Music" and explains it as an "*Idol*-promulgated school of vocal histrionics."[41] The description of the practice as *histrionic* demonstrates a peculiarly Western, and potentially gendered, understanding of melisma as something disordered—or as a sign of disorder—and even unnatural. Musicologist Andrew Oster has discussed it as representative of stuttering and disability in an example of seventeenth-century Western classical opera, and melisma certainly also plays an important role in numerous nineteenth-century (particularly female) "mad scenes." This is not to say that melisma is always associated with madness in opera but only to suggest that such an association, if it exists for a listener, might create a cultural predisposition to connect the two in other contexts. Some see the intensive application of melisma as an act of aggression. Jody Rosen, in his *New York Times* editorial, used the phrase "violent [Mariah] Carey emulation" to describe the prevalent melismatic vocal practices of *American Idol* contestants. In addition to such allegations of belligerent imitation, judgment of vocally articulated honesty is a recurring theme; melisma can be an authentic form of an artist's personal expression, or it can be unnecessary style without emotional substance. G. Brown, for example, writes that "the expressive power" of Aretha Franklin, Ray Charles, and contemporaries "has been undermined," and "melisma has been largely reduced to an identifiable artifice."[42]

The temporal gap separating *American Idol* performances from a song's original rendition can work either for or against a contestant. The distance might invite a favorable comparison, or it might parallel the generational gap between the young singers and the judges and producers. In 2003's *World Idol* event, Kelly Clarkson—*American Idol*'s first winner—competed against ten other winners from around the (global) *Idols* franchise. She sang "(You Make Me Feel Like A) Natural Woman," first recorded by Carole King, but best known as Aretha Franklin's 1967 hit. The judging panel represented both the above responses, some flatteringly invoking the song's historical past and others expressing a distaste for contemporary melismatic style. Holland's judge Henkjan Smits told Clarkson, "This is how Carole King meant this song to be," and South African judge Randall Abrahams said, "Kelly, I imagine that Carole King has two things to be very thankful for. Aretha Franklin is one of them, and I think you're the other." Diverging from Franklin's nearly melisma-free recording (King's was also very light on the melisma), Clarkson had performed the song in an intensely melismatic way during her time on *American Idol,* and increased both the frequency and pace of her melismas on this second occasion. Example 2.1 shows the way Clarkson sang the phrase "you make me feel so alive" in her *American Idol* performance,

Example 2.1. Kelly Clarkson, passage from "Natural Woman" (re-aired on *American Idol Rewind*, March 10, 2007).

Example 2.2. Kelly Clarkson, melismatic passage from "Natural Woman" (*World Idol*, December 25, 2003). Corresponds to the last three measures of Example 2.1.

ending with a three-measure, whistle-tone high F♯. The F♯ was approached in a slide from a pitch area just below, indicated in my transcription by a short glissando marking. Example 2.2 transcribes the *World Idol* melisma, on the second syllable of "alive," that replaced the prolonged F♯ in a different articulation of virtuosity.

British judge Pete Waterman (from the U.K.'s *Pop Idol*) chastised Clarkson for "all those trills and frills," and she assured him that her mother often said the same thing.[43] Any departure from a performance style associated with iconic artists can garner charges of poorly executed facsimile, as if the changes were accidental. And in cases where contestants are covering songs with well-known preexisting covers—for example, covering Mariah Carey's version of the Jackson 5 hit "I'll Be There"—the protests can be even stronger. Simon Cowell himself expressed this point of view in an interview with Terry Gross on National Public Radio's *Fresh Air*:

> **Gross:** . . . that kind of melisma where you're singing around the note (Cowell: yes), and up and down and around the note, and embellishing a lot (Cowell: yes), without doing a good job of it, without really adding anything, and it becomes really annoying. It just becomes pure mannerism. There's a lot of that on the radio; there was a lot of that on *American Idol* too. . . . Do you ever feel that way, that you're watching this kind of catalogue of things that have gone wrong in pop music?

> **Cowell:** Oh, a hundred percent, because, like you, Terry, I loathe that
> kind of singing. . . . It's almost an affectation now, because you're not
> supposed to sing like that. I absolutely loathe it . . . they are copying
> bad singers in the first place and they—because it becomes like some
> ghastly Xerox machine, you know, the original isn't very good, and
> the copies are even worse.[44]

Cowell and the critics describe *Idol* singing as, effectively, hyper-
melismatic, approaching Baudrillard's simulacrum as their covers
produce copies of copies ad infinitum, entirely abandoning the realm
of the "real"—of the beloved soul singers of the late sixties. And considering black music's discursive position as "body music,"[45] if a surfeit
of soul melisma reduces the body in the voice, then this vocal excess
means a loss of "real" blackness, of racialized authenticity.

According to Debra Byrd, executive producers and the singers'
coaches discourage the immoderation in melisma. Indeed, in San
Francisco, at the preliminary cattle-call auditions in 2004, I heard executive producer Ken Warwick admonish the waiting crowd "no riffing," following the warning with his own demonstration of melisma.[46]
However, Byrd suggests that some singers simply fall back on a deeply
ingrained habit when under the stress of live performance:

> *We give them the same critique [as the press]. However, what these
> people, and . . . There are two things that are coming to my mind: the
> first is, they are a product of their musical environment. That's what
> they hear on the radio, that's what they think people want to hear.
> That's number one. Number two is that he's not taking into account
> that no matter how much I say, "Sing it straighter," "Too many notes,"
> you know, "You're singing too many notes," when that camera is on
> them, when they've got millions of people voting for them, when the
> heat is on, they're going to fall back into their comfort zone. Period.
> And you would, too.*[47]

Melisma can supply this "comfort zone" in the sense of familiarity
but also in terms of vocal technique. In my personal experience as a
singing instructor, I have found that vocalists sometimes choose to
employ melisma, in which subglottal pressure varies,[48] when they are
unprepared to maintain the consistent breath pressure required for

holding long single notes and phrases. This occurs especially when performers feel nervous, when the physiological demands of regulating airflow can seem suddenly implausible.

Critics have complained that *American Idol*'s singers overuse melisma as a conscious device, and consistently trace this alleged abuse to the influence of Whitney Houston and Mariah Carey on R&B, hip hop, and neo-soul vocalisms. Both singers recorded highly melismatic hit ballads in the early 1990s. In his dissertation regarding African American ballad singers in the 1990s, Richard Allen Rischar describes a revival of interest in spiritual themes during the time of Carey's debut, manifested in popular music.[49] As this trend came about at the time of the First Gulf War, melisma and its gospel connotations might have offered some musical comfort to a worried nation. It is striking that *Idol*'s new wave of would-be Mariah Careys surfaced during a comparable situation of crisis, and during a similar flare of spiritual discourse (see chapter 4). Further, it is noteworthy that *American Idol* judge Randy Jackson is Carey's musical director.[50]

Mariah Carey and Whitney Houston are clearly pop paragons for aspiring Idols, as confirmed in 2004 when I conducted two limited surveys among singers at *American Idol*–related events. The first survey took place at a local competition called "Central Coast Idol", organized by the local FOX station KKFX FOX-11, with the radio station SLY 96 FM. The prize at this competition was a guaranteed audition in San Francisco for the fourth season of *American Idol*. In earlier seasons there had been a policy at *American Idol* auditions limiting the number of attendees allowed to sing, so that even camping out at the audition site did not necessarily ensure anyone a place. In recent seasons, everyone who has attended has been heard, so the "guarantee" offered through local pre-audition competitons like "Central Coast Idol" means more in the way of bypassing the waiting and ensuring local publicity. At "Central Coast Idol", of the twenty-one people who completed my survey, eleven (52.4%) included Mariah Carey or Whitney Houston, or both, in their answers to the question, "Which artists do you consider to be your major vocal/musical influences?" Of these respondents, ten were female and one was male. At the official *American Idol* Season 4 auditions in San Francisco, of the fifty-five people who completed my survey, eighteen (32.7%) cited Carey or Houston, or both, as important personal influences in answer to the same question. Of these, fourteen were female and four were male.[51] That a few of these respondents were male indicates that the influence of these popular singers does cross gender boundaries, at least to some degree. Although the percentage citing their influence was smaller in the larger pool of respondents, it is still a considerable presence.

For some, the influence of artists like Carey and Houston, and their musical descendants—Christina Aguilera, in particular—is felt and cultivated quite deliberately. Rocío Torres, who auditioned for the third season of *American Idol* in Los Angeles, described to me how she came to absorb stylistic elements like melisma from her favorite singers. I asked her how she felt about the contestants' prevalent style and the characteristic melodic "runs":

> *Yeah, it started off with—I don't know, I'll say for me, Mariah Carey. I would just mimic people singing on the radio, like Mariah Carey and Selena. Those were the two that—I always tell people they taught me how to sing. I had no vocal training. If I never sang, I mean if I never listened to the radio 24/7 or danced, it would have never happened. I just—I mimic the way they sing, that's why I have that style now.*[52]

Celina Lima auditioned for Season 5 in San Francisco and relates a similar experience. When I asked her which singers influenced her melismatic style, she told me:

> *Well, when I was growing up, you know, middle school and high school, every day for three or four hours, I would just sit in my room and listen to Whitney Houston and Mariah Carey, and Christina Aguilera and Jessica Simpson. It was them four and me in my room, seriously, every day until it got dark. And I would just sit there for hours and just imitate them exactly, and be able to sing exactly like they did. . . . So my style's changed, now, from what it was in high school, but I definitely don't copy them, you know, exactly the way they do it, [it's] my own thing now, whereas up until I was like sixteen, seventeen, I was just imitating the artists, instead of really having my own style.*[53]

Alexandra Rajaofera, who auditioned for Season 4 in both Las Vegas and San Francisco, also counts Mariah Carey as important to her ornamentation choices: "I definitely learned it by just listening to Mariah Carey or Christina [Aguilera], and just copying it exactly. Just—that's how I learned, like, *how* to do it. But then I guess you just take from that and apply the same concepts, and just change around what goes where."[54]

What Ms. Lima and Ms. Rajaofera imply is that after one learns the practice of melisma through imitation, something more original must happen. The concepts must then be applied and developed into a personal style. The following examples are excerpted transcriptions from the song "Run to You" (by Judd Friedman and Allan Rich, 1991), as performed by Whitney Houston (Example 2.3) on the soundtrack album for her 1992 film *The Bodyguard*, and Angela Peel (Example 2.4) as a semifinalist on *American Idol*.[55] Peel's version of the song was much shorter than Houston's four and a half minutes, at just over one minute and five seconds, because of the time constraints of the televised format. The *Idol* arrangement was also keyed one whole step lower than Houston's recording. There was some direct imitation on Peel's part, with nearly precise reproduction of Houston's melismatic work in the aspiring Idol's fourth and sixth measures (and these notes are not offered in the published piano/vocal score). However, Peel's seventh measure, leading into the next section of the song, diverges from Houston's. The *Idol* contestant is given less time to make the transition to the subsequent bridge and, perhaps to fit in a comparable virtuosic moment, accelerates her melismatic rhythm earlier. This practice might offer one possible basis for the perception that *Idol* contestants use too much melisma—that the pace is sped up and smaller note values used in order to offer listeners a sense of the singers' virtuosic capabilities, within the very brief moments they are given to prove themselves. Despite Randy Jackson's judgment that Peel sang "too many runs," many of her ornamentation choices, in fact, seem strikingly similar to those in Houston's performance. With her decision to both borrow from the original recording and add her own melismatic patterns, Peel was grounding her performance in the familiar, but simultaneously demonstrating her personal abilities and style. She was therefore, as each judge in turn stated in response, making the song her own.

Example 2.3. Whitney Houston, "Run to You," from the film *The Bodyguard* (Arista, 1992). Words and music by Allan Rich and Jud Friedman. Copyright © 1992 by PSO Ltd.; Music By Candlelight; Songs of Universal, Inc.; and Nelana Music. This arrangement copyright © 2010 by PSO Ltd.; Music By Candlelight; Songs of Universal, Inc.; and Nelana Music. All rights for Music By Candlelight administered by Songs of Universal, Inc. International copyright secured. All rights reserved. *Reprinted by permission of Hal Leonard Corporation.*

Example 2.4. Angela Peel, "Run to You" (*American Idol Rewind,* February 10, 2007; originally performed on *American Idol,* June 26, 2002).

In spite of the disdain from critics, *American Idol* and its singers are applying melisma to their construction of a particular brand of authenticity, something conservative of certain aspects of American culture. For African American artists, Richard Allen Rischar sees gospel-style ornamentation as "a symbol maintaining Southern (rural) emotional, even spiritual authenticity" within a complex North/South dialectic.[56] In chapter 5 I further examine how these associations are appropriated and exploited in *American Idol,* with African American vocal practices and the South adopted as metonyms for the whole of the United States and its popular music. The cultural weight assigned to African American singing styles is underlined in the pervasive presence of melismatic practice in performances of the national anthem, particularly at sporting events. All the *Idol*-critical editorials I have surveyed note the gospel- and soul-derived character of melisma as used in popular music. That many of these publications use the term "melisma," which before Rosen's 2003 *New York Times* piece was not commonly found in public press, is a testament to *American Idol's* influence on popular music discourse. Two internet encyclopedias (Wikinfo.org and DictionaryLaborLawTalk.com) have explicitly included in their definitions of "melisma" the singing on *American Idol,* as well as "celebrity performances of the 'Star Spangled Banner.'" These descriptions tell us something vital about the associations made in critical discourse regarding melisma and its cultural functions. It is particularly linked to the popular, to the sacred, and to its semi-secular relation, the patriotic (or civil-religious). As I discuss in chapter 4, the patriotic and the sacred often intersect on the *American Idol* stage, and melisma can play an important role as an aural cue. Melisma, "The Star-Spangled Banner," and *American Idol* are also linked clearly on the show. "The Star-Spangled Banner" has had a special presence on *American Idol* from its first broadcast episode, when Season 1 finalist A. J. Gil auditioned for the judges with an ornamented version of the national anthem (Example 2.5). In pre-performance video clips, Season 2's Julia DeMato and Clay Aiken were shown singing it melismatically in their hometowns, and Season 3's John Stevens was shown singing it in his hometown high school choir. The second part of the Season 3 finale, when the focus shifted from the "red carpet" to the Kodak Theater stage, began with Season 1 finalist Tamyra Gray singing the anthem. Singers who cannot remember the words, or who sing the anthem poorly, have also been featured—Season 2's eighth episode offered a montage of these, and the fourth season opened with *Idol* hopeful Leandra Jackson's unsuccessfully melismatic audition. She was rejected for her difficulties negotiating pitch in her melismas, but she was brought back to patriotically launch that season's finale.

Singers today commonly execute the national anthem with ornamentation evoking gospel and soul. The revolutionary soul performance of Marvin Gaye at the 1983 NBA All-Star game opened up
the possibility—though José Feliciano's controversially unorthodox
arrangement at the 1968 World Series also contained a degree of
melisma—and melismatic versions have increased in recent years.[57]
Mark Anthony Neal calls Gaye's performance a moment that "suggested that African-Americans had a right to 'African-Americanize'
the composition, because of the price they paid for American democracy, while highlighting African-American music's hegemony within
American popular music and perhaps American popular culture."
Whitney Houston's 1991 performance at Super Bowl XXV was influential as well. Ken McLeod notes that the recording of Houston's
bombastic performance, which included melisma, was the first to find
a place on the pop charts since Feliciano's version was released as a
single by RCA. Houston's singing at the Super Bowl was accompanied
by a flyover of F-14s, in response to the very recent start of the Gulf
War's bombing campaign.[58] Her rendition can also be associated with
the next war, as it was re-released by Arista in October 2001, during a
flood of patriotic 9/11 charity albums.

   A. J. Gil's performance of the national anthem on *American Idol*
(Example 2.5) also came in the year after the 9/11 attacks. Houston's
influence is clear, at least in the structure of Gil's ornamental motifs;
his choices are different, but some patterns are very similar. One ornament type that occurs in both Gil's and Houston's performances
is the grace note followed by an upward leap (an articulation more
distinct than a simple slide between pitches), on "by" in Gil's second
full measure, and on "stars" in Houston's "whose [broad] stripes and
bright stars" (Example 2.6). For both singers, the upward leap is accompanied by a change in vocal timbre or register, or both, although
this stands out more clearly in Gil's version. A second pattern found
in both renditions is a motif from the fifth to the seventh scale degree
(where the traditional melody stays on the seventh degree), including
a passing tone between 5 and 7, and a lower neighbor tone on the sixth
("watched," Example 2.7). In Gil's version, this occurs on "hailed" in
measure 6, "watched" in measure 14, and "night" in measure 22. Inci-
dentally, Tamyra Gray also placed the same ornament at "hailed" and

Example 2.5. A. J. Gil, "The Star-Spangled Banner" (*American Idol Rewind,* December 23, 2006; originally performed on *American Idol,* June 11, 2002).

Example 2.6. Whitney Houston, "The Star-Spangled Banner" (Arista, 2001). Passage corresponds to mm. 9–10 in Example 2.5; ornament compares to the one in m. 2 in Example 2.5.

"watched" in her a cappella Season 3 finale performance—she made the song her own, however, with a lowered seventh degree at "early" and at "perilous." In Houston's "watched," an extra flourish is added on the way to the seventh degree, with another passing tone between

Example 2.7. Whitney Houston, "The Star-Spangled Banner" (Arista 2001). Passage corresponds to mm. 13–14 in Example 2.5.

Example 2.8. Whitney Houston, "The Star-Spangled Banner" (Arista, 2001). Passage corresponds to m. 28 in Example 2.5.

Example 2.9. Tamyra Gray, "The Star-Spangled Banner" (*American Idol,* May 26, 2004). Passage corresponds to Example 2.8, and m. 28 in Example 2.5.

E♭ and G. Both Houston's and Gil's versions also highlight the word "wave" with melisma, though Gil favors an incomplete-complete neighbor combination (or echappée-neighbor), and Houston's trill is embellished from below, creating a kind of appoggiatura before the passing tone combination (Example 2.8). Tamyra Gray used an ornament almost identical to Houston's but without the last reiterated neighbor figure (Example 2.9).

Personalized melismatic technique can contribute to an audience's sense of the performer's authenticity or inauthenticity, but certain conventions must be adhered to as well. Richard Allen Rischar describes the practice of melismatic singing in the performances of artists like Mariah Carey as representative of a particularly African American "vocal etiquette," which is "based on an intimate relationship between form, expression, and vocal style."[59] The idea of vocal etiquette, although probably always racialized in popular music, can be useful in a larger context of genre as well. All singers on *American Idol* must meet standards of vocal etiquette specific to each genre they are assigned. There are exceptions to this rule, as when the authenticity of a singer's individual style trumps the need to sound stylistically appropriate to a genre. Melisma, for example, can be an aural sign-post indicating to the listener that genre borders are being crossed, as when the practice infiltrates a traditionally less-ornamented song. This occurred, for example, early in Season 6, when soon-to-be finalist Chris Richardson performed Keith Urban's "Tonight I Wanna Cry."[60] Richardson had previously proved himself adept in an eclectic range of pop genres, all the while favoring a highly melismatic, R&B-tinged style, and his rendition of Urban's country song was no different. The audience cheered for the virtuosity of a particularly long melisma. Randy Jackson approvingly linked the "runs" to Richardson's ability to add his "own twist," once again demonstrating the relationship between melisma and the perception of originality—this time an originality grounded in a correlation between vocality and genre.

Style and Individuality

That correlation is made frequently in *American Idol*, although it does not always involve melisma. The maintenance across genres of other vocal gestures and timbral specifics is also treated as a marker of orig-inality. When Season 5 finalist Chris Daughtry performed "I Walk the Line," the judges praised him for sticking to his usual rock style. Cowell even commended him as "the first artist we've ever had on this show who's actually refused to compromise."[61]

Other signs of musical authenticity and personal originality in-clude the playing of iconic genre-specific instruments—contestants were not allowed to accompany themselves until Season 7, the first year won by a guitar-playing rock singer (David Cook)—as well as sartorial decisions and hairstyle, sites indicative that *American Idol* is not only a genred phenomenon but also a gendered one. Seven female rock singers on *American Idol*, for example, have sported hairstyles enhanced by pink or scarlet dye.[62] Like the hair of the 1980s MTV stars—Madonna with her bleached blondness and dark roots, Tina Turner with her wigs, Cyndi Lauper with her rosy highlights—the dye jobs made no apologies for inauthenticity of color, at once engag-ing and reconfiguring the female sphere of appearance. Explaining the ways in which rock ideology is gendered, Lisa A. Lewis observes that dyed hair presents "a rebellious, anti-feminine, 'she's so unusual' image." For MTV's hopeful heirs on *Idol,* hair color becomes, by association, a quick, direct reference point for rock authenticity. *Idol's* women who rock have sometimes performed iconic songs by MTV's early female artists, including Pat Benatar's "Heartbreaker," Lauper's "Time After Time" and Turner's "Proud Mary." Contestants, both male and female, who align their genre loyalties with rock are extolled as emblems of authenticity. About pioneering *Idol* rockers Bo Bice and Constantine Maroulis in Season 4, Paula Abdul told *MTV News* that, in the past, rock singers on the show "never were authentic . . . these two guys are the real deal." Judges tell finalists specializing in rock, "You know who you are," "you're the real thing," or "you always stay true to yourself"—variants of "you made it your own" calibrated specifically for rock. Like Polonius's famous advice to Laertes, these are terms that illuminate the ideological relationship between sincerity and authenticity.[63] In addition to implying individuality and self-knowledge, these phrases give the impression that singers will resist the pressures of a manipulative and inauthenticating music industry. They can be counted on; they will not "sell out" the way the judges feared Micah Read would need to.

Rock and pop form one of the many binaries that *American Idol* at once collapses and reinforces. The show's shifting priorities support the idea, as Johan Fornäs has suggested, that "the rock-pop field is a contested continuum" rather than a fixed binary opposition.[64] Simultaneously operating in multiple overlapping discourses, the show underscores the porosity of genre boundaries and yet still relies on familiar dialogues of reification. These conversations are given voice, literally, in the contestants' performance practices, and in the ideological vocabulary of those who evaluate them. Participants—producers, contestants, and viewers—know this language, the lexis of authenticity that structures a complex grammar of nation, race, self, and genre. At the heart of the matter, the show is an industry project, meant to sell music-related goods in the widest market possible, and authenticity is one of the most powerful devices in the commercial arsenal.

3

WIN OR LOSE ·
SUCCESS AND FAILURE AND
THE AMERICAN DREAM

SELLING THE DREAM

"American Idol. American Music. American Dream," read an online advertisement for *American Idol*'s 2005 season.[1] This is the formula at the heart of *American Idol*'s success, where the entanglement of American myth and American music becomes a calculable equation with money as the sum. According to Simon Cowell, he and *Idols* co-creator Simon Fuller peddled the idea for the show's format unsuccessfully in the United States before they produced it in the United Kingdom in 2001. They "tried to sell it initially as the great American dream," he told Larry King, "which is somebody who could be a cocktail waitress one minute, within 16 weeks could become the most famous person in America."[2] No one bought that dream, so Cowell and Fuller took it home and turned it into the sensation *Pop Idol*. Its success in the U.K. caught Rupert Murdoch's attention—and the following year, when national crisis had thrust the reaffirmation of American culture into every media spotlight, *American Idol* entered the scene. If it seems ironic that an explicit expression of American ideology sold in the U.S. only after it became a hit across the pond, we have notable precedent. There is a history of such appropriative cycles in popular music, and the *Idols* version of the Dream has, in the end, been an undeniably victorious British Invasion.

The strongest Idol potential seems located in those whose lives can be edited to fit familiar accounts of the American Dream: local boys make good, naïve young women make it in the big city, and immigrants are made into Americans. Su Holmes notes the significance ascribed to class-related definitions of ordinariness in the *Pop Idol* version of the Dream,[3] and the same is true for *American Idol*. Here are Cowell's cocktail waitresses and other young people struggling to escape all manner of economic and social troubles. First-season winner Kelly Clarkson actually worked as a cocktail waitress. She had taken that job in her hometown of Burleson, Texas, after losing her Los Angeles apartment in a fire immediately before the audition. And third-season winner Fantasia Barrino was a struggling single teenage mother. Such experiences of hardship are displayed often throughout each season. During a broadcast that focused on interviews with the final five contestants, Barrino told host Ryan Seacrest, "I want to see Zion [her daughter] have the best, things that I didn't have, I want to see her have it."[4] This is the generational, temporal expression of the American Dream, the potential to improve the class status of one's children, to ensure a future in which the American Dream is no longer even necessary.

The American Dream is a mythology not defined by a single narrative but by a collection of overlapping stories tracing some transformation of identity—a mutability of place, class, even ethnicity. Intertwined dreams of migration or immigration, financial opportunity, and social recognition all hinge upon movement and risk; whether they are about fame or fortune (or both at once), or plainer goals such as education or home ownership, they are all dreams of moving up, moving on. Cumulatively these dreams have been interpreted as expressive of the pursuit of happiness declared along with American independence. And though related pursuits are certainly cultivated all over the world, the words "American Dream" have become an unofficial "national motto" and birthright.[5] That birthright, presumably, is also transferrable to new citizens who shed their geographic past upon naturalization—just as other Dream protagonists leave behind a birthplace for a new place in the public eye—and trade old affiliations for hyphenated Americanness.

Several such narratives of aspiration, ambition, and the hope of achievement coalesce in Hollywood, where *American Idol* explores and exploits them all. The dream of fame on the surface is the most obvious, but it is entangled with others. And although talent is the *Idol* headline, it is far from the whole story. The crux of the American Dream, according to Robert C. Rowland and John M. Jones, is not heroism but a person's ability to enact established American ideals. Extraordinariness, in the romance of the American Dream, is a quality assigned to— bestowed upon—those who perform the Dream satisfactorily. And it is a romance, in the literary sense Rowland and Jones employ, a political one in which the agency of the protagonist is defined by values, and the application of those values to opportunity. "The protagonist must be an ordinary person," they write, "who accomplishes great things because his/her actions are motivated by values he/she shares with other Americans."[6] The two following cases illustrate how in the end, when it comes to the power of the Dream, the demonstration of American values is at least as important as the successful achievement of goals.

IMMIGRANT SONG: BAO VIET NGUYEN AND HIS AMERICAN DREAM

A 2004 episode of *American Idol* told the story of contestant Bao Viet Nguyen. "His parents escaped from Indochina to realize the American Dream," viewers were told in Ryan Seacrest's voiceover. "Now *he* may just do that" (original emphasis). Mr. Nguyen's father was shown, wiping tears from his eyes, and although he was speaking English, subtitles appeared at the bottom of the television screen. They read, "My wife and I land here as Indochinese refugees. We have nothing and we hope the first generation will do something with America. Because, America gives us a lot of opportunity." Mr. Nguyen was asked by judge Simon Cowell if he believed that he could be a star. "Actually," the singer replied, "I believe in myself as a businessman. I want to make myself a lot of money, and a lot of you a lot of money."

Elated at his acceptance to the next round, he exited the audition room exclaiming that he was "representing my mom and dad here! Boat people, 1980. Went on a boat here for two weeks, ate with rats and stuff, man. That's deep love, man!"[7]

The history of Mr. Nguyen's family since their arrival in the U.S., a few years after the fall of Saigon, does indeed follow the refugee-to-thriving-middle-class outline. But in the context of *American Idol,* its apparent adherence to the contours of the American Dream became the basis of careful strategy. By the time clips from his audition aired in January 2004,[8] the judges had long since cut Mr. Nguyen from the Top 32 group of contestants, and he watched with interest as his story unfolded onscreen. He was surprised at the focus on his father's emotional statements, but he had suspected throughout his *Idol* experience that the narrative constructed around him might be angled in such a direction. Watching the broadcast, he did not initially recall having emphasized his parents' situation so strongly at the first audition, but acknowledges that when he arrived at the later rounds in Hollywood, he'd made a conscious decision to do so:

> *This wasn't shown on TV, but I actually did "Right Here Waiting" for the first day, that song. And they tell you to say something about yourself, and so my dad convinced me to kind of play up what he did, the whole American Dream thing, and I did. I did play it up, saying "I want to be the American Idol because . . .". I kind of put myself out there as representing this whole refugee American experience, like "For my parents, who have been through this."*[9]

If the Nguyens saw the potential appeal of their story, they were not alone. Footage filmed of Mr. Nguyen during the Hollywood rounds (though never aired during the highly edited early broadcasts) had continued to stress his obligation to realize his parents' American Dream.

> *It's really cheesy. The purpose is to be cheesy and to stand out, and I thought that—my dad convinced me that one way to do that, to get yourself past there, is to play up that ethnic experience, because you know they're looking for it . . . And during my interviews and stuff they would ask those questions directed there, not anything about anything*

else. You know, "How do you feel? How do you think your dad feels? How do you think your mom feels?" A lot of things dealing with parents, as if—you know, playing on that stereotype that I do report to my parents. Kind of familial, filial duty . . . The questions were kind of directed at that refugee experience—which, I was born here, so I don't get it. But a lot of it was asking about my parents, "What do they do? Yeah, they're really hardworking Americans, what do you think of that? Supporting you in this dream."

When Mr. Nguyen first appeared on *American Idol*, friends alerted him to online discussions regarding the clips from his Pasadena audition. Reading posts on several electronic message boards, he found much support but controversy as well. Some viewers objected to his father's use of the word "Indochina," and to the way host Ryan Seacrest echoed this choice. According to Mr. Nguyen, his father later explained that he had chosen the term over "Vietnam" because it encompassed "most of South East Asia," and because "[he] wanted to include everyone." However, the name, and Seacrest's repetition of it, seemed unsettlingly colonialist to some. Additionally, opinions were split over the juxtaposition onscreen of the parents' former refugee status with certain symbols of affluence—the father's digital camera, the mother's Louis Vuitton purse, the sister's Von Dutch hat. Were these accessories symbolic of the American Dream fulfilled or merely incompatible with the repeated references to an economically humble background? Furthermore, viewers asked, was the portrayal of Mr. Nguyen a positive contribution to the marginalized representation of Asian Americans in the media or simply a reprise of familiar stereotypes?

Mr. Nguyen himself is keenly aware of these contradictions and tensions. A communications major at a prestigious university (at the time of our interview), he looks back on his own choices, and the screen time he was allotted, with a critical gaze:

I mean, from a liberal standpoint you're not supposed to believe that much in that whole American Dream thing, you know, you deconstruct it, it has a lot of faults. But it did work out for my family, and I do believe—if I didn't believe in the American Dream, I wouldn't be here [at the university], or anywhere . . . So [during his Idol experi-

ence] I was just thinking, "yeah, this is very important," but then it's not until I watched it that the issues started arising.

When members of an Asian American website invited him to give an interview, he declined, concerned that they were only fishing for evidence of racism in his dismissal from the show or in the music industry in general. Since he felt that he had not experienced this kind of discrimination, he did not want to participate. He has also considered some of these issues from an academic perspective, having written a few class assignments on the topic of *American Idol*.

The portrayal of Mr. Nguyen on the show, then, shows a co-constructed Dream narrative, subject to interpretation and reinterpretation among contestant, producers, and viewers. The narrative is based in certain hallmarks of American identity discourse, particularly movement and transformation: emigration/immigration, upward economic (and social) mobility, "going to Hollywood." No matter that Mr. Nguyen was born in the U.S. and already a resident of Los Angeles when he first appeared before *American Idol*'s judges. In the few miles to Hollywood he was traversing the unquantifiable ideological space between two indivisibles—ethnicity and Americanness. His is one kind of American success story. Other *Idol* contestants, as we will see, live a very different story.

THE CELEBRATION OF FAILURE (OR HOW TO SUCCEED IN *AMERICAN IDOL* WITHOUT REALLY WINNING)

Every season of *American Idol* chronicles the dual quality of the American Dream, in its ostensible realization for a happy few and the corresponding failure of everyone else. The Dream is a fluid concept whose definition is often presupposed as a standardized, teleological success narrative. But as Scott A. Sandage points out in *Born Losers: A History of Failure in America,* success is not the sole defining characteristic of that Dream. Rather, it is defined by motivation, not action—by ambition, not its fruition, and "success" is only one possible result. Sandage writes, "Ours is an ideology of achieved identity; obligatory striving is its method, and failure and success are its outcomes." And the chiaroscuro of the *American Idol* experience, interweaving what Matthew Stahl calls "narratives of failure" with narratives of success, supports the idea that the two outcomes may better represent points on a continuum than a fixed binary.[10]

Idol celebrity can be readily won not only through approbation but through the harshest refusals as well. Producers accept many talented contestants, but they also send many away to make room onscreen for would-be Idols to be presented as entertaining laughingstocks. The early episodes of each season highlight a tragicomic parade of anti-stars, whose imperfect performances are ridiculed by the onscreen judges but nevertheless sometimes strike a true note for viewers. The popularity of the rejection segments have generated several "specials" reviewing the most cringe-inducing moments of one or more seasons, as well as a cumulative DVD devoted to the "Worst Auditions" and a 2005 program that expanded the concept to global proportions, *American Idol Presents: The World's Worst Auditions* (aired on FOX, May 19, 2005).

At first glance the persistence of these televised rejections may seem merely to reflect an enduring sadistic streak in televisual culture—in Simon Cowell's words on *Best & Worst of American Idol Seasons 1–4*, "the modern-day version of the lions and the Christians"—or just to bolster the viewer's ego ("I can sing better than that guy!"). Upon deeper inquiry, however, it becomes clear that rampant schadenfreude is not the whole story and that more than the measure of talent is at stake. To fulfill the conditions of an American Dream discourse increasingly oriented toward fame for fame's sake, *Idol* contestants may not necessarily need to be deemed talented by judges or viewers, or even to advance in the competition. Instead, I suggest that they may, alternatively, satisfy the narrative expectations of the Dream through the demonstration of ambition, evidence of valued personality traits—especially determination in response to rejection—or the performance of certain relevant mythologies. Some, it seems, must fail to succeed.

Artichoke King

On a rainy afternoon in 2006 I stood among a crowd of several hundred spectators at the Artichoke Festival in Castroville, California, waiting for a pop idol to take the outdoor stage. When he arrived, those around me rushed forward from their makeshift hay-bale seats, cheering and brandishing cameras and cell phones. One woman held up a sign toward him that asked, "Will You Marry Me?" (Figure 3.1). The singer in question, crowned Artichoke King the previous day, shared the royal title with no less than Marilyn Monroe, Castroville's first Artichoke Queen in 1947.[11] The object of adoration on this day was not a star in Monroe's conventional mold. Nevertheless, William Hung was a celebrated performer with an idol pedigree of sorts.

At the time of his audition for *American Idol*'s third season, Mr. Hung was a student in civil engineering at the University of California, Berkeley, and an avid karaoke performer. A victory in his dorm talent competition inspired him, and he auditioned for *American Idol* in San Francisco. A substantial broadcast segment, in which he sang Ricky Martin's 2000 hit "She Bangs," aired early in 2004. In that clip, before he stepped into the audition room, Ryan Seacrest interviewed him briefly about his goals, and Mr. Hung asserted that he would like to make a living in music. Simon Cowell and Randy Jackson responded to Mr. Hung's performance with laughter and dismissal, and Paula Abdul looked pleasantly amused. Despite the disappointing reaction from the judges, Mr. Hung appeared unfazed, telling them, "I already gave my best, and I have no regrets at all."[12] Cowell, Jackson, and Abdul heartily approved of this attitude but still sent Mr. Hung on his way, and that was that.

Only it wasn't. Mr. Hung caught viewers' attention, and soon after the January 27 broadcast a fan website was established, attracting four million hits in its first week. An online petition, encouraging *American Idol*'s producers to bring him to the show in Hollywood, accumulated nearly 117,000 signatures. He was indeed asked to appear again, on an episode titled "Uncut, Uncensored, and Untalented" that aired on March 1, 2004. For this performance he was surrounded by backup dancers, whose choreography was built on Mr. Hung's own distinctive movements from his audition. From there he rose to an ambiguous position that could be described either as international fame or international infamy. He has recorded three albums for Koch Records (a label unaffiliated with *American Idol*), made a music video and DVD, appeared on the FOX Television series *Arrested Development*, and played a sizable role in a Hong Kong film. In 2005 he returned to the realm of *American Idol,* appearing in a set of television commercials for one of the show's major sponsors, (then branded) Cingular Wireless.

Because Mr. Hung's remarkable career launched with a nationally televised rejection, it is arguably as much a story of failure as of success. The most renowned *Idol* failures, whose audition clips appear repeatedly across one or more seasons, are ambitious and undeterrable personalities, typically demonstrated through fiery defiance of the judges' pronouncements. But William Hung was memorable for other manifestations of determination, including his expression of a steadfast love for singing and his imperturbable good spirits in the face of rejection. The American Dream has required this sort of unshakable determination in its adherents since it first entered popular discourse in the "melting-pot" crucible of the Great Depression—the nation's archetypal expression of success, Sandage observes, emerging from the tremendous national failure of the 1929 stock market crash.[13] William Hung did not come out of nowhere; his status had illustrious precedent in that cradle of the Dream.

During the Depression a soprano named Florence Foster Jenkins was at the height of her impressively long career. Jenkins was a socialite with a passion for opera and the funds to support it. Although she enjoyed some popularity and performed in numerous recitals—culminating in a 1944 Carnegie Hall appearance at the age of seventy-six—her audience attended for reasons other than deep respect for her vocal skills. Another curious sort of respect was at work, directed toward her attitude and personality. She has been described as "sincere," "genuine," and "happy in her work." Her longtime companion, St. Clair Bayfield, said after her death, "There was something about her personality that made everyone look at her . . . People may have laughed at her singing, but the applause was real." Personality, as in this situation, becomes a fundamental element in stardom—often attributed to possession of an intangible "it factor"—and crucial to twenty-first-century ideas about success and failure. It is even an institution in contemporary American elections, as Joshua Gamson writes, in the privileging of a "politics of personality" over a "politics of substance."[14]

Like Florence Foster Jenkins's personality, William Hung's on *American Idol* epitomized ambition and cheery determination, unself-conscious sincerity, and an apparent imperviousness to humiliation. His resolute optimism about his singing also makes him innocent, *naïf.* For this quality, his celebrated status may be located within camp, though of a different quality than that of Norman Gentle (detailed in chapter 1). Susan Sontag identified the main component of "naïve" camp (or "pure" camp) as *seriousness,* specifically "a seriousness that *fails.*" "What it [camp] does," she wrote, "is to find the success in certain passionate failures." On the DVD by Koch Entertainment, Mr. Hung is heard to say, "I might not be the best singer in the world, but I sing from my heart, and I sing with passion." For Sontag's contemporary John J. Enck, camp comes from an amateur who does not recognize the limits of his skills.[15] But although Mr. Hung's sanguinity may strike his audience as an inaccurate gauging of his ability, it becomes part of his appeal and his public identity. His "honesty" and "genuine" character are referred to frequently in the media, and his unflappable reply to the *American Idol* judges ("I have no regrets") establishes him as what Glenn Dixon calls the "Nathan Hale of the karaoke nation." These qualities seem to imbue Mr. Hung with an authenticity based in sincerity rather than musical proficiency, the kind of sincerity that Frith recognizes within rock ideology as a holdover from folk discourse and Keightley as a remnant of Romanticism. This sincerity, moreover, is as crucial to American elections as it is to music, part of a "political prototype" associated with many U.S. presidents.[16]

Mr. Hung himself acknowledges that the positive outlook he presented on *American Idol* has been a crucial factor in his success. When I asked him for his thoughts about why he had attracted so much interest, he replied, "Probably because of my attitude, or inspiration. . . . Never give up, and you can succeed in life." He also repeated this last advice later in our conversation, when asked how he would counsel aspiring singers. Mr. Hung believes that his experience might encourage others to audition for *American Idol,* or other competitions, since he has demonstrated that "there's nothing wrong with losing." His statements reinforce the idea of failure as only a temporary obstacle, a fundamental and necessary experience on the road to success. He has expressed similar sentiments during public appearances. When he returned to *American Idol* about a month after his audition aired, host Ryan Seacrest asked him about his studies in civil engineering. He admitted that he was struggling a bit in school, and then continued, "I'm struggling with pretty much most of the things I do in my life." At the audience's laughter, he responded, "No, what you need to understand . . . is that everybody goes through struggles to succeed." This statement was greeted with cheers and applause, a response hinting at the relationships between failure and ordinariness, between the ordinary and the authentic, and an alternative manifestation of the desire to see celebrities as "real people."[17]

Alterities Singing

Mr. Hung's determination to experience rejection on his own terms becomes a key point in the case *Idol* makes for the agency of its viewers, and of Americans. His immigrant background (he was born in Hong Kong and came to the United States as a child) is not insignificant in this context. To some, Mr. Hung's success, or successful failure, is entangled with deeply embedded social prejudices regarding Asians and Asian Americans. This is not surprising, as the adoration is certainly not devoid of sinister qualities; his innocence is fascinating but innocence is not enough. With the captivation of his audience, he is also held captive to a combination of racializing and commercial motives. "Race, as a cultural construct," Deborah Wong asserts, "is neither natural, innocent, nor apolitical and is intimately linked to processes of commodification and control." In Season 6 semifinalist Paul Kim made an impression during his first broadcast appearance that went beyond his admirable singing skills. His audition was featured in a segment ostensibly intended to provide numbered guidelines for hopeful singers; "2. Seek Inspiration," the title card read. After a brief flashback to Mr. Hung's infamous audition, Kim was shown telling the cameras, "It kind of bothers me [that] when people think about 'Asian singer[s],' they think William Hung . . . and I'm not hatin' on William Hung, but I mean, come on—there are many talented Asian people out there, you just don't see them. I mean, they don't get an opportunity in the entertainment industry at all."[18] This is a telling statement, especially considering Mr. Hung's relative accomplishments in terms of opportunity and output. For Kim, that success doesn't count. It is an inspiration in the negative, and he is motivated to transcend it.

More than one writer has seen in Mr. Hung's portrayal an uncomfortable reference to historically essentialized performances of Asianness and Asian Americanness. Journalist Emil Guillermo believes that Koch Records and the music channel Fuse (which aired Mr. Hung's video) have made of him an updated version of Mickey Rooney's faux-Asian (Japanese) "Mr. Yunioshi" in the 1961 film *Breakfast at Tiffany's*. Sharon Mizota (who also emphasizes the impact of Mr. Hung's personality) compares this kind of representation to blackface minstrelsy, and describes the commodification of William Hung as a new form of "yellowface." She points to his performance on the *Today Show* in the spring of 2004, during which audience members enacted this analogy almost literally, holding up masks with photos of Mr. Hung's face. Additionally, both she and David Ng find his popularity an example of the discursive desexualization of Asian and Asian American men. According to Ng, when it comes to "virility, images of Asian men rank somewhere below white women." Mizota sees the Asian American man as a "heterosexual 'subaltern,'" in the mainstream perception dating from early immigration policy. Cliff Cheng discusses this history in his essay on the marginalized and the hegemonic in masculinity, tracing the (a- or) de-sexualization of Asian American men to the nineteenth-century laws that prevented immigrant Chinese laborers from either bringing their wives to America or marrying non-Chinese women. Because of these restrictions, the men lived in a social situation without women or the ability to reproduce, and in order to live they had to perform tasks that otherwise would be left to women.[19]

It is these disturbing implications that led Mizota to ask, about Mr. Hung, "Can the Subaltern Sing?" (referencing Gayatri Chakravorty Spivak's iconic question of representation and agency, "Can the Subaltern Speak?"). He is constructed not only as a marginalized ethnic/immigrant subaltern but also as an archetypal "nerd"—a socially awkward, academically inclined engineering major—who has spoken in public about his desire to remain a virgin until marriage (adding fuel to the racialized desexualization of his persona). Mizota calls him a "righteous nerd." His public nerdiness and approach to sexuality both diminish the masculinity of his image to a level acceptable for Asian Americans within the conventions of U.S. popular culture. Further, as Cheng points out, in the designation of "nerd" assigned to many Asian American men working in technical and business fields, class is a consideration.[20] This may also be part of Mr. Hung's initial failure in *American* Idol—that for an Asian American man, an immigrant without a publicized hard-luck or family refugee story (as in that of Bao Viet Nguyen), there is no apparent possibility of the familiar *Idol* transformation through the American Dream: it has, it seems, already been achieved.

Frank H. Wu writes of the important role of the American Dream in the "model minority" stereotype of Asian Americans. "In the view of other Americans, Asian Americans vindicate the American Dream," he writes, but also notes, in addition to the "disingenuous" nature of this myth, another problematic implication. If Asian Americans represent the model minority, then who is the model for? The answer, which Wu traces to an influential 1966 article by William Peterson, and through later statements from the Reagan administration, is that the myth is aimed at the African American collective minority, asking, "They made it; why can't you?"[21] In other words, the Asian American success myth places Asian Americans, in "making it," closer to whiteness. There is a paradox here, however—in the binary racialization of popular culture, that very whiteness, or at least a lack of blackness (or appropriation of blackness) can be fatal. "Do you know what a nerd is?" musician and theorist Brian Eno famously asked in an interview with an editor of *Wired*—and then answered his own question: "A nerd is a human being without enough Africa in him or her." In her groundbreaking discussion of Asian American rap artists, Deborah Wong describes how the decision of any Asian American to "move in the direction of color," that is, "away from Whiteness"—from the idea of the model minority—may be received as shocking, even unimaginable.[22] William Hung's image, then, is neither black enough nor white enough to be viable in the pop world.

Although I am not claiming that William Hung was turned away from *American Idol* simply because of racism, I do suggest that racial and related sexual discourses have played an important role both in the show's mocking portrayal of him and in his ultimate popularity. In light of these problems of representation, it might seem startling that Mr. Hung has found enthusiastic audiences in his native Hong Kong, and in other Asian communities with large ethnically Chinese populations. However, Sheng-Mei Ma sees a kind of strategic essentialism (the temporary, goal-oriented employment of essentializing ideas)[23] in the reappropriation of body and language stereotypes within Chinese American literature. In the context of increasingly globalized popular culture, the worldwide adoration of Mr. Hung could exemplify such a reappropriation. It is also possible that, for some fans, Mr. Hung is simply a different kind of karaoke hero than the type offered in actually elected American Idols. According to Deborah Wong and Mai Elliot, karaoke in Asian contexts generally emphasizes the participatory rather than exceptional skill; the authors point out that "while good singing is admired, bad singing isn't maligned."[24] In the karaoke-like atmosphere of American Idol, the categorical collapse of success and failure parallels the simultaneous collapse of amateurism and professionalism effected through the show.

William Hung the Singer

Discourse about Mr. Hung's image sometimes overlooks the details of his actual performance in the televised audition. Although his musicianship is continuously under fire, I would argue that his competence, in fact, exceeds that assigned to him by his critics. His rendition of "She Bangs," and Ricky Martin's own track from the 2000 album *Sound Loaded,* are both precisely in $F_\sharp$ minor. When I asked him if he had received his starting pitch before he began singing, he seemed confused by the question, and told me that he already knew how to perform the song from his many hours of listening and practice. And because he also said that he had not been listening to it just prior to his audition, we may infer that he sang exactly in Martin's key from memory. In addition, the range of the song exceeds the pitch (around E_3, by the system of the Acoustical Society of America) at which untrained young male voices tend to encounter problems. So if he can sing in key, and has a good ear and good pitch memory, what in the performance provokes the judges' reactions? His movement is the most visible target. Mr. Hung criticized himself, telling the University of California, Berkeley's *Daily Californian,* "My singing wasn't horrible, but my dancing really made it look silly."[25] Language expectations may also factor in the judges' response, although in spite of his accented English, his diction is entirely intelligible. However, *American Idol* already had a history of ridiculing those with discernible foreign accents. And in the season following Mr. Hung's, the audition episodes featured a segment titled "The Incomprehensibles," in which the performances of a South Asian man and a Japanese woman were presented with phonetically transcribed subtitles that amounted to nonsense. Such failure to articulate the American immigrant Dream through racialized linguistic and cultural assimilation accounts only partially for the alterity subjected to humiliation on *American Idol*. But humiliation serves its purposes, too.

Making the Dream a Reality (Show)

Humiliation is a hallmark of reality television, and, as William Hung observes, rejection from *American Idol* is "the norm, not the exception."[26] But this clear and present danger fails to deter the thousands who attend the *American Idol* cattle-calls. A "personal release" form supplied at the show's website spells out the risks involved in auditioning, requiring the potential contestant to acknowledge that information "of a personal, private, embarrassing or unfavorable nature" may be made public, "which information may be factual and/or fictional" and which might result in "public ridicule, humiliation, or condemnation."[27] The humiliation in question is most often enacted onscreen by the judging panel, typically as Simon Cowell and Randy Jackson joke about a contestant's appearance or singing ability. Their mockery is a performance that acknowledges and in a way authorizes many viewers' instincts; during her years on the show Paula Abdul countered it frequently, chastising her colleagues, standing in as the voice of America's conscience, and reminding viewers that the responsible response to unkindness is outrage.

Where do the impulses to undergo and to watch humiliation come from? Humiliation, cousin and sometime progenitor to the humility prized in American personalities, has long been an important factor in American Dream mythology, especially in fame narratives. Looking as far back as the colonial catalysis of the nation's history, George and Ira Gershwin even insist that "They all laughed at Christopher Columbus." In this song, penned for the 1937 Depression-era film *Shall We Dance*, the name of explorer Columbus precedes a litany of inventors and entrepreneurs including Edison, the Wright brothers, Eli Whitney, and Henry Ford, all of whom (the lyrics claim) overcame mocking and disbelief to become tyrants of industry and technology. In another 1937 film, before her ascendance to the silver screen, the aspiring-actress protagonist of *A Star Is Born* delivers a stinging monologue to her unsupportive family: "You think you can laugh at me? Well, someday you won't laugh at me; I'm going out and have a real life! I'm gonna *be* somebody!" An unsteady step along the path to fame, humiliation—such as that experienced by millions of destitute Americans during the Depression—is assigned the power not only to ruin lives but also to fuel the fire of American determination.

Numerous recent discussions of reality television[28] have also invoked a broader, more troubling impulse behind the continued broadcast of humiliation. Enlightenment philosopher Jeremy Bentham's *panopticon*, taken up by Michel Foucault in *Discipline and Punish*, is a prison design in which inmates are arranged in cells surrounding a guard tower, allowing the guard to watch every detail of the prisoners' lives. For Foucault, this Enlightenment concept marks a shift away from a morality that relied upon public torture and execution, and toward what John McGrath describes as "a naturalized discipline of the self," "a sense of self that is always subject to viewing by authority—and which therefore must forever engage in the measuring, grading and censoring of behaviour." In this situation, the failure that results in imprisonment is a failure of self-discipline. In reality television, fortunately, literal and legal imprisonment is not a typical outcome. But those rejected are mocked for a failure similar to that identified by Foucault and McGrath—they have failed in self-discipline, self-measurement, self-censoring, in the self-awareness that would apprise them of their own shortcomings. And the rejection handed out by the show's producers and judges, namely, a condemnation of the voice—a deeply embodied instrument—is also an indictment, and conviction and sentencing, of the body. This form of humiliation is a disciplining of the body that is painful for the contestants turned away, and it is a kind of public torture that is painful, if somewhat sadistically pleasurable, for viewers to watch. In cases like that of William Hung, the racialization of the body, and of dancing, add further layers to significance of such discipline. According to Foucault, the Enlightenment termination of public executions meant a change from spectacle to surveillance, and a "slackening of the hold on the body." But perhaps the *Idol* humiliation perfectly demonstrates how that "hold" nevertheless endures, figuratively, in surveillance culture. As Deborah Wong reminds us in her investigation of performativity and the racialized body, "The theater of the disciplined body has been redefined. But it certainly hasn't disappeared."[29]

The Risk of Rejection

The hazards inherent in deciding to audition for *American Idol* raise questions about why, nevertheless, so many make that choice, and about why viewers tune in to the mocking rejection of the "worst auditions." The answer to the first appears to involve that patented American ambition, the requirement that one seize opportunity when it appears. I spoke with several singers who told me that they auditioned "just to say I did it." I heard that phrase from a young man, Matthew Maimoni, who had auditioned four times and would try yet again. He told me that he never expected to "make it," but that a persistent "little bit of hope that you're going to make it through" can be enough to keep a singer coming back for more. He, along with others, also considered the attraction of a seemingly easy path to fame and fortune, for those who "just kind of want to go from their nothing lives to something big," and though he recognizes that much work is done behind the scenes of the show, he has a sense that "this is an easy way to go for it." Another singer, Branden James, explained it this way:

> I look at it as this. . . . It is sort of like winning the lottery. A mass, fun, mainstream get-rich-quick scheme. It allows you the opportunity to put yourself in a fantasy—in the process—and to dream big while [you are] actually seeing a road ahead that TV has created from other seasons. There is hope in that fantasy, and the possible outcome makes you feel good about yourself. That is the scary part about the power of this show, American Idol. Nonetheless, it was an experience, just like venturing to New Jersey and waiting in a line for hours for a $100 million jackpot lottery ticket is. (I did that once.) The odds are against

you, and the notion is somewhat insane, but the allure is a great force. It was a life experience. There was no enrichment as an artist or even a useful way to practice an audition. Merely an experience. An "I did that when" sort of thing.

Mr. Maimoni and Mr. James both have an understanding of the *Idol* opportunity as chiefly a televisual, manufactured, and somewhat suspect one, but the promise of an "experience" and even the very slim odds of success made gamblers of them both. After all, as Mr. Maimoni put it, "Who wouldn't want to be the American Idol?"[30]

At least one audition judge also sees the power in taking that chance. *Idol* associate music director, Michael Orland, who evaluated singers during the Season 5 audition tour, reported that, in each site he had attended, he would encounter someone who froze when his or her turn came and refuse to audition. He described his reaction:

Uh-uh, no way, you're going to do it. You just waited in line that whole time, you're going to—I don't care if you sing one line to me and do it badly, you're not going to leave here and say you didn't do it. . . . So I made these kids, just to say they did it.[31]

Taking the *Idol* opportunity is a merit badge of sorts, then, a story one can tell to prove one's sense of ambition, one's dedication to the American Dream. And the American Dream pursued at the *Idol* auditions mirrors quite precisely the one represented in the Golden Age of cinema—those who are "discovered" are literally invited to Hollywood, to the place where that Dream lives.

As for the viewers who watch the dozens of frequently cruel *Idol* rejections early in the broadcast season, there is certainly more than one possible attraction. William Hung proposes that the rejection segments are, beyond their "entertainment value," in fact educational for potential contestants. Viewers may learn from them what to do and what not to do when their turn comes, "what the *American Idol* judges are actually looking for." *Idol* vocal coach Debra Byrd suggests a kind of morbid curiosity. In response to my question regarding why audiences might be drawn to these segments, she asked, "You ever been on the freeway, when there's an accident on the other side?" But she also cites another element, which, she points out, "makes fantastic television." This is the quality of "bravado" in the hopeful singers, a sense of confidence or pride that does not match the evaluation of the judges, or possibly of the audience; as Byrd describes it, these singers engage viewers' interest when they display "more guts than talent."[32] Although the unfortunate are turned away for such hubris, Byrd's assessment is still consistent with the American admiration of ambition, of the attempt to fulfill the American Dream.

How do people deal with public *Idol* rejection? Of course, there are the rants and curses encouraged and recorded at the auditions ("If we say you suck . . . get to a camera," urged producer Nigel Lythgoe at the Season 4 auditions in San Francisco). But others, like William Hung, take the experience gracefully in stride, "grateful for the opportunity." "Regardless of how they portrayed me," he maintains, "showing me on TV is like opening doors."[33]

In May 2004, in the wake of William Hung's early success, the WB Network aired a short series in which unwitting contestants mistakenly believed that they were participating in a search for the best singer in the country. In fact, *Superstar USA* was aired as a search for the "worst" singer in America. Its format was an overt parody of *American Idol* with any singers who might have been competitive in the real *Idol* context immediately eliminated. The show came under a bit of ethical fire in the press but primarily because one of the producers had told the paid studio audience that the singers were part of a charity program for seriously ill youths (a falsehood for which an apology was eventually issued).[34] When the finalists and the winner were at last informed that they had won thousands of dollars for their incompetence, and not in recognition of their talent, no one showed the expected outrage. They had, after all, been paid handsomely, with the victor Jamie Foss receiving a hundred thousand dollar prize and a contract.[35] A soundtrack recording of the contestants was produced on KOCH Records, the same company responsible for William Hung's albums. After the show aired, Foss told *TV Guide Online* about her response to the revelation of *Superstar USA*'s hoax:

> My reaction was definitely fine. I was a little shocked, and there was
> a kind of frustration. But then I thought about it, and, like, a minute

later, I was like, "This has been the time of my life. I would have done it even if I had known it was a joke!" I mean, I got to work with chore-ographers, I got a makeover, I was in Hollywood for three weeks . . . It was awesome![36]

It seems, then, that even when fulfillment of the American Dream is just that, a brief and illusory dream, the "allure" Mr. James cited can be irresistible and the simulacrum can be fulfilling enough.

William Hung's voice has been styled as that of a bona fide every-man, of the humble but determined, of blind ambition and blind faith in the American Dream. His kind of celebrity begins to answer the question of why, in the face of almost certain rejection and the strong possibility of very public ridicule, up to one hundred thousand attend auditions each season and millions tune in to every brutal dismissal. It is about selling the American Dream, regardless of whether it re-sults in success or failure—and about the enactment of an ideology that hovers at the edges of any discourse about American morality. It is the potential of great ambition, rather than great talent, that drives these hopefuls and inspires their fans. William Hung's devotion to his new vocation evokes the famous words of Florence Foster Jenkins: "Some may say that I couldn't sing," she allowed, "but no one can say that I *didn't* sing."[37]

CONCLUSIONS

Bao Viet Nguyen and William Hung represent two sides of a particu-larly American coin, two Asian American men living different versions of the same immigrant Dream. Both demonstrated a determination, an ambition to succeed, and both achieved something with their *Idol* endeavors. But whereas one was held up as a model example of how to become American, the other was ridiculed for his efforts to do the same. Nevertheless, in the end, William Hung made more money and received far more attention than Bao Viet Nguyen. Their experiences speak far more to American understandings of the Dream than to the quality of the young men's singing, more about national values than about the evaluation or devaluation of talent. Their stories remind us that being a celebrity involves a continuous rehearsal of American ideals, and that being American is a constant performance.

Figure 3.1. A fan's request at William Hung's Artichoke Festival performance in Castroville, California, May 21, 2006.

IDOL WORSHIP ·
CIVIL AND SACRAL RELIGION
IN *AMERICAN IDOL*

LIKE A PRAYER

Waiting in San Francisco's Cow Palace at 6:45 AM for the early-morning start of Season 4 auditions, I watched a small group in the stands begin singing together. Their spontaneous outburst quickly caught on, and soon much of the entire stadium, several thousand strong, joined in a communal performance of Harry Dixon Loes's "This Little Light of Mine." It seemed a striking moment, the crowd choosing this gospel song with all its layered meanings to shore up their audition resolve. To begin with, the song's text imparts a message of empowerment: the declaration "This little light of mine, I'm gonna let it shine" is a positive mantra for those about to take the considerable emotional risks involved in the *Idol* audition process. The performance also demonstrated the foundational values of the American Dream, the dual kernels of individualism—in the song's lyrics—and complementary communitarianism—in the mass recital—that deeply inform American politics and public morality. And "This Little Light of Mine" holds a special place in the development of popular music in the U.S.; transformed into "This Little Girl of Mine" by Ray Charles, it became an early example of the controversial secularization of gospel aesthetics and repertoire into soul and R&B—a stylistic crossover that has shaped the repertoire and performance practices now prominent on *American Idol*. This sacred–secular dialectic took place in the early years of the cold war, when, as religious and moral debates raged over the new music of American youth, the U.S. became a nation "under God" because the Soviet socialist republics were not. Finally, "This Little Light of Mine" is a gospel song whose strong presence during the civil rights movement in the 1960s demonstrated the integral role of religious music in the negotiation of a changing relationship between American citizens and the state.[1]

Its lyrics, civil rights leader Fannie Lou Hamer believed,[2] came from the Beatitudes in the New Testament, the Sermon on the Mount, and the proclamation "You are the light of the world. A city that is set on a hill cannot be hidden" (Matthew 5:14). This text became an ideological cornerstone of what would become the United States, epitomized famously in John Winthrop's lay sermon, "A Model of Christian Charity." Composed in 1630 on the way to the founding of the Massachusetts Bay Colony, the sermon spoke of a covenant with God and envisioned the new "plantation" as a "city upon a hill,"[3] an example for other Protestant communities. Winthrop's words have long inspired Americans to exceptionalism, and, no matter how separate church and state, have contributed to an underlying interdependence between American religious thought and the imagination of this nation.

THE SPIRIT OF CAPITALISM:
CIVIL RELIGION AND *AMERICAN IDOL*

Religious rhetoric and actions concerning the state are expressive of *civil religion*. In the groundbreaking essay "Civil Religion in America," where Robert N. Bellah adapted the term from its first usage in Rousseau's *Social Contract,* civil religion is a public religious dimension, the articulation of sacred thinking about the nation through "a set of beliefs, symbols, and rituals."[4] Characteristic articulations rely on the confluence of the religious and political in language ("God bless America") and in ritual (the president's inaugural oath on the Bible). Civil religion publicly performed in these ways legitimizes the state, its leaders, and their actions, imbuing them with a divinely sanctioned authority,[5] and supporting the idea that particular religious beliefs and practices are legitimately American.

American civil religion can be interpreted as separate, but not isolated, from sacral religious institutions, distinguished by its focus on a relationship between the state and the citizen, as overseen by a higher power. Civil religious rhetoric generally eschews sectarian vocabulary (e.g., citing "God" but not "Jesus" or "Christ"), respectful of the First Amendment, but this does not mean that Americans never understand the nation in terms of their own sacral religious experiences. The hymnbooks of American churches often include patriotic and civil religious songs, and some congregations regularly pray for the nation's leaders, thus including the state in sacral worship even if the reverse is constitutionally unacceptable.

"Civil religion" is an academic term not widely known to the American public, and the line that separates church and state has rarely been clear, sometimes crossed subtly in political speech or policy. Resurgences of American civil-religious expression have been intricately linked to resurgences of sacral religion. September 11, 2001, found the nation already in the midst of the discourse about the "religious (or Christian) Right" that had aided the election of a born-again evangelical president. In response to a new conflict with acutely religious overtones—not so different from the early years of the cold war, when religion was used to set the U.S. apart from "godless" communist adversaries—civil and sacral religion have each worked in defense of the other. It is difficult to entirely reify civil and sacral religion in terms of their effects on political culture and cultural politics; they might best be understood as two sides of a single American coin, inscribed with the words "In God We Trust."[6]

Bellah began his study of civil religion with an analysis of John F. Kennedy's inaugural address. The religious rhetoric found in presidential addresses is typically designed to avoid crossing into the territory of sacral religion, but allusions to personal faith have become more common in recent decades. *American Idol* candidates have followed this lead. As in the American presidency, a person outside the spectrum of Christian faiths has never filled the role of American Idol. It is perhaps not coincidental that, of the American Idols to date (up to Season 9 as I edit), most have spoken publicly about their faith during their *Idol* campaigns, seven of the nine hailed from southern states—as did recent Presidents George W. Bush[7] and William Jefferson Clinton—and six were elected during the presidency of Bush, a self-proclaimed born-again Christian. The first American Idol, Kelly Clarkson, and the seventh, David Cook, even share Texas with Bush as their home state. During his presidency, Bush was criticized by some for a perceived overemphasis on his personal faith in public speeches as well as in certain policies of his administration. But the prominence of his faith also figured in his political success, winning him allies among those with similar values. Openness about faith works in favor of *American Idol*'s contestants as well, and of the show itself. Although it cannot be said that Idols hold positions equivalent in power to the presidency, the highlighting of faith in both elections reflects related sociopolitical trends.

Historian Wilfred M. McClay remarked in 2004 that "the September 11 attacks have produced a great revitalization, for a time, of the American civil religion."[8] And it was made apparent on 9/11, when members of Congress sang an impromptu "God Bless America" on the steps of the Capitol, that music would play an important role in this escalation of civil religion. The events of that day initiated a prolonged flood of language and actions invoking the mythic status of America as a "chosen" nation, blessed by God. In October 2001 the U.S. House of Representatives even passed a resolution essentially suspending the separation of church and state in the context of public education, so that schools might be allowed to display the words "God Bless America" in support of the nation.[9] Premiering in the summer of 2002, *American Idol* came to television at a time when such expressions had gained an increasingly regular presence in the media, and the show quickly joined the discourse.

Six days after the United States entered Iraq in 2003, Season 2 finalists performed a rendition of Lee Greenwood's 1984 hit "God Bless the U.S.A."—a title in which civil religion is implicit—led by one of the army's own ranks, Marine Lance Cpl. Joshua Gracin. A positive response from viewers inspired the immediate recording and release of the song on a CD single, from which partial proceeds were donated to the Red Cross. In this disc God and country and the American *Idol* Dream were tidily packaged for purchase. Rhys H. Williams and

N. J. Demerath III observed, in 1985, that "people must be motivated to act politically; the resonant symbolism of civil religion helps serve that purpose by placing the movement's goals within the frame of legitimate political discourse." *American Idol*'s "God Bless the U.S.A." indicates that the combination of civil-religious and political symbolism can also motivate people to act economically, capitalistically. And with $155,000 worth of philanthropy, *American Idol*'s "God Bless the U.S.A." became a civil-religious tool in the practice of a kind of morally "responsible capitalism," to build on a phrase from Herbert Gans. The song also became an *Idol* campaign strategy a few years later; On March 25, 2008, when the musical theme had the Top 10 finalists selecting "songs from the year they were born," hopeful Idol Kristy Lee Cook performed "God Bless the U.S.A." Judge Simon Cowell called it the "most clever song choice" he'd heard in years. It was not clever just because it was a familiar song, or even because it was patriotic, but also because the episode aired the week America marked the fifth anniversary of the Iraq War, and Cook, who had placed in the "bottom three" among the contestants the two previous weeks, performed the anthem five years almost to the day after the Season 2 finalists had performed it in 2003.[10] She stayed in the competition another three weeks.

American Idol has maintained a relationship with the United States Armed Forces beyond the showcasing of Lance Corporal Gracin and occasional references to the American presence overseas. Former *Idol* contestants have participated in USO tours abroad to Europe, Iraq, and Afghanistan (e.g., Kelly Clarkson, Diana DeGarmo, Carrie Underwood, Kellie Pickler, Bucky Covington, Elliott Yamin, and David Cook), and 2005 saw the debut of *Military Idol*.[11] The first run of this contest, webcast through Army Knowledge Online (with the final round also aired on the Pentagon Channel), included members of the U.S. Army stationed all over the world—though security concerns excluded those in Iraq and Afghanistan—and reworked the conventional army talent show into an epic *Idol*-style competition. Victor Hurtado, artistic director of the U.S. Army Soldier Show, arranged a short-term licensing agreement with FremantleMedia for use of the *Idol* name, and commandeered *Idol* coach Debra Byrd as a judge. (After the official license ended, the program dropped the "Idol" name and became *Operation Rising Star. American Idol* alumna

Kimberly Caldwell has also appeared as a guest judge on *Operation Rising Star.*) Byrd, whose father was in the army, praised the show for its morale-boosting efforts to "let people know that we're thinking of them. That's what I think the purpose of *Military Idol* serves. I think it serves a greater good than we even realize."[12]

From morale to morals, communal responsibility is a value that permeates both America's democracy discourse and the mythology of the American Dream, tied up in the same covenantal language that Winthrop broached in 1630, and which has become common civil-religious rhetoric. Presidents have favored such language, from Abraham Lincoln's famous reference to America as an "almost chosen people"; to Ronald Reagan, who frequently cited the "city upon a hill" and popularized the end-of-speech motto "God bless America"; to William Jefferson Clinton, who introduced his plan for a "New Covenant" in 1992; to George W. Bush, who in 2000 told B'nai B'rith International, "Our nation is chosen by God and commissioned by history to be a model to the world."[13] Bush also echoed Winthrop in his first national address following 9/11: "America was targeted for attack because we're the brightest beacon for freedom and opportunity in the world. And no one will keep that light from shining." Words strikingly parallel to the president's final phrase, and to "This Little Light of Mine," appeared in *American Idol*'s third-season original song, "I Believe," written as a kind of inauguration speech for the winner: "See, I strive to be the very best / Shine my light for all to see."[14] The correlation here does not end with semantics but touches upon the deeper relationship between a democratically utopian dream-America and the American Dream—the mission of the nation and the mission of the individual, the balance between communal and personal responsibility.

According to Roberta L. Coles, discourse envisioning America as a chosen nation took root in the nineteenth-century doctrine of Manifest Destiny. Coles cites two national missions as paramount in this doctrine: the development of "a democratic system that would serve as an example to the rest of the world" and "a mission to lead other states toward freedom."[15] In other words, America(ns) must work to build and maintain a nation worthy of being a *role model,* and act upon this impulse. The nation's mission is considered in this doctrine to be sanctioned, and thus justified, by God. A corollary of the American Dream touts a comparable mission, an individual striving toward achievement and status as a role model for other individuals. *American Idol* contestants frequently call upon secular "role model" rhetoric. In the questionnaires completed by each finalist on the FOX Network's pre-2006 *American Idol* website, one question asked, "What is your definition of an AMERICAN IDOL?" Fourth-season finalist Vonzell Solomon answered, "An American Idol is a person that's a role model for young people and an inspiration for all. A superstar on and off stage."[16]

A sixty-five-year-old woman told me that she "wore out two phones" voting for Clay Aiken during Season 2, because she admires him for his openness about his faith, because he "practices what he preaches," and is a good role model.[17] This comment points to the weight placed on contestants' public adherence to certain moral values, discrete but not separable from religion, and definitely tied up in the American Dream. Naming any pop culture figure as one's "idol" connotes someone one admires, a hero setting an example toward which others should strive. When second-season finalist Joshua Gracin, now a successful country singer, defined an American Idol for the FOX website, he emphasized the importance of morality: "Someone who can be a role model (never in trouble, don't smoke, don't drink, party and is down to earth)." Many idolonfox.com message threads during Season 3 debated the merits of eventual winner Fantasia Barrino as an American symbol. Her status as an unwed teenage mother became quite controversial on the official FOX website forum. For example, one viewer wrote:

> I am disgusted with the show "American Idol." Please note that our youth look to the contestants on the show and the term "Idol," is used to illustrate some sort of following. . . . How can FOX be so irresponsible in allowing this to happen? Have a single mother, high school drop out be an American icon, a symbol to our youth. This is a joke, and a disgrace to our society.

In response, another post read:

> It tells our youth that in this society it is never to late to turn your life around, to set goals and go after your dreams. That as adolescence you do and will make wrong choices . . . many adults have made

wrong choices . . . but we can grow from the lessons learned . . . pick up our lives and rise above it![18]

These and similar posts indicate that at least some viewers interpret the American Idol as a national or "societal" symbol or both, an embodiment of certain ideal moral characteristics of Americanness. Here the significant characteristics are the acquisition of education and adherence to social guidelines about marriage and sexual intercourse.

If the American Idol is positioned as an elected leader, as the voting process would imply, further parallels may be drawn to the political sphere. In *Ritual, Politics, and Power,* David Kertzer notes Bruno Bettelheim's recognition of "a general human tendency to invest the political conqueror with semi-divine characteristics" and the idea that any threat to a leader's power creates in people a "need to deny [the threat] by believing in his virtue."[19] Though education and perceived moral uprightness may not be "semi-divine" characteristics per se, the above discussion, posted the week before the final audience vote between final rivals Barrino and Diana DeGarmo, reflects a certain anxiety about Barrino's immediately potential status as American Idol. One fan even related negative posts about Barrino to the post–9/11 national climate, writing,

> This board does show you that 9-11 obviously didn't bring many Americans closer together. It also didn't open up enough peoples eyes to what is truly important. All of those innocent people who died and children who lost parents . . . and all the people on these boards can do is try to take away a young mothers dreams because she made a mistake when she was a teenager.[20]

To this viewer the morality of the voting audience is apparently as much in question as that of the *American Idol* contestants. Judgments have also been passed regarding the morality of the show itself, as the Association of National Advertisers and its Family Friendly Programming Forum gave *American Idol* a "Family Television Award" in 2003. The criteria the Association use for honoring programs is listed at the group's website: "Family friendly programming is appropriate in theme, content and language for adults and children. It has cross generational appeal, depicts real life and resolves issues responsibly."

Viewer Chris Rainey, vice president of marketing at the Christian apparel company Kerusso, says that the show appeals to him and his family because it offers "normal people having a shot at their dreams" and has the potential to inspire his children in the pursuit of their own dreams. He also sees the family act of watching *American Idol* as a teaching moment, when the words the judges use to critique contestants, and the ways in which contestants respond to that criticism, serve as positive or negative behavioral examples.[21]

These ideas correspond to the notion of the *calling*, traced in Max Weber's *The Protestant Ethic and the Spirit of Capitalism*. In its Reformation sense, according to Weber, the fulfillment of duty in the worldly calling (as opposed to the religious calling) came to be viewed as the pinnacle of moral action, proof of a favorable predestination, thus lending sacred significance to the pursuits of everyday life.[22] This formula connects American Protestantism intimately to the American Dream, in which, as Walter Fisher argued, dual myths of moralism and materialism compete for dominance. According to Fisher, the moralistic American Dream is grounded in the principles of the Declaration of Independence, and emphasizes the "freedom *to be* as one conceives himself," while the materialistic side of the story champions the "freedom *to do*." The tenets of the moralistic myth "involve the values of tolerance, charity, compassion, and true regard for the dignity and worth of each and every individual," while

> the materialistic myth is grounded on the puritan work ethic and relates to the values of effort, persistence, "playing the game," initiative, self-reliance, achievement, and success. It undergirds competition as the way of determining personal worth, the free enterprise system and the notion of freedom, defined as the freedom from controls, regulations, or constraints that hinder the individual's striving for ascendency in the social-economic hierarchy of society.[23]

In *American Idol* both myths are at work, and in friction. The Idol is a kind of ultimate convergence of several strands of commodification—of music, fame, image, identity—but has been divinely approved in the fulfillment of a calling: "Heaven knows your existence," run the lyrics to "I Believe," "and wants you to be everything you are". Weber also asserts the importance of the "moral justification of worldly activity."[24] In order to validate participation in the commercialized spheres of popular music and reality television, some singers involved in fame-oriented projects like *American Idol* feel it personally important to resist the materialistic side of the Dream. Sacral religion can play a part in that resistance. Celina Lima, a young singer with whom I attended auditions for *American Idol*'s fifth season, raised this issue. She had planned to audition with one of two recent R&B songs, either Joss Stone's "Fell in Love with a Boy" or Alicia Keys's "Fallin'," but at the last minute—even though producer Ken Warwick admonished "preferably not religious songs"—instead chose to sing the canonic gospel song "His Eye Is on the Sparrow." When I asked why she had changed her mind, she said that she had prayed about it and felt that God had wanted her to sing the gospel song. She also thought that she had been focusing too much on the "fame" aspect of her singing goals, and that if she sang one of the R&B songs it would not be "for Him." In a subsequent interview, Ms. Lima further explained her singing as a kind of calling, a "task set by God" to help her know Him:

> My singing is what really ties me close to God . . . music has always been my key, the key tie between me and God. And so I feel like he gave me this voice for a reason—I feel like my purpose in life is to kind of find out what he wants from me, you know, musically, and then just to go and do it, and kind of fulfill my purpose. And I feel that that's why I was created. . . . Singing is how I communicate with God, and that's when I feel Him strongest within me. . . . [It's] just this gift He's given me, and it's like we kind of share it, almost, because it's within me.[25]

Singers featured on *American Idol* broadcasts often express similar sentiments. Contestants, in their official FOX website questionnaires, frequently respond to questions such as "Do you have any formal singing training?" with statements like that of Season 3 semifinalist Elizabeth Letendre: "No, it is a NATURAL gift from GOD!!"[26]

This kind of language suggests two important points—first, that singers can assign the act of singing, even in the exquisitely commercialized context of *American Idol,* a sacred quality; second, it defers to a higher power any glory otherwise related to the materialistic side of success, implying a sense of humility in the singer. Contestants regularly attribute their talent and their "lucky break" on *Idol* to divine will. In the liner notes to Season 2's collective CD, *All Time Classic American Love Songs*, nine of the eleven finalists[27] thanked God, Jesus, or "the Lord." Contestants—like Academy and Grammy Award winners, and triumphant athletes—have also regularly thanked God or counted their blessings on-camera. Of course, onscreen they must also express gratitude to voting America, thus ascribing credit for individual success to both the sovereignty of God and the democratic process.

The psychological asceticism expressed by singers like Ms. Lima is key both to Weber's "spirit of capitalism" and to notions of the American Dream. The Protestant (Calvinist) ideal of self-denial in the process (and also in spite) of material achievement translates into the humble origins, humility, and struggle required in the pursuit of the American Dream. And the realization of that struggle, punctuated by its obligatory trials and failures, is also frequently attributed to divine will. Rocío Torres, who auditioned for Season 3, told me that after she had camped out at the Rose Bowl for three days and progressed to a higher round, she developed a cold and decided to go home. She interpreted her illness as part of a divine plan: "God just gave me the signal to 'just go home, you're not gonna make it.'" Another young woman, disappointed in her rejection at Season 4 auditions, was comforted in her belief that what she termed "my higher power" had a plan for her, even if *American Idol* was not a part of it.[28] All this further highlights the relationship between national and individual implications of American civil religion: although the nation or the person is "chosen" in some way, and the individual *possesses* choice or agency as a citizen, the will of God remains sovereign.

Morality is a quality not only deemed important for America as a nation and the American Idol as a personal role model, but it also marks *American Idol* as a role model for other television programs. This connection has led to the direct involvement of *American Idol* cast members in events with national civil-religious significance, ritual "action wrapped in a web of symbolism"[29] that help Americans to define America.

POLITICS, RITUAL, AND POLITICAL RITUAL

In 2002, first American Idol Kelly Clarkson was invited to perform at the first national September 11 commemoration in Washington, D.C. In the weeks leading up to that occasion, her engagement to sing the national anthem at the Lincoln Memorial became so controversial that she tried to back out. Opponents of Clarkson's appearance protested what they saw as *American Idol*'s rampant self-promotion, inappropriately timed. However, a spokesman for the Washington, D.C., youth service organization, Champions of Hope, which organized Clarkson's appearance, told a *Washington Post* columnist,

> I don't see this as commercial. . . . I see this as an individual who competed—and Americans are one of the most competitive people on the planet. . . . America is built on people like that, who strived and succeeded in their ultimate goal.[30]

This comment illustrates how American Dream values, balancing the moralistic and the materialistic versions of the narrative, are used to reconcile tensions between the civil-religious and the commercial. (No such tension was apparent when Kelly Clarkson performed for Pope Benedict XVI during his 2008 visit to the United States).

The 2002 controversy also cemented *American Idol*'s significance as an entertainment intertwined with American political ritual. The show submits easily to familiar analyses of ritual. Writing about the Dutch program in the *Idols* franchise, Stijn L. Reijnders, Gerard Rooijakkers, and Liesbet van Zoonen remark that "the entire *Idols* format revolves around the elements of community spirit and ranking" as well as a sense of communitas, and they offer an insightful application of van Gennep's (and in part Turner's) ritual models. The *Idols* stage is a liminal one, where contestants are guided by judges and producers, and sometimes undergo the humiliation typical of rites of passage. They are then returned to "the bosom of the community with their new status."[31] The *Idols* format is not just any rite of passage, however, for it evokes and invokes a democratic political process.

"Because politics is a dramatic ritual," Joshua Meyrowitz maintains, "it is ultimately impossible to separate the thread of reality from the thread of performance." These conditions make *American Idol*'s reality television milieu a perfect setting for America to rehearse one of its most defining rituals—the election. Kertzer has written about the importance of mediation in the "ritual drama" of the election: "In the United States, as elsewhere, election campaigns involve the staging of such dramas by candidates as well as the attempts to get the mass media to broadcast these dramatic productions into people's homes." Whether or not *American Idol*'s producers intend to overtly emulate the process of American political drama, the show at the very least contains strongly evocative symbols. The audience vote suggests a sense of agency that is essential in the American election ritual. A singer born in East Germany told me at the 2004 auditions that he felt it was important for *American Idol* viewers to vote, because "if you vote, you can make a change."[32]

It is worth considering, though, that both the political election and the *Idols* election incite popular speculation regarding the actual degree of agency involved—that is, does one's vote (or one vote) really make a difference? *American Idol* has technically and technologically circumvented this question by allowing virtually unlimited voting per person, though some measures are taken to avoid technologically enhanced "power voting." There are also no age restrictions to the voting process; young children and teenagers who cannot legally vote in a presidential election, for example, may make their "voices" heard by casting hundreds of votes for their favorite contestants. *American Idol* offers Americans a new brand of universal suffrage.

However, fans of the show still question the true effect of their input. Public voting only begins with the semifinalists who are selected by producers and a panel of judges from the one hundred thousand contestants at previously held auditions, and presented over the first several weeks of broadcast. This means that the viewers enter an election process already in progress (as, essentially, do American citizens, in caucuses and primaries) and that they are offered choices already limited by other parties. When fans are disappointed by voting results, they express concern, in hundreds of FOX *American Idol* forum threads, blogs, and online petitions, that their favorites' designated telephone lines were busy or blocked, that judges or other voters or even "America" are racist, or that the final result of the show is "fixed." The possibility of overloaded telephone lines is a common concern, since a number dialed is sometimes far more likely to result in a busy signal than a vote logged. Perhaps because of the deluge of protest letters addressed to FOX and the Federal Communications Commission (FCC) in 2004,[33] the final vote for *American Idol's* third season offered for the first time *three* available numbers, rather than two, that viewers might call for each of the two final contestants. Further, in the fourth season, typographical errors in the onscreen display of telephone numbers led to a special "do-over" episode and a new voting session, aired on March 24, 2004. Nevertheless, the effectiveness of viewer voting is frequently called into question. *New York Times* journalist Kate Arthur echoes fan forum postings: "much as when I go to the polls in November, I'm never sure my [*Idol*] vote makes a difference."[34]

Viewers are not alone in their concerns; 2004 semifinalist Charly Lowry wondered at the voting results that kept her from being included in the Top 12. When I asked whether she thought the voting system on *American Idol* worked, she said, "If you had asked me that for Season 1 or 2 [before she had a successful audition], I would say I guess so, but after Season 3 I had too many people tell me that they called *way* too many times for me not to advance to the next level."[35] Public anxiety about agency and power relations regarding voting on *American Idol* mirrors familiar concerns raised in genuine American political elections, for example, the 2000 scandal over "hanging chads" and ballot comprehensibility, the persistent issues of racism and inadequate minority representation in the government, and a kind of despairing apathy that prevents people from voting. Simon Cowell, however, believes in the power of *American Idol* voters, or at least he believes they feel that power:

> [LaToya London, a third-season finalist] had a little bit of criticism, and she said: "I'm not the slightest bit worried. We're all winners now. We're all going to have successful careers." When she said it, I said, "She's out." Because America decides whether they're going to have successful careers. To say that was verging on arrogance.

In his interview with Virginia Heffernan of the *New York Times,* Cowell goes on to reproach Fantasia Barrino for "behaving like a politician rather than a pop star" and, perhaps alluding to baby-kissing political candidates, bringing her toddler daughter onstage.[36]

Viewers demonstrate an acute awareness of the parallels between the show's design and the democratic process. One viewer posted this message on idolonfox.com:

> I find it amazing that most of the country is in such an uproar about this show . . . if people truly took interest in politics and voted for what is best for the country, perhaps we wouldn't be in such a mess as we are today.

Another wrote:

> But 65 million votes . . . and we have a very extreme low voting rate for Presidential race here in America . . . wow, that really says something doesn't it . . . America needs this show right now, we need something to look forward to, to remember the "dream" that was often sung about in the competition. We live in perilous times, let us not forget that . . . and remember, the "American" in American Idol . . . I do believe, the title of the show is hinting to us, that there is more than just pop market value.[37]

The question of ultimate authority in *American Idol* also involves issues analogous to those of the political election: Does the power belong to the people, to an elite group making the decisions, or to God? One viewer who decided not to vote in the fourth season chose to "let the gods decide this one," indicating a sovereignty above that of the public. As discussed below, faith in the guidance of a divine power plays a vital role for many participants in the *American Idol* experience. In *American Idol,* as in American civil religion, although God is sovereign, the nation must be, too, and it is left to its citizens to carry out divine will. On the other hand, even as the democratic process provides citizens with a certain degree of agency, "the ultimate sovereignty has been attributed to God."[38] The majority vote is critical, but it is not always the last word.

The mediation of civil religion and its rituals can contribute to the reinforcement of national solidarity. Benedict Anderson describes the nation as an "imagined community," in which members, though never directly interacting with most other members, will nevertheless maintain an imagined communal relationship in the form of "a deep, horizontal comradeship." According to Anderson, this connection

may be reinforced by simultaneous experiences such as the performance of national anthems on official holidays, creating an imagined
communal sound, or "unisonance." The broadcast of such ritual performance broadens the effects of such unisonance. Tong Soon Lee
builds on Anderson's theory in relation to the situation of Muslims
in the increasingly heterogeneous social organization of urban Singapore. In the face of radical changes that have disrupted and geographically scattered members of Muslim communities, they have
been able to maintain an imagined community chiefly "defined in
relation to the radio transmission of the call to prayer." Nationally
televised events such as *American Idol* may accomplish a similar result. Televisual mediation, along with the virtual fan experience of
the internet, creates a perceptual space even more complete than the
"shared acoustic space" that Lee discusses. Philip Bohlman has also
applied Anderson's concept of "unisonance" to the televised broadcasting of the Eurovision Song Contest, which approaches nationalized music making in ways similar to those of *American Idol.* Such
experiences create "a feeling of cultural intimacy," in Bohlman's view,
"allowing 'each' person to sing the music of the 'whole' nation with
'all' other citizens."[39] Not only does the act of watching *American Idol*
help create a sense of nationally coherent community; so, too, does
the mutual experience of listening to nearly exclusively American music performed by young American singers. Although I am not declaring that *American Idol,* in fact, unites the country, such programming
may enhance the imagination of a cohesive America through sounds
and images.

A close look at the Season 3 finale of *American Idol* provides an
entire network of civil-religious symbols of ritual. In addition to the
sacred-secular song "I Believe," the broadcast presented symbols of
three major American rituals: certain election-day campaign practices, the Academy Awards, and nationally televised sports events.
Allusions to the Oscars abounded, not least in the structure of its
mediation. A "pre-show" has aired on *American Idol*'s home network,
FOX, or on the TV Guide Channel in the hour before the final broadcast of several seasons. On May 26, 2004 it was hosted on FOX by
screen actress Jennifer Love Hewitt and first-season *American Idol*
finalist Christina Christian. Standing outside the Kodak Theater in

Hollywood (where the show was housed in its final week), Christian stopped celebrities for brief interviews on their way into the building via a red carpet evocative of an awards show. E! Entertainment Television, which traditionally provides similar coverage of the Academy Awards, offered a live broadcast beginning two hours before even the "pre-show" that included interviews with celebrity fans, as well as with the American Idol judges and former finalists. Most interviews focused on naming favorite contestants and predictions of the winner. As there is perhaps no greater celebration of the American Dream's narrative of fame than the Academy Awards, American Idol's appropriations on this occasion were entirely fitting.

The "results" portion of the show opened with a performance of the national anthem, sung by first-season finalist Tamyra Gray. She performed the anthem a cappella, a style common at athletic events.[40] Displayed on a screen behind her was the image of a billowing American flag, and the audience inside the Kodak Theater (including the judges, one of whom is British) stood. During the live broadcast brief clips were shown of large fan gatherings in the hometowns of the two final contestants (High Point, North Carolina, and Snellville, Georgia). These clips showed county commissioners, mayors, and even a state governor offering statements of support to their respective finalists. Georgia governor Sonny Perdue claimed to be wearing pink in support of finalist Diana DeGarmo, who had made her preference for the color clear early in the season. An Associated Press article[41] reported that Perdue and North Carolina governor Mike Easley made a bet with each other regarding the outcome of the final American Idol vote. Their wagers included tickets to local NASCAR races and a large quantity of their respective state fruits (the peach and the blueberry). The endorsement of local and state officials not only is a strong reference to national sports events, which also elicit gubernatorial betting,[42] but also to political, particularly presidential, campaigning. This sense is further emphasized in the opposition implied by Perdue's status as a Republican and Easley's as a Democrat. Posters and signs of support held up by fans inside and outside the show's production locations throughout the series broadcasts add to the aura of campaign procedure. Such posters are an Idol fixture early in the game, present even at the preliminary cattle-call auditions (Figure 4.1).

Figure 4.1. At the Cow Palace: Jessika with supporters
Andrew, T. J., and Glenna Marie (October 5, 2004).

Ritual pervades those auditions not only in the uniform event
structure across the nation but in the way singers experience the event.
At 7:05 on the morning of the 2004 auditions I attended, a few minutes
after "This Little Light of Mine" had swept the stands and over an hour
before the tryouts began, I saw the entire seating section to my left rise,
bow their heads, and pray together. This moment is indicative of the
occasion's personal and spiritual significance for many participants
and of the importance of even the most hastily formed communities
in the *Idols* experience. An analogy might also be drawn here to the

practice of team prayer before athletic events. The auditions did, after all, take place in a stadium, and the crowd even executed an enthusiastic "Wave" at one point. The stadium setting of the auditions, the pre-competition prayer, and a collective performance of the national anthem for the cameras all mimicked the conditions of sports-related ritual. Michael Novak identifies a kind of civil religion within the "institutions of sport," suggesting that "going to a stadium is half like going to a political rally, half like going to church."[43] Audition attendees also participate in group activities for potential inclusion in televised broadcasts, including locally themed songs ("California Dreamin'" or "Viva Las Vegas," for example) or, as in the case of the San Francisco auditions in 2004, massive performances of the national anthem.

In the absence of sports-like teams, these impressions of community are striking given *American Idol*'s otherwise cutthroat model of individual competition. And although contestants are urged to demonstrate unique identity, and to produce individualized performance styles, the counterbalancing sense of community does not end with the auditions. Voting is both an individualistic and a social act. Tocqueville observed in the nineteenth century that Americans insist on following their own judgment instead of received authority, and this is a sensibility at work somewhere in both the democratic process and the making of the active *Idol* consumer. But while the decision made in the polling booth is a private act, it is also a ritual primarily about "subjunctive" (to paraphrase Rothenbuhler) communal experience, about the desire and hope for representation. *Idol* viewers often coalesce into voting communities, interest groups supporting favorite Idol candidates based on some identity factor such as place, ethnicity, or religious faith. American television viewers participate as an integral component in a national whole, but they also watch as individuals or private family units in their living rooms. Catherine Bell sees this kind of viewing as a quality of ritual practice, different from other ritual forms privileging national solidarity at the expense of family solidarity or vice versa, that developed in the twentieth century with radio and television.[44] Additionally, although contestants get through the competition displaying personal values such as hard work, faith, and determination, it is the American community they thank and in part assign the responsibility for their successes.

That balance forms a central element of the composite American Dream mythology, whose multiple narratives celebrate individualism and communitarianism to different degrees. For Robert C. Rowland and John M. Jones, the American Dream essentially justifies the classical liberalism endorsed by the authors of the Constitution, the premise of a society in which "ordinary people have the opportunity to make a better life" for all Americans. From this ideology sprang two centuries of the political rhetoric that in turn generated the American Dream during the Great Depression. Examining this history, Rowland and Jones conclude that although the rhetoric of Teddy and Franklin Roosevelt—who represented opposing parties—and FDR's successor, Truman, equally championed individual and communal responsibilities, by the late twentieth century these strands had developed partisan associations articulated through American Dream narratives. Rowland and Jones trace this shift to Ronald Reagan's presidential oratory, which emphasized personal values such as faith, family, and work, in order to support conservative policies favored by the Republican Party. Thereafter the "dominant conflict," according to these authors, between Republican and Democratic uses of the American Dream has been "between narrative themes emphasizing personal versus societal responsibility for success"—and also whether the individual citizen or the government should be more accountable for progress. The American Dream became associated with conservative Republican discourse and policy, and disassociated from the comparatively liberal Democratic Party—recall Bao Viet Nguyen's conflicted description of his relationship with the Dream (chapter 3); although his family history followed a celebrated immigration narrative, he believed that "from a *liberal* standpoint you're not supposed to believe that much in that whole American Dream thing, you know, you deconstruct it." Rowland and Jones argue that when Barack Obama spoke as an Illinois senator at the Democratic National Convention in 2004, although he largely followed the expected rhetorical blueprints of the Democratic Party, his outlook was "received as revolutionary" because he reestablished an American Dream narrative that balanced individualist and communal values and made it a property again accessible to adherents of either party. He presented his own life as a story about individual effort and faith but also spoke of American universality and tolerance: "Alongside our famous individualism, there's another ingredient in the American saga, a belief that we are connected as one people."[45] That narrative equilibrium proved a powerful platform, propelling him to election in 2008; for *American Idol,* that same narrative has won eight elections and immense revenue. And although *Idol* discourse has often critiqued voting results as representative of a conservative "middle America," the balance of individualist and communitarian Dreams indicates that the show actually walks a middle road to fame.

The individualism touted in the American Dream comprises two strands of its own, corresponding to Herbert Hoover's rugged economic brand and Foucault's self-knowledge (see chapter 2). Robert Bellah et al. recognized these in different terms. These authors expressed a fear that certain kinds of individualism had "grown cancerous" and threatened to destroy American freedom. They understood a tension between a career-oriented "utilitarian individualism" and a more outwardly directed "expressive individualism." The former emphasizes self-interest, a striving toward increasing achievement and social prestige, and material success as evidence of strong moral character. This is an individualism linked by Bellah and colleagues to a "basically economic understanding of human existence." The American Dream, with its endorsement of fame, and its celebration of the ideal fluidity of class, fits this mode of individualism. Expressive individualism, on the other hand, aims for self-realization through the expression of a unique individual "core," by which one may potentially connect with other people, with nature, or with "the cosmos as a whole."[46] Its ideological roots, as Charles Taylor masterfully demonstrates, can be traced through the Calvinist shift toward the inward, personal commitment to a covenantal relationship with God, and the impact of naturalism in Deistic, Enlightenment, and Romanticist religious thought. For Taylor, the idea of the "inner voice" is particularly linked to an intertwining of naturalist philosophy and Christian faith (as in Deism), in which "what is primary is the voice within or, according to other variants, the élan running through nature which emerges inter alia in the voice within," and God "is to be interpreted in terms of what we see striving in nature and finding voice within ourselves."[47] This is perhaps the real task that *American*

Idol contestants are charged with in "making the song their own"—and Season 5 finalist Katharine McPhee did tell the *Idol* audience to trust "The Voice Within" (melismatic icon Christina Aguilera's 2003 Top 40 hit)—whether or not the singers personally identify it as a religious process.

RELIGION, COMMUNITY, AND RELIGIOUS COMMUNITIES

Émile Durkheim emphasized the role of religion in social solidarity, but he also posited that the division of labor led to a sacralization of the individual at the expense of other kinds of faith. *American Idol* demonstrates a "common faith" in the individual as idealized in the American Dream, however, it also supports the close relationship between morality and religion—which many believe can counteract the secularizing influences of the market—to sustain communal solidarity. To Durkheim, religion was a system that could unite adherents "into one single moral community called a Church."[48] In the Age of Information, "church" as a community can be a transient form of sacred space that no longer even requires a physical edifice in order to exist and function. The expansion of technological synergy has further contributed to this phenomenon, and the fluidity of sacred space has proven important to many *American Idol* viewers. On the FOX Network's *American Idol* message boards, viewers posting to support their favorite singers have often participated in "prayer chains." In these message threads, viewers petition God to help a singer through a difficult week, poor health, or the danger of elimination from the competition. The case of one such singer, a finalist in the third season of *American Idol,* is particularly striking. George Huff, who was regularly praised online for his own sense of faith, became the center of much viewer prayer. One post introduced a viewer to the FOX *American Idol* forum in March 2004 as the leader of Huff's church at home. He conducted message-board prayer for the singer when Huff was unwell and also at other particularly difficult points throughout the competition. A post from late in the season read:

> FATHER GOD, WE COME TO YOU TONIGHT IN THE NAME OF YOUR SON, JESUS CHRIST.

WE HOLD UP GEORGE AND YOUR OTHER CHILDREN AND PRAY
BLESSINGS ON THEM ALL.

MAY YOU BE GLORIFIED THROUGH THEM, FATHER, AS WE GIVE
YOU SPECIAL THANKS FOR THE RETURN OF THE ANOINTING ON
GEORGE.

CAN I HEAR AN AMEN?

Prayer and the electronic "amens" submitted on the message boards help to construct a virtual sacred space for worship-related ritual. With the participation of the online pastor, the newly assembled, virtual church community is also connected to the physical church community he led in Oklahoma City (where Huff attended the University of Oklahoma). Further, a post from the same contributor in the previous month had asked,

WITH GOD ON OUR SIDE WHO COULD COME AGAINST GEORGE?[49]

Analogous language has been associated with civil religion at the national level. Shortly after 9/11, President Bush addressed a joint session of Congress and the American people: "The course of this conflict is not known, yet its outcome is certain. Freedom and fear, justice and cruelty, have always been at war, and we know that God is not neutral between them."[50] Without explicitly saying so, this speech implies that God supports the position of the United States in the conflict, as the nation acts to fulfill its mission. Likewise, the online clergyman hints that George Huff will be successful in *his* calling, with God's divine endorsement.

In the online prayer threads, God is imagined as an intermediary between the audience and the characters (contestants) onscreen. This can be a two-way street: Season 3 finalist Jasmine Trias told a reporter, "I pray Tuesday night [the night votes are submitted] . . . I pray, 'Please make the people vote for me.'"[51] Bringing God into the audience equation adds a special dimension to the interaction between viewers, characters, and the powers that be in the media industry.

The example of George Huff's fan community illustrates the significance of viewer-contestant bonds based on identity markers like religious faith. "HuffNation," as members called it, was a distinct, self-defined subgroup of the *American Idol* audience, founded on loyalty to a specific contestant and on its members' mutual awareness of a specified Christian religious code. That faith is important to some *American Idol* fans is clear; the kind of role it plays in their voting practices is more ambiguous. As Rhys Williams notes, religion as an identity marker is considered to exert a potent influence in the context of the political election.[52] Discourse on the FOX message boards suggests a similar effect in the selection of the American Idol. One third-season contestant mentioned his attendance at Brigham Young University (associated with the Church of Latter-Day Saints) in his online profile. He and another singer whose Mormon affiliation was somehow surmised became the objects of frequent forum postings by co-religionists. One message thread asked the question "Mormon vote: John PETER [Jon Peter Lewis] or John PREATOR."[53] Worth noting is that these singers, among some *Idols* of other Christian denominations, counted among their experiences religious missionary work,[54] a sacral social responsibility that has informed America's mission-oriented moral and political rhetoric.

Several fans expressed to me their approval of contestants' publicly acknowledged faith, but most dismissed the idea that such factors have guided their voting. Along with George Huff, Season 2 runner-up Clay Aiken was an all-time favorite of some fans at two dress rehearsals I attended during Season 4. A mother and adult daughter from Arizona, who told me that they listened primarily to Christian rock, recognized and commended Aiken's Christianness but considered religion unimportant in their voting decisions.[55] However, even if there is not always a direct correlation between a singer's religious faith and his or her ultimate success on *American Idol*, related issues of morality and of the Idol as a role model may come into play. Like the sixty-five-year-old woman who "wore out two phones" voting for Aiken, many voters place weight on contestants' evident observance of certain moral values.

But Chris Rainey of the Christian apparel company Kerusso discussed his own *Idol* voting experience, explaining that, among other reasons, he is sometimes moved to support contestants because "they're part of the family; they're a brother or sister in Christ." He also sees a connection to both political and consumer choices:

> *You've got two people that are extremely talented, but one, their values more reflect yours. So do you vote for them? I think it's like that, for a lot of people anyway, I think it's like that across the board—whether it's politics, or American Idol, or the store you shop at, or the clothes you wear, or the brand you support. I mean, if you know that a company or a person, their values are more in line with yours, all things being equal, and that's the thing that tips the scales, I do think that influences people.*[56]

Mr. Rainey also reminded me of press reports toward the end of Season 8 that contrasted Kris Allen's Christian background with Adam Lambert's then unconfirmed homosexuality. Although many suggested that Christian voters might dominate the season's proceedings, both singers admonished at a pre-finale press conference that the competition was meant to be about singing. "For me," Allen said then, "I hope that having the 'Christian vote' doesn't help with anything. . . . I hope it has to do with your talent and the performance that you give and the package that you have. It's not about religion and all that kind of stuff." Lambert echoed the sentiment: "I don't think it has anything to do with your religious background, what color you are, your gender. . . . It's about music. That's really important to keep in mind."[57]

Religious discourse on *American Idol* begins with the semantics implied in its very title. The connotations of the word "idol" are not lost on viewers; numerous forum threads contain warnings addressing this issue:

> I believe that we shouldn't idolize anyone, but to worship God alone.

And another thread read:

> Who is your Idol????? (thread title)
> My idol is God . . . first and foremost . . . no other Idols . . .[58]

For these fans it seems important to keep the sacred separated from the secular in their viewing experiences. The celebrity must remain distinct from the celestial. These posts seem to have descended from the concerns of Daniel J. Boorstin, who feared in 1961—just a few years before Bellah's essay—that, with the "image" (in particular, film and television) overtaking the "ideal" in American thought, God was being re-imagined as a kind of ultimate celebrity. In this model God became just a holier matinee idol, whose power could "be measured by how widely he is reported, how often he is spoken about."[59]

Kerusso, where Chris Rainey is an executive, sells a T-shirt emblazoned with an icon in the style of the *Idols* logo. Inside the familiar blue oval, and in the white *Idol* font, the words "Amazing Grace" are followed in smaller letters by "How Sweet the Sound." Underneath, the words "I don't need an IDOL, I have a SAVIOR" are silkscreened. The epigram is an apparent critique of *American Idol*'s pop-star worship, intended to polarize religion and the consumer culture of which the T-shirt is a part—but for Mr. Rainey, who says he is not offended by the inclusion of the word "idol" in the show's title, it is simply meant to convey the message that the teen or pop-culture idol is not the highest role model. "They might be the best singer," he says, "and they might have got 50 million votes, but at the end of the day there's someone who's even greater, that we need to look to and we need to serve"[60] (Figure 4.2).

Any controversy over vocabulary has done little to discourage contestants from making direct expressions of faith or producers from making indirect references. Once an Idol is elected, he or she immediately records the new song written especially for the show.[61] Sometimes, as in "I Believe" or Season 4's "Inside Your Heaven,"[62] religion is implicit. Although no deity is mentioned specifically in the lyrics of either song, other words and symbols, offered at the penultimate and ultimate moments of the "campaign," allude to religious ritual. "I Believe" did so, particularly in its style, referential lyrics, and performance presentation. Fantasia Barrino made numerous references to her faith throughout the competition, both verbally and symbolically. Finishing performances, she often pointed skyward in a gesture ostensibly of thanks or praise, and in the May 18 (2004) broadcast, she wore a necklace with several dozen pendant crosses. Her performances also typically featured a hallmark dance, which she named "the BoBo" and associated with her experience singing in church. In her autobiographical book, *Life Is Not a Fairy Tale,* she says of her experience in her family's church,

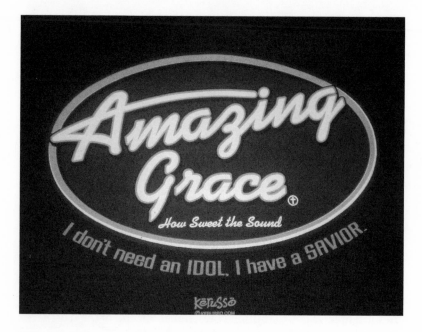

Figure 4.2. Logo on a T-shirt produced by the
Christian apparel company Kerusso.

> When someone feels the presence of the Holy Spirit, they need to
> let it out! Sometimes, the spirit makes us run up the aisles of the
> church; sometimes it makes us sit still and cry; sometimes it makes
> us faint. I have fainted. But most of the time it just makes me do my
> dance, the BoBo.

George Huff also had a specialized, characteristic movement, which
his mother identified during one episode's pre-performance video
package as a "dip" he developed singing in church.[63]

Following Barrino's performance of Barry Manilow's "It's a Miracle" on April 20, judge Randy Jackson told her, "I feel the spirit in
here tonight!" Of Manilow's *Idol*-specific rearrangement of his song,
Barrino stated, "I put a little church [and] soul into it." Manilow expressed his delight: "Now I can finally hear 'It's a Miracle' like it would
come right out of a church . . . I've always wanted to hear it like that."[64]
Her performances, then, were both calculated and received as evocative of (African American) church ritual.

Dwelling on Barrino's faith not only supported the show's family appeal, but it also served to further connect *American Idol* to the American Dream. Jennifer Hochschild writes that working-class African Americans tend to hold more tightly to that Dream than their more affluent counterparts, and suggests that religion plays an important role in that perpetuation. First, according to Hochschild, religious belief and the church community lend individuals the "strength to carry on." The church also often works with social agencies to address community issues, and church leaders sometimes even enter politics to achieve the necessary results. And Hochschild reminds us that different interpretations in Christian theology focus respectively and collectively upon fundamental human equality and hard work (tenets, as we have seen, of the American Dream). Even the Nation of Islam, she suggests, had a paragon of the American Dream in the prison conversion of Malcom X, whose history of self-improvement was an important part of his influence.[65] It seems, then, that Barrino's blackness may be even more closely tied to the show's religious tendencies than the mere (if frequent) references to gospel music might indicate. And the choice to highlight particularly *African American* forms of religious expression, quite specific in their national locality, adds to the show's performance of a spiritualized Americanness. Fantasia Barrino's association with a Holiness denomination also brings in the element of "old-time" religion, whose resurgent influence Wade Clark Roof and William McKinney identified in 1987. This was a trend continuing from the previous decade, they wrote, that had arisen in response to the radical secularity and pluralism of the 1960s.[66] Barrino and *American Idol* entered the scene just as the legacy of these developments had reached a new pinnacle of civic tension.

However, not everyone responded to Barrino in the same positive vein as Jackson and Manilow; one thread on FOX's official fan forum was filled with unfavorable opinions regarding this performance. "Fantasia's 'soul-gospel' rendition simply stunk and was an insult to the song and to Manilow (IMHO)," wrote one viewer in April 2004, and many on the forum concurred. Another viewer complained about Barrino, "This is getting annoying, everytime she points up to God and mouths something." This kind of discrepancy fits well with Kertzer's tripartite conception of symbolic meaning in ritual. The three properties he ascribes to symbols include *condensation,* a symbol's unification of diverse meanings; *multivocality,* those diverse meanings attached to a single symbol; and *ambiguity,* the lack of a single precise meaning associated with a symbol.[67] Underlying all three of these properties, of course, is polysemy, the implication that a symbol may be inscribed with multiple meanings. The negative response posted about "It's a Miracle" does not indicate that Barrino's "soul-gospel" performance had no meaning for that viewer but rather that the meaning it had was incompatible with the meaning he or she found in the song itself, or in its original recording.

Others were suspicious that the religious references were strategically conceived. When asked by journalist Virginia Heffernan about his feelings regarding "the religious element to the show," Simon Cowell answered, "Obviously a lot of people are using it to gain votes." Catherine Bell points out practice theory's approach to agency in ritual, and the assertion that ritual may be viewed as "a strategic way of acting." A ritual participant may be seen as "a ritualized agent who has acquired an instinctive knowledge of schemes that can be used to order his or her experience as to render it more or less coherent with these ritual values [values inscribed in the sacred] concerning the sacred."[68]

Barrino's actions, or at least their interpretation as politically intended, may be seen (perhaps too simplistically) as a literalization of this idea. Barrino's and other contestants' invocation of God onstage and in other venues imbue the show and its products with a kind of testimonial element. Following an early broadcast in which Barrino, grateful for being voted into the Top 12, gestured skyward and proclaimed, "I thank God. I'm happy. It's a blessing, and I love you all," one viewer posted,

> FANTASIA!!! You did it!!! Praise GOD! . . . I loved what you said tonight. God sure blessed you with true talent . . . Keep acknowledging God and I know you will come out on top everytime!

In response to this post, another wrote, "AMEN TO THAT!"[69]

Like viewers, the contestants and producers of *American Idol* seem to be keenly aware of the allusions to gospel music, church ritual, and the power of religion in electoral politics. Second-season victor Ruben Studdard confirmed an interviewer's suggestion that he "learned to sing in church" in the manner of the soul singers he grew up listening to. He and first-season winner Kelly Clarkson (who is white) appeared in September 2003 on a VH1 special titled *From the Church to the Charts,* and both acknowledge their debt to gospel singing. This was soon proven in explicit practice in the 2004 special *Kelly, Ruben, and Fantasia: Home for Christmas,* in which Clarkson and Barrino together led a rendition of the song "Jesus Oh What a Wonderful Child," complete with a gospel choir. Ruben Studdard later fronted the choir with "Amazing Grace."[70]

Clarkson's post-competition single in 2002, "A Moment Like This," was also accompanied by a multiethnic gospel choir. In the final broadcast of *American Idol*'s second season, a similar choir, assembled specially for the episode,[71] joined winner Ruben Studdard as he sang "Flying Without Wings," a 1999 single by U.K. band Westlife (another Cowell project, and contracted with *Idols*-affiliated BMG). The other remaining contestant, Clay Aiken, was also supported by the choir in his rendition of "Bridge Over Troubled Water," the 1970 platinum hit by Simon and Garfunkel. The gospel choir returned, robed, for "I Believe" in 2004, and again wearing black for Carrie Underwood's 2005 winning moment with "Inside Your Heaven," then robed once more for "blue-eyed soul" singer Taylor Hicks's victory in 2006 with "Do I Make You Proud." It was conspicuously missing at the end of Season 6, although the winning entry in the new songwriting competition had been co-written by a pastor.[72] In Season 7 the choir only appeared, robed, during a charity special in April, but in Season 8 it joined the finale again wearing black civilian garb as the Top 2 finalists sang "We Are the Champions" with the musicians of Queen. Associate music director Michael Orland suggests that the use of a gospel choir, though not necessarily intended as religious, adds a certain weight to the proceedings:

> You can't get big enough for the finale, and our producers love the gospel choir thing going on. . . . When the exec producers, Ken and Nigel, hear the songs that were picked for the kids to sing for the finale, it always feels like it needs to generate that kind of bigness.[73]

Even when the song holds little religious meaning, the gospel choir is undeniably a symbol of religious ritual. And as it did at President Clinton's 1997 inauguration,[74] the presence of a gospel choir in commemoration of an election carries specifically civil-religious significance.

CONCLUSIONS

As the democratic process and the American Dream, embedded in *American Idol,* carry American civil and sacral religion into living rooms around the world, the geopolitical implications are potentially profound. Marcella Cristi believes that most theorists neglect Rousseau's intention that civil religion exist as a phenomenon created and controlled by the *state.* In this model, civil religion can be used as a political tool, most significantly for purposes of coercion. Cristi asserts that a Durkheimian conception of civil religion, such as that followed by Bellah, is about consent, whereas Rousseau's version is about coercion. Although Antonio Gramsci is only mentioned cursorily in Cristi's work, it is important to consider the potential function of civil religion in a Gramscian framework of global hegemonic conditions.[75]

Rhys Williams, in a 1996 analysis for the *Journal for the Scientific Study of Religion,* argued for an understanding of religion in general as "both culture and ideology," a "political resource" in a Gramscian sense that is about both meaning and power.[76] This is an important model for the continuing study of *civil* religion as well, as civil religion may serve in these terms as a resource of both coercion and consent. In the *Idols* series, civil religion, the voting process, and the American Dream represent not only Gramscian tools of the entertainment trade but also a metonymically commodified democracy. And at a time when democracy is virtually proselytized through American foreign policy, the civil-religious and moral significance of *American Idol's* pseudo-election should not be disregarded.

America's most recent conflicts may have special implications here. Bellah associated the development of American civil religion with particular periods of social upheaval and division: (1) the generative war for independence, (2) the Civil War and the struggle surrounding the institution of slavery, and (3) the discord of the time he was writing in, concerning civil rights and the Vietnam War. He posited that a "successful negotiation" of that third "time of trial," entailing the achievement of a cohesive world order, would result in a reconceptualization of American civil religion as part of a larger global whole. If the crisis subsequent to 9/11 amounts to a fourth "time of trial," then we may view this reconceptualization of civil religion as ongoing, along with efforts toward the elusive "world order" Bellah predicted in 1967, what Roberta Coles foresees as "a more universal civil-religion in this post-modern world."[77] Key elements of American civil religion have been discursively important in the current endeavors toward worldwide democratization—the association of democracy with a divine covenant, articulated recently as a preoccupation with the mission of global democratization, and the concepts of the *calling* and morality in the context of the American Dream. *American Idol* broadcasts these ideological frameworks to 113 nations.[78]

American Idol, combining a highly developed formulation of consumer practice with the diversely mediated performance of ritual, effectively illustrates the convergence of religion and consumption in popular culture. It is designed in ways that underscore the moral ideals central to the American Dream, and to common understandings of American democracy. *American Idol* highlights a set of concerns at once urgently immediate and older than the nation itself. In its reflection and reinforcement of a new kind of "virtuoso" civil religion, we may observe the struggle to reconcile the ideological binaries of individualism and community, commercialism and authenticity, capitalism and democracy.

5

GOING PLACES

GOING TO HOLLYWOOD

Every summer one hundred thousand young men and women crowd into sports arenas and convention centers around the United States, sing their hearts out for twenty seconds, hold their breaths, and hope to hear this congratulatory pronouncement: *"You're going to Hollywood!"* Those happy few who do are sent forth, "golden tickets" in hand, to retrace the path of the ultimate American narrative—a story in which Manifest Destiny, the spirit of capitalism, and the allure of seizing the microphone have led inexorably west, to California.

The journey fulfills more than *Idol* dreams. It is centuries of imagining America and Americans as the sum of where they have come from and where they are going. *American Idol* reiterates old mythologies of migration and immigration, reconfirming deeply embedded ideas of Hollywood as the locus of the American Dream, as the site where that Dream becomes reality (or, at least, reality programming). But the defining relationship between Hollywood and the American Dream isn't about rising stars and starry-eyed ingénues. It is instead a set of entwined and enduring dialectics. The first is a dialectics of journey: Hollywood is part of a geographical dialogue between California and the rest of the Union, especially in relation to the region understood as the South. It is also in conversation with the past, with a national history dependent on movement and change. And within this dialectics lies another dialogue of passage, immigration, linking California and other nations across borders and oceans. Immigration is a continuing trope in *American Idol;* a montage of Season 8 auditions in New York even included a shot of contestants waving their golden tickets (saffron-colored A4) onboard a boat in front of the Statue of Liberty. (That season also brought the first auditions conducted in a U.S. territory, in Puerto Rico.) *American Idol* often features the stories of first-generation American singers like Season 8's Allison Iraheta and Anoop Desai, Irish immigrant Carly Smithson and Australian immigrant Michael Johns in Season 7 (Smithson and Johns had each lived in Georgia before moving to California), Ukrainian immigrant Anthony Federov in Season 4, and Bao Viet Nguyen, as related in chapter 3. Although his parents made the Pacific journey, Mr. Nguyen

Figure 5.1. Luggage at the San Francisco audition site, August 17, 2005.

himself was born in California and was living in Los Angeles at the time of his Pasadena auditions. "Going to Hollywood" might be an act more metaphorical than cartographical for him, but that makes it no less real. Mr. Nguyen understands his portrayal on the show as part of a mediated, multiculturalist imagining of the United States. In his words,

> They made it seem as if I just got off a boat yesterday and decided to become an R&B star, you know, or a pop star. . . . It made sense to show an Asian person on there, like, "He's here because he has this great story, not because he's just a regular American, going and trying out for American Idol." . . . It was just like, oh, the ethnic, "This is our Asian story." Because we have a lot of Black stories, Latino stories, and so this is to show multicultural America, and this is—we accept everyone.[1]

This picture reiterates the tensions between discourses of multiculturalism, in which the preservation of ethnic identities is considered important and beneficial to the nation's general social health, and the discourses of "melting pot" assimilation established via Israel Zangwill's eponymous play in 1908. In *American Idol*, this conflict is reflected in the way the show's election works through coalition voting—with viewers often voting for contestants based on shared identity factors—positioned against the election of a national representative and the (albeit appropriative) melting pot of commercial pop. In the aforementioned geographies, Hollywood figures as cultural capital. These layered dialogues write much of the script for the discursive complex called the American Dream and play a leading role in the construction of America itself.

A second crucial dialectics creates a paradox of authenticity, positioning Hollywood simultaneously as crucible of national identity and national disorder. This conflict offsets a desire to make the American Dream real in Hollywood—to *construct* American reality there—with an abiding fear that anything made in California might be inherently fake, nothing more than a manufactured prop on a movie set. This is the problem of authenticity for which Baudrillard saw only one possible solution—a complete "reversal of values" in which the reproduction, by logical necessity, has become reality, and anything once considered fake has become authentic: "It is Disneyland that is authentic here!" he marveled, "The cinema and TV are America's reality!"[2] This California is imagined coastally, even teleologically—positioned at the extremities of the nation's moral map, either as the utopian just deserts of model American behavior or, conversely, as just *desert*, Baudrillard's end-stage simulacrum in which television has superseded reality. *American Idol* is reality TV, the embodiment of Baudrillard's critique, television about manufacture. But at the same time *American Idol* offers, over and over, on Tuesdays, Wednesdays, and sometimes Thursdays, a collection of Americans genuinely trying to live their American Dreams in Hollywood. Hollywood is California telescoped into the twenty-five square miles at the center of the U.S. film industry, the heart of American imagination. It is an ultimate goal, a space that houses the spirit of the American Dream, yet, as Baudrillard saw it, the seat of all that is hyper-commercial and false about the partnership of entertainment and American capitalism in the culture industry.

And California is not the only place cursed with such ambiguity of meaning. The larger regional construction known as the South is imbued with similar connotations, inestimably vital in the cultural history of the nation, but at the same time, as Tara McPherson sees it, discursively "alternating between (if not simultaneously representing) the moral other and the moral center of U.S. society." *American Idol* celebrates both the South and Hollywood in dialogue with each other; one place is where American talent comes from, and the other the place it goes to live the Dream. Each location is understood as representative of prized American values (such as opportunity in California and, in the South, Christian religious and moral standards). On the other hand, this situation also exposes what James W. Fernandez calls "the problem of metonymic misrepresentation," in which the problems of a place considered a part stand in for the problems of a larger place considered a whole.[3] In such a scenario, the perceived fakeness of Hollywood encapsulates a broader fake America, and a history of poverty and social disorder in the South makes it the locus of national blame. *American Idol* puts forth both sides of the equation, glorifying southern music but emphasizing the struggles experienced by southern contestants in their pre-*Idol* lives—lives left behind for the chance at a bright, but clearly engineered, future in Hollywood.

California Dreamin'

Just before the 2008 season of *American Idol* began, FOX ran a commercial for the show, a montage of successful auditions overlaid with Collective Soul's 2007 single "Hollywood"—a song that symbolically positioned the singer in a romance with the eponymous center of the U.S. entertainment industry. "Yeah, Hollywood," Ed Roland sang, "You know I love you more than one man should / Well, kiss me, kiss me good." As the song played, captions and clips told the viewer, "These three words changed America forever: 'Welcome to Hollywood.'" Whether or not the words (used interchangeably on the show with "you're going to Hollywood") have, in fact, had the effect advertised, there can be no doubt that, like *American Idol* itself, they are compelling descriptors of our geographical dialectics.

Hollywood is where the later phases of the *American Idol* season are staged and filmed, once the preliminary national audition tour is completed. It is where the successful auditionees go. That directional motion is important; Hollywood is a place you go, a place you go *to,* in the imagining of America. It is not a place you leave in order to find a better life, but the place where you are at last permitted to pursue that life, that Dream. Hollywood and the American Dream are engaged in a special relationship, each contributing to the mythology of the other, together figuring in the total mythology of America. Located at the farthest edge of the space that was once the "Western Frontier," Hollywood absorbed the role of ultimate objective. "Nothing is more American than Hollywood," writes historian Larry May. As he begins his examination of Hollywood's political history, May wonders, "How does the nation's popular culture become enmeshed in debates over the meaning of good citizenship in terms of sex, race, and class?" It is not just about entertainment and family values, he believes, but about something else, "something that connects Hollywood to political power, cultural authority, and the very meaning of national identity."[4] Situated physically and ideologically in this powerful Hollywood, *American Idol* contributes to the very complex construction of this "something."

All nine seasons of *American Idol* to date have included a California city among the annual open audition sites, usually alternating between a southland location and San Francisco. During initial broadcasts every season, these sites are typically identified by footage of the enormous auditioning congregation, shouting the name of the city in unison. "San Francisco Rocks!" we screamed together at the Season 5 auditions I attended at San Francisco's Cow Palace. The producers on site encourage such localized camaraderie at each audition event, giving all a place-specific song to perform together, en masse, on camera. These assignments transform the stadium crowd from *Idol* viewers into performers, actors onscreen; for the moment all become San Franciscans, all Californians, though earlier in line I'd met singers from Oregon, Arizona, and as far away as Germany. At registration it was announced that we would collectively perform "Dock of the Bay"—which Otis Redding wrote in nearby Sausalito—although when the morning of the auditions came, we were asked to sing "The Star-Spangled Banner" instead. The Bay Area pride quickly shifted to patriotism, and a chant of "U.S.A.! U.S.A.!" broke out among the crowd. Our California location suddenly stood in for the whole of the nation. Regional or national, these performances of solidarity recall the importance of "location, location, location" in the landscape of Americanness as it is sung in popular culture—mountains, prairies, and everything from sea to shining sea.[5]

Another song, "California Dreamin'," was the chosen group number for San Diego during Season 7 auditions. Sung by thousands of potential Idols with Walk of Fame stars in their eyes, the title itself is telling—"of all the states in the union," historian Kevin Starr observes, "only California has attached to its identity the concept of dream."[6] And "California Dreamin'" has played a recurring role on *American Idol* since the Top 8 first-season finalists shot a video for one of the broadcasts. In this video the contestants suddenly appear in an empty space, as if instantly transported to the Hollywood terrace that serves as the video set. They sit outdoors around a picturesque fire pit, eight young singers representing multiethnic America—black, white, a singer whose post-*Idol* management has billed him as "The first Mexican/American, True R&B star" (http://www.emancipated-talent.com), and at least one singer who has self-identified as biracial (Justin Guarini). Hailing from different parts of the United States, they all sing the same California song, sharing the text and the tune among them before joining together in harmony.[7] These Top 8, selected by viewers from the producers' initial pool, reflect the conventionally rainbow casting of reality television shows since the 1990s, California idealized as an American leader in racial diversity, and the wishful thinking of "California Dreamin'" matched with the premature celebration of a "post-racial" America. In its worst light, the idealized *American Idol* cast looks like another instance of Baudrillard's inauthentic image become reality, America as "a hyperreality because it is a utopia which has behaved from the very beginning as though it were already achieved."[8]

When "California Dreamin'" is sung on *American Idol,* the title alone implies the dream of a fair economic forecast of money and fame that the show plays upon and preys upon. The Mamas and the Papas recorded "California Dreamin'" at United/Western's Studio 3 in Hollywood, and became the center of some tensions at Monterey Pop in 1967, for reasons entangled with rock ideology and the dialectic opposing Hollywood and authenticity. Monterey Pop was engineered in the end by John Phillips and the group's producer, Lou Adler, and although it included many artists associated with the countercultural movement, it became, effectively, counter-countercultural—what Barney Hoskyns calls "a rock and roll trade show masquerading as a love-in." To many participating San Francisco musicians, like Country Joe McDonald, the Mamas and the Papas and their Hollywood "California Dreamin'" represented "a total ethical sellout of everything that we'd dreamed of" and the moment Hoskyns pinpoints as the "inevitable, unavoidable moment when the underground went mainstream."[9] As a paragon of commercial pop, "California Dreamin'" connects genre discourse to place and strips Hollywood of its status as a national objective. And in a Season 8 *Idol* recurrence of the song, José Feliciano's interpretation served as a melancholy soundtrack to the end of dreaming, played under the onscreen drama as contestants were cut from the initial Hollywood audition rounds. Then it was a warning that California can be, to paraphrase Christopher Isherwood, like every Promised Land "a tragic country."[10]

The Monterey Pop performance, the *Idol* video, and the group-sing at the San Diego auditions all took place in California. "California Dreamin'," however, does not. It teeters on the indecisive edge of movement ("If I didn't tell her I could leave today") but firmly inhabits a place where the "leaves are brown and the sky is grey"—a place that is in dialogue with, but not situated in, the Golden State. Part of our geographical dialectics of Hollywood and the American Dream, this dialogue practically defines California in the American (and *American Idol*) imagination. By itself, California has no more or less special meaning than Arkansas or Oregon or Ohio. But no place exists in a vacuum, and in the broader map of the United States California is assigned the role of destination, of destiny.

Manifest Destiny

When John L. O'Sullivan first coined the phrase "Manifest Destiny" in an 1845 issue of the *Democratic Review,* California was still half a decade away from annexation; O'Sullivan wrote his essay in support of the final statehood of Texas. Barely four months later it served as the rhetorical focus of plans to terminate the joint occupation of Oregon with Great Britain, and ultimately the words became the generic motto of expansionist ideology, of westward movement.[11] "Manifest Destiny" was at once the call of fate and a call to American citizens to become masters of their own, and it declared the responsibility of a geopolitical role assigned by "Providence"—one that the nation's leaders take very seriously to this day. As Reginald Horsman has suggested, it was also an ideological model that helped shape American racialism.[12] The impact of this model, named and catalyzed by O'Sullivan's words, has much to do with its context; "manifest destiny" was invented during the events precipitating war with Mexico and just before the 1848 gold rush, two circumstances that whipped the Union into an expansionist frenzy directed west. By the time filmmaking came to Hollywood in the 1910s, California was already firmly cemented in the national consciousness as a national and personal aspiration.

The film industry combined the rhetoric of Manifest Destiny with dreams of relocation early on, and eventually infused this formula with the formerly Broadway narrative of small-town Americans making it in the big city. In the 1937 film *A Star is Born*—produced by David O. Selznick in the throes of the Depression that birthed the American Dream myth, and of the Dust Bowl that again drove thousands westward—Janet Gaynor's Esther Blodgett is a North Dakota farm girl longing for a film career in Hollywood. In an early scene, after her family discourages her plans, her grandmother finds her weeping and recounts her own youthful pioneer trek west. Grandmother Lettie (May Robson) comforts Esther, reminding her that everyone who dreams is laughed at in the beginning, even the pioneers, and warns her that living one's dreams always comes at a cost.

> When I wanted something better, I came across those plains in a prairie schooner with your grandfather. Oh, everyone laughed at us. . . . They said this country would never be anything but a wilderness. We didn't believe that! We were going to make a *new* country. Besides, we wanted to see our dreams come true. . . . But don't you think for one single minute that it was easy, Esther Blodgett![13]

The scene draws a parallel between the pioneers' fulfillment of John L. O'Sullivan's westward charge and the driven young woman determined to "be somebody" and to go to Hollywood to do it. (And as Esther approaches the train that will take her to California, Lettie encourages her: "Go on, there's your prairie schooner!")

American Idol returns, repeatedly, to these twin iconic journeys of geography and ideology. Every year the show includes footage of young men and women who walk in Esther Blodgett's footsteps—fictional, yet fixed in our national consciousness—to the Hollywood Walk of Fame, and fly over the phantom wagon tracks of her pioneer grandmother. The American Dream is a story of motion. The opening graphics for *American Idol*'s very first season sent a fleet of jetliners across the screen, and during early episodes each year viewers hear countless tales of first journeys, first airplane rides that take contestants to Hollywood. The airplane graphics were preceded by a flock of cameras, suggesting tourism, a sense of someone out of place, or out of one's depth, overlaid with the dual implications of transit: an airplane can take you to Hollywood, but it might just as easily take you home again.

The Hollywood where Manifest Destiny and the American Dream interlock demands an understanding that pursuit—and even achievement—risk that sort of disappointing outcome, and require personal sacrifice (as Esther Blodgett's grandmother warned her). In

American Idol hopeful singers make sacrifices of their own. In the early seasons they brought sleeping bags and necessities to an audition site, camping there for several nights in order to secure a place in line—later, changes in the audition process meant that everyone was heard and camping was not required; now camping is no longer allowed at many sites. In an interview, auditionee Rocío Torres recounted to me her extended 2002 camping experience at the Rose Bowl in Pasadena, sleeping on the ground along with thousands of others, over three nights. She described it as

> tor-ture. *Because [of] our lack of food and us not wanting to get out of line, because people are just crazy there—they'll totally take your stuff . . . But we sleep Thursday night, and it is freezing at night and so hot during the day. . . . Oh my God, it was horrible!*[14]

Her enumeration of the hardships endured through the audition process curiously echoes the words of Esther Blodgett's grandmother in *A Star is Born*, who recounts that on her westward voyage "we burned in summer and we froze in winter." In the end Rocío was invited to sing for the judges (the third round of auditions) and was called back for a second day, but she caught a cold, felt guilty for neglecting her summer school finals, and went home without finishing the audition process.

For a chance to be cast in *American Idol* and get to Hollywood, some are willing to sacrifice more than sleep, sustenance, and comfort. The first episode of Season 4 featured Regina Brooks, who explained on camera that she had pawned her wedding ring for $200 so that she could travel to the Washington, D.C., auditions. Judges Paula Abdul and Randy Jackson, along with guest judge Mark McGrath, declared their interest in her "story" after her audition, and indeed sent her on to Hollywood.[15] Such demonstrations of asceticism again hark back to Weber—the Calvinist ideal of self-denial in the process (and also in spite) of material achievement translating into the humble origins, humility, and struggle required in the Hollywood pursuit of the American Dream. Regina Brooks's story also, however, highlights a privileging of the chance for fame over other social values, even marriage. In their journeys to Hollywood, Rocío Torres and Regina Brooks walked the treacherous path of Hollywood's authenticity dialectic, a balancing act between living the Dream and selling the soul for a few moments in the spotlight.

The Best of the West

In Season 5 *American Idol* further highlighted the Hollywood history of western expansion, in concurrently satirical and earnest tones. Early broadcasts featured three "cowboys," beginning with a humorous segment on February 14, 2006 that parodied the recently released cinematic hit *Brokeback Mountain*. That film, about a complicated emotional and sexual relationship between two men, offered new symbols and possibilities of meaning for the iconic image of the American cowboy. The *Idol* spoof, titled "Brokenote Mountain," transferred these possibilities to the more musically specific icon of the *singing* cowboy. Scenes of generic male bonding, hugging, and crying provided sensitive, if satirizing, moments that retained the film's suggestion of alternate masculinities and homosocial camaraderie. The cowboys included Michael Evans of Denver, Colorado; Matthew Buckstein of Burbank, California; and Garet Johnson of Veteran, Wyoming—the state in which the movie *Brokeback Mountain* is set.

The *Idol* cowboys are linked to another emblematic notion of individualism, cemented like that of the American Dream during the Great Depression. They recall the singing cowboy celebrated in 1930s Hollywood films (although their appearances were at least once backed by the musical theme to *The Good, the Bad, and the Ugly*), a symbol that Bill C. Malone identifies as a coping mechanism during hard times. "In their search to regain a sense of purpose," he writes, "many Americans may have found comfort in identifying with a reassuring symbol of independence and mastery, a collection of traits that the nation had once possessed and might once again assert."[16] The cowboy, racialized as white, was also an antidote to the other rural white American icon, the hillbilly, offering instead an itinerant but employed figure identified with no economic class in particular.[17] *American Idol* presented the familiar solitariness and independence in the cowboy narrative but also balanced it with a message about community, touting brotherhood and solidarity. The *Idol* cowboy image was up to date, with its allusions to *Brokeback Mountain* and the group's integrated composition. (Michael Evans came on the show's scene less than a year after another African American country singer, Cowboy Troy, debuted in the No. 2 spot on *Billboard*'s country charts. Cowboy Troy also became the 2006 co-host of *Nashville Star,* an *Idol*-like competition for country singers on the USA Network.)

The story of the Brokenote Cowboys' youngest member, Garet Johnson, had begun during the preliminary audition episodes with a segment detailing his tiny hometown and family ranch, his home schooling and social isolation, his financial difficulties, and the fact that his only singing experience had been in front of a turkey. Although he preferred Elton John to country music for his audition, he did refer to himself explicitly as a cowboy. Though Johnson was the most completely drawn cowboy character of the three, together they presented a new breed of Hollywood cowboys, blending the sensitive *Brokeback Mountain* image with the more familiar character of cinematic country-singer cowboys like Gene Autry. And together they defied the figure of the lonesome cowboy, exchanging rugged individualism for the comfort of community. Eventually the trio's group audition during the Hollywood rounds foundered because of one member's weak harmonies, and all three went home. But they had served their purpose, their story both reaffirming and satirizing the tenuous balance in American culture between individualism and community, and a geographically centered dialogue between Hollywood and the American Dream.

California Is a State of Mind

The geographical dialectics of Hollywood is muddied by the show's widely spread production processes. *Idol* doesn't only happen physically in California, but California is always present—even when it is absent. As Gerald Haslam suggests, "California remains at least as much state of mind as state of the union."[18] In many ways *American Idol*'s California, and its Hollywood, become dislocated, re-mappable places. Although the judges congratulate auditionees with the words "You're going to Hollywood," until 2009 the initial "Hollywood rounds" usually took place in Pasadena, before producers and judges had narrowed down the contestant pool and production had moved on to CBS Television City for the start of viewer voting. In the eighth season these rounds were actually relocated to Hollywood, to the Kodak Theater, adjacent to the Hollywood Walk of Fame.

And about half the time in any season's early-audition episodes, instead of "You're going to Hollywood!" the *Idol* judges crow, "*Welcome* to Hollywood!" This happens regardless of where the auditions are taking place—in Dallas, Jacksonville, Philadelphia, or Honolulu—as if the judges' desk were itself a part of Hollywood existing outside time and space, requiring an invitation to permit approach. Hollywood, like some omnipotent god, is everywhere, *judging* you, declaring you worthy or unworthy of entry.

The shape of this transposable California can be charted more clearly in the American imagination than on any map. It is a site returned to again and again in times when the definition and redefinition of America occupies public attention. It becomes a symbol of motion and of change—the latter of which recent electoral politics have underlined as an early-twenty-first-century concern—and of the reassuring continuity of American ambition, American possibility. Baudrillard once described cities as definable by the kinds of disasters they have undergone, or await, with Los Angeles identified by the experience of "seismic challenge."[19] At an uneasy historical moment, with the ground shifting disconcertingly beneath us in the shaky new twenty-first century, *American Idol*'s California also perhaps offers Americans the comforting example of a place built directly on (and on top of) the potential for movement, a place that has repeatedly survived the most literal upheaval.

Where does America go when the going gets tough? Well, come each January, once again, it's going to Hollywood.

THE SOUTH RISES AGAIN

In 2009 *American Idol* opened an attraction at Disney's Hollywood Studios theme park, in Lake Buena Vista, Florida—stunningly recalling Baudrillard's California vision of Disneyland, of film and television as America's new reality. The performer voted the winner by a live audience earns a "Dream Ticket" marking "the next Cinderella story" and offering the vague "opportunity to make a reservation to sing in front of an American Idol representative at an actual regional audition of the American Idol TV show, where it's your moment to shine!"[20] This is *American Idol's* conflicted Hollywood discourse removed to Florida, offering Dream tourism on the far side of the country. The connection between Hollywood and Orlando cannot be accidental. If the American Dream, in its most prevalent form, has "its apotheosis in California," it has its "roots in the South."[21]

The prominence of southern singers in the competition has been the subject of much gossip in the press coverage of recent seasons, with ubiquitous allusions to the historical position of the post–Civil War South; an Associated Press piece titled "Rise of the South on 'American Idol,'" for example, and a *New York Times* essay titled "On 'Idol,' the South Rises Again . . . and Again."[22]

In June 2006 the NPD Group, a global marketing research firm, released the results of a study concluding that *American Idol's* contract with Cingular Wireless (branded AT&T Wireless until 2004, and rebranded AT&T Mobility in 2007) could be responsible for the dominance of southern contestants on the show. Almost half of Cingular cellular customers resided in southern states, the study claimed, and twice as many subscribers used Cingular's text-messaging services than in any other region. Because text-messaging is the only sure way an *Idol* vote may be placed—no busy signals, no tied-up lines— and because Cingular was the only permissible avenue through which text-messaged votes may be placed, the NPD Group suggested that southern viewers and their southern Idols might have an advantage. The study defined "southern" states according to U.S. Census criteria: Texas, Oklahoma, Louisiana, Arkansas, Tennessee, Mississippi, Kentucky, Alabama, West Virginia, Washington, D.C., Virginia, North Carolina, South Carolina, Florida, Georgia, Delaware, and Maryland. However, as Owen Thomas and Oliver Ryan of CNNMoney.com have noted, the Atlanta-based Cingular only became associated with *American Idol* after it initially absorbed AT&T Wireless in 2004, when the first two seasons had already yielded southern Idols. NPD's study, then, does not offer a complete explanation for the southern inclinations of the show.[23] Predictably the situation is more complex, involving not only the location of capital and consumer but also certain perceptions, understandings, and ideologies regarding the union and division of the United States.

Throughout all of its seasons to date, *American Idol* has increasingly relied on the presence of campaign-like hometown support for its contestants. This accomplishes two primary results: a focus on where a candidate/singer is from can help establish not only a dependable voting bloc but also, down the line, a ready market for post-*Idol* projects. To this end there has been consistent emphasis on a monolithic South, stretching across the South Atlantic states, the Deep South (East South Central states), and the West South Central states (including Texas and Oklahoma). This South can claim seven out of the nine winners up to 2010[24]—from Texas, Alabama, North Carolina, Oklahoma, Alabama again, Texas again, and Arkansas, respectively—and a majority of top finalists as native sons and daughters. *American Idol*'s ranks have been filled each season with singers of soul, R&B, and country music who project southern personas and act out stereotypes that remain persistent in American popular culture. These representations are racialized and gendered, and moored in intricately associated conventions of nostalgia, electoral politics, and the mythology of the American Dream.

Place holds a key position in the narrative of transformation, from ordinary to extraordinary, from anonymous to celebrity. Contestant Idols, in the legacy of the silver screen legends, must begin somewhere Other than Hollywood, far removed by some combination of geographical, economic, vocational, or ideological distance. As Gavin Campbell writes in his analysis of pop icon Britney Spears, "The American Dream is most satisfying when the hero grows up in [straitened] circumstances, busting out from somewhere constraining, from somewhere good enough to nurture them but too small to contain their genius." The South, then, becomes a "talent hot-house," which will initially nurture a budding talent but will not be able to sustain it; instead, the talent must be "transplanted, or it will wither, uncultivated."[25] Cultivation invariably—and ironically, in the context of this agricultural metaphor—must occur in a bustling urban setting, Hollywood being among the most celebrated. Executive producer Ken Warwick confirms this narrative as a potential reason for the southern domination of *American Idol*:

The thing is, if they're [from the] North and they're talented, then they tend to go professional.... They go to New York, they come to L.A., they go to San Francisco and they get jobs. But if they're in the South, maybe there's a little less opportunity, so there's more talent ... floating around. And that's what we're after. We like the fact that the kid comes from nothing and becomes a huge star.

"The South" can even be an anti-Hollywood in this dialogue between places; it can be a place that grounds would-be stars and inoculates them against the forfeit of their home-grown "realness" as they make the journey toward fame. After especially successful Season 5 auditions in Greensboro, North Carolina, Warwick stated, "Now we're reviewing the places we actually go to, because the [southern] kids are ... not more genuine, but they're less affected by showbiz." And Season 2 winner Ruben Studdard declares on his official website, "I'm from Alabama and it's hard for us to get to Hollywood. If you are who you say you are and you're real, it should be hard to change your personality overnight."[26] Hollywood, then, can not only be a geographical location but also an attitude or even a pose in opposition to the glamour and clamor of the entertainment industry's northern outposts.

Placing the South

What "the South" means deserves some discussion here. There is no "single South," writes Tara McPherson, "so specific understandings of how the South is represented, commodified, and packaged become key." It can be a place or a space full of places; Ruben Studdard's "205" jerseys throughout his appearances on *American Idol* referred to his Birmingham area code, "representing," and establishing, what Murray Forman describes as a "narrowed sense of *place*" to which authenticity is closely linked in hip-hop culture. Birmingham was perhaps the narrowest kind of place linked onscreen to an *Idol* campaign until 2009, when finalist Anoop Desai repeatedly shouted out an institution: the University of North Carolina, Chapel Hill, where he had earned his bachelor's degree and begun a graduate program in folklore (researching barbecue in southern culture). The South is also a site of American history or at least, as presented in popular culture, a site of reconstructed history—relying particularly on Reconstruction history—and nostalgia. This kind of nostalgia communicates an idealistic imagining, which, according to Fabio B. DaSilva and Jim Faught, "offers a bucolic image of unrestrained social relations in which hardships are overcome by good intentions." Some kinds of hardships are understood as specific to southern history, having been, supposedly, surmounted and relegated to the past. Teresa Goddu asserts that the South is "perceived as having overcome much of what made it distinctive," including racial discrimination and violence; if this is so, then it offers a very satisfactory utopian version of America-in-general to *Idol* viewers. The musical history that is traced and canonized on *American Idol* glosses over the racial interactions and tensions that characterized its very birth and is happily celebrated by an interracial cast. On the other hand, some of the other southern associations Goddu mentions, such as "economic impoverishment, educational ignorance, and religious fundamentalism," have all appeared in the portrayals of southerners on the show, apparently waiting for the singers to overcome them on a personal level on their way to the American Dream.[27]

The South is an "imagined community," David A. Davis writes, after Benedict Anderson. It is "the U.S. social, political, racial, economic, ethical, and everyday-life imaginary written as 'regionalism,'" and it is also a region written as nation. Historically the South has been "a foil of the North," an Otherized and exoticized direction polarized against the "liberal vision" claimed by other parts of America.[28] Nonsoutherners have sometimes seen the South as a symbol of everything wrong with America—the poverty portrayed in the Depression-era photographs of Walker Evans, the racial violence and segregation televised during the Civil Rights movement (a *movement,* another kind of American motion). But, as James C. Cobb observes, eventually it becomes clear that problems found in the South are not confined to the South, and that trouble there means trouble everywhere. And in this moment of realization, when the North and the whole of America are in trouble, the crucial foil of the South is paradoxically called upon to reaffirm a national identity.

This is a moment Cobb identifies in the election of President Jimmy Carter and his "liberal vision" in 1976, a political shift in response to the disillusioning events of the civil rights years—during which the South was the seat of disorder—the Vietnam War, and Watergate. During the election process, Cobb notes, "a nation plunged into a downward spiral of uncertainty and self-doubt was suddenly looking to the South not simply to break its fall but to seize the controls and pull its nose up before it crashed." He points to a 1976 *Saturday Review* issue that designated "the South as the New America" and suddenly extolled the recently problematic region. It is notable that the same issue also featured admiring write-ups of southern music, including an article positioning "The Spiritual as Soul Music" and the seed from which "truly" American music sprang, as well as a piece on country music and its "crossover" to the pop charts.[29] *American Idol* shows a contemporary, comparable reliance on images and music of the South, constructed in a time of crisis as both conservative of social values and liberal in its racial-musical pluralism.

The Mason-Dixon Line might mark the South as a bordered geography, but across that boundary regional and national popular cultures have flowed and intersected, converged and diverged. In the context of music, these bi-directional processes have resulted in a nationalization of southernness, a southernization of the national, so that "Southern music"—to paraphrase Bill C. Malone, and to parallel the *Saturday Review* theme—becomes "American music," and vice versa. Even so the South figures as a distinctive, if multivalent, symbol—maintaining, in Tara McPherson's words, "recognizable forms of southernness, points of rupture and disjuncture in 'Americanness' as a whole."[30] These forms and points of rupture include certain characterizations familiar from the very first stages—theatrical and developmental—of our national popular culture, in the blackface minstrel shows that swept the country, and in works like the parlor songs of Pennsylvanian composer Stephen Foster. Nostalgia, a *"preference for things as they are believed to have been"* in the past,[31] or even as they are believed to be in a distant, romanticized present, has persisted in the stories of the young men and women who follow their dreams from farms and rural poverty to *American Idol*, personifying small-town or "country" naïveté and expressing a homesickness for southern cooking. During Season 5 auditions in San Francisco, producer Ken Warwick reminded the crowd that previous winners had succeeded unexpectedly, exemplified by Carrie Underwood, a girl from a "little country town."[32] This fetishism of smallness exemplifies the similar preferences pointed out by Herbert Gans as elemental in the "enduring values" of news media. Gans attributes "small-town pastoralism" to an anti-industrialist desire for nature, endangered by industrial growth, the use of land for the development of suburbs, and the ongoing energy crisis. "The virtue of smallness" is also, Gans writes, positioned opposite the "faults of bigness" in government and business.[33] *American Idol*'s championing of seemingly small-town talent does something to deflect the astounding bigness of the *Idols* enterprise, to celebrate a virtuosity of place.

Place and Race and the Imagined South

Southern characterizations (sometimes caricatures) on *American Idol* appear regularly, are easily identifiable, and are highly racialized. Some African American contestants represent urban black communities in the South, such as Ruben Studdard with his area-code apparel, and others, like Fantasia Barrino, symbolize the rural and poverty-stricken. The show also features southern identities racialized as white, characters Campbell describes as "hicks, hillbillies, and belles."[34] Superficially the power of these stereotypes is clear. A 2008 Google search for the names of Bucky Covington and Kellie Pickler, two Season 5 contestants from North Carolina, in conjunction with the word "hillbilly," yield approximately five thousand and eleven thousand hits, respectively, mostly on message boards and blogs; to be fair, some of these contain arguments against the use of that term, but the fact remains that it is part of *Idol* discourse. "Hillbilly," as John Hartigan has asserted, is a racially marked white identity dependent not only upon the relationship between blackness and whiteness but between place and class as well. It is part of a vocabulary of difference that turns a southward gaze on rural life and poverty, and also on the incongruity of these conditions with the goal of white upward mobility in urban spaces. Once an intraracial epithet applied to out-of-place, rural (especially Appalachian) white Southerners who had moved post–World War II to northern cities for employment, "hillbilly" retains regional associations even north of the Mississippi and generations later.[35] Other, related designations of denigrated whiteness have entered *Idol* discourse as well; in 2004, during the Hollywood rounds, Houston contestant Kiira Bivens, who is white, railed at the judges for sending her home and keeping "trailer trash" in the competition.[36] Although the terms do not designate any possibility of class elevation, "hillbilly" and "trailer trash" do keep alive the associations of marked whiteness with transplantation, with geographical movement.

American Idol underlines the interdependence of discursive identity categories. As Judith Butler cautions, gender, race and ethnicity should never be treated as "fully separable axes of power."[37] In *American Idol* the onscreen characters built around several female contestants illuminate racialized and place-specific constructions of femininity. Some contestants, constructed as stereotypes of white southern women, have proven the endurance of Britney Spears's youthful model for success: a fusion of naïveté and chaste sexuality, of "hick" and a kind of girl-next-door "belle." The Season 3 runner-up and Georgia native Diana DeGarmo was announced during a performance on the 2004 "Idols Live" tour as "the southern belle of the group."[38] She was one of only two southern women on that tour, and the other one was African American and therefore not eligible for the historically white-specific term "belle." Fourth-season winner Carrie Underwood, from Checoteh, Oklahoma, projected a notably farm-bred image in one of her earliest appearances on the show (and she actually did grow up on a farm). She said onscreen that she had not flown in an airplane before her initial trip to Hollywood, as noted above, a commonly referenced marker of the rural *American Idol* persona, naïve and out of place in the bustle of Los Angeles. Memorably, when host Ryan Seacrest asked Underwood if she had seen any stars in Hollywood, Underwood, misunderstanding the question, replied that she had not because it was too cloudy.[39]

In Season 5 another air travel novice took up Underwood's mantle. Top-10 finalist Kellie Pickler, from Albemarle, North Carolina, was known for her unfamiliarity with haute cuisine and some vocabulary, beginning with a pre-performance video in which she spoke of her unfamiliarity with foods such as spinach salad and calamari. Later she did not understand Cowell's meaning when he called her a "minx." Malapropism, from Shakespeare to the TV situation comedy, has long been an established satiric indicator, in popular culture, of region and rurality and their ties to differences in economic class—and for some (especially blonde) figures, like Pickler, of gender. This kind of comedic innocence of worldly knowledge makes the sexuality of the young women in question safe for the show's family demographic, and offers up a characterization that is familiar and easy for viewers to remember when voting. Like Britney Spears, both Underwood and Pickler also had some experience with beauty pageants—a kind of theater for playing out belle-hood aspirations, another Dream-saturated stage for the dramatized transcendence of class limitations. This narrative is also recognizable as the story of an Otherized white Vaudeville archetype, the "rustic, hayseed, country bumpkin character" who must undergo a transformation and, "like his ethnic brethren," become "'Americanized' into the urban bourgeois mode."[40] The finishing-school urbanity required of pageant contestants somewhat counteracts the singers' "hick" image, without tarnishing their sheen of naïveté. As a construction, "hick," like its ethnographic cousin "folk," also distances the contestant from the assumed superficiality and industry of Hollywood, thereby endowing her with opposite qualities that make her "real" and "natural." Implications of poverty and hard times also contribute to that sense of authenticity, with Pickler revealing in her first *Idol* moments that her father was in prison, her mother had long been absent, and the grandmother who raised her had recently passed away.[41] Against the backdrop of those "straitened circumstances," the prospect of the American Dream is strikingly compelling.

Pickler's personal misfortunes are also part of her gendered, white southern image. Louis A. Ruprecht Jr. writes that the idea of tragedy is paradoxically about lost causes but "dedicated ultimately to the idea of redemption—and it is in this sense that the South's is a tragic landscape." And in that landscape, viewed with a nostalgic and idealizing white gaze, the "strong Southern woman" has become an enduring archetype. It is a specifically white archetype, even *especially* white, as Amy Schrager Lang notes the descriptions of extreme paleness permeating songs about the female figure of poverty. "Hard times," she writes in her essay on the Stephen Foster song of that name, are feminized and racialized as white in musical discourse about the South. Lang sees this concept as persistent today, when "current public discourse about poverty, after all, precludes absolute sympathy for the young black woman—represented [encoded] as the calculating (and always by implication promiscuous) 'welfare mother.'"[42]

The power of such prejudices was tested, and both confirmed and challenged, during *American Idol*'s third season. The 2004 contestant pool offered an earlier analogue to Underwood's farm girl persona in the context of southern black femininity. Season 3's eventual winner, Fantasia Barrino of High Point, North Carolina (Pickler's state as well), was a self-proclaimed "country girl" but could never be assigned the cultivated innocence associated with Underwood and Pickler as she was a single, teenaged "welfare mother." Even so, there were intentional signs of a lack of sophistication (though by whose intention it is not certain), including a performance in April 2004 during which Barrino sat on the stage floor in a couture dress and bare feet. This eschewing of shoes evokes once more the natural and folk-ness, as well as youth, innocence, and even childishness. In a performance on the "Idols Live" tour of the Top 10 finalists, she wore shoes to sing "Summertime" but not to sing "I Believe," and another African American finalist (from California), LaToya London, was inspired to forego shoes during one of her own numbers.[43]

The choice of "Summertime" is significant in its own right, the song having originated in George Gershwin's musical amalgamation of western classical, blues, jazz, and folk styles, *Porgy and Bess* (1935), and enduring as a cross-genre standard. Gershwin himself called the work a "folk opera," a designation in keeping with the folkloric quests of the 1920s and 1930s. The search for, and construction of, national cultural authenticity during those years seeded the popular recording industry and some of the same entertainment stereotypes we are talking about today. And the projects of the 1930s—the Archive of American Folk Song (est. 1928), the research of John and Alan Lomax, their management of Lead Belly—highlighted African American music in new ways. In this context many hailed *Porgy and Bess,* written by white Americans about the black American experience, as a paragon of Americanness in general.[44] Barrino's performance, created for an episode with a cinematic theme (her choice possibly alluding to the 1959 film, which was eventually effectively withdrawn at the demand of the Gershwin estate), was built on this complicated history and helped make the singer herself another paragon of Americanness, the American Idol.

Following her victory Barrino released a candid and earnest autobiography, *Life Is Not a Fairy Tale*. In its first pages (written with collaborator Kim Green), she alludes to her barefoot performances, admitting that "I am just a country girl who loves the Lord and loves to have a good time. I still kick off my shoes every chance I get—even on TV!" She refers to herself and to her family as "country" numerous times in those initial pages, and as if to prove this, the text is littered with truncated gerunds: "I just kept cryin', prayin', huggin', smilin', and askin' the Lord to get me through those moments like a professional singer, not the messy country girl who had never been too far out of North Carolina."[45]

The juxtaposition of "country" with Barrino's religiosity is notable, as we have seen (in chapter 4) that her expressions of faith also contributed to her image during her time on *American Idol*. It also points to the perception on the show of southern religion and its influence on American music and musicians—executive producer Nigel Lythgoe has said "I think there's a lot of church-going [in the South] where they literally learn their craft and they're singing there every single week and [perfecting] the performance that goes with that. . . . And I think there's a lot of soul there."[46]

Voicing the South

The speech patterns laid out in Barrino's narrative are perhaps linked to one of the personal disclosures of her book; Barrino made national headlines for revealing her struggle with literacy. Speech patterns and southern accents have been of great importance in the history of American popular music, and even in popular music created outside the U.S. In a 1979 piece for the journal *American Speech*, S. J. Sackett pointed to the "very nearly de rigueur" presence of southern U.S. accents in the performances of rock singers, whether born in the South, other parts of the country, or even in England. Sackett heard the American South in the early Beatles and in the Rolling Stones' Mick Jagger, and understood this seeming incongruity as connected to the influence of African American artists and styles in the formative years of British rock. We should recall here that the creators and producers of *American Idol* are British, and have tended to favor the music of the period in which Sackett was writing. The influence of African American artists' speech/singing patterns would, of course, become fundamental in stateside music, too, as Sackett also noted, in addition to the impact of southern studios (Sun Records, Stax-Volt, Muscle Shoals) and the role of southern gospel, "white, black, and integrated." Sackett suggested two further explanations for the pervasive southern accent, linked to its "social associations with the proletariat and the rebellious." Moreover, as waves of migration followed the Dust Bowl, and the Second World War shifted scores of impoverished Southerners toward the North and the West, the accent took on increasing connotations of hardship, of "the Disadvantaged."[47]

Although *American Idol* may not showcase the "rebellious" in its ranks of finalists, economic and social class is more of a priority. A working man or woman trying to make it in the music industry is sympathetic, remaining a bastion of authenticity in the highly commercial context of *American Idol*. And if a singer with a southern accent is indeed disadvantaged (and indeed southern), as Pickler and Barrino appeared to be, then his or her struggle to achieve the American Dream resonates all the more. An accent can also be treated as integral to a person's voice—a connection I would venture to guess might be owing in part to the role of vowel shape and formats in the way vocal timbre is perceived, though certainly also to the social connotations attached to these perceptions. In any case, after a performance in Hollywood, judge Randy Jackson complimented the "speaking voice" of Season 3 contestant Charly Lowry, declaring that it reminded him of his own "southern heritage" (he grew up in Louisiana). Lowry, from Pembroke, North Carolina (again), had said onscreen that she thought her accent distinguished her from the other singers, and later saw it as a key part of the persona presented on *American Idol*.[48]

It is important to understand that, just as there is no single South, there is no single southern accent, and there are sub-regional, ethnic, and racialized distinctions. However, ears outside the South may gloss over these distinctions, perceiving a generic aural symbol inscribed with any of the meanings that attend "The South"—including the conflating influences Bill C. Malone sees in the equation "Southern Music/American Music." In his conclusion, Sackett wondered whether the southern accent in rock, which he perceived as antiestablishment, might have a future effect on the "prestige dialect," the "speech of the Establishment" outside the South. The presence of the southern accent, as Sheldon Hackney writes, in a "hugely disproportionate number of the leaders of both national parties" today, indicates a fulfillment of Sackett's prediction.[49] And its audibility in the speech of seven out of nine American Idols, as well, speaks to the power of history and tradition in the twenty-first-century music industry.

FINAL FRONTIERS

Places in the United States are defined through their relationships with one another, and through complex networks of dynamic, locality-specific identity politics. The places in question comprise not only "America" but also geographical subdivisions that each dialectically affects the imagination of the others, and of the national whole. The essentializing structures built into reality television highlight the cultural weight given to place-related representations and interactions. But Arjun Appadurai warns against essentializing region, contending that "ideas that claim to represent the 'essences' of particular places reflect the temporary *localization* of ideas from *many* places."[50] Thus regionally inflected depictions on *American Idol* characterize much more than just a sense of local ideology or culture, more than simply Otherizing or exoticizing stereotypes but, rather, always composites assembled from dialogue among all these factors at a particular historical moment.

Place and space must have special connotations for a show broadcast around the U.S. and much of the world, involving not only multiple configurations of physical space—the studio audience, the widespread audition locations, and the living room—but also virtual space and globalizing place. Akhil Gupta and James Ferguson have suggested:

> Something like a transnational public sphere has certainly rendered any strictly bounded sense of community or locality obsolete. At the same time, it has enabled the creation of forms of solidarity and identity that do not rest on an appropriation of space where contiguity and face-to-face contact are paramount.[51]

Communication online accomplishes this reconfiguration of community in *American Idol*, allowing viewers a space in which to articulate and (re-)negotiate regionalisms and localisms in ways that incorporate their Idols. The *Idol* audience may be constructed in geographically defined terms, but as we have seen, these are not necessarily residential terms. Place still matters in cyberspace. Like the West in which Hollywood is located, cyberspace is thought of as somewhere that awaits expansion—a political, cultural, economic, and personal "frontier" with no foreseeable bounded limits. If the "electronic frontier" is "a region without physical shape or form,"[52] then it can also be a part of the negotiation of physical regionalism, as *Idol* viewers across the nation—and around the world—exchange ideas and ideologies in the discourse of place.

But the obsolescence of locality is not complete. Gupta and Ferguson also understand that, as the scope of places widens and boundaries become increasingly unclear, "*ideas* of culturally and ethnically distinct places become perhaps even more salient."[53] Although they are positioning these changes in the context of de- and re-territorialization, displacement, and memory, the concept is equally applicable to the dynamics of place within the United States, and to the place of locality as America continually relocates itself in an increasingly global space.

POLITICS AS USUAL

In the final moments of *American Idol*'s fifth season, host Ryan Sea-crest marveled at the 63.4 million votes recorded the previous night—more votes, he said, "than any president in the history of our country has ever received."[1] Critical speculation throughout *Idol*'s run has frequently remarked upon the enthusiastic participation of *American Idol* viewers, contrasted with voter turnout in the election of political leaders. The *Idol* advantage certainly depends at least in part upon the show's nationwide unlimited electoral franchise and the allowance of multiple votes per person. However, there is more to this phenom-enon than suffrage for preteens with mobile phones and preternatural texting skills.

American Idol offers voters something powerful and relatively rare: the chance to see themselves represented on television, and to elect a representative in the music industry. Demographic diversity has historically played an integral part in the American political sys-tem, with regional or ethnic "coalition building" or both—between politicians and identity-based constituent groups—as key factors in the campaign process. Such coalition building can also be a corner-stone, in *American Idol,* for auditioning, campaigning, marketing, or voting strategies, where some find serious parallels to electoral politics: when Ruben Studdard attained the *Idol* title in Season 2, five years before the election of Barack Obama, an opinion writer at AfricaHome.com suggested that "Ruben, believe it or not, on Wednesday night was, on that very stage, elected the first black president of the United States."[2]

Though it might be a stretch to draw a direct parallel between the *Idol* process and the presidential election, coalition-based voting on *American Idol* does signal an important trend, the adoption of political strategy in the mediated marketplace. Henry Jenkins locates the phenomenon as part of a media industry strategy he names "affective economics," in which television networks use information about consumer desires—"emotional, social, and intellectual investments"—to learn how to reshape them toward specific purchasing choices and brand loyalty. Jenkins notes a paradox, too, as the commodification of identity at once makes marginalized American identities more visible and effects a troubling kind of cultural exploitation in the name of multiculturalism and diversity.[3] Music, of course, is instrumental (and vocal) in the commodification of identity, and such commodifying tendencies thread through the full history of popular music in the U.S. Even in its infancy the record industry helped to shape national discourses of whiteness, blackness, and American ethnicities, and of the South, the West, and parts of the map Othered in established imaginings of the nation. *American Idol* reminds us that all these discourses are close relations, and shines a glaring spotlight on their continuing influence in U.S. popular culture. This chapter examines the show's racialized politics of musical genre, and then offers five case studies in which coalition voting has helped to shape *Idol* political process.

GENRE POLITICS

Although each week demands that contestants tackle different repertories, the early seasons of *American Idol* especially showcased canonic selections in limited genres, in particular first soul and then country—genres that have each had a turn in the electoral limelight, and so serve as natural resources for *Idol* candidates looking for a constituency. In fact, soul and country figured significantly in the soundtracks for the 2008 presidential campaigns of Barack Obama and John McCain, respectively. Although McCain's run with vice-presidential candidate Sarah Palin was plagued by complaints from several artists (Ann and Nancy Wilson of Heart, John Mellencamp, Bon Jovi, the Foo Fighters, Jackson Browne, and country songwriter Gretchen Wilson) about the unsanctioned use of their music, country stars John Rich and Hank Williams Jr. dedicated songs to the Republican team. And the musical accompaniment of many 2008 campaign appearances by Barack Obama and Joe Biden relied heavily on soul. As the election neared, Stevie Wonder's 1970 "Signed, Sealed, Delivered," Jackie Wilson's 1967 "(Your Love Keeps Lifting Me) Higher and Higher," and Curtis Mayfield's 1970 "Move On Up," were featured prominently. Soul and country are genres with implicit political histories, mined enthusiastically whenever either presidential or *Idol* candidates are courting voters.

The Soul of Idol-ness

Soul as a named genre entered mainstream marketing in 1969. The change in category terminology (from "rhythm and blues") signified an industry acknowledgment of black music's powerful impact in American popular culture, as well as its salability among white consumers. The label was applied to both black and white artists whose performance practices showed the influence of blues or gospel.[4] It is partly this flexibility that makes soul particularly useful for *American Idol*, where the genre is recontextualized, and repoliticized, in a variety of ways. Aretha Franklin's rendering of Otis Redding's "Respect," for example, ceases to be a black feminist anthem, and becomes instead an exhibition of individual virtuosity demanding a different kind of recognition, the "respect" of celebrity itself. And first-season winner Kelly Clarkson's ability to handle Franklin's "Respect" proved to her audience that she was deserving of the Idol title. It also showed that she was something historically desirable—a white singer who could perform the repertoire and stylistic symbols of blackness. This requirement has heavily informed the construction of whiteness in American popular music, and, evoking too familiar narratives of segregation and appropriation, becomes a multivalent mark of authenticity.

Soul has had a special presence on *American Idol*, not only in its repertoire but also in the appearances of several key figures over the seasons—particularly icons of Motown soul. On March 30, 2004, the then surviving core members of Motown's house band, The Funk Brothers, appeared on *American Idol*, backing each contestant's performance.[5] The band had been the subject of a recently released (2002) film, *Standing in the Shadows of Motown*, had won a 2003 Grammy for the movie's compilation soundtrack, and, in February 2004, a Grammys Lifetime Achievement award. Fantasia Barrino's rendition of "I Heard It Through the Grapevine" received rave reviews from the show's three judges, and also from Nickolas Ashford of Motown's songwriting team Ashford and Simpson, who appeared together as guest judges on that *Idol* episode (the broadcast did not include a response from Valerie Simpson). In eliciting the approval of Motown greats, including original members of the historic black-owned label's integrated band, Barrino simultaneously demonstrated both a racial "authenticity" and her ability to fit into the crossover-market aesthetic of both Motown and *American Idol*.

Other Motown figures have been featured on *American Idol* as well; for example, Diana Ross appeared as a guest mentor in 2007, and Lamont Dozier of the songwriting team Holland-Dozier-Holland was a guest judge in 2003—the same year that the trio won the BMI Pop Icon award. The invocation of Motown also illuminates a certain historical continuity, or cycle, between the structure of the Motown factory model and that of the *Idols* factory model. Journalist Phil Gallo noted in his report on the Holland-Dozier-Holland BMI award that the honor

> arrive[d] at a time when the music business has been reviving the Motown model of a label handling the whole ball of wax for a performer, beginning with aligning young singing talent with songwriters and producers and then shaping the performers—Kelly Clarkson, for example.[6]

19 Entertainment executive Simon Fuller has described his comprehensive management plan as advantageous to the artist. In a 2004 news item he is quoted as saying:

> Most artists working on the old-fashioned model, how do you keep
> track of your publisher, your record company, your merchandise,
> your sponsorship agent, your touring agent? There could be 10 differ-
> ent people dealing with different areas of your life. This is one-stop
> shopping.[7]

Although the advantage of Motown in its heyday lay in the prospect
of opportunity for black artists in an industry that traditionally ne-
glected them on the basis of race, *American Idol* also offers a trade-off
between tight contractual control and a success that might otherwise
have eluded its contestants. Of course, the show lacks the extensive
process of artist development famously associated with Motown, substituting instead a kind of whirlwind, season-length makeover before
the consumer's eyes.

Berry Gordy's Motown and the *American Idol* program also share
an institutional concern with family values. *American Idol*'s focus on
soul genres, whether Motown, southern, or "blue-eyed," speaks to
this matter. Soul, according to Robert W. Stephens, has historically
had a place in the maintenance of African American solidarity, especially "in changing times." Among the effects Stephens summarizes,
in part related to soul's origins in gospel style, are the affirmation
of "belief in conventional morality," and the promotion of "familial
stability and parental responsibility."[8] Again, somewhat re-racialized
and recontextualized, these qualities fit in well with *American Idol*'s
family-entertainment tone and the broad reach desired of any campaign. The emphasis on soul repertoire and style is also significant
for what the songs do *not* represent. The majority of selections on the
show and on its albums are ballads and love songs, aesthetically in-
nocuous genres with moderate tempi that also support the addition
of virtuosic ornamentation suitable for competitive singing. They are
thematically "safe" and, more important, related to safe aspects of
African American and popular culture; the religious implications of
gospel vocal style possibly play a role here. Richard Allen Rischar
points out that ballad singers are "not gangsta's ... they are not heavy-
metal artists ... they do not reflect the inner city."[9] This quality also
characterized the soul used in the Obama-Biden campaign—not the
soul of Black Power but the upbeat, integrationist style that flooded

the cross-racial market in the late 1960s and early 1970s. In a new iteration of the "changing times" Stephens cited, and in a campaign explicitly urging America to "vote for change," the choice of soul could only have been deliberate—and perhaps the Obama-Biden campaign took its musical cue from the success of *American Idol*'s intergenerational, accessible playlist.

The inclusive tone of *Idol* soul does not preclude statements of position entirely. During Season 8's last performance episode, the Motown legacy added an unprecedented undercurrent for the top two finalists' repertoire.[10] Each of the two contestants sang three times: one selection chosen by a judge, one representing the contestant's own preference, and one submitted by Simon Fuller. Fuller's choices, though the singers were both white, were two iconic civil rights anthems—Sam Cooke's 1963 "A Change Is Gonna Come" for Adam Lambert, and, for Kris Allen, Marvin Gaye's 1971 call to lay down arms, "What's Going On?" The purpose these songs served on the show had little to do, at least immediately, with race. For months press speculation, online chatter, and water-cooler gossip had revolved around the question of Adam Lambert's sexuality. As discussed in chapter 1, neither Lambert nor the show's producers ever publicly addressed any of those questions during the broadcast season. But Lambert personalized his performance of Cooke's song, even at one point substituting the word "my" for "a" to insert the phrase "*My* change is gonna come." (Political songs have been rare and risky on the *Idol* stage, although "A Change Is Gonna Come" has been a perennial fixture in the preliminary televised audition rounds, and Season 7's Syesha Mercado chose it for a Motown-themed episode.) In the end Kris Allen won, and Lambert came out in *Rolling Stone* a few weeks later. Although he told the interviewer, "I'm trying to be a singer, not a civil rights leader," he also said about the song: "This civil rights movement is near to my heart and it felt really good to sing that."[11] The decision to assign such emblematic anthems could have been arbitrary, but it could also have represented acknowledgment of the 2008 presidential election or tacit producer support for Lambert and the very political situation he was navigating on *Idol*.

The often unspoken issues surrounding the racial recontextualization of soul on *American Idol* have occasionally been obliquely acknowledged during the show. In 2006 the term "soul" took on specific
new meanings for the series, when eventual winner Taylor Hicks attracted a fan base with the name "Soul Patrol." Hicks, a white singer,
recognized the Soul Patrol from the stage in episode after episode,
making the phrase his signature (campaign) slogan. Because of Hicks
and his second runner-up, Elliott Yamin, the words "blue-eyed soul"
began to crop up frequently in the judges' comments and in the press,
and Paula Abdul was moved more than once to call Yamin a "funky
white boy."[12] These designations simultaneously call attention to and
discount the problems of appropriation and racialized subjectivity
pervasive throughout the history of American popular music, as if
naming the explosive might defuse it—another instance of concurrent boundary crossing and reinforcement of reification.

Race and ethnicity are no less a public concern in *American Idol*
than they are in any other cultural or political context. Rumors have
surfaced online, at the beginning of several seasons, regarding suspi-
cions of a possible racial angle to producers' plans. After two consecu-
tive African American winners, some believed, the producers would
want the show to yield a white Idol. Christopher Allen, a fan I met in
line for a 2005 public dress rehearsal, related to me his experience as
an extra in some of the finalists' weekly Ford commercials, and said
that he thought his favorite, Nadia Turner, had been eliminated for
reasons related to race. He "knew that the black people weren't going
to make it" that year or the show would lose the significant white portion of its audience. "It's all about the money," he concluded. When I
heard Ken Warwick admonish the 2004 San Francisco crowd waiting to audition, "No riffing,"—a warning he followed with a demonstration of melisma—I wondered if he had said the same at previous
auditions and if it meant a change in the preferred repertoire for the
show.[13] Others looked further into Warwick's words and suspected
a more specific design for the season; already at the auditions the
rumors were flying about producers' racial preference for the 2005
Idol. One post on FOX's *American Idol* forum early in the broadcast
expressed anxiety about this possibility:

When a friend of mine told me that a producer stated "no riffing" at
AI tryouts, I immediately felt that something was amiss. My fears
were confirmed tonight with the choice of the final 24. With the exception of David Brown, no gospel influenced singers were chosen ...
I personally think this is sad, because most African American singers
developed their skills in church. I don't mean to be racial, but I think
AI was wrong for what they did this season. Why should the producers push the audience in a certain direction, when they are going to
get ratings anyway?[14]

It seems, then, that the racial connotations of soul, and associated
stylistic markers like melisma, do not escape viewer notice. Carrie
Underwood, 2005's Idol, was indeed white and, as a country singer,
was outside the previously favored genre and style boundaries of the
show.

Country Voices

The show's shift toward an interest in country and country-pop in
2005 was surprising but not entirely without warning. In 2003 there
had been an outcry in the press against the "melismatic" singing styles
associated with the show's soul repertoire (see chapter 2). African
American singers had won Seasons 2 and 3, and as the 2004 season
neared rumors began circulating on the internet that the next winner
would be white. Many studies of country music[15] have investigated
the relationship of the genre to discourses of America's white working class, although it is also important to acknowledge that not all
country musicians are white, or even American—the USA Network's
country-focused Idol imitation, Nashville Star, has featured as a host
Cowboy Troy, an innovative and genre-stretching country singer who
is African American, and Australian country artist Keith Urban (born
in New Zealand) has had great success in the United States. However,
all finalists who have favored country on the show have been white.
It is significant that by the 1950s, when the chart designations of R&B
and country had gained widespread usage, songs (but usually not artists) could cross between those genres and the "pop" category that
often included white artists' covers of songs first recorded by black
artists.[16] Such crossover is a key element in American Idol, where self-

identified country singers must also prove their capabilities in repertoire from many other genres.

Let us look, for example, at Season 2 finalist Joshua Gracin, whose
2004 debut album entered the *Billboard* country charts at No. 2. Gracin, at the time he appeared on *American Idol,* was on active duty as
a Lance Corporal in the U.S. Marine Corps and, whenever possible,
demonstrated a preference for country music in his song choices.
While on the show, he covered country songs by Garth Brooks, Lonestar, and Neal McCoy, and led a group performance of Lee Greenwood's "God Bless the U.S.A." With the debut in 2003 of *Nashville
Star,* one might wonder why Gracin chose to audition for *American
Idol* instead. After he left the show, he told MTV.com that he made
the decision "because there's a larger audience and simply because of
the fact that all the kids, you knew, were going to sing R&B or pop,"
potentially giving him the advantage of genre distinction. He had a
specific stylistic goal during his time on the show, and a musical strategy, to "make a new sound." To accomplish this, he said, he "tried to
picture country music, and I tried to picture songs that I could probably re-do as a country song. Then I looked at a country song, and I
tried to pick a country song that sounded like the song I wanted to
sing. I incorporated the two and came up with a middle ground."[17]
In a competition format that previously had not been particularly
country-friendly, Gracin's solution is intriguing. It describes careful
song selection, as well as thorough preparation of a moderate, crossover style designed to connect with a wide range of listeners without
abandoning his identity as a country singer.

Sustaining this identity was a choice he was counseled to make.
Early in the finals Gracin sang the Four Tops' "Baby I Need Your
Lovin'," (March 11, 2003), followed the next week by Aerosmith's "I
Don't Want to Miss a Thing" (March 18, 2003), a 1999 cover which
had also been a hit for country singer Mark Chesnutt. Gracin's two
performances were markedly different in style, although both were
praised by the judges. In the Aerosmith song Gracin, who grew up
in Michigan, sang with a pronounced southern accent that had been
largely missing in the previous week's Motown selection. The little
melisma he used in the Four Tops song vanished in the other, but
the small number of "cry-breaks" in the earlier song was dramatically

increased for the Aerosmith. The practice of cry-breaks is particularly associated with country music vocality, described by Aaron A. Fox as a nuanced effect that interrupts a sung note with either silence or a fleeting grace-note motion to a lighter (Fox identifies it as "falsetto") register. It is strongly attached to diction, Fox writes, especially in the transitions from liquid (l and r), fricative (f, s, z, sh), or nasal (m, n, ng) consonants to vowels.[18] For Gracin, consonants and vowels themselves contribute to his timbre as factors in the southern accent, with a strongly retroflexed "r" and rhotacized vowels. Vowels also come into play, with the diphthong removed from the word "I" to make it simply "ah" and added to make "this" into a two-syllable effort. Gracin's vocal timbre changed as well, sounding more distinctly "country" in the Aerosmith song. Descriptions of vocal timbre in country music often rely on the timbral concept of *twang,* a perceptual term that has been linked to vocal technique in which a narrowed pharyngeal area, shortened vocal tract, and decreased open quotient (the amount of time the glottis is open during a phonatory cycle) are characteristic.[19] Studies also have suggested greater similarities between speech and singing practices in country singers than in singers of Western classical music.[20] Specifically country singers approach breath management more similarly in speech and singing than do opera singers, and the formant frequencies (major acoustic factors in timbre) of speech and singing are more markedly similar in country singers. Stone et al. also posit that articulation (diction) practices are closely matched as well in the speech and singing of country artists.[21] This is important information in terms of Gracin's timbral shift to a speech-like, "twangy" country sound—but in his case we certainly cannot compare speech and singing articulations neatly, since his speech on *Idol* altogether lacked the southern accent and the accompanying vowel timbres so prominent in his singing.

After "Baby I Need Your Lovin'," judge Randy Jackson told Gracin that he had had some trouble locating the singer's personality in his sound. After "I Don't Want to Miss a Thing," Simon Cowell and Gracin had the following exchange onscreen:

> **Cowell:** You did not sound like that last week. Two different voices. So I don't know what your voice is. So, what's it going to be next week?

Gracin: Same thing. Country from now on.

Cowell: Okay, no, that's fine. But you've just got to stick to what you are, so you can't change it around now. You're now a country singer. But we're doing disco next week.[22]

Gracin survived the disco theme and added to his list songs by Elton John, Neil Sedaka, 'N Sync, and the Bee Gees, and just one more song originally associated with country, Lonestar's "Amazed." The southern accent and twang persisted throughout, lending Gracin southernness and implying personal authenticity (staying true to "his" sound) in the carrying of a genre-specific sound across genre territory. After performances of "Jive Talkin'" and "To Love Somebody," guest judge Robin Gibb of the Bee Gees repeated that he loved the "country feel" Gracin brought to the songs.[23] In Gracin's *Idol* run, the all-important personal touches, the "making the song your own," came primarily from genre crossover—the infusion of non-country repertoire with country timbre, diction, and vocal gestures. With his adoption of country vocality, his onscreen image is constructed as a southern/ American musician.

Following his respectable fourth-place finish, Gracin signed with Lyric Street Records, a label associated with country groups SHe-DAISY and Rascal Flatts, who according to his official website (www .joshgracin.com) helped orchestrate Gracin's deal. He released a highly successful country-themed album in the summer of 2004, debuting at No. 2 on the *Billboard* Top Country Albums chart and quickly attaining No. 20 on the *Billboard* 200 chart, which includes all marketing genres. It was also among the first albums to benefit from the RIAA's "digital sales award program,"[24] after going "digital gold." With proof that a country Idol could succeed, the new highlighting of country singers would provide welcome variety and a sure market for the next winner. The 2005 season was different, maintaining some of the earlier themes but more heavily integrating implicitly white genres like country and southern rock. This led to the impressive success of winner Carrie Underwood in the world of country music, and to the less widespread success of the runner-up, country-rock singer Bo Bice. Regardless of racialization, however, the music has contributed to the same version of Americanness consistently championed on the show, if now contextualized in regional terms. While country music is in no way contained by southern regional borders, Teresa Goddu has surmised that "country, long caricatured as hillbilly music, is now selling the nation an idealized image of America by mass marketing more wholesome images of the South: rural nostalgia, conservative politics, and traditional values."[25] Country music's role as an idealized stand-in for all of America, not just the South, is one reason that the genre featured prominently in the 2008 McCain-Palin campaign. It is a tried and true campaign tool, and *Idol* contestants know it.

Like much of the show's soul repertoire, country music provides a fairly safe pool of repertoire for family entertainment, that is, for an intergenerational audience. It may obliquely (or somewhat openly) address country-standard social problems such as prostitution (Reba McEntire's "Fancy," sung by Kellie Pickler) or domestic abuse (Martina McBride's "Independence Day" and the Dixie Chicks' "Sin Wagon," both covered by Carrie Underwood), but these topics seem to be acceptable on the *Idol* stage. The dangerous elements missing from *American Idol*'s music history include explicitly sexual lyric content, race relations, and antiestablishment politics. Robert W. Van Sickel points out that overtly racial themes are largely absent in country music owing to the genre's largely white niche. He also surmises that, contrary to conventional wisdom, country songs are rarely political, and he finds that even the patriotic ones seem to express "Southern pride rather than American nationalism."[26] Van Sickel's data pool did not extend to country songs released after 9/11, but it is still conceivable that a few very recognizable, very nationalistic songs would not alter his results much. Although Van Sickel's content analysis does not address the possible reasons behind the common association of country music and politics, some extramusical considerations are significant.

Southern, especially Republican, presidential candidates have, in recent years, frequently relied on existing patriotic country songs for campaign themes—notably Lee Greenwood's "God Bless the U.S.A." for Ronald Reagan in 1984 and for George H. W. Bush in 1988, as well as Brooks and Dunn's "Only in America" for George W. Bush in 2004 (and, actually, both John McCain and Barack Obama in 2008). Patriotic country was highly visible and audible in the days after 9/11, on the airwaves and at public memorials, and at benefit concerts. Genre stars including Willie Nelson, Faith Hill, and the Dixie Chicks appeared on the televised, cross-network benefit concert *America: A Tribute to Heroes* (September 21, 2001). The next few years brought escalating political tensions, the onset of the war in Iraq, and several high-profile country songs, such as Toby Keith's 2002 "Courtesy of the Red, White, and Blue (The Angry American)" and Darryl Worley's 2003 "Have You Forgotten." In July 2005 Joshua Gracin was featured in a CMT Network program dedicated to the *Greatest Patriotic Songs*.[27] Wartime patriotism has historically been a perennial theme in country music, although more songs have projected a "support-the-troops" position, consistent with the genre's emphasis on the condition of the working man, than a pro-war or pro-government angle. According to Van Sickel, the flood of "jingoistic" country songs following 9/11 was "without precedent." But this cannot be considered an entirely isolated effect, as Malone and Stricklin have detailed the emergence—in addition or in response to the powerful surge in antiwar music—of "ultrapatriotic" country during the later years of the Vietnam War:

> It was not simply an extension of southern working-class values into a national setting. It also reflected the polarization of the period and the country industry's attempts to gain acceptance by identifying with national trends and attitudes and capitalizing on public fears and neuroses.

It is possible to see the more recent jingoistic songs noted by Van Sickel as contextualized in a similar setting, revitalizing and reinforcing the "equati[on] of 'country music' and 'Americanism.'"[28]

Country music is not the only genre with ties to southern presidents. Phil Walden, the father of what Mike Butler terms "the Southern Rock Movement,"[29] was a staunch supporter of Jimmy Carter, and his bands were booked to perform at many campaign benefits. Two of these groups, the Marshall Tucker Band and the Charlie Daniels Band, were featured at President Carter's inaugural ball. Southern rock was Walden's project, intended to create opportunity for southern artists who were overlooked by "Yankee" labels because of their regionally idiosyncratic styles. He established Capricorn Records in 1969, and soon bands like the Allman Brothers, Lynyrd Skynyrd, and Black Oak Arkansas headed his roster. Southernness was a crucial theme in the production and consumption of southern rock in the 1970s and 1980s. The music was strongly influenced by blues and country, was marketed using symbols of the Old South (e.g., Confederate flags), and was discursively associated with images of white southern masculinity. These images were reconfigured in the changing politics of social class and race relations, and the genre became "emblematic of the South's struggle for redefinition after the Civil Rights movement." That quality was complicated by the association of southern masculinity with white supremacy, and some southern rock bands explicitly expressed related sentiments (although some, like the Allman Brothers Band, were integrated); the implications of Confederate imagery, whether intended as white-supremacist or not, also added to the complexity.[30]

These complications have put Lynyrd Skynyrd's "Sweet Home Alabama" (1974) at the center of some controversy. The song's lyrics, one section in particular ("and the governor's so true"), have been interpreted variously as a "glorification of Alabama's segregationist governor George Wallace" and as a "rejection of George Wallace's segregationist politics and a celebration of Muscle Shoals' integrated recording culture."[31] In either case, "Sweet Home Alabama" was unquestionably intended to defend the South, specifically to counteract the negative images portrayed in Canadian country-rock artist Neil Young's earlier singles, "Southern Man" (1970) and "Alabama" (1972). Considering the song's volatile political history, it might be surprising that it has been performed more than once on *American Idol*. More remarkable is that it first came to the *Idol* stage as sung by Ruben Studdard, the Season 2 winner.[32] Studdard, an African American singer, included the verse about the governor but gave no noticeable indication of his stance on the song's meaning. The singer's allegiance to his Birmingham home was emblazoned on his black and gold "205" shirt; perhaps his devotion to the state of Alabama trumped any concerns about race relations. If so, then Studdard's decision to sing "Sweet Home Alabama" is an instance in which musical regionalism was privileged over musical racialization, possibly aiding Studdard in his successful pursuit of victory.

The other important *Idol* performance of "Sweet Home Alabama" came in Season 4, when runner-up Bo Bice sang with members of Lynyrd Skynyrd during the season finale. The band has appeared in several incarnations since a fatal 1977 plane crash that killed lead singer and songwriter Ronnie Van Zant, guitarist and singer Steve Gaines, and singer Cassie Gaines, as well as the pilots and the band's road manager. The appearance on *American Idol* did include three musicians connected to Lynyrd Skynyrd since the 1970s: Rickey Medlocke, Gary Rossington, and Billy Powell. They were joined by bassist Ean Evans, who had played with the group since 2001 (Evans died in 2009). Throughout the season, Bice had also sung other southern rock standards, including the Allman Brothers' "Whipping Post" (1969) and Lynyrd Skynyrd's iconic "Free Bird" (1973), and he had declared Lynyrd Skynyrd his favorite band. But "Sweet Home Alabama" came at the end of his *Idol* campaign, and a certain kind of tribute was required. Bice called Helena, Alabama, his home, so, like Studdard, he had a specific geographical connection to the song and a regional connection to the band.

COALITION VOTING

Jasmine Trias and the Hawai'i Vote

Bice first met the members of the band on an *Idol*-arranged visit home to Helena. Toward the end of each season, the top three contestants return to their hometowns, where footage is shot of the singers meeting fans and participating in locally specific activities. Politicians representing the hometown, even the home state, may make appearances with contestants and confer some honor, for example, a key to the city or an honorary day-long mayorhood. This is only the tip of the iceberg, however. One of the most impressive examples of hometown campaigning occurred in 2004 and involved eventual third-place contestant Jasmine Trias. In May Trias arrived in Hawai'i, accompanied on her trip by producer Simon Lythgoe, to attend not only a hometown welcome but a statewide celebration in her honor.[33] Hawai'i's lieutenant governor, James Aiona, proclaimed May 13, 2004, "Jasmine Trias Day,"[34] and the following week her home county of Honolulu had its own "Jasmine Trias Day." It was a special season for Hawaiian viewers; because *Idol* auditions were held in Honolulu, a large segment of the early broadcasts were dedicated to Hawaiʻi. Two of the finalists were residents of Hawaiʻi, including Trias and another young woman, Camile Velasco. Hawaiʻi's region-specific interest in *American Idol,* in fact, had shown a promising start during the previous season (2003), with the appearance of Jordan Segundo in the Top 32 round (when audience voting began to narrow the pool down to twelve). It has been reported that the number of Hawaiʻi residents watching *American Idol* during Segundo's critical round rivaled the ratings from the home area of eventual Season 2 winner Ruben Studdard.[35] This trend continued, even more intensely, in the case of Trias's home-state support.

The choice of Honolulu for *Idol* auditions was not random. It was, in fact, orchestrated by the Hawaiʻi Visitors and Convention Bureau, whose representatives "thought an Emmy-nominated TV show could add excitement and energy to Hawaii's image," as David McNeil, a partner at the Bureau's public relations affiliate, told *Pacific Business News.* The same article reports that the Bureau began efforts to secure an audition slot the previous spring, with hotels and airlines offering free service to *Idol* crew. Because of budget restrictions, the Bureau could not purchase advertising spots on network television, but saw in this solution promising opportunities for tourism and local business. These instincts proved correct. The auditions drew an estimated one thousand from the mainland, boosting hotel and travel revenue. During the broadcast season some restaurants in Honolulu and elsewhere became *Idol* bars, inviting customers to watch the show on Tuesday nights; one restaurant reportedly drew in several thousand dollars in extra sales with this strategy. Even little things counted: the *Star Bulletin* reported a sharp increase in sales of flower hair ornaments like the ones Trias wore throughout much of the season, and of the reggae-associated red, yellow, and green wristbands favored by Velasco.[36]

In early 2004 Velasco and Trias rose to the Top 32 group along with the Honolulu-born Jonah Moananu, whose performance, however, did not generate even half the land-line votes (dialed through Verizon Hawaii) recorded for each of the two women. Toward the end of the season, after Velasco had been cut, 98 percent of the votes from Hawai'i residents were placed in Trias's favor. When she made her last stand, as one of the final three contestants, the numbers of Hawai'i calls reached 5.9 million.[37] It should be noted that these calls are reported as "attempts," since high call volume and busy lines may prevent many calls from resulting in successful votes. Throughout Velasco's and Trias's time on *American Idol*, local newspapers such as the *Honolulu Advertiser* and the *Honolulu Star-Bulletin* followed each episode of the show closely, detailing the status of the two women every week. In April, during the last week that both contestants remained on the show, the *Star-Bulletin* reported some voting statistics:

> Verizon Hawaii reported yesterday that its land-line calls to the "American Idol" numbers from Hawaii totaled 926,878. While that figure was lower than last week's 1.68 million and 2.98 million from two weeks ago, it still represents the third largest volume of calls for that time period in Verizon's nationwide network, behind the states of New York and New Jersey.[38]

It is evident that both Trias and *American Idol*'s producers intended to portray her as a representative of Hawai'i and that members of the audience readily received her as such. The singer's reception, and her audience, were cooperatively engineered by producers, by Trias as a "character" on the show, and by viewers as fans. Throughout the broadcast season, Trias spoke often on air of Hawai'i. For most episodes she wore a flower above her right ear, and its disappearance toward the end of the season did not go unnoticed among fans. Several verbal, gesticulatory, and sartorial symbols served as essentializing (if strategic) accessories, establishing Trias as an embodiment of regional Hawaiianness. In one of her earliest appearances on the show, she was shown smiling and calling "aloha" as she exited a vehicle, and flashing the "shaka" sign. The significance of this hand gesture, in which the three middle fingers are folded down, leaving the thumb and little finger visible, is strongly associated with Hawai'i, and with surf culture in both Hawai'i and California. It also has ties to politics, popularized as a logo by Honolulu politician Frank Fasi during his third successful mayoral campaign in 1976, and throughout his tenure. Trias's campaign was national, whereas Fasi's was local, and in this larger context Trias's "shaka" gesture carried a heavier political burden—the election this time had the potential to establish a national representative both *from* and *of* Hawai'i. Trias also saw the broader significance of her hoped-for success. Later in that early segment she was briefly seen teaching hula motions to other contestants and to her vocal coaches, and she firmly declared her mission to "bring Hawai'i to the rest of the world."[39] Considering *American Idol's* worldwide distribution, she may have succeeded.

Trias's case is also remarkable for the double roles of place and race in her success, as her *Idol* identity not only relied on localized regional support but also on the complicated ethnic histories of Hawai'i, the Philippines, and a pan-ethnic Asian American community. The idea of ethnic coalition voting has been a primary source of controversy for *American Idol*. In voting for representation, viewers of *American Idol* are also voting for *representations*. Producers and contestants collaboratively construct onscreen characters, often drawing attention to racial and ethnic identity. Even a contestant whose ethnicity remains invisible and unmentioned on the show may gather fans based on a surmised, or even hoped-for, ethnic identity. Joane Nagel has written of the dialectic construction of ethnic identity, formed through both self-identification and identification imposed from external sources. In this process, she proposes,

> the individual carries a portfolio of ethnic identities that are more or less salient in various situations and vis-a-vis various audiences. As audiences change, the socially-defined array of ethnic choices open to the individual changes. This produces a "layering" (McBeth 1989) of ethnic identities which combines with the ascriptive character of ethnicity to reveal the negotiated, problematic nature of ethnic identity.[40]

American Idol's audience is layered, geographically and demographically, and the available "ethnic choices" are accordingly dynamic.

These conditions are particularly evident in the context of Jasmine Trias's situation, in that, in addition to her explicitly Hawai'i-based fan community, she also drew significant support from both fellow Filipino Americans and Filipino viewers outside the U.S., in the Philippines. (*American Idol* is broadcast to the Philippines, but votes may only be cast by telephone from within the U.S.) The *Honolulu Advertiser* ran an item with the title "Filipino Pride Flows for State's 'Idol' Finalists," with the subtitle "Competition: State's Filipinos Unite behind Finalists." The paper reported dozens of daily e-mails regarding Trias and the paper's coverage of *American Idol*, sent "from the Mainland and the Philippines." Toward the end of the season, one post on *American Idol*'s official Web forum urged: "Fellow Filipinos, Fil-Ams, people from Hawai'i and Asia . . . please don't forget to vote for *Jasmine Trias*."[41] Messages sometimes included text in Tagalog (the Filipino language), establishing certain electronic threads as a point of contact for a specified group of viewers. Following her tenure on *American Idol*, Trias began to develop a career strongly reliant on her overseas support. She performed during the fall of 2004 in the Philippines, where she met with President Gloria Macapagal Arroyo, and the palace in Manila issued a statement calling Trias an inspiration to Filipinos.[42]

It is worth noting the inclusion in the aforementioned post of "Asia" among the several targets in its exhortation to fans to support Trias. Numerous additional posts were submitted praising the singer as a representative of "Asian Americans." Thus Trias's onscreen character is constructed, in a telescoping fashion, as a representative of Hawai'i, of Filipino Americans, of the Philippines, and of Asian American pan-ethnicity. Detailed analysis of the etiology and implications of this identity network, through which are woven threads of imperialism and the political institutionalization of ethnicity, in all its "multiple levels,"[43] regrettably lies outside the scope of this book. However, it must be mentioned that, in Trias's case, the juxtaposition of Hawaiian symbols onscreen with identification among Filipino American, Filipino, and Asian American viewers highlights the complicated and intertwined construction of ethnicity and regional identity in Hawai'i.

Race and Voting Controversy

The diversity of thinking and terminology surrounding Trias's appearances on *American Idol* sparked a flurry of internet discussion threads about labels and definitions, the practice of voting based on ethnic identity, and racism. Online dialogue regarding racism escalated in late April, when an African American finalist, early favorite Jennifer Hudson, was eliminated from the competition. Viewers were incensed not only because of her departure but because all three of the contestants with the lowest votes (Hudson, La Toya London, and Fantasia Barrino) were African American women. The following week Ryan Seacrest addressed the public outrage in his opening remarks, noting a deluge of letters, phone calls, and threats in response to the loss of Hudson. At the studio audience's angry shouts, he insisted that the unsatisfactory result was the responsibility of no one but the voting audience. "That's how *you* voted. Or maybe you didn't call in at all, because you thought there was no need. That's what can happen. Remember," he reproached America, "*You* vote, *you* decide."[44] The (British) producers thereby absolve themselves of fault—if anyone is racist, these statements imply, it is America.

Jungmin Lee, professor of economics at Florida International University, has conducted a statistical analysis of *American Idol*'s Nielsen ratings in order to determine the role racial preference plays in viewing and voting. Lee finds that the involvement of more black viewers means that black contestants are less likely to be eliminated, although this is only significantly the case when the number of total contestants has been reduced to fewer than half the final twelve. He also concludes that a larger number of black contestants leads to an increase in the number of black households tuned in to the show and that non-black viewership drops a bit in this situation. A larger number of black viewers decreases the probability that a black contestant will be voted off, but the research also finds that, overall, "black contestants are disproportionately more likely to be voted off." But it is difficult, Lee writes, to disentangle same-race viewing and voting preferences from a preference for programming that demonstrates casting diversity in general.[45]

Lee's study provides the most comprehensive analysis possible using Nielsen household data, especially considering the inaccessibility of specific voting statistics. A number of intriguing questions are raised as well—for example, how does Nielsen determine which contestants are "black"? Season 1 runner-up Justin Guarini has referred to himself as "biracial,"[46] and Season 6 winner Jordin Sparks came from a similar background. How do multiracial contestants (or households) fit into the Nielsen scheme? Lee explained to me that, in his project, he relied on press references to contestants in order to determine which contestants count as "black." He did not include Guarini in that description. It would be interesting, too, to find out what other ethnic voting coalitions might be represented in "non-black" households. Lee clarified that although Nielsen research includes data on Hispanic households, he chose not to examine that data because *American Idol* was not one of the Top 10 programs in the Hispanic demographic.[47] This situation seems to have changed even since the study was published in 2008; the magazine *Hispanic Business* reported, in early 2009, that *American Idol* was then the most-watched English-language show among Nielsen's Hispanic audience category.[48] Some *Idol* contestants, including 2009's Alison Iraheta (who introduced her Salvadorian family onscreen) and Jorge Nuñez (who auditioned in San Juan, Puerto Rico), have self-identified onscreen as "Latin American," "Latino/a," or "Mexican American," though none has won the competition at the time of this writing. Other questions for future research might address the occurrence of coalition voting among white viewers, or the issue of whether viewers identifying outside the "white" and "black" demographics watch and vote more frequently for non-white contestants. Lee's is certainly a thought-provoking study and suggests the potential significance of further inquiry.[49]

Hudson herself had doubts about the reasons behind her elimination, telling FOX News: "I don't know what it was based on, but it wasn't talent . . . Because if it was, all three of us wouldn't have been in the bottom three. Maybe one, but not all three." The controversy was subsequently furthered by reports of a comment Elton John had made during a "promotional appearance" in New York. John had been a guest coach for the week of April 7, when contestants were assigned to perform his songs. Three weeks later he told the press:

> The three people I was really impressed with—and they just happened to be black, young female singers—all seem to be landing in the bottom three . . . They have great voices. The fact that they're constantly in the bottom three—and I don't want to set myself up here—but I find it incredibly racist.[50]

American Idol vocal coach Debra Byrd, who is herself African American, relates a behind-the-scenes perspective on this incident:

> *Just before that [Elton John's statement in the press] came out, before that happened, Elton John was profiled on the show. [KM: right.] And that meant that the contestants spent time with him singing Elton John songs. So on that particular day, Elton John was asked by Nigel [Lythgoe] and Ken [Warwick] who were his favorite singers. And he mentioned the three ladies. He mentioned Fantasia, Jennifer Hudson, and La Toya London. And I asked him, "Do you think America will let three black women be the first, second, and third?" He said, "No. No way." And I agreed with him. Now, for him to go with the press—to go to the press, you know, for his quote, I don't—I can't defend him or say anything else about it, except that I know that he and I felt that it just won't happen in America, that there are three black women in the forefront. It's not going to happen. Which is very interesting, okay? It is what it is. Now, I spoke with Nigel about that particular day when the three ladies were in the bottom three, and the theory being that because they're all wonderfully talented, it was felt that they split the African American vote. And people do vote in clumps—they just do. I can speak about Jasmine Trias, with Hawai'i, I can speak about second season's Carmen Rasmussen, with the Mormons. And that's what they found, is that people vote in clumps, and it was felt that the African American vote was split between the three ladies. And that's what that was about.*[51]

Byrd's statements confirm that producers and other individuals important in the making of the show are keenly aware of the power of coalition voting. But audience dissatisfaction regarding voting results, even cries of discrimination, can also be an opportunity to encourage the further involvement of viewers. In response to speculation about racism as a cause for Hudson's departure, *American Idol* judge and producer Simon Cowell said, "There are a lot of passive viewers who complain about the results but don't pick up the phone or text a message . . . We needed a shake-up and I think it will change."[52] In his scenario the allegations of racism could result in greater viewer investment, in a more highly interactive audience.

Around the time of the Hudson/Elton John uproar, the content of the forum messages became so heated that website moderators deleted dozens of posts deemed "mean-spirited" or offensive.[53] A week later producers stepped in. For a brief time FOX replaced an advertisement for its new show *The O.C.* at the top of the forum screen with a banner that successively flashed the phrases:

Be a fan. Not a hater.
It's about talent.
Hard work and dedication.
Not racism.
Be a fan. Not a hater.[54]

With the introduction of this banner FOX and the show's producers submitted a direct response to the concerns preoccupying forum members at the time. It also seems an apparent attempt to ensure that voting is undertaken for what the producers feel are the "right" reasons. We are to understand that because it is "about talent," voting practices based on ethnic identity are inappropriate. The language of the admonition is also noteworthy, a world of layered implications present in the loaded use of hip-hop jargon ("hater") and the epigrammatic reinforcement of the myth of the American Dream.

Ethnicity as Individuality: Charly Lowry

Each season *American Idol* asserts that producers are looking for someone "unique." On a February 2004 audition episode set in Atlanta, this criterion was explicitly defined in ethnic terms, as Ryan Seacrest's voiceover introduced Charly Lowry's audition segment. "Not only was she talented," he said, "she was also unique." A quick cut to her performance for the judges implied that this quality was located in her ethnic identity, as she told the judges, "I'm Native American. I'm proud of that. I'm very proud of it, I like to make it known. I'm from the Lumbee tribe of North Carolina. It's a tribe of about 48,000 proud, strong, beautiful people."

In his closing comments after the singer was admitted through to Hollywood, Seacrest calls her audition "a lesson to everyone who wants to make it to Hollywood: be an individual. Be proud."[55] The text and subtext of Seacrest's voiceover script raise some important issues surrounding the role of ethnicity in mediated culture. His statements imply that the concept of ethnicity may be interpreted not only as functioning in terms of community but also as a factor in American individuality, and that on television an ethnic identity outside the mainstream can be taken as equivalent to personal "uniqueness." It also appears that *American Idol* is urging Americans to express pride in their ethnic identities, that this might even be a requirement (for non-whites) in the journey to Hollywood and the fulfillment of the American Dream. Significantly this contradicts other *Idol* implications regarding the importance of *assimilation* on that journey, and this is perhaps a key paradox today in U.S. popular culture industries—to achieve celebrity, one has to simultaneously stand out and blend in, and if one stands out ethnically, the conspicuous distinction must be somehow balanced on the other side of the scales.

Ms. Lowry was, overall, pleased with her early segments on the show, and expressed surprise that she was given so much screen time. She had expected (and participated in) the emphasis on her identity as Native American and as southern but was also delighted with the inclusion of a complimentary appraisal by Paula Abdul after her audition segment aired. This exposure, she felt, helped viewers recognize her when the time came for the live performance shows and audience voting. She was also careful during the filming of the early Hollywood rounds to avoid the possibility of negative exposure, making an effort to "stay away from the camera as much as possible" and allowing her on-camera story to be shaped with the information she provided. Ms. Lowry, who at the time of our interview was a communications major at the University of North Carolina, Chapel Hill, developed an acute sense of this process during her participation in *American Idol*:

> I figured that, one, they would try to market the fact that I was Native American, and I figured they would say a lot about the way I talk, so I figured those were just—because after a while, after being around all that stuff, you start picking up on things, like you start realizing that they want you to have a story. It's almost like they're creating characters. And so my thing was, "she's Native American, and she's from North Carolina and she has this accent that, you know, [is] crazy, or unreal," or whatever.

When I asked how she felt about the way she was presented on the show, she told me that she had been "one of the lucky ones." "The way they presented me," she said, "that was me."[56] It is noteworthy that her own strategy helped produce the satisfactory onscreen portrayal; in her filmed audition she gave a very specific delineation of her views regarding her ethnic identity, and tried to stay in control of how much information viewers would receive. In the end her representation on the show was not essentialized onscreen in the racialized, gendered, or regionalized ways applied to some other contestants. Rather, her image was shaped by her own strategic essentialism.

Her ethnicity became important in the way some viewers experienced her *American Idol* appearances. While at home between the first Hollywood rounds and the start of the performance episodes, for which she would return to Los Angeles, she watched the preliminary broadcasts and kept a close eye on the *American Idol* message boards. Online, she found a great deal of support and encouragement to bolster her for the second trip to California. Many such posts were made by viewers identifying themselves as members of the Lumbee tribe or as Native Americans or as residents of Ms. Lowry's hometown of Pembroke, North Carolina. Other messages came from residents of Robeson County, in which Pembroke is located, and where the Lumbee population is estimated to make up close to one-third of the county's total. The town of Pembroke is "predominantly Indian."[57] Ms. Lowry was "representin da lumbee tribe," and "representing all Native Americans," her fans wrote.

The Lumbee tribe has inspired several in-depth anthropological studies, and has been seen as particularly remarkable not only for its large membership but also for its maintenance of a cohesive identity without the specific unifying linguistic or cultural customs, ties to a reservation, or (until recently) the political organizing required of American tribes for federal recognition.[58] Lumbee efforts to secure full federal recognition over the past 120 years have been categorically refused, largely because of such failures to meet the established expectations of Native American ethnicity. As Anne Merline McCulloch and David E. Wilkins have written, "The ability of an Indian tribe to become and remain a federally recognized tribe is dependent on how well that tribe 'fits' the social construction of 'Indian tribe' as

perceived by federal officials."[59] Other problems in the establishment
of an "official" Lumbee ethnicity are historiographical in nature—
in conflicting historical and anthropological accounts of the tribe's
line of descent, related to internal divisions in tribal identity and
in name changes throughout the time line of North Carolina state
recognition.

Amid these conditions, and the continued struggle for federal
recognition, Ms. Lowry's passion for performing has long been attended by a sense of ethnic responsibility:

> I grew up singing in the church, but when I was twelve—our tribe
> has pageants. We have "Little Miss Lumbee," "Junior Miss Lumbee,"
> "Miss Lumbee," and about two years ago we added "Teen Miss Lum-
> bee." Well, when I was twelve, I entered "Junior Miss," and I won. And
> as the winner, you know, you become an ambassador for the Lumbee
> tribe, and that required traveling all over the nation, traveling on a
> local level, state level, and national level, speaking about your people,
> about where you come from, about your culture, and that gave me an
> opportunity to start singing in public—because that was my talent.
> I sang as entertainment, or as a guest speaker, and that got me inter-
> ested in performing in public. And I noticed that people enjoyed hear-
> ing me perform, and I liked that feeling. I liked being able to—you
> know, just to spread the word through song. So that got me interested
> in pursuing a career as a singer.

I asked her how she felt about inhabiting the role of a representative,
as her online fans called her.

> I knew that I was going to be a spokesperson for my people. Our people
> have such a negative—it's kind of like a negative rep[utation], not
> only in the state of North Carolina, not only along the east coast, but
> over the nation, because of stuff that's happened because of our plight
> for federal recognition. And I knew that I wanted to give our people
> a positive name and be a representative of our tribe and put it in a
> positive light, and show them that, you know, negative stuff—crime,
> just all kind of negativity—that's not the only thing that our people
> are about, that we have some very talented individuals that do want
> to make something of their lives, and that's the way I knew that I

> *wanted to represent them, and myself, on a national level; and I knew*
> *I had that opportunity, so I had to take advantage of it. And just to*
> *know that I did make a difference, and that I did inspire people from*
> *home is just—I don't know, I'm thankful that I had the opportunity*
> *to do that.*[60]

For Ms. Lowry, being an individual in ethnic terms entails not only personal achievement but also the work of challenging stereotypes. The viewer response to her *American Idol* appearances indicates that an essentializing image is not necessarily required for the establishment of an identity-based audience.

How I Voted for Elliott Yamin

In the tradition of the reality-TV confessional, I briefly turn the lens inward here to bring into focus a moment of participant-observation clarity (and confusion) that surprised me during the middle stages of this project. Throughout the previous seasons of *American Idol* I had shared some general identifying factors with the contestants— mostly, that I was a singer, too—and during auditions for a singing class I was teaching, I sometimes empathized with the judges; however, I had never experienced a sense of identification related to commonalities of region, religion, or ethnicity. Then, on April 18, 2006, I voted for Elliott Yamin, a finalist from Richmond, Virginia, who eventually became Season 5's second runner-up. Although I liked Elliott's voice, it was another factor that made the *Idol* experience unusual for me that season. He was Jewish, like me, an unprecedented identity in *Idol*'s Top 12, and though he never mentioned this fact onscreen or in the press, I knew it, and it made a difference. His surname was my first clue early in the season, but names can be misleading or ambiguous, and even though I approved of his singing, I did not anticipate feeling motivated to vote. But in April the *Virginia Jewish News* named Yamin "Jewish Idol,"[61] and I ended up placing several votes.

The issue of televised Jewishness is a tricky one and a problem I had encountered previously as an *Idol* viewer. Paula Abdul did not discuss her own Jewish heritage with the press until Yamin was a contestant; she appeared on CNN's *Larry King Live* in May 2006, and King suggested that Abdul and Yamin had shared a special bond based on their Jewishness.[62] Prior to this revelation there was another *Idol* contestant of unclear but possibly Jewish identity. In 2005, during Season 4, a contestant who reached the Top 12 became the object of my personal speculation. It turned out that although seventeen-year-old Mikalah Gordon's father was Jewish, she was raised Catholic by her mother in Las Vegas. In online forums and in the press, even though the word "Jewish" almost never appeared in association with Mikalah, she was compared to Bette Midler, Barbra Streisand, and especially Fran Drescher, all performers with distinct modes of publicly articulating their (gendered) Jewishness. But in her profile for idolonfox.com, Gordon listed her *rosary* as a good-luck charm. For me, her Catholicism canceled out her paternal heritage, and I did not feel that she was Jewish enough for me to identify with her (or vote for her) based on either religion or ethnicity. Jacob Neusner has written of this common and conflicted perspective in an essay illuminating the tangle of religion, politics, culture, and ethnicity facing turn-of-the millennium American Jewry. "While not all Jews practice Judaism," he writes, "Jews who practice Christianity cease to be part of the ethnic Jewish community in the iron consensus among contemporary Jews."[63]

The very concept of Jewishness as an *ethnicity,* or as *an* ethnicity, is problematic, of course. Elliott Yamin's father is an Iraqi-Israeli Jew, and my family is composed of Ashkenazim from Russia and Poland. But in the United States, Jewishness is more than either a religious ("Judaist"), cultural, ethnic, or political identity. It is a construction of all these, intertwined in various combinations of sub-identities. However, the American Jewish experience has often been viewed as a minority success story, a historical paragon of the American Dream, as Milton Gordon (as far as I know, no relation to Mikalah) suggested, "the greatest collective Horatio Alger story in American immigrant history."[64]

Mikalah Gordon seemed "Jewish" onscreen, but how? Culturally? Ethnically? In retrospect, I think it may have been the result of a purposeful technique, more of an impressionist effort, an impersonation of other Jewish individuals, than an essentialist portrait. My understanding of her as Catholic made me wonder if she might be strategically performing Jewishness, to fit her preference for Streisand's repertoire and solidify her musical niche on the show. In the microcosm of pop music history that plays out on *American Idol*, why should there not be an example of such masquerading, or what Susan Gubar calls "racial camp,"[65] or, perhaps relying on her paternal heritage, another kind of strategic essentialism?

During Season 8, while press speculation about finalist Adam Lambert revolved around the issue of his then unspoken but assumed homosexuality, the other question that sent some viewers rushing to the internet had to do with his unspoken Jewish identity. YouTube videos surfaced showing Lambert performing during an anniversary memorial for Yitzchak Rabin, singing "Shir L'Shalom" ("Song for Peace," by Yaakov Rotblitt and Yair Rosenblum—the song Rabin famously sang with a peace rally crowd just before his assassination) in Hebrew and English. Though Lambert never brought it up during the *Idol* season, he has since mentioned his Jewish background in interviews, once expressing discomfort with Christian-themed gifts and letters he had received from fans. "It's awkward," he told a college news reporter, "because that's not my belief system. I respect people for the intention in which they're giving these gifts, because I know it's out of love and hope, but it doesn't match my belief system at all, so I kind of wish there'd be a little bit more respect for that."[66] Respect might not have played into the situation, however; because most of Lambert's presence in *Idol* discourse among critics, bloggers, and fans did not even broach his Jewishness in passing, it's likely that the Christian viewers he inspired simply did not know.

Much recent, excellent literature has addressed the problems of Jewish representation in scripted television. Decades of televisual worry about seeming "too Jewish" set a long precedent that still haunts Hollywood, and the question of American Jews' standing in 1990s multiculturalist discourse arrived at no easy answers.[67] In Vincent Brook's analysis of Jewishness and situation-comedy programming, he writes of a late-twentieth-century American crisis in Jewish identity fueled by intermarriage rates, anxieties about the political/ ethnic/religious conflict in Israel, the controversy over Israel's Law of Return, and the "particularist pressures—and opportunities— of multiculturalism." Regarding the latter, he also notes that "Jews' comparatively recent widespread acceptance in mainstream, white America has come at a moment when identity politics and multiculturalism have put a premium on difference." With ethnic, cultural, and religious expression among American Jews growing increasingly abstract, representation has become a complicated project. Brook proposes that, in response to this crisis, sitcom creators have relied upon two primary ways to deal with Jewishness onscreen. The first, what Brook calls "conceptual Jewishness," occurs when writers, producers, or actors *conceive* of a character as Jewish, even if a show's script includes no explicit reference.[68] Brook draws his theorization from Herbert Gans's idea of "symbolic Judaism" (this term was introduced in Gans 1994, but Gans also dealt with a broader "symbolic ethnicity" in 1979). The second is a "perceptual Jewishness," when a character is *perceived* by viewers as Jewish but was not conceived that way.

Because personas in reality television are often carefully constructed as characters drawn from familiar televisual experiences of identity, Brook's theory is to a degree transferable. Onscreen, Yamin and Lambert were conceptual Jews, literally, from birth, and recognizable to other Jews through cultural signifiers such as Yamin's surname and Lambert's extra-*Idol* performance video of the Rabin memorial. Gordon's *Idol* character was a perceptual Jew, with an ambiguous ethnic and cultural affiliation that some equated with the same performative signifiers of Jewishness discursively assigned to her own idols, such as Streisand. And, as Lambert's other nondisclosure indicates on a more publicly acknowledged level, certain marginal identities on *Idol* are made conspicuous and significant—and still powerful—for some viewers through their omission.

The Occupational Vote

In Walt Whitman's poem, "I Hear America Singing," singers and their songs are designated by occupation, the carols of "mechanics, each one singing his," of the carpenter and the mason singing theirs, "the boatman singing what belongs to him in his boat."[69] Season 4's second runner-up Vonzell Solomon, a "rural carrier associate" in Florida for the U.S. Postal Service, demonstrated the presence of nationwide *Idol* solidarity based on occupation—one associated with a federal agency, even. According to ethnomusicologist and longtime postal worker Juan Zaragoza, Solomon became "unofficially the face and the voice of the postal service" while she was on *American Idol.* Her image was featured on closed-circuit television in post offices and sorting stations, in the newsletter *Link,* and on the official website for the U.S. Postal Service. The postal service even established a post office box where congratulatory messages might be sent to Solomon through the NetPost CardStore. Postal workers were encouraged to vote for her, and, as Mr. Zaragoza saw, many did. In a postal service press release, Dale Holton, president of the National Rural Letter Carriers' Association, stated,

> The nearly 120,000 men and women of the United States Postal Service who are dedicated to delivering the mail to rural America salute their idol . . . Many of them undoubtedly tune in every week to watch, cheer for and vote for Vonzell. I'm now asking all of my fellow postal employees and their families who support Vonzell to vote and make her America's idol!

Solomon also acknowledged onscreen her fellow postal workers and her former occupational community, at one point twice exclaiming, "United States Postal Service—I love you (guys)!" In Mr. Zaragoza's view, the postal service's appropriation of Solomon as a symbol helped raise employee morale, easing their struggle with long hours and difficult deadlines.[70] In this case, a young southern, rural, African American working-class woman became the "face" and "voice" of a national, state-run organization.

CONCLUSIONS

The overlapping identity discourses that contribute to *American Idol*'s persistent success are a reminder that the construction of place, race, and ethnicity in the United States is firmly tied to political processes. In *American Idol* the processes of construction are built on a self-perpetuating dialectic: onscreen constructions of American identities create a framework for the strategic participation of viewers, and the commercial success of this framework, in turn, makes identity construction an appealing strategy for those involved in what happens onscreen. Choices regarding music and language, as well as dress and appearance, serve as cues for voters, as signs of specific identities that factor in the definition of a broader national one. As Simon Frith writes, "An identity is always already an ideal, what we would like to be, not what we are. In taking pleasure from black or gay or female music I don't thus identify as black or gay or female . . . but, rather, participate in imagined forms of *democracy and desire,* imagined forms of the social."[71] Through the use of familiar music and familiar identities, *American Idol*'s producers, contestants, and viewers provide a cultural and political blueprint for Americanness.

7

THE UNITED NATIONS OF POP ·
GLOBAL FRANCHISE
AND GEOPOLITICS

WORLD IDOL

Simon Fuller recalled, in 2003, "when I dreamt up the idea of *Pop Idol*, I always saw it as a global concept."[1] As increasingly transnational processes drive cultural flow across geographic, economic, and political boundaries, the significance of reality television programming broadens, too, far beyond mere diversion. Licensed in more than forty versions across six continents, the *Idols*-format show has become a worldwide pastime perhaps rivaled only by certain athletic events. Although *American Idol* and *Pop Idol* have been seen via satellite television in nations beyond their geographically delimited voting audiences, most of the programs are scarcely known outside their country or region of production. But between December 25, 2003, and January 1, 2004, a two-episode series titled *World Idol* confirmed *Idols* as a global phenomenon.

Formulated as a climactic synthesis of the first two years of the franchise, *World Idol* presented a competition in which the winners of eleven *Idols* programs met in London to vie for the world title. They included representatives from Germany, Australia, Canada, the Netherlands, South Africa, Poland, the United States, (Flemish) Belgium, the United Kingdom, Norway, and what was referred to as the "Pan

Arab" region. *World Idol* was broadcast to the participating countries and several others, although voting could only take place within the nations involved. A weighted voting system, emulating that of the Eurovision Song Contest, took varying population size into account.

World Idol, in the end, highlighted some widespread ideological convictions about the nature of popular music, and demonstrated the enduring relationship between popular music and politics. Viewers in disparate locations tuned in to find out whether their own national or regional Idol could make it on the "world stage." This oft-repeated phrase was even illustrated literally during the first broadcast's opening graphics, as the globe spinning inside the *World Idol* logo in fact flattened into the image of a stage. As *American Idol* creates an arena for the performance of nationally specific identity politics, *World Idol* offered a collection of such performances on a wider scale.

The show was imagined and presented as a kind of international summit. Half an hour into the FOX broadcast edited for U.S. audiences, co-host Anthony McPartlin exclaimed, "Look at what we're doing here—it's like the United Nations of pop!" Correspondingly, introductory graphics during the preliminary credits featured a glossy, computer-generated figure striding along an avenue of flags evocative of those lined up outside U.N. headquarters in Manhattan.[2] This allusion was augmented as the camera panned the assorted flags clutched by audience members inside the Fountain Studios. The eleven contestants were critiqued by eleven judges from their respective series, judges whose nationalities were further indicative of the fluid boundaries and dominant industrial voices of the worldwide music business. It is noteworthy that not only the judge representing the U.K.'s *Pop Idol* but also the U.S., Australian, and German judges were British in origin. Nevertheless each judge championed the singer representing his or her particular show, although U.S. judge Simon Cowell also verbally supported the winner of the British series he had co-created.

Language used by judges and hosts, albeit jokingly, placed the United Kingdom in a position of cultural authority. The British representatives even passed judgment on other participating countries; the Polish judge antagonized the panel to the degree that Polish contestant Alicja Janosz ("Alex") was asked if everyone in her country was mad. Comedy-duo hosts Anthony McPartlin and Declan Donnelly

("Ant and Dec") offered a brief, essentializing description of each nation before its representative went onstage. "Belgium, home of waffles, chocolate . . . that's about it, really," they announced, or "Now, what has Canada ever given us, huh? Ice hockey, enormous moose, and Céline Dion."[3] And drawing on historical discourse in the U.S. broadcast, they shouted, "The British are coming!" by way of announcing U.K. Pop Idol Will Young.

World Idol demonstrated both the individualized national character of each *Idols* series and the ostensibly universal qualities that unite them all. To begin with, although every *Idols* logo looks approximately the same (with few exceptions, a blue oval with silver writing),[4] the titles show some discrepancies. While most of the programs include the word "Idol," a few are instead called *Super Star* or something similar. David Lyle of *Idols* production company FremantleMedia has explained this as an issue of semantics: certain meanings of the word "idol" made its use seem unwise in specific nations. According to Lyle, it "harked back to the [F]ührer a little" in Germany, where the series has been titled *Deutschland sucht den Superstar.* Despite such differences, the uniformity of the *Idols* design and the influence of its British prototype were evident in the approaches of several *World Idol* judges. In the original *Pop Idol* Cowell had made indispensible his straight-to-the-point, often ruthless persona. Lyle has admitted, "By and large we have encouraged most markets to find a character who's going to tell it like it is." Likewise Cowell says of his fellow *World Idol* judges, "Every one of these people has based themselves on my character. They think it's cool to be me."[5] As in much of reality television, the prospect of participants' humiliation has become part of the attraction in the *Idols* shows. Both the December 25 and January 1 broadcasts featured segments ridiculing the performances of those rejected during each show's preliminary audition process. These former hopefuls were presented as bad singers, bad dancers, or just plain odd, but clearly elicited the same mockery everywhere, regardless of nationality.

Some of the most striking commonalities among the *Idols* shows involve the musical selections performed. Of the eleven songs performed by the *World Idol* contestants, ten were covers of songs by American, British, or Irish artists (U2) well known in anglophone/phile nations. Of these, only three were composed after 1985. Singers whose choice of material stood out from these criteria were subject to some criticism from the judging panel, or at least to the judges' evident bewilderment. The structure and content of *World Idol* expressed a tension between multiculturalist or pluralist thinking and the hegemonic configuration of the global entertainment industry. It also implicitly promoted the idea that "pop music" may everywhere be defined through English-language songs and U.K., U.S., or Irish musicians.

The issue of language proved to be an area of both convergence and conflict, at once unifying and diversifying the multinational franchise. Clips from each series showed that aspiring Idols often auditioned in English and sang in English throughout the broadcast season, although the narration and dialogue was apparently carried out in an assortment of national languages. The *World Idol* competition was conducted in English, but there were exceptional moments— Polish judge Kuba Wojewódzki spoke in Polish to his nation's representative, as well as during occasional outbursts at other points.

Only the "Pan Arab" contestant, a young Jordanian woman named Diana Karazon, sang in a language other than English.[6] Her performance also elicited some discomfort among the judging panel. Karazon occupied a unique place among her colleagues in *World Idol*. The other ten contestants all sang popular selections in English, covers of songs associated with performers recognizable to much of the largely North American and European audience of the *Idols* franchise. These included compositions made famous by Elton John ("Sorry Seems to Be the Hardest Word"), Aretha Franklin (Carole King's "Like a Natural Woman"), U2 ("Beautiful Day"), and Aerosmith ("I Don't Want to Miss a Thing"). Karazon's selection, "Insāni ma binsāk" (Forget Me, I Won't Forget You) was a new song, not a cover, from her debut album, which had premiered in September 2003. Her *Idols* show, *Super Star*, did not include English-language music; her album was entirely in Arabic, and she sang in Arabic at the international competition. She has also said that, although she is able to sing in English, she preferred to sing in Arabic at *World Idol*.[7] Her decision to perform in Arabic left both Karazon and the music she sang reduced to a linguistic incongruity. American contestant Kelly Clarkson, who offered on-camera comments for the benefit of U.S.

audiences, thought it was "cool that she sang her own . . . style and her own language." Belgian judge Nina De Man warned Karazon that her "language impose[d] restrictions on the votes"; Dutch judge Henkjan Smits called her "brave" for singing in Arabic; and Australian judge Ian Dickson invoked the metaphor of music as a universal language, declaring after her performance that "the true beauty of music is that it translates [sic] language barriers." In the broadcast on FOX in the U.S., British hosts McPartlin and Donnelly announced Karazon as "the only person not to sing a Western song." They asked the television audience, "Can she secure the world's vote?"[8]

Karazon's performance contained many choices that may be interpreted as implicitly or explicitly political. Her stylized dress suggested visually that she would be contributing something different, neither European nor American, to the competition. Because she represented a large group of nations, she was identified throughout the World Idol program as the "Pan Arab" contestant. In spite of this generality, and broad responsibility, when the camera turned to Karazon's cheering fans during her time onstage, they were waving specifically Jordanian flags. Super Star's delegated judge in World Idol, Elias Rahbani, was also given the captioned designation "Pan Arab."[9] Although McPartlin and Donnelly alluded during the World Idol broadcast to an undisclosed "twenty-two nations" participating in Super Star, they did not name the Arab League, to which those twenty-two nations belong. Though neither Idols-related websites nor press ever explained the relationship of the twenty-two countries, the label "Pan Arab" conflated all of them into a presumably unified geographical and cultural region. This idea belies the deep competition and underlying political discord among participant nations in Super Star, whose first season culminated in a small riot at the Beirut studios where the program was being filmed. The label may, however, have prevented an explosion of more inflammatory politics.

The judges' comments included in the FOX broadcast highlighted international diversity but also suggested universality. American Idol judge Simon Cowell insisted that he had no idea whether Karazon's performance was "any good." Approaching the performance as if it were something political, Belgian judge Nina De Man assessed it as "inspiring" despite the language issue, and told Karazon, "I'm sure people all over the world will . . . feel the strength in your voice." However, De Man believed that the singer's decision to perform in Arabic would prevent her from acquiring the title "World Idol." Australian judge Ian Dickson thanked Karazon for representing "a huge part of the world" and declared that he was "very proud to be part of a program that can embrace a culture like [Karazon's]."[10] Karazon's performance was thus addressed in terms that reinforced both a sense of cultural distance and of multiculturalist inclusiveness, at once exoticizing—even fetishizing difference—and superficially assimilating.

Although *World Idol* was not repeated the following year, the franchise was not finished with the idea of a pan-*Idols* competition. An *Asian Idol* contest was held in 2007, including winners and judges from South and Southeast Asian shows *Indian Idol, Indonesian Idol, Philippine Idol, Malaysian Idol, Super Star KZ* (Kazakhstan's version), *Vietnam Idol,* and *Singapore Idol.* The overall Asian Idol title went to Singapore's second-season winner, Hady Mirza. American Idol Taylor Hicks joined the contestants to sing his Season 6 winner's song, "Do I Make You Proud" in the results broadcast. However, the only larger global *Idols* perspective following *World Idol* aired in an hour-long 2005 special titled *American Idol Presents: The World's Worst Auditions.* It featured clips of auditions from several *Idols* shows, many familiar from a similar, if shorter, segment during *World Idol.* The World's Worst Auditions offered a global view of equal-opportunity ridicule from an American point of view, a multilingual pastiche of the same problematic musicianship and insults broadcast in every season's early audition episodes. This special, however, gave humiliation a universal cast, all *Idols* contestants—all world citizens, perhaps—united by the capacity to be unsuccessful: "It is estimated that over a million people have auditioned to be their country's idol . . . There's one thing they have in common," the narrating voiceover announced over an off-key rendition of "Rhinestone Cowboy," "—they suck, big time."[11] While the original *World Idol* in the end highlighted cultural and linguistic differences, *The World's Worst Auditions* emphasized the universal ordinariness of the rejected contestants. Singers who did not make the grade in Arabic were portrayed as no worse, and no better, than those who failed in English or Polish or German. The humiliation celebrated in reality television becomes a great equalizer, where anyone can become either a star or an international laughing-stock (or in cases like William Hung's, as we've seen, both at once).

The international audience vote, weighted in a manner appropriated from the Eurovision Song Contest, resulted in the victory of Norwegian singer Kurt Nilsen as "World Idol." Karazon placed near the bottom in the results from most of the eleven national/regional counts. Voting nations were not permitted to vote for their own representative, and each contestant was automatically awarded the maximum of twelve points from his or her own contingency. All other contestants were given between one and ten points (ten being the high end). Aside from the "Pan Arab" vote, Karazon received her highest rating from the United States, which placed her fourth overall in its vote. Her relatively high placement in the U.S. and German votes is striking. Thomas Solomon observes that in the case of the Eurovision Song Contest, "there is nothing to prevent migrants residing outside their country of origin from voting for their home country."[12] If it is possible that diasporic Arab communities in the United States contributed to Karazon's standing in the similar context of World Idol, Super Star's "Pan Arab" qualities might be raised to another level.

In addition to spoken rhetoric, other political signs also played a role in World Idol. Although audience members waved Jordanian flags in support of Karazon, she flashed the two-fingered "V" sign as she came onstage with the other Idols. In parts of the Middle East, this motion has been strongly associated with Yasser Arafat and Palestinian causes, indicating "victory." It is possible, of course, that the sign had a more general meaning for Karazon, but as a Jordanian of Palestinian origin, she had been vocal during the first season of Super Star about her support for Palestinian concerns. Still, the "V" sign clearly has polysemic properties; Belgian Idol Peter Evrard made the same gesture. In his case, the "V" likely came from Evrard's devotion to rock, where the gesture has also been inscribed with multiple meanings.

Evrard's own performance of Kurt Cobain's "Lithium" caused some consternation as well. Since the conception of Idols with the aptly titled Pop Idol, producers had only specific genres of music in mind, and the possibility of including music designated as "rock" was initially only reluctantly considered. Nina De Man explained during

World Idol that she and her Belgian colleagues on the *Idool* (Belgian spelling) judging panel had, at first, thought that Evrard did not "fit the mold" of their competition. They had changed their minds, however, as he came to "carve a brand new mold" with songs like Nickelback's "How You Remind Me" and Neil Young's "Keep on Rockin' in the Free World" (which had more recently been covered by Pearl Jam). But *World Idol* judges were not convinced. German representative Shona Fraser believed that Evrard should sing with a band, rather than execute the karaoke-like performance style of *World Idol*. "This isn't the place for you," she concluded. Cowell and *Pop Idol* judge Pete Waterman seemed appalled by the intrusion of rock into the *Idols* world. In a tense exchange with Evrard, Cowell pronounced that "this would be Kurt Cobain's biggest nightmare . . . because you were conforming, and rock 'n' roll is about *not* conforming." Waterman was adamant on this point as well, telling Evrard, "If you were serious, you wouldn't be on this show."

Such statements, paradoxical in the mouths of *Idols* originators, plainly delineate what *Idols* must be about: pop music, not rock; money and fabrication, not authenticity. Implicitly condemning their own show, the sentiments of Cowell and Waterman expressed rock ideology (a situation similar to that of Micah Read's audition for *American Idol,* detailed in chapter 2). Rock is discursively associated with personal and musical authenticity, and hard work, whereas "pop," as a distinct genre group, is conversely characterized as inauthentic, manufactured, and commercial.[13] The grunge rock icon Kurt Cobain, as Cowell and Waterman insisted respectively, "did it through being real" and "by working nine years." With these words, they also implied that *Idols* represents the opposite, a shortcut to fame that neglects questions of artistic integrity.

Evrard took the time to challenge the judges' assessment of his own authenticity, and, in his post-performance interview with hosts McPartlin and Donnelly, maintained that he was sure of who he was, and that his "homies" believed in the honesty of his songs. Addressing the judges, he also accused them of contributing to the same inauthenticity they had just rejected. "You guys made it this way," he told them, "the industry made it this way, that young artists can't find another contract anymore, where I'm from." Curiously, a month before

the *World Idol* competition was announced, FremantleMedia executive David Lyle had invoked the example of Belgium to imply that
Idols was doing just the opposite. On NPR's *On the Media,* he claimed
that *Idols* gave small countries a chance to produce singing stars in the
face of international entertainment oligopoly:

> Like in Belgium, where we've done it. They don't really have their
> own pop industry. For them to create a singing sensation is almost
> impossible, because they are just monstered by the large recording
> companies. So in Belgium, in Holland and in, in Scandinavia . . .
> we've allowed the public to create a new pop star.[14]

Idols, however, is itself linked to "large recording companies"—to
BMG and, through that corporation's impressive 2004 merger, to
Sony.

In addition to the discourse of rock authenticity, *Idols* emphasizes
the visual aspect of popular music, and "pop" in particular—that is,
the "image." This has led to frequent discussion of physical appearance, and its potential consequence in the selection of a pop star. In
World Idol, South African singer Heinz Winckler was praised for his
"matinee idol" looks, while Norway's representative, Kurt Nilsen,
was mocked for resembling "a hobbit." However, the importance of
appearance is often controversial in *Idols* programs. Canadian judge
Zack Werner told Winckler that being attractive was not enough for
World Idol; this was not the "Mr. Universe pageant," he insisted, but a
"singing contest." He was contradicted by Australian judge Ian Dickson, countering with a firm belief that looks did indeed matter in a
televised competition. Similarly Cowell assured Nilsen that, were
World Idol a radio competition, he would certainly win. All the same,
both Cowell and Waterman pronounced Nilsen the "dark horse," on
the basis of his voice. Jan Fredrik Karlsen, representing the Norwegian judges, reminded Nilsen that he had been an underdog on his
own nation's show and that he was an underdog at *World Idol* because
of Norway's modest global stature. On January 1, 2004, Nilsen was
crowned World Idol, over bookies' favorite Kelly Clarkson.

World Idol saw the demonstration and reinforcement of particular
concepts about genre in popular music. It also illustrated the ways in
which British and American music has been employed in the service

of creating national stars in an international industry. And we have seen that on a "world stage" performance is bound to be political. Through a range of signs and layered meanings, a singing competition can become a theatrical allegory for the politics of globalization. Andrew Strenk points out that the Olympic Games "offer a symbolic arena and an alternate channel for international competition."[15] (Appropriately, the Pythian events of the ancient Panhellenic games included singing contests.) *World Idol* represents a comparable process, highlighting the tensions brought to light through the persistent spread of a global franchise.

AMERICAN IDOL GIVES BACK

During Season 6, in an encounter of *Idol* politics and American politics that was perhaps inevitable, the president of the United States appeared on *American Idol*. His videotaped visit was directly tied to the previous week's special format. 19 Entertainment executive Simon Fuller, in collaboration with Richard Curtis, had organized a two-episode *American Idol* charity event called "*Idol* Gives Back," which aired on April 24 and 25, 2007. The celebrity-saturated show enlisted viewers and a number of large corporations, including News Corporation (News Corp.), which owns FOX, to donate to a newly established aid organization. Curtis's and Fuller's new Charity Projects Entertainment Fund was designed to function as a sort of one-stop distribution center (much like Fuller's "one-stop shopping" music industry ideal), collecting donations and passing the money on to several existing aid groups that address the problems of poverty, illiteracy, and health care in the U.S. and Africa.[16]

The two broadcasts featured corporately sponsored films of Ryan Seacrest and Simon Cowell visiting families devastated by HIV/AIDS in Africa—the only places explicitly mentioned were Kisumu and Kabira, Kenya—Randy Jackson in a FEMA trailer park in post-Katrina Louisiana (his home state), Ryan Seacrest in Atlanta (his hometown), and Paula Abdul at a Boys and Girls Club center in Hollywood, as well as footage from a Navajo reservation in Chinle, Arizona, film of students at the Beckham Bates Elementary School in Kentucky's Letcher County, a food bank in Los Angeles, and mobile health care units at unspecified locations. In a voiceover describing the video from Louisiana, Randy Jackson pointed out that, in 2005, ten thousand had auditioned for *American Idol* at the Louisiana Superdome in New Orleans, the very site where, one year later, ten thousand evacuated hurricane victims later spent the awful aftermath of the disaster waiting for aid. The *Idol* contestants sang new "We Are the World"-like songs composed by Quincy Jones and by archetypal musician-activist Bono, whose contribution was called "American Prayer."

On Tuesday the Top 6 finalists also sang "inspirational songs," alternatively referred to in press releases and on the *American Idol* website as "life anthems." These included cover performances of John Lennon's "Imagine," Eric Clapton's "Change the World," Garth Brooks's "The Change," the 2004 official *American Idol* song "I Believe," the *Carousel* standard (and Liverpool Football Club anthem) "You'll Never Walk Alone," and Faith Hill's "There Will Come a Day." Notably "Imagine," "There Will Come a Day," and "Bridge Over Troubled Water," which Annie Lennox brought to "*Idol* Gives Back," had all been performed during the immediately post-9/11 benefit concert "America: A Tribute to Heroes," aired on dozens of television and radio stations on 21 September 2001. On Wednesday musical guest stars on "*Idol* Gives Back" included Earth, Wind, and Fire, Annie Lennox (whom Simon Fuller manages), Il Divo (Simon Cowell's "opera band"), Josh Groban and the African Children's Choir[17] (the choir was also present at charity rock guru Bob Geldof's Live8 event in 2005), Rascal Flatts, former American Idols Carrie Underwood and Kelly Clarkson (with guitarist Jeff Beck, in Patty Griffin's gospel-inflected "Up to the Mountain [MLK Song]"), and a time-bending duet between Céline Dion and a digitally resurrected Elvis Presley.

The presence of Annie Lennox and Céline Dion implied that *Idols* has a place in the dynastic legacy not only of American pop but also international pop. Elvis's spectral attendance extended the Idol genealogy to the fullest, underlining the idea that, democratic elections aside, the Idols are part of the royal lineage established by the "King" of American pop at the very outset of rock 'n' roll—that racialized moment when Sam Phillips famously hired Presley as a white man with a "Negro sound."[18] The choice of Elvis was no casual decision. Robert F. X. Sillerman of CKX, Inc., who acquired 19 Entertainment in early 2005, also acquired Elvis Presley Enterprises just months before. The website for Elvis Presley Enterprises quotes Sillerman: "I believe Elvis to be the single most significant icon in American pop culture."[19] The Dion/Presley duet was a technological and temporal feat, an exercise in *Idol* time, with Ryan Seacrest announcing Dion's journey "back in time" to 1968, when Elvis's performance of "If I Can Dream" first aired in an NBC special. In (virtual) reality, it was Elvis's performance that visited *American Idol* in 2007, thanks to masterful editing and the application of a technique called rotoscoping. Commonly used in animation since its invention in 1915, rotoscoping originally allowed the motion of live actors to inform that of drawn figures.[20] Technological advances, including digitalization, have changed the practice of rotoscoping over time, and the *Idol* reanimation of Elvis did not involve cartoon animation. It was instead effected through a process of repetition, decontextualization, and recontextualization, in which Dion was first filmed singing her part of the duet, without an audience and without any Elvis; then again with a lip-syncing Elvis impersonator carefully following Presley's 1968 movements and gestures; and, finally, Presley's NBC performance was extracted from the 1968 footage, and combined with the footage of Dion alone and Dion with the body-double.[21]

Similar processes had been used before, familiar from a reverse version in the film *Forrest Gump,* in which Tom Hanks' character is shown interacting with John F. Kennedy. At the end of 2006 BBC1 launched a special in the U.K. called *Duet Impossible,* which used the Dion/Elvis effect to pair English boy band McFly with a teenaged Lulu (who is still alive but no longer a teenager), Westlife (for whose success Simon Cowell is responsible) with Roy Orbison, the girl band the Sugababes in black and white with Dusty Springfield, and Boy George with his own younger self.[22] Some of these performances are not only intergenerational but also international. The phenomenon of impossible duets is a fitting addition to *American Idol*'s world, the world of reality television, where ideas about reality are already sold with confidence and received in a kind of doubtful trust. As John Whitfield writes in a *Nature* piece about rotoscoping, "What counts as real . . . depends on technologies of representation; as technology has changed, so has our perception of the hallmarks of reality."[23]

The benefit program was deeply referential in terms of American history, music history, and, self-referentially, *Idol* history. The selection of songs associated with the national response to 9/11 demonstrates awareness of not only the recent U.S. past but also of previous charity events. Carrie Underwood's video of "I'll Stand By You" also echoes a benefit concert, this time the Concert for the Gulf Coast after Hurricane Katrina, when Patti LaBelle sang the song. The participation of Bono, Quincy Jones, and the African Children's Choir positioned "*Idol* Gives Back" in the genealogy of charity rock as a descendant of "USA for Africa" (Quincy Jones conducted and produced "We Are the World" for that benefit in 1985), "Live Aid" (1985), and Live8 (2005, where the African Children's Choir performed). The inclusion of two former Idols serves to intensify that position. Underwood's appearance in her music video, surrounded by dozens of African children, also echoes the construction of other white American and European female celebrities as humanitarians and diplomats in Africa—from Audrey Hepburn as UNICEF ambassador, to Sally Struthers with the Christian Children's Fund, to the recent adoption efforts of Angelina Jolie and Madonna. Raka Shome explains this persistent image as part of the way "the nation writes its transnational re/visions," suggesting that "the production of white femininity in relation to natives of 'other worlds' continues to be a mode through which western cultural postcolonial modernity writes itself."[24] Of course, that modernity does not so much write itself as it *is written,* and it is vital to consider the authors. Shome's essay is about the U.K.'s beloved Princess Diana, a symbol of this phenomenon with whom the British *Idol* executives and "*Idol* Gives Back" producers must be thoroughly familiar. Locating Underwood in such an ideological context strategically legitimizes both the singer and *American Idol* in the postcolonial history of Western humanitarian aid efforts. Additionally, it further reinforces the idea of the United States as role model and civil-religious missionary. The next year "*Idol* Gives Back" featured footage of Fantasia Barrino and Elliott Yamin visiting Namibe province in Angola to survey the results of the 2007 donations on efforts toward malaria prevention. Yamin wept on camera as a family named their newborn after him, and he presented the mother—"on behalf of *American Idol* and ExxonMobil and UNICEF" with a mosquito-protection bed net.[25]

In 2007 News Corporation pledged to donate ten cents per *Idol* vote on Tuesday, up to 50 million votes, though there were 70 million placed. The *"Idol* Gives Back" event was constructed as a demonstration of what Herbert Gans calls "altruistic democracy," in which "politics should follow a course based on the public interest and public service."[26] "*Idol* Gives Back" raised around $70 million with its broadcasts on of April 24 and 25, 2007, and the following week the show aired a statement by President George W. Bush and First Lady Laura Bush thanking America and *American Idol* for showing "the good heart of America." The president closed the statement with "Thanks, and God bless."[27] With the apparent altruism of corporate giants, the contributions of American viewers, the approval of the nation's leader, and the implication of divine corroboration, the "*Idol* Gives Back" effort officially established *American Idol* as an exemplary Model of American Charity—of civil-religious morality.

"*Idol* Gives Back" returned in 2008, but in 2009 the onscreen philanthropic spectacle was limited to a brief video and a single appearance by teenaged, HIV-positive Rwandan rapper Noah Mushimiyimana, introduced by R&B star Alicia Keys and representing the Keep a Child Alive Foundation.[28] His performance was available on iTunes, with proceeds donated to the foundation. Before Mushimiyimana took the stage, Ryan Seacrest announced that the *Idol* Gives Back program had raised more than $140 million since the first event in Season 6. In October 2009 *American Idol's* website (americanidol.com) announced plans for a 2010 special, again set to contribute to an array of organizations focusing both on the U.S. and overseas distribution: the Children's Health Fund (founded by singer-songwriter Paul Simon and Irwin Redlener, M.D., in 1987), Feeding America, Malaria No More, Save the Children, and the United Nations Foundation.[29]

In harnessing the *Idol* voting process for raising charity funds, "*Idol* Gives Back" has made further use of its preexisting implications of empowerment. During the first week of May 2007, when phone lines for the first "*Idol* Gives Back" were still open for donations, former Idols Ruben Studdard, Fantasia Barrino, and Taylor Hicks appeared in taped segments urging viewers to contribute. The message was the same for all three: I was nothing until America voted for me, and now you can change the lives of others, too, by giving money. "You believed in me, now believe in someone else," Barrino pleaded.[30] The *American Idol* Dream depends on viewer agency, whether it is expressed in votes or in cash. In its juxtaposition of the election process, religion, music history, and the implications of charity as a mitigator to the concentrated capitalism of the *Idols* franchise, "*Idol* Gives Back" provided an intensive course in American culture, located in a larger global context.

GLOBALIZATION, TRANSNATIONALISM, AND DEMOCRACY

In the summer of 2009 FremantleMedia's Web page for the *Idols* format declared a worldwide sum of more than three billion votes, submitted in the franchise's dozens of programs. Its pseudo-democratic structure has unquestionably had a tremendous discursive effect since the earliest *Idols* programming, although it is only one ingredient in the successful formula. The extraordinary reach of the franchise may ultimately be understood as part of larger phenomena: in particular, the twin processes of globalization and consolidation in the media industry, and the most recent worldwide wave of democratization. These processes embody the enduring model of global landscapes proposed by Arjun Appadurai. For Appadurai, the globalized economy comprises a set of five interconnected but disjunctive dimensions: "ethnoscapes" (the landscape of people in motion), "technoscapes" (the "global configuration of technology"), and "financescapes" (landscapes of global capital), as well as "mediascapes" and "ideoscapes." Appadurai links the last two as "landscapes of images," but he distinguishes them: mediascapes are "image-centered, narrative-based accounts of strips of reality," whereas the images of ideoscapes involve political ideologies and counter-ideologies.[31]

As each *Idols* show is simultaneously tailored to a nation, or group of nations, and positioned as part of a transnational cultural topography, the interlocking mechanisms of multiple ethnoscapes grow more apparent. As Penelope Coutas has written, "the framework may be foreign, but the story is local"[32]; each program stages a specific landscape of identity politics. In terms of technoscapes, *Idols* draws attention to the distribution of technology. Voting usually depends on access to the internet, to telephones, and to text-messaging systems, the availability of which varies from country to country and among individual viewers. Aswin Punathambekar, writing about *Indian Idol's* viewership, coins the phrase "mobile publics" to encapsulate the essential role of "mobile media technologies and practices . . . in the formation of publics, and to underscore the shifting and transient nature of such publics."[33] In some cases, including *Super Star,* the outcomes of the competition have been heavily linked to voting technology. Future TV, the network that airs *Super Star,* reported that in the first season most votes from Kuwait and Saudi Arabia were placed through the internet.[34] But SMS (short messaging system) has played an increasingly important role, and the national mobile phone service of a country will often offer discounts on voting calls and text messages placed in favor of the *Super Star* finalist from that nation. It is possible, then, that pricing competition between rival companies in different nations may contribute to the final results of the singing competition. Samer Bazyan, data services manager for the Jordanian mobile phone service Fastlink, has attributed the first-season victory of Jordanian Diana Karazon partly to Jordan's comparatively low voting costs.[35] In *World Idol* the weighted voting system was intended to reduce the effects of general population disproportion, but financial considerations across a world of multiple ethnoscapes may still have made a difference in the accessibility of voting equipment.

   Idols is also a testament to the increasingly concentrated corporate oligopoly that makes up the global media industry. If Appadurai's financescapes relate to landscapes of global capital and production, then the current topography of the music and entertainment industries is increasingly relevant. The *Idols* enterprise, working on both localized and global levels, comprises a complex of technological and financial landscapes, and a small number of powerful transnational corporations. 19 Entertainment's Simon Fuller and BMG executive Simon Cowell developed the format, which 19 owns jointly with FremantleMedia.[36] BMG, formerly one of the "Big Five" companies in

the recording industry oligopoly, was the music division of Bertelsmann AG and encompassed several subsidiary labels. It merged with
Sony in 2004 so that the combined entity is now one of the "Big Four"
(Sony Music Entertainment, Universal Music Group, EMI, and Warner Music Group). FremantleMedia is also connected to Bertelsmann
through its parent company, the RTL Group, 90 percent of which
Bertelsmann owns. Bertelsmann at one time also held joint ownership of AOL Europe with Time Warner, whose recording division has
been attached (as well as the Music Master International label and
BMG) with the winners of *Super Star.* The structure of the transnational music industry, dominated by a handful of recording labels, is
evident in these convoluted corporate relationships. In Appadurai's
analysis, production may be fetishized in terms of locality, masking
the global nature of the productive process.[37] *American Idol,* for example, highlights its very American content and does not reveal its
international corporate roots or British origins. But these roots are
essential to understanding *Idols* in its global context.

Globalization, writes sociologist William I. Robinson, can be
considered a new "epoch" in the history of capitalism. To Robinson, in the global economy not only capital but also the processes
of production are decentralized and fragmented, and the local and
globalized "circuits of production" whose interrelationships form the
structure of "transnational corporations" are ever more difficult to
extricate from one another. He views the globalization of capital and
production as catalytic in the establishment of a "transnational capi-
talist class." Emerging from elite strata that underwent a politicization
between the 1970s and the 1990s, a kind of global ruling class developed that created transnational institutions (e.g., the WTO or the
G-8) and acted as a *"manifest agent"* of global change. In light of these
power structures, transnational corporations play an important part
in what Robinson posits as an overarching *transnational state,* where
individual nation-states are subsumed in a larger network with supra-
national economic and political institutions.[38]

Could *World Idol,* then, be a product and indicator of the new
world order that Bellah predicted in 1967? If this is so, then the transmission abroad of *American Idol* and its ideologies carries deep political and economic implications. Robinson shares and expands simi-

lar concerns about individualism to those detailed by Bellah et al. in *Habits of the Heart* (see chapter 4), observing that:

> The spread of a homogenous consumer culture and the "spirit of individualism" it brings justifies social differentiation and also acts as a mechanism of social control by deflecting attention away from collective demands for social justice and toward the individual and competitive pursuit of consumption.[39]

If Bellah's predicted world order has come to pass, then instead of the transcendent civil religion he hoped for, it is one in which a global economic and political hegemony balances on the fulcrum of the American Dream.[40] That Dream, like *Idols,* is now reconfigured in the emergent context of the transnational state. With the rise of the *Idols* franchise it becomes plain that the Dream is not the exclusive geographical property of America but, dislocated and de-territorialized, takes on new definitions in a larger setting.

The multiple mediascapes of *Idols* produce diverse images, narratives, and metaphors upon which imagined lives and imagined worlds are constructed. Linked to these mediascapes, *Idols* depends heavily on Appadurai's more political ideoscapes, which commonly involve Enlightenment concepts such as "freedom," "representation," and, notably, "the master term *democracy.*" In the *Idols* format, democratic choice has been replaced with consumer choice, epitomizing Cornel West's concerns about contemporary understandings of American democracy. West worries that certain "dogmas" are stripping democracy of its meaning—for example, through a conflation, or confusion, between *freedom* and *free-market* in which the market becomes "*idol* and fetish." And if, as Sheldon Wolin suggests, "electoral politics [have become] assimilated to the practices of the market place," then the *Idols* format captures the early-twenty-first-century political zeitgeist.[41]

Although the economic power in the *Idols* franchise is shared among a very few transnational corporations, the audience vote serves to imply that power is distributed more democratically. The *Idols* vote has become a geopolitical symbol. A 2003 remark made by David Lyle, president of Entertainment and Drama for Fremantle-Media North America, hints at the idea that the *Idols* format might factor directly in the worldwide expansion of democracy. After voting toward the end of *Super Star*'s first season resulted in a conflict that made international headlines, he stated:

> Well, we did a pan-Arabic version . . . And as that got to the sort of pressure point, there was a small riot in which some members of the audience . . . did resort to bringing out blades. You've got to realize that for many countries that pan-Arabic show went out in, this was the first time the public ever had to cope with something as unusual as voting, so it was a very novel moment for them—the idea of casting a vote, and probably even more novel, that the votes actually were counted correctly and the right person won.[42]

Idols certainly was not the first Arab experience of democracy, but this theme has remained connected discursively to the format. In 2006 another incident sparked press speculation regarding the consequences of the *Idols* design in global democracy. A story broke that the State Administration of Radio, Film, and Television in China had begun curbing television programming modeled on the *Idols* design. The administration had issued a statement declaring that talent competitions must contribute to the upholding of socialism, and "have a favourable influence on morality."[43] CNN's Larry King broached the topic with Simon Cowell soon after the news item began circulating in the U.S. Cowell responded, "Well, because it's a democracy, isn't it? You know, I mean, it's the public voting. So you can understand why they're getting slightly nervous about it . . . And the public got to vote. And suddenly there were demos, and it was democracy."[44]

While some television viewers in Iraq have, in the past, received broadcasts of *American Idol* and the U.K.'s *Pop Idol,* an Iraqi show in a voter-driven format similar to *Idols* (but not part of the same franchise) created a stir in 2005. *Iraq Star* airs on the Beirut-based satellite network al-Sumaria and came to Western attention for a twelve-year-old contestant's emotional performance in tribute to a devastated Iraq. *Iraq Star* has held early qualifying rounds in the difficult setting of war-torn Baghdad, besieged by helicopter noise at a studio adjacent to the International ("Green") Zone—working in literally the same space as U.S. democratization efforts. Also significant is that a show called *Talents* debuted in 2004 on al-Iraqiya, a channel funded by the

U.S. Pentagon. Western press hailed it as "Iraq's answer to *American Idol*," but its origins are less commercial. *Talents* began as a project of the psychological operations team of the 101st Airborne Division in Mosul, to direct Iraqi attention away from satellite programming with anti-American sentiment. Although the format for *Talents* program diverged from that of the *Idols* franchise, some of the democracy-friendly discourse remains. Anne Garrels of NPR reported that "the idea behind the *Talents* show was to show that in post-Saddam Hussein's Iraq, there's a chance for everyone to share the spotlight regardless of family position or personal politics."[45]

Havana Marking's award-winning documentary *Afghan Star* (released in the U.S. in 2009) offers similar words about Tolo TV's singing competition in troubled Afghanistan after the end of Taliban rule. According to Marking's film, the television show *Afghan Star* encourages voting across traditionally fraught ethnic lines, thus promoting a sense of national unity. About the mobile-phone voting system, the film's website declares that "for many [viewers] this is their first encounter with democracy."[46] The *Idols* design and its progeny, intertwined with heavy political rhetoric, have thrived in the current period of intensive international democracy promotion. Although *Pop Idol*, the first effort, emerged before 9/11 escalated U.S. discourse and action toward these ends, the timing turned out to be ideal, for the ideals of the time.

Whether recent regime changes represent part of a new wave of democratization, or a ripple of an earlier wave, remains to be seen. The idea that democratization has historically occurred in "waves" was introduced in Samuel P. Huntington's 1991 book, *The Third Wave: Democratization in the Late Twentieth Century*. A wave, Renske Doorenspleet summarizes, consists of a cluster of regime transitions from non-democratic (particularly authoritarian) to democratic. The designation of "wave" also applies specifically to a time when more transitions *to* democracy take place than regime transitions *from* democracy. For example, Huntington identified the era in which he conducted his study as a "third" wave, spanning the years between the 1974 coup in Portugal to the collapse of the Soviet Union. Some analyses of democratization after Huntington's initial appraisal have proposed that the years of decommunization, through the end of the twentieth century, might represent a recent "fourth wave". And Doorenspleet observes that following 9/11 the U.S. administration appeared to expect that the regime change in Iraq would initiate a fresh wave of democratization throughout the Middle East.[47]

As Doorenspleet recommends, it is important to *define* the democracy that serves as the goal of democratization, and after Huntington, Robert Dahl (1971), and Joseph Schumpeter (1976), she stresses the necessity of *competition* and *inclusion* in that definition.[48] The first provides a system of checks and balances, and the second unlimited suffrage for adult citizens. Further, relying upon the measurements of democratic competition proposed by Ted Robert Gurr et al. in 2005 for the Polity IV project—a database of regime information in independent states—Doorenspleet notes the importance of conditions in which "subordinates" have "equal opportunities to become superordinates."[49] These values of democratic competition are also central to the competitive individualism that stars in the early-twenty-first-century American Dream.

According to 19 Entertainment, *American Idol* itself—the seat of American Dream idolatry and all its attendant ideological articulations—has been broadcast by satellite to 113 nations. If, as the U.S. State Department reports, in 2009 there were 194 independent nations in the world (this number does not include dependent territories), the numbers make *American Idol* available in 58.2 percent of all sovereign states. These have included, among others, territories served by Sony Entertainment Television in Latin America, and by the Star World satellite feed in South and Southeast Asia (including India, Pakistan, Indonesia, the Philippines, Singapore, Malaysia, Thailand, and the Hong Kong Special Administrative Region). The show has also been watched in Israel, first on Star World and then on YES Channel 3, in Turkey on e2, on CTV in Canada, and throughout the United Kingdom.[50] It should be noted that *American Idol* does not air in precisely the same way in all countries; for example, the initial (for the judges) audition of Thomas Lowe, hailing from Manchester, England, but living in Boston during the tryouts for Season 6, was not shown on FOX in the U.S. but was included in an episode broadcast on ITV and ITV2 in the U.K. In 2007 *American Idol* British television personality Cat Deeley hosted *American Idol* on ITV2, in a version repackaged for the U.K. and aired at a delay of a few days.[51] In the U.S., other *Idols* shows may be glimpsed primarily through fan posts offering uploaded videos on the internet. Although each version I have seen retains unique qualities, many familiar elements are also apparent—the opening graphics, the theme, the glossy/neon stage, the sweeping camera angles from above, sometimes even the judges' onscreen personalities. Even the repertoire is often shared. In the summer of 2006 I watched a brief excerpt of the new *Philippine Idol* program that had been posted on the then brand new video site, YouTube.[52] It was a group performance of "I Believe" (see chapter 4).

If Doorenspleet insists on defining the democracy in democratization, then it is also essential to examine the *kind* of democracy associated with recent regime transitions—and, correspondingly, with *Idols* and with *American Idol*. Daniel J. Boorstin cautioned nearly fifty years ago that the global export of American culture, including film and television, transmitted more than just goods. The twentieth-century American displacement of "ideal" by "image," he warned, was also being spread around the world. The *Idols* format transmits an image of democracy dominant in the most recent wave of democratization. In 1996 William Robinson studied the processes of U.S. democracy promotion, concluding that since the early 1980s foreign policy has emphasized a particular ideation of democracy called *polyarchy*. Polyarchic democracy is not holistic; it tends to disregard the development of economic and social systems in favor of a focus on governmental forms. It emphasizes the election, a process that serves as the only available site for participatory policy decisions, although even that is managed by competitive groups of elites.[53] The concept of voting is highlighted and globally disseminated in *Idols* in a way that treats the election similarly, an emblematic stand-in for the totality of democracy. Polyarchic democracy privileges process (i.e., voting) over outcome; the sense of popular empowerment is imperative. This is consistent with the metonymic *Idols* democracy, in which a symbolic ritual (act) is conflated with an implied but absent whole, and the results (who wins) are given less importance than the *process* of creating a salable product—as exemplified during the final weeks of *American Idol*, when the "results" episodes consist of approximately fifty-eight minutes of recap, guest appearances, and filler material, a special commercial filmed for Ford starring the *Idol* finalists, and about two minutes revealing the voting results.

Robinson asserts that economic globalization (the same process that led to transnational programming like *Idols*) is partly responsible for polyarchy's status as an "emergent global political 'superstructure,'" because it "breaks down the autonomy of national political systems" and makes distinct systems difficult to maintain. The development of transnational capitalism, then, contributed to the parallel development of polyarchy, which "provides the basis for the first time in history for world order based on a Gramscian hegemony." Robinson casts polyarchy as exemplary of a hegemonic political system that favors consensual domination, in contrast with the primarily coercive methods of authoritarianism—although the systems each rely on both coercion and consent to different degrees. The empowering political symbol of the democratic election becomes an important element in the establishment of consent.[54]

In *Battle of Symbols,* marketing entrepreneur John Fraim investigates the hegemonic potential of American popular culture in the aftermath of 9/11. Building on Joseph Nye's model of "soft" and "hard" power, he discusses symbols as "the core of soft power,", the co-optive complement to the coercion of military and economic "hard power." For Nye, both soft and hard power are necessary for the U.S. to institute a "successful foreign policy in a global information age," because "the soft power that comes from being a shining 'city upon a hill' . . . does not provide the coercive capability that hard power does." *American Idol*'s democratic symbols—American music, the election, civil religious rhetoric, and American Dream narratives—represent "Institutions, Values, Culture," and "Brands, services, software," and information technology, implying the application of soft power, and underscoring the relationship between global capitalism and global democratization.[55]

The *Idols* election makes the franchise a vehicle for the transmission of a democracy that, like polyarchy, is reduced to its hallmark component, the act of voting. John Hartley notes the significance of mediation in contemporary citizenship, and, as mentioned in chapter 4, calls programs that educate their audiences in this way "democratainment." For Hartley, the idea is connected to globalization, and the potential transnational implications of democratainment have become central to *Idols* discourse. In the context of a transnational state, the impact of Fuller's and Cowell's American Dream is also modified and expanded. Jim Cullen imagines the American Dream, in terms of globalizing effects in the U.S., as a "kind of lingua franca, an idiom that everyone—from corporate executives to hip-hop artists—can presumably understand."[56] If it can work like this, as the nation's common idiom, how might it function in a transnational context?

Considering *Idols* in terms of transnational economic, political, and cultural hegemony raises further questions about genre as well. In the discourse that polarizes "pop" and "rock," the acts of listening to or performing rock are often considered acts of Do-It-Yourself resistance. If there is any degree of resistance in *Idols*, it is to be found in the voting practices of the audience, and in the fostering of a pop version of DIY. In October 2005 FremantleMedia and the Los Angeles internet company Fluid Audio Networks launched a website called "American Idol Underground" (idolunderground.com), a platform separate from the show where artists or bands could pay ($50 per track) to post their music for review by listeners and music celebrities, and potentially win prizes. Promotional literature distributed at Season 5 auditions claimed, "We choose winners democratically based on the ratings of our listeners."[57] The site functioned as an interactive music community and listening station, building on the popularity of other self-publishing formats (including YouTube). The title implied resistance, although whether it resisted the mainstream pop industry or had gone "underground" in relation to the *American Idol* television program is not clear. Sony joined the venture in 2007 offering a series of contests, but as of the summer of 2009 the site was no longer extant.

Beginning in 2005 another "site" of resistance has perennially produced quite a lot of buzz. Although "VoteForTheWorst.com" had existed the previous season, during Season 4 its campaign in "support" of finalist Scott Savol was the subject of numerous newspaper articles. "Vote For the Worst" (VFTW) selects contestants based on perceived characteristics such as lack of talent, entertaining/mockable personalities, or having earned the judges' disdain. The FOX

Broadcasting Company has insisted that the website has no effect on voting,[58] but VFTW claims partial credit for the victory of Season 5's Idol, Taylor Hicks, who is pictured on the site's home page smilingly holding a shirt with the VFTW logo. By Season 6 VFTW had gained so much notoriety that media commentators routinely attributed the Idol longevity of finalist Sanjaya Malakar to the site's efforts, and the name and voice of VFTW founder Dave Della Terza were, like Malakar's, suddenly everywhere. Della Terza created the site, he says, "mostly as a joke after watching season 2," when he "realized that it was a carefully crafted reality TV show and not a talent competition, so I figured it'd be fun to liven it up by voting for the bad singers." On his site he points out that the show begins by glorifying "the bad singers" and the entertaining characters, and even profits from a "Worst of American Idol" DVD, making VFTW actually consistent with some of American Idol's own structure. Della Terza, a community college instructor, considers himself a fan of the show, even a fan of Sanjaya Malakar. "I love the show because it's so terrible," he told me in an e-mail, "I love Sanjaya and all of our VFTW picks . . . and I would love to see him become a huge success!" However, some supporters of the site have understood it in a subversive capacity, as radio personality Howard Stern did while promoting it and campaigning for Sanjaya Malakar on his show. Stern told the New York Times, "We're corrupting the entire thing . . . All of us are routing 'American Idol.' It's so great. The No. 1 show in television and it's getting ruined." Either way, Della Terza sees a point to his site, drawing a connection between its encouragement of Idol voting and the benefits of political voting: "I think VFTW is a prime example of what happens when one person states their opinion and tries to start a cause. Is it important? Not at all. But VFTW shows that everyone has a voice, and that is obviously true in politics, where so many people don't bother to vote because they think their vote doesn't count."[59]

But though viewers may question the level of agency actually afforded them in the innovative Idols voting processes, the implications of agency remain crucial. Some see a kind of symbolic power, or power over symbols, in this millennial reconfiguration of consumer choice. John Fraim asserts that, today, "leading symbols in an electric consumer democracy like America are products, people, places, and events, 'voted' into ascendancy (bottom up) rather than proclaimed into ascendancy (top down) by producers and leaders." Others have understood that "democracy" of consumption as directly linked to monopolies and oligopolies of production. Appadurai contends that in global cultural landscapes "the consumer is consistently helped to believe that he or she is an actor, where in fact he or she is at best a chooser."[60] Regardless of which viewpoint one takes, clearly the choices consumers and television viewers make can be enormously political, inseparable from the politics of their daily lives and from the politics of the new transnational world.

The influence of the *Idol* election is now omnipresent, with viewer-voting shows nearly de rigeur for every major television network in the world and consumer choice suddenly dressed *everywhere* in the trappings of the democratic process. The annexing of the term "Idol" to virtually any other word has come to be nearly synonymous with competition, especially one in which the outcome is determined by voting.[61] Watching other programming, Americans have voted for favorite celebrity dancers (*Dancing With the Stars*), new dance stars (*So You Think You Can Dance*), potential Hollywood directors (*On the Lot*), and a new lead vocalist for rock band INXS (*Rock Star: INXS*). On the internet a recent trend has consumers voting for new snack flavors and even for favorite *American Idol*–branded ice cream, and the government asked to hear Americans' voices in the race for special stamp designs (*Star Wars* in 2007, *The Simpsons* in 2009). On CNN's website there is a continuous series asking viewers to "vote" on topics like the fairness of Paris Hilton's 2007 jail sentence or whether the recession had ended by the fall of 2009. Here the totality of democracy is again concentrated into that single act of voting, abandoning other principles and practices. Apart from Hillary Clinton's use of the *Idol*-esque popular vote to select her 2008 campaign song (which she later changed), such choices unsurprisingly have little direct political consequence. But this ubiquity does not diminish the import of voting; on the contrary, it underscores the central place of the act in contemporary discourse about democracy. *Idol* voting is no idle act—this reality-show definition of democracy is intertwined with the reality of democracy promotion in the deadly serious realm of geopolitics.

CONCLUSIONS

Although the cultural-political relevance of *American Idol* in the United States may not feel as starkly, urgently apparent in 2010 as that of *Afghan Star* or *Iraq Star,* it is no less considerable in the long-term development of national identity. In 2006, during the premiere of *American Idol*'s fifth season, host Ryan Seacrest announced that "the show is now an integral part of American culture." With this avowal, those behind the scenes declared America thoroughly *Idol*-ized, and confirmed their awareness of the potential power in their prize invention. That power, and *American Idol*'s phenomenal success, hinge largely on the show's employment of established ideas and ideologies of Americanness—on its provision of a flashy, chrome-and-neon stage for the performance of a historically familiar and always emergent politics of American identity.

Reiterating one of the paradoxes of popular culture, *American Idol*'s very popularity consistently earns it critical derision and frequent relegation to the status of embarrassing guilty pleasure. My research grew out of questions about this contradictory quality, and about why the show matters. In the end I have found that what superficially appears to be a form of light entertainment is, in fact, doing serious cultural work, and is a powerful tool in the process of deciding, and selling, who we are.

This book, in editing in 2010, has considered the first nine seasons of *American Idol*. Each year since 2002, the program's structure has changed subtly, adapting and expanding to acknowledge multiple discourses of music, politics, and identity, and appealing to the interests of as inclusive an audience as possible. I have argued that, in doing so, *American Idol* presents an idealized litany of national ideals, born of the country's foundational philosophical, political, and religious principles, and constantly reinvented. In the performative process, *American Idol* also simultaneously confirms the erosion of numerous discursive boundaries and illuminates the marking of identity as a campaign strategy, as a source of both cultural and financial capital, and as a core practice in American music. The show's continued resonance rests largely on two sets of disemic[62] codes that summarize the current shape of American culture: (1) as I noted in my introduction, a need for the reinforcement of clearly defined identities at a time when lines are blending toward dialecticism everywhere else, between production and consumption, and actor and viewer, between musical genres, the public and the private, and between politics and entertainment; and (2) a related series of paradoxical dynamics—the difficult equilibrium between cultural value and market value, between values such as individuality and community, between the unique and the familiar, skepticism and fandom, between desired political power and undesirable exploitation. Furthermore, the show documents a complicated entwinement of authenticities, suggesting that to elect an American Idol is to both name and celebrate an authentic American, and to *act as* an authentic American, as a participant in the construction and marketing of democracy. The Idolizing of America is more than a fetishism of fame and fortune, but a fetishism of democracy, and—in all its multivocality—of Americanness itself.

As my writing comes to a close many are speculating that 2011, the end of *American Idol*'s current contract, will be its last season on television. Considering the 2010 replacement of Paula Abdul, the impending departures of Simon Cowell, Ellen DeGeneres, and Kara DioGuardi, and the upcoming U.S. version of Cowell's megahit *The X Factor,* this book could indeed serve as a long good-bye. But whatever its ultimate legacy will be, *Idol* has had an undeniable impact on the way the world hears America singing, and in how we chart the place of music and media in the continual making of a nation.

EPILOGUE · CRYSTALLIZED

Ohio is pivotal in any national election. The balance of red and blue in its political allegiances has lately tended toward purple, fueling some intense partisan anxiety. But in the *Idol* election of 2010, there was no question who had the Buckeye vote, or who had captured the Heartland's heart. I had the extraordinary fortune to be living in the northwest region of the state (in Bowling Green) during Season 9, when local singer-songwriter Crystal Bowersox coasted through to the Top 2. From the moment she was inducted into the Top 24, it seemed that the only newsworthy topic for miles around was Crystal's performance every Tuesday night, and for the first time, I watched firsthand as an *American Idol* contestant galvanized a community.

Crystal's story was simultaneously a standard *Idol* idyll and anything but typical. Raised in a farm town called Elliston in Ottawa County, she followed the classic American Dream path through hard times, and the rock narrative of the Dream paying small-time dues toward Hollywood. Like Season 3 winner Fantasia, she was a single mother and vocally devoted to the idea of making a better life for her child (fans, following Randy Jackson's lead, took to calling her "Mama Sox" early in the season, as she frequently talked about her toddler son onscreen). But she was also unusual, one of several Season 9 singers touted for their anti-commercial sensibilities, an "artist," the judges insisted repeatedly, who rarely appeared onstage without her guitar, and covered Janis Joplin and Tracy Chapman instead of Whitney Houston and Mariah Carey. Though there had been signs of interest in earlier seasons, it nevertheless seemed a startling about-face for *Idol* to promote singers like Crystal, disavowing the preceding years of proud pop promotion in favor of contestants with acoustic folk and indie rock inclinations. (Kara DioGuardi identified her as a singer of "Americana rock.") She epitomized the genred *Idol* ideology of rock, asserting a strategy of "stay[ing] true to myself." In the same jargon of authenticity and individuality they had applied to previous rockers, the judges praised Crystal continually for being "real" and told her "this is what we talk about, when people know who they are."[1]

Crystal had begun performing publicly as a child—toward the end of the *Idol* season videos circulated of her performing, aged thirteen, at a county fair—both because of her love for music and to help her father make ends meet.[2] Though she left home to live in Chicago for nearly five years, by the time of her departure for *Idol* in Hollywood, the 24-year-old was once again a fixture at East Toledo's Papa's Tavern, and had played every Monday for a year and a half at a combination pizzeria/bar on Conant Street in Maumee. It was there, at the Village Idiot, that I first encountered the fierce local pride that would characterize the Season 9 experience for Ohioan viewers.

The first time I entered the Village Idiot, that pride was in abundant evidence. A larger-than-life portrait of Crystal graced the wall, gazing down upon around thirty boisterous patrons and staff. The room radiated excitement, even nervous tension—the first thing I heard as my party sat down was the resounding command, "when Crystal comes on, everyone shut the fuck up!" Everyone did, raptly turning their attention to the three screens above the bar as Crystal sang "Me & Bobby McGee." They only broke their silence to add their cheers to the judges' praise, and when Crystal's regular bassist Frankie May appeared onscreen in the studio audience. May, a locally known artist and close friend of Crystal, had played the Monday night set with her since the beginning. He was one of several Village Idiot associates who traveled to California to attend *Idol* tapings during the season, and before the last week of the show, the venue held a fundraiser so that he could fly there for the finale (the money donated exceeded his needs, and the surplus was donated to the Juvenile Diabetes Research Foundation). Others had gone out to Hollywood to support their Idol as well, including manager Nathan Woodward, who regularly kept in touch with Crystal while she was in California.[3]

Neither Mr. Woodward nor bar co-owners John and Nikki Schafer had been fans of *American Idol* in previous seasons ("I thought it was cheesy," admitted Mr. Schafer), but they were always fans of Crystal, and by the end of March Nathan could list, in order, every selection Crystal had sung to date. "Our girl," Ms. Schafer called her. The staff and patrons admired her talent and her "down-to-earth" demeanor long before they knew she had auditioned for the show, and their faithful attendance at her Monday night performances soon turned into Tuesday night gathered around the bar's televisions. Everyone was aware that Crystal was a priority then. Staff told me that Mark Mikel, whose band played the Village Idiot on Tuesdays at 9:00, always waited to start if Crystal's segment hadn't aired by that time. The moment she stepped off the *Idol* stage, though, the show was over for the crowd, and no one watched the remaining contestants. Mr. Woodward wrote Crystal's 1-866-IDOLS number on the chalkboard next to the bar, and when we talked, estimated that he and bartender Ed Lopez had voted 500 times together the week before.[4]

During her time on *American Idol,* Ohio came to Crystal. Her son and her then-boyfriend stayed in California for the duration, her father attended the show (once provoking Crystal to a brief bout of onscreen tears much discussed in *Idol*-related media), her bass player visited, and the Village Idiot staff, too. And she brought even more pieces of home to Hollywood. Midway through the season, she began to make herself quite literally at home onstage when she sent for her old mic stand, the one she'd built out of a lamp given to her by the owner of Papa's Tavern.[5]

As the season finale approached, she also brought Hollywood to Ohio. On May 14, the Toledo area had a chance to show Crystal its support in person. When the Top 3 contestants left California for their hometown visits, Crystal returned not to just one place, but to a parade in Toledo, a family celebration in Elliston, and a fairgrounds stage in nearby Oak Harbor. Officials offered her the keys to both Toledo (a crystal key, even) and Elliston. Her agenda comprised both producers' plans for *Idol* footage and some personal stops (including a secret visit to play at Papa's Tavern) that were never announced or attended by the media.

In the late morning, fans lined Summit Street and swarmed after Crystal's motorcade as it turned down Water Street—clusters of little girls clutching homemade signs, men and women in t-shirts proclaiming their support, teenagers from the Toledo School for the Arts, where Crystal had been a student. She emerged from her limousine to sit on top of the sun roof, waving and taking her own photographs as the crowd thrust their mobile phones and cameras in the air, while a Fox crew captured it all for *Idol* footage. Disembarking from the limousine to transfer to her parade vehicle (a Ford Mustang), she stopped to greet those thronging around her. She handed out her signature sunflowers, shook hands, showed a child her insulin pump, and kissed a student on his cheek. Area newspapers counted the attendance close to 10,000 as the party moved to Levis Square to see Crystal honored by mayor Mike Bell and hear her short concert.[6] She sang Alanis Morissette's "One Hand in My Pocket," and "Holy Toledo," a composition she'd written at 17. Her recording of "Holy Toledo" dominated the rotations of two local radio stations during the last weeks of the *Idol* season. After the home-visit footage aired on *American Idol,* Crystal told Ryan Seacrest that she was pleased the producers had used "Holy Toledo" for the soundtrack, since she had been "fighting all season long for some originals." And she recognized the significance assigned to the song, and to her stardom, at home. Northwest Ohio, she explained, had been "in kind of a slump for a while," and "Holy Toledo" had become an anthem for her city, had "given the area so much hope, something to look forward to."[7]

As she sang in Toledo, thousands pressed into the square, holding signs and children aloft—one little girl, atop her father's shoulders near where I stood, raised a tiny guitar above her head in solidarity with Crystal. (Acoustic and toy guitars, in fact, were a common sight among the masses there.) In the crush of people, I spoke with a longtime Toledo resident who said he'd never heard of Elliston until Crystal made the town famous—an indication that she had brought her community together geographically as well as emotionally. After Crystal left downtown Toledo for Elliston, between five and six thousand people made their way to Oak Harbor for the event advertised as "Bowerstock."[8] On my way, all along the interstates and county roads heading to the Ottawa County fairgrounds, I saw further signs of local devotion—signs planted on farmhouse lawns and spelled out on Mc-Donald's marquees, soaped onto the windows of local businesses and strung across the streets. "We love you, Crystal," they proclaimed. "We believe in you. You're our Idol. Welcome home."

By early evening, I stood in another crowd under the highly personalized "Bowerstock" banner, which was decorated with a peace sign, a cross in place of the letter "t," an acoustic guitar like Crystal's, a motorcycle (Crystal's father belongs to a local group, and the Toledo mayor had led the parade that morning on his own motorcycle), and, to symbolize local crops, an ear of corn. The event was set up like a show at a county fair, complete with funnel cakes and souvenirs—I bought a commemorative t-shirt from representatives of Elliston's Trinity Church; inscribed above a list of the songs she had performed on *American Idol* was the epigraph "She left Elliston a singer and came home a star." It was sold rolled up in a plastic, jumbo-sized Coca-Cola cup, but at Crystal's request all proceeds went to the Diabetes Youth Services (DYS). The earnings from another T-shirt, designed by Toledo School for the Arts alumnus Jacob Parr, were donated to the Juvenile Diabetes Research Foundation (JDRF). The JDRF's special events manager, Shelley Crossley, told me that Crystal herself had attended a DYS summer camp to learn how to manage her health after her Type 1 diagnosis. She also said that Crystal had needed to make some adjustments while on *American Idol:* a sudden hospitalization in early March had required the show to reorganize its performance schedule. Season 5 finalist and JDRF spokesman Elliott Yamin, according to Ms. Crossley, had been mentoring Crystal in such matters.[9] Crystal had become an inspiration to other young people dealing with a Type I diagnosis, she added, an assertion supported by the sign I had seen held proudly up at the Toledo event: *Diabetics Rock!*

As May 14 was officially declared "Crystal Bowersox Day" in Ottawa County, Crystal received the key to Elliston from the Trinity Church council president and an American flag from congresswoman Marcy Kaptur, who called her "America's precious daughter of song." She sang with Frankie May in a set that included "Holy Toledo" and

Figure E.1. The crowd begins to gather at Bowerstock, about 2½ hours before Crystal's arrival. Ottawa County Fairgrounds in Oak Harbor, May 14, 2010.

another original song, and two selections she had previously performed on *American Idol.* Chatting easily with her audience, she thanked them for their votes and support in a statement evocative of civil religious electoral language: "God bless you all for carrying me this far."

She left the fairgrounds to open a Toledo Mud Hens' game with the first pitch and the "Star Spangled Banner," drawing record-setting ticket sales of 13,200. And minor league baseball wasn't the only local enterprise to benefit from Crystal's success. Two weeks later, when I arrived at the Village Idiot to watch the final *Idol* performance night, I was part of an assembly nearly five times the size of the one I had experienced in March. People were packed into corners, and filling the standing room on the same stage where Crystal had played her

Monday night gigs. Bartender Jason Szczublewski said that the establishment had become something of a pilgrimage site in the preceding weeks, the staff fielding phone calls and visitors looking for a Crystal sighting.[10] If the first evening I had spent there seemed energized, the excitement for the finale was palpable. This time, as we watched Crystal sing Patty Griffin's gospel-tinged tribute to Martin Luther King, Jr., "Up to the Mountain," there was more pizza and less tipsiness. The room was more diverse in age and ethnicity, there were more families with children, and the cheering more than matched that of the enormous studio audience shouting at high volume on the bar's televisions.

As the competition played out between Crystal and Chicago-area resident Lee DeWyze, to some it felt more like watching a sporting event than a singing competition. For John Schafer, it was "like rooting for our home team in the championships." (He could not have been alone; the season finale the next day included a group performance of Delta Goodrem's "Together We Are One," written for the 2006 Commonwealth Games.) And Jodi Szczublewski, Jason's sister and a regular at the weekly *Idol* watch, imagined the final vote as a rivalry between Chicago and Toledo; the Idol would be determined by "whichever one's got a bigger heart." Nearly every viewer I talked with expressed staunch conviction that Crystal would win. When she lost the next night, edged out by what Ryan Seacrest announced was less than two percent, it didn't seem to matter. The thousands watching via a huge screen in Toledo's Huntington Center hooted in dismay, but then some resolutely raised their signs again. On television, Fox Toledo kept flashing its "Congratulations, Crystal!" screen all night, regardless of the outcome. The news also caught at least one prematurely celebratory fan by surprise, leading to a kind of "Dewey Defeats Truman" moment for the digital age. In the last minutes before Telescope, Inc. delivered its results to Ryan Seacrest on the Nokia stage in Hollywood, a friend wrote to tell me that Crystal had already been recorded on Wikipedia as the winner.[11] At 9:55 PM when I checked the Wikipedia page for *American Idol,* Crystal's name was indeed highlighted along with all of the previous seasons' winners. Since we were on Eastern Standard Time and the announcement had not been made yet, it could not have been an informed entry. By the time I refreshed the page at 10:08, after winner Lee DeWyze's name had been called and the credits had rolled, the information had been corrected.

Since the finale, Crystal has remained a persistent focus here. Weeks later, I still overheard frequent conversations about the shock of her unexpected loss, and in early July as I add this epilogue, "Holy Toledo" continues as part of the regular lineup on Toledo's KISS FM. Perhaps most locally appropriate, there are currently plans in the Ohio village of Whitehouse for a corn maze based on images of Crystal and her guitar (www.whitehousecornmaze.com). The consensus among Northwest Ohio residents and media, it seems, is that she is still a hero.

While only in my second year as a resident of Northwest Ohio, I could not help feeling swept up in the local enthusiasm, nor could I deny my eventually partisan leanings. And as I watched and lived the engagement of my community in the chronicles of Crystal, I saw that her story drew together several of *American Idol*'s elemental themes: the relationship between discourses of musical authenticity and the American Dream, the compelling design of participatory television, the powerful political experience of place displaced onto the television screen—the ways that twenty-first century Americans entwine old tropes of democratic representation, of community and individuality, into their negotiation of identity. I saw the nation writ small, and Northwest Ohio writ large, on a hand-inked t-shirt in the crowd at Bowerstock: a Sharpied declaration that Northwest Ohio had incontestably "been Crystal-ized"—as, through the singing contest, America has been Idolized.

NOTES

Introduction

In this book all ethnographic quotations and quotes from idolonfox.com strive to maintain the original language and spellings of the speaker or writer, even when unconventional.

1. "No Boundaries" was co-written by Cathy Dennis, Season 8 judge Kara DioGuardi, and Mitch Allan (for EMI Music Publishing, Ltd.; Bug Music; Sunshine Terrace Music; Bughouse; Matzoh Ball Music; and Art for Art's Sake Music).

Fredric Jameson's quote is from *The Cultural Turn: Selected Writings on the Postmodern, 1983–1998* (London: Verso, 1998), 2. Regarding Lévi-Strauss, see James Boon, "Claude Lévi-Strauss" in *The Return of Grand Theory in the Human Sciences,* ed. Quentin Skinner (Cambridge: Cambridge University Press, 1990[1985]), 165.

2. Jack Citrin, et al., 2001, "Multiculturalism in American Public Opinion," *British Journal of Political Science* 31, no. 2 (1998).

3. The quotes can be found, respectively, in Bill Brown, "Identity Culture," *American Literary History* 10, no. 1 (1998): 165 (emphasis in original); and Akhil Gupta and James Ferguson, "Beyond 'Culture': Space, Identity, and the Politics of Difference," *Cultural Anthropology* 7, no. 1 (1992): 12.

4. Both quotes are from Josh Kun, *Audiotopia: Music, Race, and America* (Berkeley: University of California Press, 2005), 30.

5. On identities, see Henry Jenkins, *Convergence Culture: Where Old and New Media Collide* (New York: New York University Press, 2006), 62–63. On relational interaction, see James Clifford *The Predicament of Culture: Twentieth-Century Ethnography, Literature, and Art* (Cambridge, Mass.: Harvard University Press, 1988), 12. Sara Cohen's quote is from "Ethnography and Popular Music Studies," *Popular Music* 12, no. 2 (1993): 132.

6. FremantleMedia, the international production company that distributes these programs, lists *Idols* on its website as the name of the franchise in its totality (www.fremantlemedia.com, May 20, 2007). In this volume I use the plural term *Idols* to refer to the franchise as a whole, but the singular *Idol* as an abbreviation for *American Idol.*

229

7. Not everyone who attends is there to audition; many come only to support friends or family who plan to sing.

8. In this book I use the term "semifinalists" to refer to the "top 30" contestants in Season 1; the top 32 in Seasons 2 and 3; the top 24 in Seasons 4, 5, 6, and 7; the top 36 in Season 8; and the top 24 in Season 9. I use the term "finalists" to indicate the top 10 of Season 1, and the top 12 of the subsequent seasons until Season 8, which had a top 13 group. Season 9 returned to a top 12.

9. Corey Moss, "Think You Know Everything about 'American Idol'? Think Again," MTV.com, May 25, 2004, www.mtv.com/news/articles/1487448/20040525/id_1235723.jhtml.

10. According to *American Idol,* FOX Network, www.americanidol.com.

11. Cingular acquired AT&T Wireless in late 2004 and the name "Cingular Wireless" replaced AT&T's in the lineup of major *American Idol* sponsors. Not long after, SBC Communications acquired the AT&T Corporation and appropriated its brand name, so that by January 2007 the name AT&T Mobility was the one associated with *American Idol* sponsorship.

12. FOXNews.com, "Wednesday's 'American Idol' Draws 36.9 Million Viewers," January 19, 2007, www.foxnews.com/story/0,2933,244888,00.html.

13. For the Telescope report, see Telescope Creative Interactive Solutions 2003a, "Case Studies: American Idol 'Season1' DRTV Viewer Voting," www.telescope.tv/americanIdol1.html. The 2009 announcement was made on *American Idol,* FOX Network, May 20, 2009.

14. First season data is from CBSNews.com 2002. Eighth season data is from *American Idol,* FOX Network, May 20, 2009.

15. Season 7 data on viewers is from Nielsen Media Research, "The Nielsen Company Measures the 'American Idol' Phenom," May 1, 2008, www.nielsen.com/media/2008/pr_080515.html. Information on ratings that same night is from Benjamin Toff, "Ratings: 'Idol' Can't Quite Hit the High Note," *New York Times,* January 16, 2008, http://tvdecoder.blogs.nytimes.com/tag/american-idol/page/2/.

16. In the summer of 2002 major sponsors paid less than $10 million for a season-long *Idol* marketing package (Theresa Howard, "Real Winner of 'American Idol': Coke," *USAToday,* n.d. 2002, www.usatoday.com/money/advertising/2002-09-08-idol_x.htm); by 2008 the price tag had gone up to $35 million (Gail Schiller, "Idol" Sponsors Now Paying $35 Million Each, Reuters.com, January 16, 2008, www.reuters.com/article/sphereNews/idUSN1620948620080116?sp=true&view=sphere), and Season 7 earned $903 million in advertising revenue outside of product placements (Alex Dobuzinskis, "Clouds on Horizon for 'American Idol' Juggernaut?" Reuters.com, May 17, 2009, www.reuters.com/article/entertainmentNews/idUSTRE54G1BP20090517). As of 2002 previous reality television advertising had not reached these levels (Michael Starr, "'Idol' Rich: 26 Million for Show's Ads," October 15, 2002, www.foxnews.com/story/0,2933,65664,00.html).

17. For more on the first and third scenarios, see chapter 7, this volume. For the second, see Ashling O'Connor "Riots as TV Win Splits Communities," *Times Online,* September 29, 2007, www.timesonline.co.uk/tol/news/world/asia/article2553740.ece.

18. See also Timothy J. Cooley, Katherine Meizel, and Nasir Sayed, "Virtual Fieldwork" in *Shadows in the Field: New Perspectives for Fieldwork in Ethnomusicology,*

ed. Timothy J. Cooley and Gregory F. Barz, 2nd ed. (Oxford: Oxford University Press, 2008).

19. On diffuse time-space, see George E. Marcus, "Ethnography in/of the World System: The Emergence of Multi-Sited Ethnography," *Annual Review of Anthropology* 24 (1995): 96. On multisite research, see Christine Hine, *Virtual Ethnography* (London: Sage, 2000), 41. See also Cooley, Meizel, and Sayed "Virtual Fieldwork," 91.

20. Timothy Rice, "Toward a Mediation of Field Methods and Field Experience in Ethnomusicology," in *Shadows in the Field: New Perspectives for Fieldwork in Ethnomusicology*, ed. Gregory F. Barz and Timothy J. Cooley (Oxford: Oxford University Press, 1997), 107.

21. Marcus, "Ethnography in/of the World System," 105.

22. Gregory F. Barz and Timothy J. Cooley, eds., *Shadows in the Field* (see n19 above); also see my experiences recounted in Cooley, Meizel, and Sayed, "Virtual Fieldwork."

23. See Cooley, Meizel, and Sayed, "Virtual Fieldwork."

24. Jameson, *The Cultural Turn*, 2; and Frederic Jameson, *Postmodernism, or, The Cultural Logic of Late Capitalism* (Durham, N.C.: Duke University Press, 1991), 2.

25. Quotes are from Jameson, *The Cultural Logic of Late Capitalism*, 275; and Reebee Garofalo, *Rockin' Out: Popular Music in the USA*, 2nd ed. (Needham Heights, Mass.: Allyn & Bacon, 2002), xi.

1. Facing Reality

The author has applied Bielby's and Harrington's model of audience bonds previously in Katherine Meizel, "'Be a Fan, Not a Hater': Identity Politics and the Audience in American Idol," *Pacific Review of Ethnomusicology* 12 (2006), www.ethnomusic.ucla.edu/pre/Vo112/Vo112html/V12Meizel.html.

1. Phillip Sherwell, "Women Fans May Sue over Pop Idol Who 'Wasn't All He Seemed,'" Telegraph.co.uk, March 5, 2006, www.telegraph.co.uk/news/main.jhtml?xml=/news/2006/03/05/wido105.xml.

2. Aiken's statements quoted, respectively, in Erik Hedegaard, "Cover Story: New Kid on the Block," *Rolling Stone,* July 10, 2003, www.rollingstone.com/news/story/23218342/new_kid_on_the_block/2003; Carrie Borzillo-Vrenna, "Clay Aiken Speaks out about Rumors," *People,* September 20, 2006, www.people.com/people/article/0,,1536827,00.html; and David Caplan, "Clay Aiken: I'm a Gay Dad," *People,* September 24, 2008, www.people.com/people/article/0,,20228488,00.html.

3. Brooke Anderson, "Showbiz Tonight," interview transcript at CNN.com, September 22, 2006, http://transcripts.cnn.com/TRANSCRIPTS/0609/22/sbt.01.html.

4. Steve P, "Pop News: Top of the Pops," BBC.co.uk, March 23, 2006.

5. Joshua Gamson, *Claims to Fame: Celebrity in Contemporary America,* (Berkeley: University of California Press, 1994), 146.

6. Interview October 22, 2004.

7. It has received only two awards: one a special Governors' Award for its charity special *Idol Gives Back;* and one, in 2009, for Directing for episode 883. In 2005, the televised Emmy Awards ceremony included an "Emmy Idol" feature involving entertainment stars singing for viewers' votes.

8. Columbia Pictures, 1997. The film was released in the United States at the beginning of 1998.

9. The Spice Girls were initially formed under the direction of Heart Management, but they soon signed with Fuller at 19 Entertainment.

10. Michael G. Robinson, "The Innocents Abroad: S Club 7's America," *Popular Music and Society* 27, no. 3 (2004): 1.

11. Anna McCarthy, "'Stanley Milgram, Allen Funt, and Me': Postwar Social Science and the 'First Wave' of Reality TV," in *Reality TV: Remaking Television Culture*, ed. Susan Murray and Laurie Ouellette (New York: New York University Press, 2004), 24. Bradley Clissold, "*Candid Camera* and the origins of Reality TV: Contextualising a Historical Precedent," in *Understanding Reality Television*, ed. Su Holmes and Deborah Jermyn (London: Routledge, 2004), 35.

12. Phillip Auslander, "LIVENESS: Performance and the Anxiety of Simulation," in *Performance and Cultural Politics*, ed. Elin Diamond (London: Routledge, 1996), 198, 203–208.

13. Pressbox.co.uk 2006, "Former Clay Aiken Fans Respond to Simon Cowell Comments from Larry King Live," March 21, www.pressbox.co.uk/detailed /Entertainment/FORMER_CLAY_AIKEN_FANS_RESPOND_TO_SIMON _COWELL_COMMENTS_FROM_LARRY_KING_LIVE_58613.html.

14. Edward Wyatt, "'Idol' Group Numbers: Not So Live After All," *New York Times*, March 25, 2009, www.nytimes.com/2009/03/26/arts/television/26idol .html?_r=2.

15. Gil Kaufman, "Jennifer Hudson Lip-Synched Super Bowl Performance," MTV.com, February 2, 2009, www.mtv.com/news/articles/1604041/20090202 /hudson__jennifer.jhtml.

16. Interview, September 8, 2005.

17. Definition of the *hyperreal* and the *simulacrum* from Jean Baudrillard, *Jean Baudrillard, Selected Writings*, ed. Mark Poster (Stanford, Calif.: Stanford University Press, 1988), 169. Remarks on hyperrealist logic from Baudrillard, *The Gulf War Did Not Take Place* (Bloomington: Indiana University Press, 1995), 27. The essay was originally published as *La Guerre du Golfe n'a pas eu lieu*, a series of articles in *Liberation*, in 1991. Baudrillard also responded to the 9/11 attacks, in *Le Monde*, with his piece "The Spirit of Terrorism," November 2, 2001.

18. Jenkins, *Convergence Cultures*, 60, 78.

19. *American Idol* executive producer Nigel Lythgoe appeared as one of the regular judges on *Popstars* in the U.K. before he joined 19 TV (www.BBCNews .com, "New Job for 'Nasty Nigel.'" March 29, 2001, http://news.bbc.co.uk/1/hi /entertainment/tv_and_radio/1249681.stm).

20. James Friedman, *Reality Squared: Televisual Discourse on the Real* (New Brunswick, N.J.: Rutgers University Press., 2002), 7; also cited in Su Holmes and Deborah Jermyn, "Introduction," in *Understanding Reality Television*, ed. Su Holmes and Deborah Jermyn (London: Routledge, 2004), 5.

21. Holmes and Jermyn, "Introduction," 1–15.

22. Catherine Lumby, "Real Appeal: The Ethics of Reality TV," in *Remote Control: New Media, New Ethics*, ed. Catharine Lumby and Elspeth Probyn (Cambridge: Cambridge University Press, 2003), 12.

23. Quote from Jenkins, *Convergence Culture*, 88. On product placement, see Mary-Lou Galician, *Handbook of Product Placement in the Mass Media* (London: Routledge, 2004), 12.

24. Statistics from Mike Brunker, "'Idol' Empire Conquers New Multimedia Worlds," MSNBC.com, January 15, 2007, www.msnbc.msn.com/id/16580677/; and from Steven Zeitchik and Nicole Laporte, "The Money Tree: Everyone Seems to Be Joining the 'Idol' Rich," Variety.com, May 7, 2006, www.variety.com/article/VR 1117942693.html?categoryid=16&cs=1.

25. In this paragraph, Lumby, "Real Appeal," 12; Jean Baudrillard, *America,* trans. Chris Turner (London: Verso, 1989), 58–59.

Statistics for American Idol come from American Idol, *The Search for a Superstar,* dir. Bruce Gowers, Nigel Lythgoe, and Ken Warwick (videocassette), and from *American Idol* broadcasts, beginning with the tally announced on January 18, 2005. The disconsolate teenager quoted appeared on *American Idol,* FOX Network, January 16, 2007.

26. Robert Stebbins, *Amateurs, Professionals, and Serious Leisure* (Montreal: McGill-Queen's Press, 1992), 38.

27. Jose Antonio Vargas, "How a Villager Became the Queen of All Media," *Washington Post,* April 20, 2009, www.washingtonpost.com/wp-dyn/content /article/2009/04/19/AR2009041900508.html?nav=hcmodule.

28. In this paragraph, Andrew Keen quoted from *The Cult of the Amateur: How Today's Internet Is Killing Our Culture* (New York: Random House, 2007), 36. Ellen Page is cited in Luchina Fisher, "Susan Boyle's Talent Revealed Early," ABCNews .com, May 4, 2009, http://abcnews.go.com/Entertainment/SummerConcert/story ?id=7496425&page=12009.

For a stunningly thorough discussion of the origins and meanings of the term "noble savage," see Ter Ellingson, *The Myth of the Noble Savage* (Berkeley: University of California Press, 2001).

29. In this paragraph, Stebbins cited from *Amateurs, Professionals, and Serious Leisure*; Todd Gitlin from "Prime Time Ideology: The Hegemonic Process in Television Entertainment," in *Television: The Critical View,* ed. Horace Newcomb, 6th ed. (Oxford: Oxford University Press, 2000), 584.

On the demystification of television, see Lumby, "Real Appeal," 11–12. For discussion of reality TV's emphasis on the importance of information as cultural capital, see Lisa A. Lewis, *The Adoring Audience: Fan Culture and Popular Media* (London: Routledge, 1992).

30. Sonia Livingstone and Peter Lunt, *Talk on Television: Audience Participation and Public Debate* (London: Routledge, 1994), 172; after Erving Goffman, *The Presentation of the Self in Everyday Life* (New York: Anchor Books, 1959), and Anthony Giddens, "Time, Space and Regionalisation," in *Social Relations and Spatial Structures,* ed. Derek Gregory and John Urry (Basingstoke, England: Macmillan, 1985).

31. Mary Beth Haralovich and Michael W. Trosset, "'Expect the Unexpected': Narrative Pleasure and Uncertainty Due to Chance in Survivor," in *Reality TV: Remaking Television Culture,* ed. Susan Murray and Laurie Ouellette (New York: New York University Press, 2004), 76, 93. Ryan Seacrest quoted from *American Idol,* FOX Network, January 19, 2004.

32. John McGrath, *Loving Big Brother: Performance, Privacy and Surveillance Space* (London: Routledge, 2004), vi.

33. For discussion of *The Real World*, see Jon Kraszewski, "Country Hicks and Urban Cliques: Mediating Race, Reality, and Liberalism on MTV's *The Real World*," in *Reality TV: Remaking Television Culture*, ed. Susan Murray and Laurie Ouellette (New York: New York University Press, 2004).

34. Livingstone and Lunt, *Talk on Television*, 172.

35. The above discussion is based on L. S. Kim and Gilberto Moisés Blasini, "The Performance of Multicultural Identity in U.S. Network Television: Shiny, Happy *Popstars* (Holding Hands)," *Emergences* 11, no. 2 (2001): see especially 281, 290–91. (Lisa Lowe also argues that better media representation does not equal actual racial equity in her book *Immigrant Acts: On Asian American Cultural Politics* [Durham, N.C.: Duke University Press, 1996], 88.) For my piece in *Slate*, see Katherine Meizel, "Idol Loves Idol: Sweater Vests and Presidential Candidates, from Katherine Meizel to Jody Rosen," May 23, 2007, www.slate.com/id/2158332/entry/2166866/.

36. Holmes and Jermyn, "Introduction," 5.

37. In 2003 the motto "fair and balanced" attained widespread currency, when Fox News sued satirist Al Franken over his appropriation of the words in his book title *Lies and the Lying Liars Who Tell Them: A Fair and Balanced Look at the Right*. Fox had registered its slogan as a trademark in 1998 (CBSNews.com, "FOX News Drops Franken Lawsuit," August 25, 2003, www.cbsnews.com/stories/2003/08/12/entertainment/main567800.shtml).

38. Henry Jenkins, "Covergence Is Reality," *Technology Review*, June 6, 2003, www.technologyreview.com.

39. For theories of audience formation by the media industry, see Ien Ang, *Desperately Seeking the Audience* (London: Routledge, 1991); John Hartley, "Invisible Fictions: Television Audiences, Paedocracy, Pleasure," *Textual Practice* 1, no. 2 (1987); Shaun Moores, *Interpreting Audiences: The Ethnography of Media Consumption* (London: Sage, 1993); Estella Tincknell and Parvati Raghuram, "*Big Brother*: Reconfiguring the 'Active' Audience of Cultural Studies?" in *Understanding Reality Television*, ed. Su Holmes and Deborah Jermyn (London: Routledge, 2004), 253.

40. For theories on the active role of audiences, see Louis Althusser, "Ideology and Ideological State Apparatuses: Notes Toward an Investigation," in *Lenin and Philosophy and Other Essays*, trans. Ben Brewster (New York: Monthly Review Press, 2001 [1970]); J. G. Blumler and Eliu Katz, eds., *The Uses of Mass Communications: Current Perspectives on Gratifications Research* (Beverly Hills, Calif.: Sage, 1974); Stuart Hall, "Encoding/Decoding," in *Culture, Media, Language: Working Papers in Cultural Studies*, ed. Stuart Hall (London: Hutchinson, 1980); David Morley, *The "Nationwide" Audience: Structure and Decoding* (London: British Film Institute, 1980), and "Active Audience Theory: Pendulums and Pitfalls," *Journal of Communications* 43, no. 4 (1993); Ien Ang, "Wanted: Audiences. On the Politics of Empirical Audience Studies" in *Remote Control: Television, Audiences, and Cultural Power*, ed. Ellen Seiter (London: Routledge, 1989); and John Fiske, *Television Culture* (London: Methuen, 1987).

41. For theories of the interactive audience, see John Cruz and Justin Lewis, *Viewing, Reading, Listening: Audiences and Cultural Reception* (Boulder, Colo.: Westview, 1994); Will Brooker and Deborah Jermyn, eds., *The Audience Studies*

Reader (London: Routledge, 2003); C. Lee Harrington and Denise D. Bielby, "Constructing the Popular: Cultural Production and Consumption," in *Popular Culture: Production and Consumption,* ed. C. Lee Harrington and Denise D. Bielby (Malden, Mass.: Blackwell, 2001).

42. The idea of reality television overflowing the TV screen itself is taken from Will Brooker, "Living on *Dawson's Creek:* Teen Viewers, Cultural Convergence, and Television Overflow," *International Journal of Cultural Studies* 4, no. 4 (2001): 457. Jenkins is quoted from *Convergence Culture,* 86.

43. MSNBC.com, "Report: Phone Logjams Thwart 'Idol' Voters," May 16, 2004, www.msnbc.msn.com/id/4992204/.

44. *Wireless Week,* "AT&T Wireless Sets Messaging Records," June 4, 2003, www.wirelessweek.com.

45. The site advised, "Some videos may have a different camera feed than what was shown on LIVE TV" (http//www.americanidol.com).

46. Jenkins, *Convergence Culture,* 2, 59.

47. Julia Kristeva, *Desire in Language: A Semiotic Approach to Literature and Art,* ed. L. S. Roudiez, trans. T. Gora, A. Jardine, and L. S. Roudiez (New York: Columbia University Press, 1980), 69. Brooker, "Living on *Dawson's Creek,*" 457.

48. Tincknell and Raghuram quotes are from "*Big Brother,*" 267 (emphasis in original), and 258, respectively. Su Holmes, "But This Time *You* Choose! Approaching the 'Interactive' Audience in Reality TV," *International Journal of Cultural Studies* 7, no. 2 (2004): 222.

49. Briefly, when the site moved to www.americanidol.com, it was accessed from a link labeled "My Idol" and a sublink, "Boards"; as of 2009 it was again found under "Community."

50. Denise Bielby and C. Lee Harrington, "Reach Out and Touch Someone: Viewers, Agency, and Audiences in the Televisual Experience," in *Viewing, Reading, Listening: Audiences and Cultural Reception,* ed. Jon Cruz and Justin Lewis (Boulder, Colo.: Westview, 1994), 83.

51. Gray Cavender, "In Search of Community on Reality TV: *America's Most Wanted* and *Survivor,*" in *Understanding Reality Television,* ed. Su Holmes and Deborah Jermyn (London: Routledge, 2004), 157; after Robert Putnam, *Bowling Alone: The Collapse and Revival of American Democracy* (New York: Simon and Schuster, 2000).

52. Derek Foster, "'Jump in the Pool': The Competitive Culture of *Survivor* Fan Networks," in *Understanding Reality Television,* ed. Su Holmes and Deborah Jermyn (London: Routledge, 2004), 270.

53. Previously at idolonfox.com, now americanidol.com, 2005.

54. Re-aired in *American Idol Rewind,* FOX Network, February 10, 2007.

55. Simon Cowell, *I don't mean to be rude, but . . .: Backstage Gossip from American Idol and the Secrets That Can Make You a Star* (New York: Broadway Books, 2003), 8–9.

56. Daragh O'Reilly and Kathy Doherty, "Music B(r)ands Online and Constructing Community: The Case of New Model Army," in *Cybersounds: Essays on Virtual Music Culture,* ed. Michael D. Ayers (New York: Peter Lang, 2006), 140. For their definition of "brand community," O'Reilly and Doherty cite Albert M. Muniz and Thomas C. O'Guinn, "Brand Community," *Journal of Consumer Research* 27, no. 4 (2001): 412–432; and James H. McAlexander, John W. Schouten, and Harold F. Koenig, "Building Brand Community," *Journal of Marketing* 66, no. 1 (2002): 38–54.

57. Bielby and Harrington, "Reach Out and Touch Someone," 85–88. Bielby and Harrington base their understanding of these types of text on John Fiske's (1987) usage in *Television Culture.*

58. This discussion based on Judith Shklar, *American Citizenship: The Quest for Inclusion* (Cambridge, Mass.: Harvard University Press, 1991), 3, 64–65. Quotation is from page 64.

59. In *The Origins of Totalitarianism* (New York: Harcourt, Brace and World, 1966 [1951]), Arendt wrote about the rise of the Third Reich: "In an ever-changing, incomprehensible world the masses had reached the point where they would, at the same time, believe everything and nothing, think that everything was possible and that nothing was true" (382).

60. Quote from Francesca Coppa, "A Brief History of Media Fandom," in *Fan Fiction and Fan Communities in the Age of the Internet,* ed. Karen Hellekson and Kristina Busse (Jefferson, N.C.: McFarland, 2006), 56–58. For "Real Person Fiction," see Henry Jenkins, *Textual Poachers: Television Fans and Participatory Culture* (London: Routledge, 1992), 12; also cited in Coppa, 56.

61. Coppa explains (48) that the word "slash," as in *popslash,* refers specifically to homoerotic fan fiction; the term is derived from the description of the story, as in "Kirk/Spock," indicating a romantic or sexual relationship, or both, between two characters.

62. MSNBC.com, "Gay Group Questions 'American Idol' Judges," MSNBC .com, January 25, 2006, www.msnbc.msn.com/id/10994783/.

63. Helton's statements are reported in Greg Hernandez, "American Idol's Big Gay Closet," Advocate.com, April 24, 2007, www.advocate.com/issue_story _ektid44063.asp2007; Lambert is quoted in Vanessa Grigoriadis, "Wild Idol: The Psychedelic Transformation and Sexual Liberation of Adam Lambert," *Rolling Stone,* no. 1078 (2009): 53.

64. Quoted in Grigoriadis, "Wild Idol," 52.

65. The preceding discussion of glam is based on Phillip Auslander's book *Performing Glam Rock* (Ann Arbor: University of Michigan Press, 2006). Glam, like *American Idol,* began as a British project but developed through a dialogue between British and American culture (45). For glam as a sociological construct see p. 50; on style, fashion, and gender construction see pp. 60–61 and 66–67.

66. Quoted in Mark Harris, "Adam Lambert: Shaking Up 'Idol,'" *Entertainment Weekly,* EW.com, 2009, www.ew.com/ew/article/0,,20007164_20171835_20277643,00 .html.

During the final stages of this book, Lambert made headlines again, this time for an S&M-infused performance and onstage same-sex (male) kiss at the 2009 American Music Awards. Aired on ABC, the performance ended up censored by the time it was aired on the West Coast. Lambert expressed disappointment with the network's decision, citing a double standard in his post-performance *Rolling Stone* interview, "Female performers have been doing this for years—pushing the envelope about sexuality—and the minute a man does it, everybody freaks out" (Shirley Halperin, "Adam Lambert Says Censorship of American Music Award Song Would Be 'Discrimination,'" *Rolling Stone,* November 23, 2009, www.rollingstone.com).

67. In some sources the name is listed as "Normund Gentle," although on the *American Idol* screen the spelling "Norman" was consistent.

68. The video in which Mitchell explains the need for an alter-ego can be found on americanidol.com. Like Mitchell, Lambert also took on iconic diva fare in the early Hollywood rounds with Cher's "Believe" (February 3, 2009).

69. Jack Babuscio, "Camp and the Gay Sensibility," in *Camp Grounds: Style and Homosexuality,* ed. David Bergman (Amherst: University of Massachusetts Press, 1993); quotes from pages 33 and 26, respectively.

Also in this paragraph, "[F]lamboyant diva bad lounge act" quoted from Ken Levine, "American Idol: Top 36," *Huffington Post,* July 31, 2009, www.huffington-post.com/ken-levine/iamerican-idoli-top-36_b_167630.html 2009; "bad art or kitsch" from Susan Sontag, "Notes on Camp," in *Camp: Queer Aesthetics and the Performing Subject: A Reader,* ed. Fabio Cleto, Repr. (Ann Arbor: University of Michigan Press, 1999 [1964]), 55.

70. Burkeman's analysis of the origin of "gay adjacent" is from Oliver Burkeman, "Are You Gay-Adjacent?" January 13, 2002, www.guardian.co.uk/world/2006/jan/13/gayrights.media. He cites Chuck Kim's article, "The Real World Goes Straight," *The Advocate,* October 1, 2002, www.Advocate.com as the first source for the term. The reference to "gay-adjacent" in "The Buzz" appears in *The Advocate,* October 14, 1997.

2. Facing the Music

1. *American Idol,* FOX Network, February 2, 2004. Seger's "Old Time Rock and Roll" is a Capitol release, 1978.

2. For Frith's remarks on defining pop, see his "Pop Music," *The Cambridge Companion to Pop and Rock,* ed. Simon Frith, Will Straw, and John Street (Cambridge: Cambridge University Press, 2001), 92–93, 95. For his view of "rock ideology," see Simon Frith, *Sound Effects: Youth, Leisure, and the Politics of Rock* (London: Constable, 1981). Kelefa Sanneh, "The Rap Against Rockism," *New York Times,* October 31, 2004, www.nytimes.com/2004/10/31/arts/music/31sann.html?_r=1. Among others who have used this designation, see Lisa A. Lewis, "The Making of a Preferred Address," in *Gender Politics and MTV* (Philadelphia: Temple University Press, 1990), 27-42; and Phillip Auslander, *Liveness: Performance in a Mediatized Culture,* (London: Routledge, 1999). The past two decades (especially the 2000s) have also seen some of America's most influential music writers wrestle with the pressures of "rockism" and "poptimism" in their business; see Robert Christgau, "Decade: Rockism Faces the World," *Village Voice,* January 2, 1990, www.robertchristgau.com/xg/rock/decade-89.php; Sasha Frere-Jones, "When Critics Meet Pop," *Slate,* August 22, 2003, www.slate.com/id/2087321/; Douglas Wolk, "Thinking about Rockism," *Seattle Weekly,* May 4, 2005, www.seattleweekly.com/2005-05-04/music/thinking-about-rockism/; and two pieces by Jody Rosen: "G-d's Reggae Star: How Matisyahu Became a Pop Phenomenon," *Slate Magazine,* March 14, 2006, www.slate.com/id/2138032/, and "The Perils of Poptimism," *Slate,* May 9, 2006, www.slate.com/id/2141418/.

3. Simon Frith, "'The Magic That Can Set You Free': The Ideology of Folk and the Myth of the Rock Community," *Popular Music* 1 (1981), 163. Keir Keightly "Reconsidering Rock," in *The Cambridge Companion to Pop and Rock,* ed. Simon Frith, Will Straw, and John Street (Cambridge: Cambridge University Press, 2001), 136. A distinguished pantheon of work on this theme further highlights the central position of

authenticity in the rock/pop discourse, Philip Auslander's "Liveness" ("Performance and the Anxiety of Simulation," *Performance in a Mediatized Culture*) theorizes it in terms of anxieties about mediation, Lisa Lewis reveals the ways that the "ideology of rock" has been gendered and racialized (see her three titles in the bibliography), and Daphne Brooks examines how it has shaped both the racialized experience of music and music criticism in "The Write to Rock: Racial Mythologies, Feminist Theory, and the Pleasures of Rock Music Criticism," *Women and Music* 12 (2008).

4. Michel Foucault, *The Care of the Self: The History of Sexuality*, vol. 3, trans. R. Hurley (New York: Pantheon, 1986), 42.

5. Regina Bendix, *In Search of Authenticity: The Formation of Folklore Studies*, (Madison: University of Wisconsin Press, 1997); quote is from page 9.

6. Quotes are from two books by Lawrence Grossberg, "The Media Economy of Rock Culture: Cinema, Post Modernity and Authenticity," in *Sound & Vision: The Music Video Reader*, ed. Simon Frith, Andrew Goodwin, and Lawrence Grossberg (London: Routledge, 1993), 206 (also cited in Phillip Auslander, "Good Old Rock and Roll: Performing the 1950s in the 1970s," *Journal of Popular Music Studies* 15, no. 3 [2003], 186); and "'You [Still] have to Fight for Your Right to Party': Music Television as Billboards of Post-Modern Difference," *Popular Music* 7, no. 3 [1988]: 326). In his outstanding book, *Let's Talk about Love, A Journey to the End of Taste* (New York: Continuum International, 2007), music critic Carl Wilson relates a conversation we had about Grossberg's concept, "'Authentic inauthenticity,'" he declares, "is really just another way of saying 'art'" (71).

7. Cowell *I don't mean to be rude, but...*, 88.

8. Interview, September 24, 2004.

9. Interview, January 31, 2006.

10. As of March 2006, when Brown performed it, "Unwritten" had peaked in the U.S. at number 6 on the Billboard Hot 100 chart. She was dismissed in the March 9, 2006 episode of *American Idol* (FOX Network).

11. I quote producers' directions to audition attendees from my field notes, August 17 and 18, 2005, and Michael Orland from an interview, September 10, 2005.

12. Interview, September 10, 2005.

13. *American Idol,* FOX Network, February 28, 2006.

14. Interview, September 24, 2004.

15. Several of these artists, while visiting *American Idol,* have themselves taken the opportunity to perform during the Wednesday "results" show, sometimes to promote a new or retrospective album. Often they appear in order to promote a new release. For example, disco artist Donna Summer performed on *American Idol*'s Season 7 finale on the same day (May 20, 2008) that her album *Crayons* hit the shelves. Summer's label is Sony, part of the same label (Sony/BMG) that backs most *Idol* singers' post-season contracts.

16. The episode aired on April 25, 2006, and Yamin's statement was confirmed in the *International Herald Tribune* article "'American Idol' Backup Singers Deliver Every Time" (April 4, 2007, www.iht.com/articles/ap/2007/04/04/arts/NA-A-E-TV-US-Idol-Angels.php).

17. Both quotes from Fabio B. DaSilva and Jim Faught, "Nostalgia: A Sphere and Process of Contemporary Ideology," *Qualitative Sociology* 5, no. 1 (1982): 49. For Frith's views, see Frith, "'The Magic Can Set You Free,'" 160.

18. Ranking data from FremantleMedia, 2005. Orland and Byrd, interviews, Association of National Advertisers, "Family Television Awards Honor Six for Family Friendly Programming," August 15, 2003.

19. Auslander, "Performance and the Anxiety of Simulation," 207.

20. Interview, August 10, 2005; my emphasis.

21. Jacques Attali, *Noise: The Political Economy of Music,* trans. Brian Massumi (Minneapolis: University of Minnesota Press, 1992 [1985]), 141.

22. Each season until 2010 a newly composed song was featured during the final week, performed by the final two contestants, and released as a single either by the eventual winner or by both. While the first five seasons showcased the work of established songwriters, in 2007 and 2008 the show held an open competition for songwriters, allowing viewers to select the song from among finalists whose entries were posted on www.americanidol.com.

23. Typically for Sony (formerly Sony/BMG) labels, particularly RCA and J Records at Arista, although some finalists who do not win end up outside of Sony entirely. (The label was to change as of summer 2010.)

24. Christine R. Yano, "Covering Disclosures: Practices of Intimacy, Hierarchy, and Authenticity in a Japanese Popular Music Genre," *Popular Music and Society* 28, no. 2 (2005): 200.

25. During the results show judge Randy Jackson attributed the arrangement to Jeff Buckley, but I have found no evidence that Buckley ever performed or recorded any such arrangement.

26. George Plasketes 2005, "Re-flections on the Cover Age: A Collage of Continuous Coverage in Popular Music," *Popular Music and Society* 28, no. 2: 152. Copycats are called out (for example) on *American Idol Rewind,* March 17, 2007. A similar dynamic of praise and chastisement also occurred on *Pop Idol,* as documented in Su Holmes, "'Reality Goes Pop!' Reality TV, Popular Music, and Narratives of Stardom in *Pop Idol,*" *Television & News Media* 5, no. 2 (2004): 155–156.

27. Earl Stewart, *African American Music: An Introduction* (Belmont, Calif.: Schirmer/Thomson Learning, 1998), 7.

28. Deborah Ann Wong, *Speak It Louder: Asian Americans Making Music* (New York: Routledge, 2004), 181.

29. *American Idol,* FOX Network, January 19, 2004. To be clear, the melismatic singing preferred on *American Idol* is not the only melismatic practice in the world. Certain styles of Bulgarian music, for example, depend on melisma just as strongly to identify genre and a national vocal sound. On one 2007 episode of the Bulgarian program *Music Idol,* a globalizing and humorous assignment from the producers led eventual first-season winner Nevena Coneva to perform "I Will Always Love You" with a Balkan brass band and, instead of Houston's iconic "runs," used the melismatic vocal style associated with *obrabotki*—the genre, exemplified on the *Mystère des Voix Bulgares* albums, that Donna Buchanan discussed as a political tool of the Bulgarian government during the last years of communism there in "Bulgaria's Magical Mystère Tour: Postmodernism, World Music Marketing, and Political Change in Eastern Europe," *Ethnomusicology* 41, no. 1 (1997). (Thanks to Plamena Kourtova, who discussed the performance in an unpublished paper, "The Power of Imitation in *Music Idol,* Popular Music, Media Markets, and the Politics of Identity in post-Communist Bulgaria," at the national meeting of the Society for

Ethnomusicology, October 25, 2008). In this case melisma once again denoted a national musical style, even in a song from outside the implied genre. To become the Music Idol Coneva, in fact, had to prove her facility with both (African) American melisma and Bulgarian melisma, auditioning for the judges with Christina Aguilera's hit "The Voice Within" and "Daniova Mama," a song that has famously been recorded by Binka Dobreva with the *Mystère des Voix Bulgares* choir.

30. Quotes from Aaron A. Fox, *Real Country: Music and Language in Working-Class Culture* (Durham, N.C.: Duke University Press, 2004), 272–273. Eric Lott cited from *Love and Theft: Blackface Minstrelsy and the American Working Class* (Oxford: Oxford University Press, 1993).

31. Quoted in Jackson Griffith, "Must Not See TV!" *SN&R* (*Sacramento News & Review*), July 18, 2002, www.newsreview.com/issues/sacto/2002-07-18/arts.asp. The other moments described were re-aired on *American Idol Rewind,* February 10, 2007.

32. Niccolò Machiavelli, *The Prince,* trans. Harvey C. Mansfield (Chicago: University of Chicago Press, 1998 [1532]). Robert Walser, "Eruptions: Heavy Metal Appropriations of Classical Virtuosity," *Popular Music* 11, no. 3 (1992): 278. Martyn de Bruyn, "Machiavelli and the Politics of Virtù," (Ph.D. diss., Purdue University, 2003), 35.

33. Machiavelli, *The Prince,* 22.

34. de Bruyn "The Politics of Virtù," 21, after Neal Wood, "Machiavelli's Concept of Virtù Reconsidered," *Political Studies* 15 (1967).

35. Jody Rosen, "The State of American Singing as Heard on 'I-I-I-I-I-I-Idol,'" *New York Times,* May 18, 2003, 3.

36. "The body in the voice" is a phrase from Roland Barthes, *Image, Music, Text,* trans. Stephen Heath (New York: Hill and Wang, 1977), 188. Barthes discussed *pheno-song* in the same work on page 182.

37. Richard Crocker, "Melisma," *New Grove Dictionary of Music and Musicians,* ed. Stanley Sadie (344–346), 2nd ed., vol. 6 (New York: Grove, 2000), 344, my emphasis.

38. See, for example, Corey Moss, Raquel Hutchinson, and Angela Lu, "The Scourge of *American Idol:* Oversingers," MTV.com, February 6, 2006, www.mtv.com/news/articles/1523040/20060202/story.jhtml.

39. Jeniece Brock, personal communication, January 20, 2009.

40. *American Idol,* FOX Network, May 20, 2009. Immediately after the music ended, Seacrest and DioGuardi explained to the audience that she had only agreed to the stunt on the condition that money would be donated to her "favorite charity."

41. *Blender,* "The 50 Worst Things to Happen to Music," April 2006, www.blender.com/guide/articles.aspx?id=1913.

42. Historical examples from Andrew Oster, "Melisma as Malady: Cavalli's *Il Giasone* and Opera's Earlies Stuttering Role," in *Sounding Off: Theorizing Disability in Music,* ed. Neil Lerner and Joseph N. Straus (New York: Routledge, 2006). Quotes from Rosen, "The State of American Singing," 3; and G. Brown, "Serial Triller: Mariah Carey's Musical Crime: Leading the Growing Trend toward Overblown, Roller-Coaster Vocals," *Denver Post,* August 10, 2003: 3.

43. *World Idol,* FOX Network, December 25, 2003.

44. Terry Gross, *Fresh Air,* National Public Radio, broadcast January 15, 2004 (my transcription).

45. Frith, *Sound Effects,* 21.

46. My field notes, October 5, 2004.

47. Interview, January 31, 2006.

48. Graham F. Welch and Johan Sundberg, "Choir," in *The Science and Psychology of Music Performance,* ed. Richard Parncutt and Gary McPherson (Oxford: Oxford University Press, 2002), 259.

49. Richard Allen Rischar, "One Sweet Day: Vocal Ornamentation and Style in the African American Popular Ballad, 1991–1995" (Ph.D. diss., University of North Carolina at Chapel Hill, 2000), 171.

50. CBSNews.com, "FOX News Drops Franken Lawsuit," August 25, 2003, www.cbsnews.com/stories/2003/08/12/entertainment/main567800.shtml.

51. Data for "Central Coast Idol" competition from my field notes, August 28, 2004. Data for official *American Idol* Season 4 auditions from my field notes, October 4, 2004.

52. Interview, February 23, 2004.

53. Interview, August 23, 2005.

54. Interview, November 2, 2004.

55. Re-aired on *American Idol Rewind,* February 10, 2007.

56. Rischar, "One Sweet Day," 147.

57. Mark Clague, "'What So Proudly We Hail'd': Performing Meaning in the Star-Spangled Banner" (unpublished paper presented at the 2003 joint meeting of the Society for Ethnomusicology, the College Music Society, and the Association for Technology in Music Instruction, Miami, Florida, October 2, 2003).

58. Mark Anthony Neal, *What the Music Said: Black Popular Music and Black Public Culture* (New York: Routledge, 1998), 72. Ken McLeod, "'We Are the Champions': Masculinities, Sports, and Popular Music," *Popular Music and Society* 29, no. 5 (2006): 534.

59. Rischar, "One Sweet Day," 28.

60. *American Idol,* FOX Network, March 6, 2007.

61. *American Idol,* FOX Network, March 21, 2006.

62. Singers who favored pink or scarlet-toned hair included rockers Nikki McKibbin in Season 1, Vanessa Olivarez in Season 2, Amy Adams in Season 3, Gina Glocksen in Season 6, and Alexis Grace and Alison Iraheta in Season 8. Amanda Overmyer, Season 7's female rocker, sported two-toned black and blonde hair, but so did her R&B rival Ramiele Malubay. Season 9's twelfth-place contestant, Lacey Brown, brought a more indie-rock sensibility to the rose-dyed hair.

63. In this paragraph, Lisa A. Lewis, "Female Address on Music Television: Being Discovered," in *Jump Cut: A Review of Contemporary Media* 35 (2006 [1990]), www.ejumpcut.org/archive/onlinessays/JC35folder/GirlsMTV.html; Paula Abdul quoted in Corey Moss, "Can You Still *Rock* if You're on 'American Idol'? Bo Bice and Constantine Maroulis Are Out to Prove You Can," *MTV News: Headlines* at *MTV.com,* March 18, 2005, www.mtv.com/news/articles/1498298 /03182005/abdul_paula.jhtml.2005a. On sincerity and authenticity, see Lionel Trilling, *Sincerity and Authenticity* (Cambridge, Mass.: Harvard University Press, 1972), 3.

64. Johan Fornäs, "The Future of Rock: Discourses That Struggle to Define a Genre," *Popular Music* 14, no. 1 (1995), 112.

3. Win or Lose

The section "Immigrant Song, Bao Viet Nguyen's American Dream" contains material previously published in Meizel, "'Be a Fan, Not a Hater.'" The section "William Hung and the Celebration of Failure (Or How to Succeed in *American Idol* without Really Winning)" is based on, and includes material from, Katherine Meizel, "Making the Dream a Reality Show, The Celebration of Failure in *American Idol*," *Popular Music and Society* 32, 4 (2009), 475–488. Available at www.informaworld.com.

1. idolonfox.com, accessed December 3, 2004.

2. Larry King, interview with Simon Cowell, *CNN Larry King Live*, CNN, March 17, 2006 (transcript accessed at CNN.com, http://transcripts.cnn.com /TRANSCRIPTS/0603/17/lkl.01.html).

3. Su Holmes, "'Reality Goes Pop!'"

4. Kelly Clarkson's pre-*Idol* story is recounted in Josh Tyrangiel, "Miss Independent," *Time Magazine*, February 4, 2006, www.time.com/time/magazine /article/0,9171,1156534,00.html. Barrino's interview is quoted from a special episode of *American Idol*, FOX Network, May 3, 2004.

5. This discussion of the American Dream mythology is based on Jim Cullen, *The American Dream: A Short History of an Idea that Shaped a Nation* (Oxford: Oxford University Press, 2003), 5–6.

6. Robert C. Rowland and John M. Jones, "Recasting the American Dream and American Politics: Barack Obama's Keynote Address to the 2004 Democratic National Convention," *Quarterly Journal of Speech* 93, no. 4 (2007): 431.

7. *American Idol*, FOX Network, January 27, 2004.

8. Early rounds are filmed in the summer and fall, with audience voting beginning a few weeks into the broadcast season that premieres in January.

9. This and the following three Nguyen quotes come from an interview on September 15, 2005.

10. Scott A. Sandage, *Born Losers: A History of Failure in America* (Cambridge, Mass.: Harvard University Press, 2005), 265; Matthew Stahl, "A Moment Like This: *American Idol* and Narratives of Meritocracy," in *Bad Music*, ed. Christopher Washburne and Maiken Derno (London: Routledge, 2004), 224.

Sandage has recognized, to a degree, the idea of a continuum rather than a binary of success and failure in an interview published in *Cabinet* in 2002 (Sina Najafi and David Serlin, "The Invention of Failure: An Interview with Scott A. Sandage," *Cabinet* 7, no. 2 [2002], www.cabinetmagazine.org/issues/7/inventionoffailure.php).

11. Kirsten Fairchilds, "William Hung Will Be King at Artichoke Festival," *Santa Cruz Sentinel*, May 18, 2006, www.santacruzsentinel.com/archive/2006/May /18/local/stories/0710cal.htm.

12. *American Idol*, FOX Network, January 27, 2004.

13. Sandage, *Born Losers*.

14. Descriptions of Florence Foster Jenkins quoted from Brooks Peters, "Florence Nightingale," *Opera News* 65, no. 12 (2001): 22, quoting Alix B. Williamson; Pablo P. Helguera, "Florence Foster Jenkins: La Diva del Cuarto Tono," *Pauta* 75–76 (2000), 102 ("*genuina*"), quoting Roger Bager in *New York World Telegram*; Peters "Florence Nightingale," 23. Gamson, *Claims to Fame*, 189.

15. Sontag "Notes on Camp," 59 (my emphasis) and 65. Hung quoted from *Hangin' With Hung*, KOCH (DVD, 2004). John J. Enck, "Campop," *Wisconsin Studies in Contemporary Literature* 7, no. 2 (1966), 174.

16. Glenn Dixon, "What It Means to Be Hung," *Washington City Paper,* May 7, 2004; Frith 1981a, 164; Keightley "Reconsidering Rock," 136. On the quality of sincerity, see Joseph L. DeVitis and John Martin Rich, *The Success Ethic, Education, and the American Dream,* (Albany: State University of New York Press, 1996), 54.

17. My interview with Hung February 23, 2006; *American Idol,* FOX Network, special episode, March 1, 2004.

18. Wong quoted from *Speak It Louder,* 4; Kim from *American Idol,* FOX Network, February 7, 2007.

19. Emil Guillermo, "William Hung: Racism, or Magic?" SFGate.co, April 6, 2004, www.sfgate.com/cgibin/article.cgi?file=gate/archive/2004/04/06/eguillermo .DTL&type=printable; Sharon Mizota, "Can the Subaltern Sing? Or, Who's Ashamed of William Hung?, *Pop Matters,* May 4, 2004, www.popmatters.com/tv /features/040504-williamhungmizota.shtml; David Ng, "Hung Out to Dry: What We Laugh about When We Laugh about *American Idol*'s Most Famous Reject," *Village Voice,* April 6, 2004, www.villagevoice.com/news/0414,ng,52441,1.html; Cliff Cheng, "Marginalized Masculinities and Hegemonic Masculinity: An Introduction," *Journal of Men's Studies* 7, no. 3 (1999).

20. Mizota, "Can the Subaltern Sing?"; Chen, "Marginalized Masculinities and Hegemonic Masculinity."

21. Frank Wu, *Yellow: Race in America beyond Black and White* (New York: Basic Books, 2002), 49.

22. Eno's quote from Kevin Kelly, "Eno: Gossip Is Philosophy," *Wired* (May 1995): 149; also cited in Ron Eglash, "Race, Sex, and Nerds: From Black Geeks to Asian American Hipsters," *Social Text* 20, no. 2 (2002), 52. Wong *Speak It Louder,* 187, 189. See also Mary Bucholtz's essay, "The Whiteness of Nerds: Superstandard English and Racial Markedness," *Journal of Linguistic Anthropology* 11, no. 1 (2001), 87, where she discusses the "nerd" as a racially marked identity in white high school students, one that eschews symbols of "trendy whiteness" and thus the associations of blackness that underlie them.

Idol has in fact featured some Asian American performers who notably buck the presumption in favor of whiteness; Paul Kim sang a heavily melismatic "If I Ever Fall in Love," by the 1990s R&B boy band Shai, and Bao Viet Nguyen sang Stevie Wonder's "Lately." In these cases the "move toward color" had positive results. The performances of Ricky Martin and William Hung of "She Bangs" did not include melisma, and without that aural marker of blackness, a particular musical authenticity may have been perceived as absent.

23. Sheng-Mai Ma, "Orientalism in the Chinese American Discourse: Body and Pidgin," *Modern Language Studies* 23, no. 4 (1993), after Gayatri Chakravorty Spivak, "Can the Subaltern Speak?" in *Marxism and the Interpretation of Culture,* ed. Cary Nelson and Lawrence Grossberg (Urbana: University of Illinois Press, 1988).

24. Deborah Wong and Mai Elliot, "'I Want the Microphone': Mass Mediation and Agency in Asian-American Popular Music," *TDR (1988–)* 38, no. 3 (1994): 158.

25. Hung's remarks to me from an interview February 23, 2006; the *Daily Californian* interview quoted in Alicia Wittmeyer, "Berkeley Junior Shot Down in American Idol Tryout," *Daily Californian,* February 2, 2004, www.dailycal.org.

26. Interview, February 23, 2006.

27. idolonfox.com, 2005.

28. See Deborah Jermyn, "'This *Is* about Real People!': Video Technologies, Actuality and Affect in the Television Crime Appeal," in *Understanding Reality Television,* ed. Su Holmes and Deborah Jermyn (London: Routledge, 2004); Mark Andrejevic, *Reality TV: The Work of Being Watched* (Oxford: Rowman and Littlefield, 2004); McGrath, *Loving Big Brother,* 2004 (quote below is from page 7).

29. Michel Foucault, *Discipline and Punish,* trans. Alan Sheridan (New York: Vintage Books [Random House], 1995 [1977]), 10; Wong, *Speak It Louder,* 164.

30. All Maimoni quotes from an interview October 22, 2004. James, personal communication, October 9, 2004.

31. Interview, September 10, 2005, my emphasis.

32. Hung interview, February 23, 2006. Byrd interview, January 31, 2006.

33. Lythgoe quoted from my field notes, October 5, 2004. Hung interview, February 23, 2006.

34. Michael Shain, "'Superstar' Producers Lied to Studio Audience," FoxNews.com, May 11, 2004, www.foxnews.com/story/0,2933,119593,00.html. A May 10, 2004, item in the *Los Angeles Times* (Scott Collins, "In Reality, It's a Super-Duping; The Coming Series 'Superstar USA' Trips Up the Audience in a Bid to Turn 'Idol' Upside-Down") inspired apologies from the WB Network, as well as some further media commentary about the public's appetite for (public) humiliation (e.g., Shain, "'Superstar' Producers Lied to Studio Audience"; Lisa de Moraes, "Fox Puts Foot in Its Mouth, Kicks Self," *Washington Post,* May 14, 2004, www.washingtonpost.com/wp-dyn/articles/A25870-2004May13.html; Ann Oldenburg, "Can't Sing or Dance? Give 'Superstar' a Shot," *USA Today,* May 17, 2004, www.usatoday.com/life/television/news/2004-05-16-wb-superstar_x.htm).

35. Oldenburg, "Can't Sing or Dance?"

36. Ben Katner, "Superstar Jamie Squeals!" *TVGuide Online,* June 15, 2004, http://144.198.225.50/News/Insider/default.htm?cmsRedir=true&rmDate=061500 4&cmsGuid=%7B4FEF0722-A7F7-4C4C-ABD9-DF1FB5E6F8DA%7D.

37. Peters, "Florence Nightingale," 23, my emphasis.

At least some contestants recognize the requirement of ambition and risk-taking as inherent in the *Idol* process. On the official *American Idol* website, Season 6 finalist Brandon Rogers defined an "American Idol" as "someone who represents the American dream of anything can happen through hard work and risk" (www.americanidol.com, 2007).

4. Idol Worship

1. This incident is described in my field notes, October 5, 2004. Ray Charles's "This Little Girl of Mine," Atlantic, 1955. I discuss the sacred–secular dialectic of the Cold War in Katherine Meizel, "A Singing Citizenry: Popular Music and Civil Religion in America," *Journal for the Scientific Study of Religion* 45, no. 4 (2006), 499.

2. An interview with Dale Gronemeier, 1964, cited in Kay Mills and Marian Wright Edelman, *This Little Light of Mine: The Life of Fannie Lou Hamer,* (Lexington: University Press of Kentucky, 2007), 21.

3. John Winthrop, "A Model of Christian Charity," in *The American Studies Anthology,* ed. Richard P. Horowitz (Lanham, Md.: Rowman and Littlefield, 2001), 18.

4. Robert Bellah, "Civil Religion in America," *Daedalus: Journal of the American Academy of Arts and Sciences* 96, no. 1 (2001 [1967]): 4.

5. R. H. Williams and N. J. Demerath, "Civil Religion in an Uncivil Society," *Annals of the American Academy of Political and Social Science* 480 (1985).

6. A two-cent piece in Civil War–torn 1864 was the first American coin to bear the phrase "In God We Trust." When a new pattern of gold coins in 1907 lacked the words, public complaints led to legislation making them mandatory on coin types that had already used them. They reappeared periodically on newly issued coins, during World War I and in 1938, the same year Kate Smith debuted Irving Berlin's civil-religious Armistice-Day tribute "God Bless America" on the radio. In 1955 new Cold War legislation put the slogan on all U.S. currency, and the following year "In God We Trust" became the official national motto.

7. Bush, though born in Connecticut, was raised in Texas and became its governor in 1994.

8. Wilfred M. McClay, "The Soul of a Nation," *The Public Interest,* no. 155 (Spring 2004).

9. H. Con. Res. 248 introduced by Rep. Henry Brown, Republican, S.C.
I address the relationship between the Irving Berlin song titled "God Bless America" and civil religion in Meizel, "A Singing Citizenry."

10. On the choice of "God Bless the U.S.A." in 2003, see also Meizel "A Singing Citizenry;" and Williams and Demerath, "Civil Religion in an Uncivil Society," 166. Herbert Gans, *Deciding What's News* (Evanston, Ill.: Northwestern University Press, 2004 [1979]), 42. Cowell quote from *American Idol,* FOX Network, March 25, 2008.

11. Competitors included soldiers on active duty and those in the U.S. Army Reserve and the U.S. Army National Guard.

12. Information in this paragraph comes from Leo Shane III, "Guardsman Is Military Idol Winner," October 24, 2005, www.military.com/features/0,15240,79208,00.html; Tim Hipps, "'Military Idol' Competition Begins on Army Installations," August 5, 2005, United States Department of Defense, www.defense.gov/news/newsarticle.aspx?id=16956; and www.armymwr.com, accessed March 30, 2010 (Kimberly Caldwell's appearance). Byrd interview, January 31, 2006.

13. During the same 2000 election in which Bush made his declaration to B'nai B'rith, the Jewish Anti-Defamation League asked Democratic vice-presidential candidate Senator Joseph Lieberman to stop making overt religious references in his speeches (Niebuhr, "The 2000 Campaign"). For quotes see Robert N. Bellah, *The Broken Covenant: American Civil Religion in Time of Trial* (Chicago: University of Chicago Press, 1992 [1975]); Rowland and Jones, "Recasting the American Dream," 432; Bruce Murray, "With 'God on Our Side'? How American 'Civil Religion' Permeates Society and Manifests Itself in Public Life," *FACSNET,* March 28, 2002, http://facsnet.org/issues/faith/civil_religion.htm; Gustav Niebuhr, "The 2000 Campaign: The Religion Issue; Lieberman Is Asked to Stop Invoking Faith in Campaign," *New York Times,* August 29, 2000, www.nytimes.com/2000/08/29/us/2000-campaign-religion-issue-lieberman-asked-stop-invoking-faith-campaign.html.

14. George W. Bush, "Statement by the President in His Address to the Nation," September 11, 2001, www.whitehouse.gov/news/releases/; also quoted in Roberta L. Coles "Manifest Destiny Adapted for 1990s' War Discourse: Mission and Destiny Intertwined," *Sociology of Religion* 63, no. 4 (2002), 423. "I Believe" lyrics, Biancaniello, Watters, and Gray 2003.

15. Coles "Manifest Destiny Adapted," 407, after Tiryakian 1982.

16. idolonfox.com, 2004.

17. Personal communications, field notes, May 24, 2005.

18. Gracin quoted from idolonfox.com, 2003. Both block quotes are from posters on the idolonfox forum; the ellipses in the second quote are present in the original.

19. David Kertzer, *Ritual, Politics, and Power* (New Haven, Conn.: Yale University Press, 1988), 38, after Bruno Bettelheim, *The Informed Heart* (Glencoe: Free Press, 1960).

20. idolonfox.com, forum.

21. Definition of family-friendly programming from the Association of National Advertisers, familyprogramawards.com, 2007. Rainey interview, August 21, 2009.

22. Max Weber, *The Protestant Ethic and the Spirit of Capitalism,* trans. Talcott Parsons (London: Routledge, 2004 [1930]), 40.

23. Walther Fisher, "Reaffirmation and Subversion of the American Dream," *Quarterly Journal of Speech* 47 (1973): 161.

24. "I Believe," see n14 above. Weber, *The Protestant Ethic,* 41.

25. The songs Lima first considered are copyrighted, respectively, by S-Curve Records, 2003; and J Records, 2001. "His Eye is on the Sparrow" is by Civilla D. Martin and Charles Gabriel, 1905. This song was, coincidentally, featured in the 2004 Idols Live tour, sung by the top ten finalists as the penultimate number. It received a partial standing ovation from the audience at the Arrowhead Pond auditorium in Anaheim, California (field notes, September 23, 2004). Ms. Lima had not seen any of the tour concerts.

Lima quotes come from a personal communication August 18, 2005, and an interview August 23, 2005. The phrase "task set by God" is from Weber, *The Protestant Ethic,* 39.

26. *American Idol on FOX,* February 2004; capitals in original.

27. The twelfth is not included on the recording, an omission ostensibly related to his early elimination from the show because of a previously undisclosed arrest record.

28. Torres interview, February 23, 2004. The second young woman, who is in fact now part of a band with a national following, I quote from a personal communication and field notes, October 5, 2004.

29. Kertzer, *Ritual, Politics, and Power,* 9.

30. de Moraes, "'American Idol' Seizes the Day."

31. Quotes from Stijn L. Reijnders, Gerard Rooijakkers, and Liesbet van Zoonen, "Community Spirit and Competition in *Idols:* Ritual Meanings of a TV Talent Quest," *European Journal of Communication* 22, no. 3 (2007): 282, 285.

32. Joshua Meyrowitz, *No Sense of Place: The Electronic Media of Social Behavior* (Oxford: Oxford University Press, 1985), 277. Kertzer *Rituals, Politics, and Power,* 11. Idol auditionee, personal communication, August 17, 2005.

33. www.people.com, "Public Complains to FCC over *Idol* Voting," May 20, 2004, www.people.com/people/article/0,,640492,00.html.

34. Kate Arthur, "How 'American Idol' Got Hijacked by Its Viewers," *New York Times,* May 24, 2004, www.nytimes.com/2004/05/23/arts/television/23AURT. html?scp=1&sq=How%20'American%20Idol'%20Got%20Hijacked%20by%20 Its%20Viewers&st=cse.

35. Interview August 10, 2005.

36. Cowell quoted in Virginia Heffernan, "Here Comes the Judge: Take Cover, Would-Be Idols," *New York Times,* May 19, 2004, www.nytimes.com/2004/05/19 /arts/here-comes-the-judge-take-cover-would-be-idols.html?scp=1&sq=Here%20 Comes%20the%20Judge:%20Take%20Cover,%20Would-Be%20Idols&st=cse.

37. Both quotes from idolonfox.com forum; ellipses in originals.

38. The anonymous viewer is quoted from personal communication, field notes, May 24, 2005. The latter quote is from Bellah, "Civil Religion in America," 4.

39. Benedict Anderson, *Imagined Communities: Reflections on the Origin and Spread of Nationalism* (London: Verso, 2002 [1983]), 7, 145. Tong Soon Lee, "Technology and the Production of Islamic Space: The Call to Prayer in Singapore," *Ethnomusicology* 43, no. 1 (1999): 92. Phillip Bohlman, *World Music: A Very Short Introduction* (Oxford: Oxford University Press, 2002), 95.

40. *San Francisco Chronicle* music critic Joshua Kosman has compared *American Idol* to a sporting event, drawing a parallel between the show and ancient Greek dramatic competitions. He notes democratic components in both situations. In fact, singing was part of Pythian Games in early Olympic tradition. ("'Idol' Hews to Ancient Traditions," *San Francisco Chronicle,* March 27, 2004, www.sfgate.com.) FremantleMedia, the production company for *Idols* shows, draws a similar comparison in an advertisement that includes announcements both for a special on ancient Olympic history and for *American Idol*: "From one gladiatorial competition to another" begins the transition between announcements (www.fremantlemedia .com, accessed March 10, 2004).

41. MSNBC.com, "Governors Place Bets on 'Idol' Winner," May 26, 2004, http://msnbc.msn.com/id/5060958/.

42. Governor Easley also made a series of food-based wagers in 2004 with Pennsylvania's governor Edward Rendell regarding the projected outcomes in the National Football Conference championships (*Governor's Newsletter,* January 16, 2004, www.virtualtours.state.pa.us).

43. Observations of the Idol audition from my field notes, October 5, 2004. Michael Novak, *The Joy of Sports: End Zones, Bases, Baskets, Balls, and the Consecration of the American Spirit* (New York: Basic Books, 1976), 18–19.

44. Alexis de Tocqueville, *Democracy in America,* vol. 2, trans. George Lawrence, ed. J. P. Mayer (New York: Doubleday, Anchor Books, 1969 [1840]); also cited in Robert N. Bellah et al., *Habits of the Heart* (Berkeley: University of California Press, 1996 [1985]), 147–148. Eric W. Rothenbuhler, *Ritual Communication: From Everyday Conversation to Mediated Ceremony* (Thousand Oaks, Calif.: Sage, 1998), 15. Catherine M. Bell, *Ritual: Perspectives and Dimensions* (Oxford: Oxford University Press, 1997), 242.

45. The preceding discussion of the work of Rowland and Jones is based on their 2007 article "Recasting the American Dream and American Politics"; quotes are from pages 430, 431, and 433; their description of Reagan's oratory is from page 427. The Nguyen quote is from an interview, September 15, 2005; emphasis is mine. Barack Obama, "Reclaiming the Promise to the People," *Vital Speeches of the Day* 70 (2004), 625; also cited in Rowland and Jones, 435.

46. This discussion based on Bellah et al., *Habits of the Heart;* quotes from pp. xlii, 336, 334.

47. Charles Taylor, *Sources of the Self* (Cambridge, Mass.: Harvard University Press, 1989), 371.

48. See Émile Durkheim's *The Elementary Forms of Religious Life,* trans. Karen Elise Fields (New York: Simon and Schuster, 1995 [1912]) for his views on the role of religion in social solidarity; on the same topic see also Bellah et al., *Habits of the Heart.* On the sacralization of the individual, see Durkheim, *The Division of Labor in Society,* 2nd ed., trans. W. D. Halls (New York: Free Press, 1997 [1893]), 122. Quote is from *The Elementary Forms of Religious Life,* 44.

49. Both posts from idolonfox.com forum; capitals in original.

50. George W. Bush, "Address to a Joint Session of Congress and the American People," September 20, 2001, www.whitehouse.gov/news/releases/2001/09 /20010920-8.html.

51. Quoted in Wayne Harada, "'Idol' Judge Simon Not Counting on Jasmine at All," *Honolulu Advertiser,* May 5, 2004, http://the.honoluluadvertiser.com/article /2004/May/05/il/i1103a.html.

52. Rhys Williams, "Religion as Political Resource: Culture or Ideology?" *Journal for the Scientific Study of Religion* 35, no. 4 (1996): 368–369.

53. Message thread, idolonfox.com forum; capital letters in original.

54. Lindsie Taylor, "'Idol' Finalist Has Been on Exciting Ride," *Deseret News,* July 8, 2004, www.deseretnews.com/article/1,5143,595075876,00.html2004; Tad Walch, "Utahns Hope to Make It as 'Idols,'" *Deseret News,* January 18, 2004, www .deseretnews.com/article/1,5143,590037094,00.html.

55. Personal communications, field notes, May 24, 2005.

56. Interview, August 21, 2009.

57. Those who predicted a predominance of Christian voters include Ramin Setoodeh ("Religion and 'Idol': Could Adam Lambert Be Heading Home?" May 12, 2009, http://blog.newsweek.com/blogs/popvox/archive/2009/05/12/religion-and-idol-could-adam-lambert-be-heading-home.aspx); Ann Powers ("'American Idol's' Bigger Message," *Los Angeles Times,* May 18, 2009, http://latimesblogs.latimes.com /americanidoltracker/2009/05/american-idols-bigger-message.html); and Gil Kaufman ("American Idol Spotlight on Christian Singers Reels in Religious Viewers," March 13, 2009, www.mtv.com/news/articles/1606966/20090313/story.jhtml). Allen and Lambert quoted in Gill Kaufman, "Adam Lambert and Kris Allen Talk 'American Idol' Finale," MTV.com, May 19, 2009, www.mtv.com/news/articles/1611707 /20090519/story.jhtml.

58. Both posts from idolonfox.com forum; ellipses in original.

59. Daniel J. Boorstin, *The Image; or, What Happened to the American Dream,* 2nd ed. (New York: Atheneum, 1962), 183.

60. Interview, August 21, 2009.

61. "Flying Without Wings" was an exception, as it had already been a hit, released in 1999 by the U.K. boy band Westlife. Season 9 had no original song.

62. "Inside Your Heaven" by Andreas Carlsson, Pelle Nylén, and Savan Kotecha, 2005. (For "I Believe" see n14 above.)

63. Fantasia Barrino on the BoBo from Lee Hildebrand, "Fantasia is Living Post-'Idol' Dream," SFGate.com, September 19, 2004, www.sfgate.com/cgibin /article.cgi?file=/chronicle/a/2004/09/19/PKGPN8MEUP1.DTL; Fantasia's quote from the book she published under her first name, *Life is Not a Fairy Tale* (New

York: Fireside [Simon and Schuster], 2005), 20. Huff's mother, *American Idol,* FOX Network, March 16, 2004.

64. *American Idol,* FOX Network, April 20, 2004.

65. Jennifer Hochschild, *Facing Up to the American Dream: Race, Class, and the Soul of the Nation* (Princeton, N.J.: Princeton University Press, 1995), 168–169.

66. Fantasia mentions the Holiness denomination in Fantasia, *Life is Not a Fairy Tale,* 20; this description of it comes from Wade Clark Roof and William McKinney, *American Mainline Religion: Its Changing Shape and Future* (New Brunswick, N.J.: Rutgers University Press, 1987), 30–31.

67. Anonymous viewer, idolonfox.com forum. Kertzer, *Ritual, Politics, and Power,* 11.

68. Cowell quoted in Heffernan, "Here Comes the Judge." Bell, *Ritual,* 82.

69. The episode aired on FOX Network, February 11, 2004, and both fan comments are from the idolonfox.com forum, capitals in original.

70. Studdard quoted in Rod Harmon, "'Idol' Winner Studdard Reaches to the Past to Make a Future," *North County Times,* February 25, 2004, www.nctimes.com /articles/2004/02/26/entertainment/music/2_25_0414_24_55.txt. *From the Church to the Charts,* September 20, 2003. *Kelly, Ruben, and Fantasia, Home for Christmas,* FOX Network, November 24, 2004. When, on the latter show, Clarkson announced the song "Jesus Oh What a Wonderful Child," she told the audience that she had suggested it for the special, as it was a favorite of hers. The song had also appeared on Mariah Carey's album *Merry Christmas* (Sony, 1994), and both Carey's and the Idols' performances were strongly melismatic.

71. Interview with Michael Orland, September 10, 2005.

72. americanidol.com; accessed May 2007.

73. Interview, September 10, 2005.

74. Jennifer Mattos, "The 1997 Presidential Inauguration: We Are the Solution: Speech Does Not Offend, nor Does It Break New Ground," *Time* (1997), www.time .com/time/inaugural/part5.html.

75. Marcela Cristi, *From Civil to Political Religion: The Intersection of Culture, Religion, and Politics* (Waterloo, Ontario: Wilfrid Laurier University Press, 2001). Her account of Rousseau's intention is on pages 6–7; the mention of Gramsci is on page 238.

76. Williams, "Religion as Political Resource," 377.

77. Bellah, "Civil Religion in America,"18. (Bellah has recently contributed to *Deepening the American Dream: Reflections on the Inner Life and Spirit of Democracy,* ed. Mark Nepo [San Francisco: Jossey-Bass, 2005].) Coles, "Manifest Destiny Adapted," 423.

78. The website for 19 Entertainment (www.19.co.uk) listed this figure as of December 3, 2005. As of August 2009 the site had been restructured, and this information is no longer included.

5. Going Places

1. Interview, September 15, 2005.

2. Baudrillard, *America,* 104.

3. Tara McPherson, *Reconstructing Dixie: Race, Gender, and Nostalgia in the Imagined South* (Durham, N.C.: Duke University Press, 2003), 17. James W. Fernan-

dez, "Andalusia on Our Minds: Two Contrasting Places in Spain as Seen in a Vernacular Poetic Duel of the Late 19th Century," *Cultural Anthropology* 3, no. 1 (1988), 22.

4. Larry May, *The Big Tomorrow: Hollywood and the Politics of the American Way* (Chicago: University of Chicago Press, 2000), 1.

5. Observations of the Season 5 auditions from my field notes, August 18, 2005; observations of the registration from my field notes, October 5, 2004.

6. Kevin Starr, "California, A Dream," in *California: A Place, a People, a Dream,* ed. Claudia K. Jurman and James J. Rawls (San Francisco, Calif.: Chronicle Books, 1986), 18.

7. *American Idol,* FOX Network, July 24, 2002. Guarini identified himself as biracial in an interview for *PBS Kids Go!* 2005.

8. On rainbow casting, see Tincknell and Raghuram, "Reconfiguring the 'Active' Audience of Cultural Studies?" Quote from Baudrillard, *America,* 28–29.

9. Both quotes from Barney Hoskyns, *Hotel California: The True-Life Adventures of Crosby, Stills, Nash, Young, Mitchell, Taylor, Browne, Ronstadt, Geffen, the Eagles, and Their Many Friends* (Hoboken, N.J.: Wiley, 2007), 18.

10. Christopher Isherwood, *Exhumations* (London: Methuen, 1966), 159.

11. Julius Pratt, "The Origin of 'Manifest Destiny,'" *American Historical Review* 32, no. 4 (1927): 795–798.

12. Reginald Horsman, *Race and Manifest Destiny: The Origins of American Racial Anglo-Saxonism* (Cambridge, Mass.: Harvard University Press, 1981).

13. *A Star Is Born,* dir. William A. Wellman, 1937; citation omitted for further references to the film.

14. Interview, February 23, 2004.

15. *American Idol,* FOX Network, January 18, 2005.

16. Bill C. Malone, *Singing Cowboys and Musical Mountaineers: Southern Culture and the Roots of Country Music* (Athens: University of Georgia Press, 2003 [1993]), 91.

17. Peter Stanfield, *Horse Opera: The Strange History of the 1930s Singing Cowboy* (Chicago: University of Illinois Press, 2002).

18. Gerald W. Haslam, *Many Californias: Literature from the Golden State* (Reno: University of Nevada Press, 1999), 1.

19. Jean Baudrillard, *America,* Trans. Chris Turner (London: Verso, 1989), 122.

20. www.disneyworld.disney.go.com/parks/hollywood-studios/attractions /american-idol/.

21. Cullen, *The American Dream,* 161.

22. MSNBC.com, "Rise of the South on 'American Idol,'" May 26, 2004, www .msnbc.msn.com/id/5053569/; Melba Newsome, "On 'Idol,' the South Rises Again . . . and Again," *New York Times,* March 25, 2007, www.nytimes.com/2007/03/25 /arts/television/25news.html?scp=1&sq=On%20'Idol,'%20the%20South%20 Rises%20Again&st=cse.

23. NPD data cited from NPD.com 2006. Owen Thomas and Oliver Ryan, "Did Text Messages Skew 'Idol' Votes?" CNNMoney.com, June 20, 2006, http://money .cnn.com/blogs/browser/2006/06/did-text-messages-skew-idol-votes.html.

24. Jordin Sparks, the 2007 Idol, was born in Arizona. 2010 winner Lee DeWyze, was born in Illinois.

25. Gavin James Campbell, "'I'm Just a Louisiana Girl': The Southern World of Britney Spears," *Southern Cultures* 7 (2001): 84.

26. Both Warwick quotes cited in Corey Moss, "Maybe We Should Just Call It 'Southern Idol,'" VH1.com, April 27, 2006, www.vh1.com/news/articles/1529538/20060426/index.jhtml?headlines=true; Ruben Studdard from www.rubenstuddard.com.

27. In this paragraph, McPherson *Reconstructing Dixie,* 18; Murray Forman, "'Represent': Race, Space, and Place in Rap Music," *Popular Music* 19, no. 1 (2000), 77; Dasilva and Faught "Nostalgia," 55; Teresa Goddu, "Bloody Daggers and Lonesome Graveyards: The Gothic and Country Music," in *Reading Country Music,* ed. Cecelia Tichi (Durham, N.C.: Duke University Press, 1998), 46.

28. David A. Davis, book reviews, *Southern Cultures* 11, no. 3: 105; Houston A. Baker and Dana D. Nelson, "Preface: Violence, the Body, and 'The South,'" *American Literature* 73, no. 2 (2001): 235; Sheldon Hackney, "The Contradictory South," *Southern Cultures* 7, no. 4 (2001): 71; James C. Cobb, "An Epitaph for the North: Reflections on the Politics of Regional and National Identity at the Millennium," *Journal of Southern History* 66, no. 1 (2000), 7.

29. Cobb quoted from "An Epitaph for the North," 7. The 1976 article he cites is "The South as the New America," by Horace Sutton, *Saturday Review,* September 4, 8; the other two articles mentioned on Southern music are "The Spiritual as Soul Music," by Dorothy Maynor, *Saturday Review,* September 4, 1976, and "Blues, and Other Noises, in the Night," by John Rockwell, *Saturday Review,* September 4, 1976.

30. Bill C. Malone and David Stricklin, *Southern Music/American Music,* rev. ed. (Lexington: University Press of Kentucky, 2003 [1979]). McPherson, *Reconstructing Dixie,* 254.

31. On minstrel shows, W. T. Lhamon, Jr., "Ebery Time I Wheel About I Jump Jim Crow: Cycles of Minstrel Transgression from Cool White to Vanilla Ice," in *Inside the Minstrel Mask: Readings in Nineteenth-Century Blackface Minstrelsy,* ed. Annemarie Bean, James V. Hatch, and Brooks McNamara (Hanover, N.H.: Wesleyan University Press, published by University Press of New England, 1996), 279. On nostalgia, Arthur P. Dudden, "Nostalgia and the American," *Journal of the History of Ideas* 22, no. 4 (1961), 517; emphasis in original.

32. Field notes, August 18, 2005.

33. Gans, *Deciding What's News,* 48–50.

34. Campbell, "'I'm Just a Lousiana Girl.'"

35. John Hartigan, Jr., *Racial Situation: Class Predicaments of Whiteness in Detroit.* (Princeton, N.J.: Princeton University Press, 1999), 90, 18.

36. *American Idol,* FOX Network, February 3, 2004.

37. Judith Butler, *Bodies That Matter: On the Discursive Limits of "Sex"* (London: Routledge, 1993), 116.

38. Field notes, Anaheim, Calif., September 23, 2004.

39. *American Idol,* FOX Network, February 9, 2005.

40. Richard A. Peterson and Paul Di Maggio, "From Region to Class, the Changing Locus of Country Music: A Test of the Massification Hypothesis," *Social Forces* 53, no. 4 (1975).

41. *American Idol,* FOX Network, January 24, 2006.

42. In this paragraph, Louis Ruprecht, Jr., "The South as Tragic Landscape," *Thesis Eleven,* no. 85 (2006): 56, 38; Amy Schrager Lang, "Jim Crow and the Pale Maiden: Gender, Color, and Class in Stephen Foster's 'Hard Times,'" in *Reading*

Country Music: Steel Guitars, Opry Stars, and Honky Tonk Bars, ed. Cecelia Tichi (Durham, N.C.: Duke University Press, 1998), 387.

43. Barrino's original barefoot moment aired on *American Idol,* FOX Network, April 14, 2004. (This performance episode aired on a Wednesday, postponed because of a Tuesday night address by President George W. Bush.) More shoelessness on the "Idols Live" tour noted in my field notes, Anaheim, Calif., September 23, 2004.

44. Ray Allen, "An American Folk Opera? Triangulating Folkness, Blackness, and Americanness in Gershwin and Heyward's 'Porgy and Bess,'" *Journal of American Folklore* 117, no. 465 (2004); Benjamin Filene, *Romancing the Folk: Public Memory and American Roots Music* (Chapel Hill: University of North Carolina Press, 2000), 58–75.

45. Fantasia, *Life is Not a Fairy Tale,* 2, xii.
The book also inspired a 2006 made-for-TV movie on the Lifetime network titled *The Fantasia Barrino Story: Life Is Not a Fairy Tale.* Barrino starred as herself.

46. Moss, "Maybe We Should Just Call It 'Southern Idol.'"

47. S. J. Sackett, "Prestige Dialect and the Pop Singer," *American Speech* 54, no. 3 (1979): 235–236.

48. *American Idol,* FOX Network, February 24, 2004; and interview, August 10, 2005.

49. In this paragraph, Malone and Stricklin, *Southern Music/American Music;* Sackett "Prestige Dialect and the Pop Singer," 237; Hackney "The Contradictory South," 70.

50. Arjun Appadurai, "Putting Hierarchy in Its Place," *Cultural Anthropology* 3, no. 1 (1988): 46, emphasis in original).

51. Gupta and Ferguson, "Beyond 'Culture,'" 9.

52. Paul C. Adams, "Cyberspace and Virtual Places," *Geographical Review* 87, no. 2 (1997): 160.

53. Gupta and Ferguson, "Beyond 'Culture,'" 10, emphasis in original.

6. Politics as Usual

Material about the Hawaiian vote and the posting of the epigram "Be a Fan, Not a Hater" has been published previously in Katherine Meizel, "'Be a Fan, Not a Hater': Identity Politics and the Audience in American Idol."

1. *American Idol,* FOX Network, May 24, 2006.

2. D.M.M., "Racism in America: Has 'American Idol' Changed the Face of White America?" www.AfricaHome.com, May 24, 2003.

3. Jenkins, *Convergence Culture,* 62–63.

4. Portia Maultsby, "Soul Music: Its Sociological and Political Significance in American Popular Culture," *Journal of Popular Culture* 17, no. 2 (1983): 58.

5. These members at the time included Jack Ashford, Eddie Willis, Joe Messina, Bob Babbitt, Uriel Jones, and Joe Hunter. Jones and Hunter have since passed away.

6. Phil Gallo, "Motown Trio Still in Groove," Variety.com, May 11, 2003, www.variety.com/article/VR1117885947?categoryid=16&cs=1.

7. MSNBC.com, "Simon Fuller: 'American Idol' Svengali—Music Mogul's Earnings at Issue," January 20, 2004, www.msnbc.msn.com/id/3943498/.

8. Robert W. Stephens, "Soul: A Historical Reconstruction of Continuity and Change in Black Popular Music," *The Black Perspective in Music* 12, no. 1 (1984): 36–37.

9. Rischar, "One Sweet Day," 155.

10. *American Idol,* FOX Network, May 19, 2009.

11. Quoted in Grigoriadis, "Wild Idol," 56.

12. For example, *American Idol,* FOX Network, May 16, 2006.

13. In this paragraph, Christopher Allen interview, May 24, 2005; Warwick quoted from my field notes, October 5, 2004.

14. idolonfox.com forum.

15. Richard A. Peterson, "From Region to Class, the Changing Locus of Country Music: A Test of the Massification Hypothesis," *Social Forces* 53, no. 4 (1997); Fox, *Real Country*; Peterson and Di Maggio, "From Region to Class"; James Gregory, "Southernizing the American Working Class: Post-war Episodes of Regional and Class Transformation," *Labor History* 39, no. 2 (1998); Bill C. Malone, *Don't Get Above Your Raisin': Country Music and the Southern Working Class* (Urbana: University of Illinois Press, 2002).

16. Peterson, *Creating Country Music,* 192.

17. MTV.com, "Booted 'American Idol' Returns to Marines, Corps Will Let Him Tour," May 15, 2003, www.mtv.com/news/articles/1471888/20030515/id_1235745.jhtml.

18. Fox, *Real Country,* 281.

19. Titze et al., "Source and Filter Adjustments Affecting the Perception of the Vocal Qualities Twang and Yawn," *Logopedics, Phoniatrics, Vocology* 28 (2003). The open quotient is the proportion of a glottal cycle (a period divided into phases, closed-to-open and open-to-closed) during which the glottis is open. It is defined as follows: O_q = open phase/T, where T is the total duration of the glottal cycle (R. J. Baken and Robert F. Orlikoff, *Clinical Measurement of Speech and Voice,* 2nd ed. [San Diego: Singular Publishing Group, 2000], 408–409). Sometimes O_q is written as Q_o.

20. A majority of scientific studies addressing the voice in music deal with Western classical techniques. These studies of country singers are therefore extremely important, not only in the field of voice science but to any analysis of country singing. Although comparisons to Western classical singing might present certain problems in an ethnomusicological framework, these studies offer significant inquiry into the relationship between what Cornelia Fales identifies as three major perspectives in discourse on sound: the perceptual, acoustic, and productive "domains" (Cornelia Fales, "Short-Circuiting Perceptual Systems: Timbre in Ambient and Techno Music," in *Wired for Sound: Engineering and Technologies in Sonic Cultures,* ed. Paul D. Greene and Thomas Porcello [Middletown, Conn.: Wesleyan University Press, 2005]).

21. Jeanette D. Hoit et al., "Respiratory Function during Speech and Singing in Professional Country Singers," *Journal of Voice* 10, no. 1 (1996); Thomas F. Cleveland et al., "Estimated Subglottal Pressure in Six Professional Country Singers," *Journal of Voice* 11, no. 4 (1997); R. Stone, Jr., et al. "Formant Frequencies in Country Singers' Speech and Singing," *Journal of Voice* 13, no. 2 (1999): 167.

22. *American Idol,* FOX Network, March 18, 2003.

23. *American Idol,* FOX Network, May 6, 2003.

24. www.riaa.com, 2006.

25. Goddu, "Bloody Daggers and Lonesome Graveyards," 46.

26. Robert W. Van Sickel, "A World without Citizenship: On (the Absence of) Politics and Ideology in Country Music Lyrics, 1960–2000," *Popular Music and Society* 28, no. 3 (2005): 325–326, 328.

27. CMT Network, July 4, 2005.

28. In this paragraph, Van Sickel, "A World without Citizenship," 317; Malone and Stricklin, *Southern Music/American Music,* 132 (block quote); Van Sickel, "A World without Citizenship," 132.

29. Mike Butler, "'Luther King Was a Good Ole Boy': The Southern Rock Movement and White Male Identity in the Post–Civil Rights South," *Popular Music and Society* 23, no. 2 (1999).

30. Preceding discussion based on Malone and Stricklin, *Southern Music/American Music,* 113–114; Butler, "'Luther King Was a Good Ole Boy.'" Quote from Butler, 43.

31. Butler "'Luther King Was a Good Ole Boy,'" 46–47; Les Back, "Voices of Hate, Sounds of Hybridity: Black Music and the Complexities of Racism," *Black Music Research Journal* 20, no. 2 (2000): 144.

32. *American Idol,* FOX Network, March 25, 2003.

33. Zenaida Serrano, "Jasmine Overwhelmed by Aloha from Local Fans," *Honolulu Advertiser,* May 14, 2004, http://the.honoluluadvertiser.com/article/2004 /May/14/il/i101a.html/.

34. Jasmine Trias Proclamation May 13, 2004, www.hawaii.gov/ltgov/copy _of_headlines/Jasmine-Trias-proclamation5.15.04/view.

35. Michael Tsai, "'Idol' Hooked Hawai'i from Start," *Honolulu Advertiser,* May 23, 2004, http://the.honoluluadvertiser.com/article/2004/May/23/ln/ln02a.html.

36. In this paragraph, Nina Wu, "Hawaii Lures Viewers to Spend 'Idol' Time Here," *Pacific Business News,* October 3, 2003, http://pacific.bizjournals.com/ pacific/stories/2003/10/06/story4.html; Nina Wu describes the lucky restaurant in "'American Idol' Brought Hawaii Dollars and Exposure," *Pacific Business News,* May 28, 2004, http://pacific.bizjournals.com/pacific/stories/2003/10/06/story4.html; and the *Star Bulletin* article is "Wristband Sales Jump After Velasco's Showing on 'Idol,'" *Honolulu Star-Bulletin,* by Shawn "Speedy" Lopes, April 6, 2004, http://star bulletin.com/2004/04/06/features/story2.html.

37. Statistics from Wayne Harada, "'Idol' Judge Simon Not Counting on Jasmine at All," *Honolulu Advertiser,* May 5, 2004, http://the.honoluluadvertiser.com /article/2004/May/05/il/i103a.html; and from Tsai, "'Idol' Hooked Hawai'i from Start."

38. Lopes, "Simon said Velasco Would See 1 More Week," *Honolulu Star-Bulletin,* April 1, 2004, http://starbulletin.com/2004/04/01/features/story3.html.

39. *American Idol,* FOX Network, March 2, 2004.

For a fascinating account of lore regarding the origins of the "shaka" sign that Trias employed on *Idol,* and its name, see June Watanabe, "Kokua Line: Wherever It Came from, Shaka Sign Part of Hawaii," *Honolulu Star-Bulletin,* March 31, 2002, www.starbulletin.com/2002/03/31/news/kokualine.html.

40. Joane Nagel, "Constructing Ethnicity: Creating and Recreating Ethnic Identity and Culture," *Social Problems* 41, no. 1 (1994): 154.

41. Michael Tsai and Wayne Harada, "Filipino Pride Flows for State's 'Idol' Finalists," *Honolulu Advertiser,* March 23, 2004; Tsai, "'Idol' Hooked Hawai'i from Start."; idolonfox.com forum.

42. MSNBC.com, "'Idol' Finalist a Huge Hit in Philippines," October 12, 2004, www.msnbc.msn.com/id/6233535/. Her concert was titled "Jasmine: Fil-Am Idol."

The *Manila Times* reported then that she "is a descendant of the revolutionary hero, General Mariano Trias" (Rome Jorge, "Jasmine Trias: Everyone's Idol," *Sunday Times* [*Manila Times Internet Edition*], October 10, 2004).

43. Yen Le Espiritu, *Asian American Panethnicity: Bridging Institutions and Identities* (Philadelphia: Temple University Press, 1992), 7–12.

44. *American Idol,* FOX Network, April 27, 2004.

45. Lee 2009: 12, 16.

46. See chapter 5, n7.

47. Personal communication, June 21, 2006.

48. Richard Kaplan, "Hispanic Viewers again Crown 'American Idol' as Most-Popular Show, Followed by 'CSI', 'The Mentalist,'" *Hispanic Business,* January 22, 2009, www.hispanicbusiness.com/entertainment/2009/1/22/hispanic_viewers_again_crown_american_idol.htm.

49. Tong Soon Lee, "Technology and the Production of Islamic Space," 17.

50. All three quotes above from Catherine Donaldson-Evans, "Elton John: 'American Idol' Is Racist," April 28, 2004, www.foxnews.com/story/0,2933,118432,00.html.

51. Interview, January 31, 2006.

52. *BBC News World Edition,* "Cowell Denies Idol 'racism' claim," April 29, 2004, http://news.bbc.co.uk/2/hi/entertainment/3668883.stm.

53. Forum moderator, personal communication, February 9, 2005.

54. idolonfox.com, May 6, 2004.

55. This and Lowry's quote above from *American Idol,* FOX Network, February 2, 2004.

56. This and block quote above from an interview August 10, 2005, my emphasis.

57. Gerald Sider, *Living Indian Histories: Lumbee and Tuscarora People in North Carolina* (Chapel Hill: University of North Carolina Press, 2003 [1993]), xxviii.

58. Karen I. Blu, *The Lumbee Problem: The Making of an American Indian People* (Lincoln: University of Nebraska Press, 2001 [1980]), 1. This, along with Sider's *Living Indian Histories,* is one of the foremost studies of the Lumbee.

59. Anne Merline McCulloch and David E. Wilkins, "'Constructing' Nations within States: The Quest for Federal Recognition by the Catawba and Lumbee Tribes," *American Indian Quarterly* 19, no. 3 (1995): 365.

60. Both quotes from an interview, August 10, 2005.

Federal recognition acknowledges a tribe as sovereign, and creates a political connection between the tribe and the United States, establishing certain governmental obligations (McCulloch and Wilkins, "'Constructing' Nations within States," 362–363).

61. Allie Vered, "Virginia's Jewish Idol," *Virginia Jewish News,* April 10, 2006. Guest mentor Tommy Mottola was shown telling him in rehearsal footage that his performance should not "sound like a bar mitzvah song," but Mottola himself converted to Judaism, so it is especially unclear whether his comment actually alluded to Yamin (*American Idol,* FOX Network, May 8, 2006).

62. Larry King interview with Paula Abdul, *CNN Larry King Live,* CNN, May 19, 2006. Transcript accessed at http://transcripts.cnn.com/TRANSCRIPTS/0605/19/lkl.01.html.

63. Jacob Neusner, "The Religion, Judaism, in America: What Has Happened in Three Hundred and Fifty Years?" *American Jewish History* 91, no.s 3–4 (2003): 368.

64. In this paragraph, information on Yamin's ancestry comes from Vered, "Virginia's Jewish Idol"; the term "Judaist" from Raphael Loewe, as cited in Neusner, "The Religion, Judaism, in America," 364; and Milton M. Gordon cited from *Assimilation in American Life* (Oxford: Oxford University Press, 1964), 185 (also quoted in Stephen Steinberg, *The Ethnic Myth: Race, Ethnicity, and Class in America* [Boston: Beacon, 1989 (1981)], 84).

65. Susan Gubar, "Racial Camp in *The Producers* and *Bamboozled*," *Film Quarterly* 60, no. 2 (2006).

66. Anna Altheide, "Backstage Pass: American Idol Season 8—Part Two," *The Chaparral: The Student's Voice of College of the Desert*, May 11, 2009, http://media.www.thechaparral.com/. Lambert also spoke of his heritage in an interview with Vanessa Grigoriadis ("Wild Idol").

67. Edward Alexander, "Multiculturalism's Jewish Problem," *Academic Questions* 5, no. 4 (1992). On worries about seeming too Jewish, see *Talking Back: Images of Jewish Women in Popular American Culture,* ed. Joyce Antler (Waltham, Mass.: Brandeis University Press, 1998); Joyce Antler's "Not 'Too Jewish' for Prime-Time," in *Televisions Changing Image of American Jews,* ed. Neal Gabler, Frank Rich, and Joyce Antler (Los Angeles: American Jewish Committee and the Norman Lear Center, 2000); and Frank Rich, "Journal; The 'Too Jewish' Question," *New York Times,* March 16, 1996, www.nytimes.com/1996/03/16/opinion/journal-the-too-jewish-question.html.

68. Vincent Brook, *Something Ain't Kosher Here: The Rise of the "Jewish" Sitcom* (New Brunswick, N.J.: Rutgers University Press, 2003), 127, 2, and (on conceptual Jewishness) 24.

69. Walt Whitman, "I Hear America Singing," in *Leaves of Grass* (New York: Bantam Books, 2004 [1855]), 9.

70. In this paragraph, information comes from an interview with Zaragoza June 13, 2006, and from USPS.com, 2005, "Fans of *American Idol* Finalist and Mail Carrier Vonzell Solomon Can Say 'Congratulations,'" May 10, 2005, www.usps.com/communications/news/press/2005/pro5_042.htm. Solomon's onscreen comment is from *American Idol,* FOX Network, May 3, 2005.

71. Simon Frith, *Performing Rites: On the value of Popular Music,* 2nd ed. (Cambridge, Mass.: Harvard University Press, 1999), 274, my emphasis.

7. The United Nations of Pop

The author has also addressed discourse about *Idols* and democracy in Katherine Meizel, "Idol Thoughts: Nationalism in the Pan-Arab Vocal Competition *Superstar*," in *A Song for Europe: Eurovision, Popular Music, and the Politics of Kitsch,* ed. Ivan Raykoff (Farnham, Surrey: Ashgate, 2007); Meizel, "A Singing Citizenry: Popular Music and Civil Religion in America"; and Katherine Meizel "Real-politics: *Super Star* and Democracy Promotion in the Middle East," in *Music and Media in the Arab World,* ed. Michael Frishkopf (Cairo: American University in Cairo Press, 2010).

1. FremantleMedia.com, "Idols Compete on the Global Stage to Become World's Favourite Pop Superstar," November 13, 2003, www.fremantlemedia.com/page.asp?partid=198.

2. A similar avenue of only American flags appeared in the opening graphics to *American Idol,* Seasons 2 and 3, and to *American Idol Rewind.*

3. *World Idol,* FOX Network, December 25, 2003.

4. France's *Nouvelle Star* changed the coloring of its logo to purple, as did the Arab program *Super Star.*

5. In this paragraph, David Lyle quotes from "Idol Worship," an interview by Bob Garfield for *On the Media,* WNYC, October 17, 2003, www.onthemedia.org /yore/transcripts/transcripts_101703_idol.html; Simon Cowell from Ellen Tumposky, "World of 'Idol' Pursuit," *New York Daily News,* December 23, 2003, www .nydailynews.com/entertainment/story/148413p-130943c.html.

6. See also two of my essays, Meizel, "Idol Thoughts," and Meizel, "Real-politics."

7. Where@Lebanon.com, "Music: Diana Karazon," January 18, 2004, www .lebanon.com/where/entertainment/musicnews230.htm.

8. *World Idol,* FOX Network, December 25, 2003.

9. Rahbani, a renowned Lebanese composer, is the youngest brother of Assy and Mansour Rahbani, with whom he sometimes worked during their famous association with celebrated Lebanese singer Fairouz.

10. This and all further quotations from participants in *World Idol* come from the *World Idol* broadcast on FOX Network, December 25, 2003.

11. *American Idol: World's Worst Auditions,* FOX Network, May 19, 2005.

12. Thomas Solomon, "'Every Way That I Can?' Turkey and the Eurovision Song Contest" (unpublished paper presented at the 2004 conference of the Society for Ethnomusicology, Tucson, Arizona, November 5, 2004), 11.

13. Lisa A. Lewis, "The Making of a Preferred Address," in *Gender Politics and MTV* (Philadelphia: Temple University Press, 1990), 27–33.

14. Lyle, "Idol Worship," www.onthemedia.org/yore/transcripts/transcripts _101703_idol.html.

15. Andrew Strenk, "What Price Victory? The World of International Sports and Politics," *Annals of the American Academy of Political and Social Science* 445 (1979): 140.

16. Richard Curtis is a film writer and director, and also a co-founder of the Comic Relief organization in the United Kingdom. Additionally he co-founded the U.K. charity holiday known as Red Nose Day, as well as the Make Poverty History coalition, and he worked with Bono and Bob Geldof on the Live8 event in 2005 (CPEF Press Release 2007). The groups supported by Charity Projects Entertainment Fund included America's Second Harvest, the Boys & Girls Clubs of America, the Children's Health Fund, the Global Fund (to fight AIDS, Tuberculosis, and Malaria), Malaria No More, Nothing But Nets, Save the Children, and the United Nations Children's Fund (UNICEF). Corporate sponsors were solicited by Ryan Seacrest onscreen in the weeks before the event, and in addition to News Corporation and regular *American Idol* sponsors Coca Cola, AT&T, and Ford, included Allstate, ExxonMobil, ConAgra Foods, and myspace.com. iTunes also participated, making "*Idol* Gives Back" performances available for purchase, with the proceeds going to Charity Projects Entertainment fund (CPEF).

17. The African Children's Choir is part of the Music for Life Institute, according to the choir's 2007 website a "Christian humanitarian relief and development organization" (www.africanchildrenschoir.com/aboutus/aboutus.php).

18. For the most oft-repeated variations of this quote, see Gilbert Rodman, "A Hero to Most? Elvis, Myth, and the Politics of Race," *Cultural Studies* 8, no. 3 (1994).

19. Elvis Presley Enterprises, "Robert F. X. Sillerman and Elvis Presley Enterprises Announce Partnership," December 16, 2004, www.elvis.com/news/full_story .asp?id=738.

20. Lisa Bode, "From Shadow Citizens to Teflon Stars: Reception of the Transfiguring Effects of New Moving Image Technologies," *Animation* 1, no 2 (2006): 177.

21. ABCNews.com, "Elvis on 'Idol': How It Was Done," April 27, 2007, http: //abcnews.go.com/GMA/story?id=3091081.

22. *Duet Impossible* also featured a performance by Katie Melua and the posthumously famous Eva Cassidy, who tragically died at the age of thirty-three in 1996, but this time the duet effect was accomplished with Melua onstage partnered with Cassidy projected on a large video screen.

23. John Whitfield, "Science in the Movies: From Microscope to Multiplex— An MRI Scanner Darkly," *Nature* 441 (2006).

24. Raka Shome, "White Femininity and the Discourse of the Nation: Re/ membering Princess Diana," *Feminist Media Studies* 1, no. 3 (2001): 333. It's worth noting in this context that Madonna appeared briefly on "*Idol* Gives Back" in a videotaped segment shot in Africa, speaking among several African children.

25. "*Idol* Gives Back."

26. Gans, *Deciding What's News,* 43.

27. *American Idol,* FOX Network, May 1, 2007.

28. Press speculated that the decision was made because of the global economic crisis (Michael Starr, "'Idol' Takes Back Charity 'Give Back,'" *New York Post,* December 12, 2008), although Cécile Frot-Coutaz, executive producer at FremantleMedia, said, "I don't think you should go back to the country and ask them to donate every single year. I think it's too much. Every two years to me feels right" (Andy Denhart, "Report: 'Idol' to Make Changes in 2009," December 11, 2008, www.msnbc.msn.com/id/28183600/).

29. Seacrest's statement about past fundraising was broadcast on *American Idol,* FOX Network, May 13, 2009. The beneficiaries of the planned 2010 special were listed on americanidol.com, October 5, 2009.

30. *American Idol,* FOX Network, May 2, 2007.

31. Arjun Appadurai, *Modernity at Large: Cultural Dimensions of Globalization* (Minneapolis: University of Minnesota Press, 1996), 34–36. See also Meizel, "Idol Thoughts"; and Penelope Coutas, *Modernity at Large: Cultural Dimensions of Globalization* (Minneapolis: University of Minnesota Press, 2008).

32. Coutas, *Modernity at Large,* 114.

33. Aswin Punathambekar, "Reality Television and the Making of Mobile Publics: The Case of *Indian Idol,*" in *Real Worlds: Global Perspectives on the Politics of Reality Television,* ed. Marwan Kraidy and Katherine Sender (New York: Routledge, 2009).

34. Arab Advisor's Group, "Arabic SuperStar's Voting Grosses over U.S. $4 Million in Voting Revenues Alone," August 24, 2003, www.arabadvisors.com/Pressers /presser240803.htm.

35. "Entertainment: Millions Vote For Middle East Pop Idol," August 26, 2003, www.160characters.org/news.php?action=view&nid=92.

36. In early 2005, 19 Entertainment was acquired by Robert F. X. Sillerman's New York–based company, CKX.

37. Appadurai, *Modernity at Large*, 41–42.

38. William Robinson, *A Theory of Global Capitalism: Production, Class, and State in a Transnational World* (Baltimore, Md.: Johns Hopkins University Press, 2004), 4 (epoch), 20 (circuits of production), 87 (elite politicization), and 48 (*manifest agent*; emphasis in original).

39. Robinson, *A Theory of Global Capitalism*, 84.

40. Meizel, "A Singing Citizenry," 502.

41. In this paragraph, Appadurai, *Modernity at Large*, 37 (emphasis in original); Cornel West, *Democracy Matters: Winning the Fight against Imperialism* (New York: Penguin, 2004), 3 (my emphasis); and Sheldon Wolin, *Tocqueville between Two Worlds: The Making of a Political and Theoretical Life* (Princeton, N.J.: Princeton University Press, 2001), 571 (also quoted in West, *Democracy Matters*, 24).

42. Lyle, "Idol Worship," www.onthemedia.org/yore/transcripts/transcripts _101703_idol.html.

43. Bill Savadove, "CHINA: Brakes Put on TV Talent Programmes," *Asia Media: Media News Daily*, March 17, 2006, www.asiamedia.ucla.edu/article-eastasia .asp?parentid=41120.

44. King, interview with Simon Cowell.

45. Information about *Iraq Star* from Ali Jaafar, "'Star' Lights Up Auds in Iraq," *Variety* at Variety.com, August 28, 2005, www.variety.com/index.asp?layout=print _story&articleid=VR11179812&categoryid=1445. On the twelve-year-old singer, see also Sudarsan Raghavan, "In Iraq, Singing for a Chance at Hope and Glory," Washington Post, Page A01, September 1, 2006, www.washingtonpost.com/wp-dyn /content/article/2006/08/31/AR2006083101675_pf.html; USAToday.com, "Who Will Become the Next 'Iraq Star'? Stay Tuned," usatoday.com, July 13, 2006, http: //www.usatoday.com/news/world/iraq/2006-07-13-iraq-star_x.htm; BBCNews .com, "Iraqis Cheered by Pop Idol Show," August 24, 2005, http://news.bbc.co.uk /2/hi/middle_east/4181696.stm. Information about *Talents* comes from Anne Garrels, "Analysis: Efforts to Enliven Iraq's New Television Network," All Things Considered, National Public Radio, broadcast January 28, 2004.

46. www.afghanstardocumentary.com/.

47. In this paragraph, Renske Doorenspleet, *Democratic Transitions: Exploring the Structural Sources of the Fourth Wave* (Boulder, Colo.: Rienner, 2005), 163; Samuel P. Huntington, *The Third Wave: Democratization in the Late Twentieth Century* (Norman: University of Oklahoma Press, 1991), 3; on the "fourth wave," see Doorenspleet and also Michael McFaul, "The Fourth Wave of Democracy and Dictatorship: Noncooperative Transitions in the Postcommunist World," *World Politics* 54, no. 2 (2002).

48. Doorenspleet *Democratic Transitions*, 15.

49. Ted Robert Gurr, "Persistence and Change in Political Systems," *American Political Science Review* 68, no. 4 (1974): 1483; also quoted in Doorenspleet, *Democratic Transitions*, 24.

50. Number of nations in the world, State Department, www.state.gov/s/inr /rls/4250.htm. The figure 113 for the nations *Idol* broadcasts to comes from an old version of the 19 Entertainment website, www.19.co.uk. As of August 2009 the site had been restructured, and the number of countries broadcast to is no longer listed,

nor was I able to obtain a complete list by request. The partial list provided is based on data from Sony Entertainment Television, www.canalsony.com/; Star World, www.startv.com/world/americanidol/index.htm; Ruta Kupfer, "Its Star Has Fallen," Haaretz.com, January 16, 2007, www.haaretz.com/hasen/spages/811361.html; and e2, www.e2.tv.tr/dizi.asp?code=americanidol.

51. Deeley did not return the following season, but he has also hosted the American show *So You Think You Can Dance,* another FOX reality program developed by *Idols* co-creator Simon Fuller and *American Idol* executive producer Nigel Lythgoe.

52. *Philippine Idol* switched host networks for its second season and became *Pinoy Idol.*

53. In this paragraph, Boorstin, *The Image,* 241; William I. Robinson, "Globalization, the World System, and 'Democracy Promotion' in U.S. Foreign Policy," *Theory and Society* 25, no. 5: 623–24. Polyarchic democracy is introduced and discussed extensively in Robert Dahl, *Polyarchy: Participation and Oppositions* (New Haven, Conn.: Yale University Press, 1971).

54. Robinson, "Globalization, the World System, and 'Democracy Promotion,'" 654 (all quotes), 628 (on polyarchy vs. authoritarianism).

55. In this paragraph, John Fraim, *Battle of Symbols: Global Dynamics of Advertising, Entertainment and Media* (Einsiedeln, Switzerland: Daimon, 2003), 34; Joseph S. Nye, Jr., "The American National Interest and Global Public Goods," *International Affairs* 78, no. 2 (2002): 239; Fraim, *Battle of Symbols,* 32 (on America's democratic symbols).

56. In this paragraph, John Hartley, "Democratainment," in *The Television Studies Reader,* ed. Robert C. Allen and Annette Hill (London: Routledge, 2004), 526 (emphasis in original); and Cullen, *The American Dream,* 6.

57. Field notes, August 17, 2005.

58. Lisa de Moraes, "'American Idol,' Ready for an Unflattering Close-Up?" *Washington Post,* May 3, 2005, www.washingtonpost.com/wp-dyn/articles/A32720-2005May3.html.

59. All Della Terza quotes from personal communication, April 12, 2007. Howard Stern quoted in Edward Wyatt, "Howard Stern Tries to Kill 'American Idol' with Kindness for a Weak Link," *New York Times,* March 31, 2007, www.nytimes.com/2007/03/31/arts/television/31idol.html?scp=1&sq=Howard%20Stern%20Tries%20to%20Kill%20'American%20Idol'%20with%20Kindness%20for%20a%20Weak%20Link&st=cse.

60. In this paragraph, Fraim, *Battle of Symbols,* 47; Appadurai, *Modernity at Large,* 42.

61. FremantleMedia has taken legal action against at least one such unlicensed competition, the "Stripper Idol" contest held at the Palazio Men's Club in Austin, Texas (*New York Daily News,* "American Idol Producers Sue Texas Club Over 'Stripper Idol' Competition," January 14, 2009, www.nydailynews.com/entertainment/americanidol/2009/01/14/2009-01-14_american_idol_producers_sue_texas_club_0.html).

62. The concept of disemia, as advanced by Michael Herzfeld, suggests a set of "co-domains" through which "individuals are able to negotiate social, national, ethnic, or political boundaries" (Herzfeld, "Disemia," in *Semiotics 1980: Proceedings of the Fifth Annual Meeting of the Semiotic Society of America,* ed. Michael Herzfeld and Margot D. Lenhart [New York: Plenum, 1982], 205).

Epilogue

1. The Kara DioGuardi quote is from *American Idol*, Fox Network, March 2, 2010 and Crystal Bowersox's assertion is from *American Idol*, Fox Network, April 6, 2010. An example of judges' praise for Bowersox as "real" occurred on *American Idol*, Fox Network, March 30, 2010; judges cited Bowersox as an example of "what they talk about, when people know who they are" on *American Idol*, Fox Network, March 9, 2010.

2. Kirk Baird, "Toledo Area Singer Takes On 'Idol' Pursuits," *Toledo Blade*. February 22, 2010, www.toledoblade.com/apps/pbcs.dll/article?AID=/20100222/ART18/2220325/0/NEWS02.

3. Details on the dispensation of proceeds from the Village Idiot fundraiser are from Kristen Rapin, "$856 donated to JDRF in May's Name," *Toledo Free Press*, May 25, 2010, www.toledofreepress.com/2010/05/26/856-donated-to-jdrf-in-may's-name/; Crystal's support from her hometown and from Woodward were discussed in an interview, March 23, 2010.

4. The Nikki Schafer quote, Ed Lopez's discussion of staff and patron admiration for Crystal; staff's assertion that the show didn't start until Crystal's performances ended, and Mr. Woodward's estimate of the number of times he and Ed Lopez had voted for Crystal are all from interviews, March 23, 2010.

5. Gil Kaufman, "Crystal Bowersox's Hometown: A Tale of Two Bars," May 5, 2010, http://newsroom.mtv.com/2010/05/05/crystal-bowersox-hometown/.

6. The description of Crystal's motorcade and interaction with the crowd is from field notes, May 14, 2010; attendance figures are from FoxToledo.com, "Mama Sox Performs for 10,000," May 14, 2010, www.foxtoledo.com/dpp/entertainment/Mama-Sox-performs-for-10-000.

7. Confirmatory evidence for the "slump" Crystal mentioned comes from the Bureau of Labor Statistics at the U.S. Department of Labor: unemployment rate in Toledo had begun the year in January at 13.6 percent, nearly 4 percent higher than the national rate of 9.7 percent (www.bls.gov, accessed July 5, 2010). Crystal's quotes on the topic of "Holy Toledo" are from *American Idol*, Fox Network, May 19, 2010.

8. Toledo resident's awareness of Elliston because of Crystal, field notes, May 14, 2010. Attendance figures for "Bowerstock" from Sarah Weber, "Ottawa County Cashes in on Crystal," May 18, 2010, www.sanduskyregister.com/oak-harbor/2010/may/18/ottawa-county-cashes-crystal.

9. Interview, May 14, 2010.

10. Toledo Mud Hen attendance, Catharine Hadley, "A Record Crowd for Mud Hens, 'Idol' Star," May 15 2010, www.thenews-messenger.com/article/20100515/NEWS01/5150312/A-record-crowd-for-Mud-Hens-Idol-star. Jason Szczublewski interview, May 25, 2010.

11. Jodi Szczublewski interview, May 25, 2010. For the premature listing of Crystal as winner on Wikipedia, many thanks to Branden James.

WORKS CITED

ABCNews.com. 2007. "Elvis on 'Idol': How It Was Done." April 27. http://abcnews
.go.com/GMA/story?id=3091081 (accessed May 7, 2007).

Adams, James Truslow. 1933 [1931]. *The Epic of America.* Boston: Little, Brown.

Adams, Paul C. 1997. "Cyberspace and Virtual Places." *Geographical Review* 87 (2):
155–171.

Adler, Jerry. 2005. "Special Report: Spirituality 2005, In Search of the Spiritual."
Newsweek 146 (9/10) (August 29/September 5): 48–64.

Adorno, Theodor, and Max Horkheimer. 1993. "The Culture Industry: Enlightenment as Mass Deception." In *The Cultural Studies Reader,* ed. Simon During.
London: Routledge.

The Advocate. 1997. "The Buzz: The Inside Scoop on Entertainment," October 14: 26.

Alexander, Edward. 1992. "Multiculturalism's Jewish Problem." *Academic Questions*
5 (4): 63–68.

Allen, Ray. 2004. "An American Folk Opera? Triangulating Folkness, Blackness,
and Americanness in Gershwin and Heyward's 'Porgy and Bess.'" *Journal of
American Folklore* 117 (465): 243–261.

Altheide, Anna. 2009. "Backstage Pass: American Idol Season 8—Part Two." *The
Chaparral: The Student's Voice of College of the Desert.* May 11. http://media.www
.thechaparral.com/media/storage/paper570/news/2009/05/11/Entertainment
/Backstage.Pass.American.Idol.Season.8.Part.Two-3752265.shtml (accessed July
31, 2009).

Althusser, Louis. 2001 [1970]. "Ideology and Ideological State Apparatuses: Notes
Toward an Investigation." In *Lenin and Philosophy and Other Essays,* trans. Ben
Brewster. New York: Monthly Review Press, 85–126.

American Idol. FOX Network. June 2002–present.

American Idol. *The Search for a Superstar.* 2002. Dir. Bruce Gowers, Nigel Lythgoe,
and Ken Warwick. Videocassette. R2 Entertainment, 19 Entertainment, FremantleMedia, StudioWorks.

American Idol on FOX, Community (Forum). Prospero Forums. www.idolonfox.com
and http://forums.prospero.com/foxidol/messages.

American Red Cross. 2003. "Sale of 'American Idol' Finalist CDs Raises $185,000."
    October. www.redcross.org/pressrelease/0,1077,0_314_1746,00.html (accessed
    July 26, 2006).

Anderson, Benedict. 2002 [1983]. *Imagined Communities: Reflections on the Origin and
    Spread of Nationalism.* London: Verso.

Anderson, Brooke. 2006. "Showbiz Tonight." Interview transcript at CNN.com.
    September 22. http://transcripts.cnn.com/TRANSCRIPTS/0609/22/sbt.01.html
    (accessed September 23, 2006).

Andrejevic, Mark. 2004. *Reality TV: The Work of Being Watched.* Oxford: Rowman
    and Littlefield.

Ang, Ien. 1989. "Wanted: Audiences. On the Politics of Empirical Audience Stud-
    ies." In *Remote Control: Television, Audiences, and Cultural Power,* ed. Ellen Seiter,
    96–115. London: Routledge.

———. 1991. *Desperately Seeking the Audience.* London: Routledge.

Antler, Joyce, ed. 1998. *Talking Back: Images of Jewish Women in Popular American
    Culture.* Waltham, Mass.: Brandeis University Press.

———. 2000. "Not 'Too Jewish' for Prime-Time." In *Televisions Changing Image
    of American Jews,* ed. Neal Gabler, Frank Rich, and Joyce Antler. Los Angeles:
    American Jewish Committee and the Norman Lear Center.

Appadurai, Arjun. 1988. "Putting Hierarchy in Its Place." *Cultural Anthropology* 3
    (1): 36–49.

———. 1996. *Modernity at Large: Cultural Dimensions of Globalization.* Minneapolis:
    University of Minnesota Press.

Arab Advisors Group. 2003. "Arabic Superstar's Voting Grosses over U.S. $4 Mil-
    lion in Voting Revenues Alone." August 24. www.arabadvisors.com/Pressers
    /presser-240803.htm (accessed February 7, 2004).

Arendt, Hannah. 1966 [1951]. *The Origins of Totalitarianism.* New York: Harcourt,
    Brace and World.

———. 1993 [1961]. *Between Past and Future: Eight Exercises in Political Thought.* New
    York: Penguin Books.

Arthur, Kate. 2004. "How 'American Idol' Got Hijacked by Its Viewers." *New York
    Times.* May 24. www.nytimes.com/2004/05/23/arts/television/23AURT.html
    ?scp=1&sq=How%20%27American%20Idol%27%20Got%20Hijacked%20by%20
    Its%20Viewers&st=cse (accessed May 24, 2004).

Association of National Advertisers. 2003. "Family Television Awards Honor Six
    for Family Friendly Programming." 15 August. www.familyprogramawards.com
    (accessed June 2, 2007).

Attali, Jacques. 1992 [1985]. *Noise: The Political Economy of Music.* Trans. Brian Mas-
    sumi. Minneapolis: University of Minnesota Press.

Auslander, Philip. 1996. "LIVENESS: Performance and the Anxiety of Simula-
    tion." In *Performance and Cultural Politics,* ed. Elin Diamond, 196–213. London:
    Routledge.

———. 1999. *Liveness: Performance in a Mediatized Culture.* London: Routledge.

———. 2003. "Good Old Rock and Roll: Performing the 1950s in the 1970s." *Journal
    of Popular Music Studies* 15 (3): 166–194.

———. 2006. *Performing Glam Rock.* Ann Arbor: University of Michigan Press.

Babuscio, Jack. "Camp and the Gay Sensibility." 1993. In *Camp Grounds: Style and Homosexuality,* ed. David Bergman, 19–38. Amherst: University of Massachusetts Press.

Back, Les. 2000. "Voices of Hate, Sounds of Hybridity: Black Music and the Complexities of Racism." *Black Music Research Journal* 20 (2): 127–149.

Baird, Kirk. 2010. "Toledo Area Singer Takes On 'Idol' Pursuits." *Toledo Blade.* February 22. www.toledoblade.com/apps/pbcs.dll/article?AID=/20100222/ART18/2220325/0/NEWS02 (Accessed July 5, 2010).

Baken, R. J., and Robert F. Orlikoff. 2000. *Clinical Measurement of Speech and Voice.* 2nd ed. San Diego: Singular Publishing Group, a division of Thomson Learning.

Baker, Houston A., and Dana D. Nelson. 2001. "Preface: Violence, the Body, and 'The South.'" *American Literature* 73 (2): 231–244.

Banton, Michael. 1977. *The Idea of Race.* London: Tavistock.

Barot, Rohit, and John Bird. 2001. "Racialization: The Genealogy and Critique of a Concept." *Ethnic and Racial Studies* 24 (4): 601–618.

Barthes, Roland. 1977. *Image, Music, Text.* Trans. Stephen Heath. New York: Hill and Wang.

Barz, Gregory F., and Timothy J. Cooley, eds. 1997. *Shadows in the Field: New Perspectives for Fieldwork in Ethnomusicology.* Oxford: Oxford University Press.

Baudrillard, Jean. 1983. *Simulations.* Trans. Paul Foss, Paul Patton, and Philip Beitchman. New York: Semiotext(e).

———. 1988. *Jean Baudrillard, Selected Writings.* Ed. Mark Poster. Stanford, Calif.: Stanford University Press.

———. 1989. *America.* Trans. Chris Turner. London: Verso.

———. 1990. [1983]. *Fatal Strategies.* Trans. Philip Beitchman and W. G. J. Niesluchowski. New York: Semiotext(e).

———. 1995. *The Gulf War Did Not Take Place.* Bloomington: Indiana University Press.

———. 1998. *Selected Writings.* In *Simulations,* ed. Mark Poster, 166–184. Stanford University Press. www.egs.edu/faculty/baudrillard/baudrillard-simulacra-and-simulations.html (accessed May 20, 2004).

———. 2001. "The Spirit of Terrorism." *Le Monde.* November 2.

Bayton, Mavis. 1998. *Frock Rock: Women Performing Popular Music.* Oxford: Oxford University Press.

BBCNews.com. 2001. "New Job for 'Nasty Nigel.'" March 29. http://news.bbc.co.uk/1/hi/entertainment/tv_and_radio/1249681.stm (accessed February 18, 2007).

BBCNews.com. 2006. "Iraqis Cheered by Pop Idol Show." August 24. http://news.bbc.co.uk/2/hi/middle_east/4181696.stm (accessed July 1, 2007).

BBC News World Edition. 2004. "Cowell Denies Idol 'racism' claim." April 29. http://news.bbc.co.uk/2/hi/entertainment/3668883.stm (accessed February 9, 2005).

Bell, Catherine M. 1997. *Ritual: Perspectives and Dimensions.* Oxford: Oxford University Press.

Bellah, Robert N. 1976. Response to the panel on civil religion. *Sociological Analysis* 37:153–159.

———. 1992 [1975]. *The Broken Covenant: American Civil Religion in Time of Trial.* Chicago: University of Chicago Press.

———. 2001 [1967]. "Civil Religion in America." *Daedalus: Journal of the American Academy of Arts and Sciences* 96 (1): 1–21. Reprinted at RobertBellah.com. http://robertbellah.com/articles_5.htm (accessed March 19, 2005).

Bellah, Robert N., Richard Madsen, William M. Sullivan, Ann Swidler, and Steven M. Tipton. 1996 [1985]. *Habits of the Heart.* Berkeley: University of California Press.

Bendix, Regina. 1997. *In Search of Authenticity: The Formation of Folklore Studies.* Madison: University of Wisconsin Press.

Benjamin, Walter. 1968. "The Work of Art in the Age of Mechanical Reproduction." In *Illuminations,* ed. Hannah Arendt, trans. Harry Zohn, 217–251. New York: Schocken Books.

Bettelheim, Bruno. 1960. *The Informed Heart.* Glencoe: Free Press.

Bielby, Denise, and C. Lee Harrington. 1994. "Reach Out and Touch Someone: Viewers, Agency, and Audiences in the Televisual Experience." In *Viewing, Reading, Listening: Audiences and Cultural Reception,* ed. Jon Cruz and Justin Lewis, 81–100. Boulder, Colo.: Westview.

Blender. 2006. "The 50 Worst Things to Happen to Music." April. www.blender.com/guide/articles.aspx?id=1913 (accessed March 11, 2007).

Blu, Karen I. 2001 [1980]. *The Lumbee Problem: The Making of an American Indian People.* Lincoln: University of Nebraska Press.

Blumler, Jay G., and Elihu Katz, eds. 1974. *The Uses of Mass Communications: Current Perspectives on Gratifications Research.* Beverly Hills, Calif.: Sage.

Bode, Lisa. 2006. "From Shadow Citizens to Teflon Stars: Reception of the Transfiguring Effects of New Moving Image Technologies." *Animation* 1 (2): 173–189.

Bohlen, Celestine. 2001. "No. 1 Anthem: 'God Bless America.'" *New York Times,* September 19. www.nytimes.com/2001/09/19/arts/no-1-anthem-god-bless-america.html?scp=1&sq=No.%201%20Anthem:%20%27God%20Bless%20America&st=cse&pagewanted=1 (accessed July 26, 2006).

Bohlman, Philip. 2002. *World Music: A Very Short Introduction.* Oxford: Oxford University Press.

Bonafante, Jordan. 1967. "Mrs. Miller Is Off-pitch for Profit: A Most Unlikely Lark." Originally printed in *Life* magazine, September 22. Reprinted at MrsMiller's World.com. No date. www.mrsmillersworld.com/story_bin/STunlikelylark.html (accessed February 20, 2006).

Bondanella, Peter, and Mark Musa. 1984. "Translator's Note to this Edition." In *The Prince* (Oxford World's Classics), xvii–xviii. Oxford: Oxford University Press.

Boon, James. 1990 [1985]. "Claude Lévi-Strauss." In *The Return of Grand Theory in the Human Sciences,* ed. Quentin Skinner. Cambridge: Cambridge University Press. 159–176.

Boorstin, Daniel J. 1962. *The Image; or, What Happened to the American Dream.* 2nd ed. New York: Atheneum.

Borzillo-Vrenna, Carrie. 2006. "Clay Aiken Speaks out about Rumors." *People.* September 20. www.people.com/people/article/0,,1536827,00.html (accessed July 20, 2009).

Bristol, Michael. 1985. *Carnival and Theater.* New York: Methuen.

Bronson, Fred. 2003. "Aiken, Studdard Storm Billboard Chart." *Billboard.* June 18. www.billboard.com/bbcom/news/article_display.jsp?vnu_content_id196290 (accessed March 26, 2006).

———. 2005. "The Year in Charts." *Billboard*. December 24. www.billboard.com
/bbcom/yearend/2005/charts/recap.jsp (accessed February 20, 2007).

Brook, Vincent. 2003. *Something Ain't Kosher Here: The Rise of the "Jewish" Sitcom*.
New Brunswick, N.J.: Rutgers University Press.

Brooker, Will. 2001. "Living on *Dawson's Creek*: Teen Viewers, Cultural Convergence,
and Television Overflow." *International Journal of Cultural Studies* 4 (4): 456–472.

Brooker, Will, and Deborah Jermyn, eds. 2003. *The Audience Studies Reader*. London:
Routledge.

Brooks, Daphne A. 2008. "The Write to Rock: Racial Mythologies, Feminist
Theory, and the Pleasures of Rock Music Criticism." *Women & Music* 12:54–62.

Brown, Bill. 1998. "Identity Culture." *American Literary History* 10 (1): 164–184.

Brown, G. 2003. "Serial Triller: Mariah Carey's Musical Crime: Leading the Growing Trend toward Overblown, Roller-Coaster Vocals." *Denver Post*. August 10.
www.denverpost.com/Stories/0,1413,36%257E1558216,00.html (accessed August
10, 2003).

Brunker, Mike. 2007. "'Idol' Empire Conquers New Multimedia Worlds." MSNBC
.com. January 15. www.msnbc.msn.com/id/16580677/ (accessed March 19, 2007).

Buchanan, Donna A. 1997. "Bulgaria's Magical Mystère Tour: Postmodernism,
World Music Marketing, and Political Change in Eastern Europe." *Ethnomusicology* 41 (1): 131–157.

Bucholtz, Mary. 2001. "The Whiteness of Nerds: Superstandard English and Racial
Markedness." *Journal of Linguistic Anthropology* 11 (1): 84–100.

Burkeman, Oliver. 2006. "Are You Gay-Adjacent?" January 13. www.guardian.
co.uk/world/2006/jan/13/gayrights.media (accessed July 29, 2009).

Bush, George W. 2001a. "Statement by the President in His Address to the Nation."
September 11, 2001. www.whitehouse.gov/news/releases/2001 (accessed October
20, 2005).

———. 2001b. "Address to a Joint Session of Congress and the American People."
September 20. www.whitehouse.gov/news/releases/2001/09/20010920-8.html
(accessed October 20, 2005).

Butler, Judith. 1993. *Bodies That Matter: On the Discursive Limits of "Sex."* London:
Routledge.

Butler, Mike. 1999. "'Luther King Was a Good Ole Boy': The Southern Rock Movement and White Male Identity in the Post–Civil Rights South." *Popular Music
and Society* 23 (2): 41–62.

Campbell, Colin. 1987. *The Romantic Ethic and the Spirit of Modern Consumerism*.
Oxford: Blackwell.

Campbell, Gavin James. 2001. "'I'm Just a Louisiana Girl': The Southern World of
Britney Spears." *Southern Cultures* 7: 81–97.

Caplan, David. 2006. "Clay Aiken: I'm a Gay Dad." *People*. September 24. www
.people.com/people/article/0,,20228488,00.html (accessed July 20, 2009).

Cavender, Gray. 2004. "In Search of Community on Reality TV: *America's Most
Wanted* and *Survivor*." In *Understanding Reality Television*, ed. Su Holmes and
Deborah Jermyn, 154–172. London: Routledge.

CBSNews.com. 2002. "Kelly is 'American Idol.'" September 4. www.cbsnews.com
/stories/2002/09/04/entertainment/main520858.shtml (accessed February 22,
2007).

———. 2003a. "FOX News Drops Franken Lawsuit." August 25. www.cbsnews.com
/stories/2003/08/12/entertainment/main567800.shtml (accessed February 10,
2007).

———. 2003b. "Mariah: A 'Save the Music' Hero." June 12. www.cbsnews.com
/stories/2003/06/12/earlyshow/leisure/music/main558293.shtml (accessed
March 12, 2004).

CNN.com. 2008. "Newest 'American Idol' Crowned; Ratings Up." May 22. www
.cnn.com/2008/SHOWBIZ/Music/05/21/american.idol.ap/index.html (accessed November 28, 2008).

Chapell, Steve, and Reebee Garofalo, eds. 1998. *Rock 'n' Roll is Here to Pay*. New
York: Nelson Hall.

Cheng, Cliff. 1999."Marginalized Masculinities and Hegemonic Masculinity: An
Introduction." *Journal of Men's Studies* 7 (3): 295–315.

Chi, Minnie. N.d. "William Hung: Biography." http://music.yahoo.com/ar-308192
-bioWilliam-Hung (accessed May 8, 2005).

Christgau, Robert. 1990. "Decade: Rockism Faces the World." *Village Voice*. January
2. www.robertchristgau.com/xg/rock/decade-89.php (accessed July 10, 2009).

Citrin, Jack, David O. Sears, Christopher Muste, and Cara Wong. 2001. "Multiculturalism in American Public Opinion." *British Journal of Political Science* 31 (2):
247–275.

Clague, Mark. 2003. "'What So Proudly We Hail'd': Performing Meaning in the
Star-Spangled Banner." Unpublished paper presented at the 2003 joint meeting
of the Society for Ethnomusicology, the College Music Society, and the Association for Technology in Music Instruction, Miami, Florida. October 2.

Cleveland, Thomas F., R. E. (Ed) Stone Jr., Johan Sundberg, and Jenny Iwarsson.
1997. "Estimated Subglottal Pressure in Six Professional Country Singers." *Journal of Voice* 11 (4): 403–409.

Clifford, James. 1988. *The Predicament of Culture: Twentieth-Century Ethnography,
Literature, and Art*. Cambridge, Mass.: Harvard University Press.

Clissold, Bradley D. 2004. "*Candid Camera* and the origins of Reality TV: Contextualising a Historical Precedent." In *Understanding Reality Television*, ed. Su
Holmes and Deborah Jermyn, 33–53. London: Routledge.

Cobb, James C. 2000. "An Epitaph for the North: Reflections on the Politics of
Regional and National Identity at the Millennium." *Journal of Southern History* 66
(1): 3–24.

Cohen, Sara. 1993. "Ethnography and Popular Music Studies." *Popular Music* 12 (2):
123–138.

Coles, Roberta L. 2002. "Manifest Destiny Adapted for 1990s' War Discourse: Mission and Destiny Intertwined." *Sociology of Religion* 63 (4): 403–426.

Collins, Scott. 2004. "In Reality, It's a Super-Duping; The Coming Series 'Superstar
USA' Trips Up the Audience in a Bid to Turn 'Idol' Upside-Down." *Los Angeles
Times*. May 10, E1.

———. 2009. "Ratings for 'American Idol' Season 8 Premiere Fall 10% Below Season 7's." *Los Angeles Times*. 15 January. http://articles.latimes.com/2009/jan/15
/entertainment/et-idolratings15 (accessed August 16, 2009).

Connell, John, and Chris Gibson. 2003. *Soundtracks: Popular Music Identity and
Place*. London: Routledge.

Cooley, Timothy J., Katherine Meizel, and Nasir Sayed. 2008. "Virtual Fieldwork." In *Shadows in the Field: New Perspectives for Fieldwork in Ethnomusicology,* ed. Timothy J. Cooley and Gregory F. Barz. 2nd ed. Oxford: Oxford University Press.

Coppa, Francesca. 2006. "A Brief History of Media Fandom." In *Fan Fiction and Fan Communities in the Age of the Internet,* ed. Karen Hellekson and Kristina Busse. Jefferson, N.C.: McFarland.

Cornell, Stephen, and Douglas Hartmann. 1998. *Ethnicity and Race: Making Identities in a Changing World.* Thousand Oaks, Calif.: Pine Forge.

Coutas, Penelope. 2008. "Fame, Fortune, Fantasi: Indonesian Idol and the New Celebrity." In *Popular Culture in Indonesia: Fluid Identities in Post-Authoritarian Politics,* ed. Ariel Heryanto, 111–129. London: Routledge.

Cowell, Simon. 2003. *I don't mean to be rude, but . . .: Backstage Gossip from American Idol and the Secrets That Can Make You a Star.* New York: Broadway Books.

"Cowell Denies Idol 'Racism' Claim." 2004. *BBC News World Edition.* April 29. http://news.bbc.co.uk/2/hi/entertainment/3668883.stm (accessed February 9, 2005).

CPEF Press Release. 2007. "'Idol Gives Back' Two-Night Special to Benefit Children and Young People in Need in America and Africa. 8 March. http://cpefund.org (accessed April 24, 2007).

Cristi, Marcela. 2001. *From Civil to Political Religion: The Intersection of Culture, Religion, and Politics.* Waterloo, Ontario: Wilfrid Laurier University Press.

Crocker, Richard L. 2000. "Melisma." *New Grove Dictionary of Music and Musicians,* ed. Stanley Sadie, 344–346. 2nd ed. Vol. 6. New York: Grove.

Cruz, Jon, and Justin Lewis, eds. 1994. *Viewing, Reading, Listening: Audiences and Cultural Reception.* Boulder, Colo.: Westview.

Cullen, Jim. 2003. *The American Dream: A Short History of an Idea that Shaped a Nation.* Oxford: Oxford University Press.

Dahl, Robert A. 1971. *Polyarchy: Participation and Oppositions.* New Haven, Conn.: Yale University Press.

DaSilva, Fabio B., and Jim Faught. 1982. "Nostalgia: A Sphere and Process of Contemporary Ideology." *Qualitative Sociology* 5 (1): 47–61.

Davis, David A. 2005. "Boundaries and Surveyors." Review of *Look Away! The U.S. South in New World Studies,* ed. Jon Smith and Deborah Cohn; *The American South and the Global World,* ed. James L. Peacock, Harry L. Watson, and Carrie Matthews; and *Globalization and the American South,* ed. James C. Cobb and William W. Stueck Jr. *Southern Cultures* 11 (3): 104–108.

de Bruyn, Martyn. 2003. "Machiavelli and the Politics of Virtù." Ph.D. diss., Purdue University.

Deleuze, Gilles, and Félix Guattari. 1988 [1977]. *A Thousand Plateaus.* Trans. Brian Massumi. Minneapolis: University of Minnesota Press.

de Moraes, Lisa. 2002. "September 11: 'American Idol' Seizes the Day." *Washington Post,* September 4, C01.

———. 2004. "Fox Puts Foot in Its Mouth, Kicks Self." *Washington Post.* May 14. www.washingtonpost.com/wp-dyn/articles/A25870-2004May13.html (accessed December 20, 2007).

———. 2005a. "'American Idol' Belts Out a Huge Opening Number: 33.6 Million." *Washington Post.* 20 January. www.washingtonpost.com/wp-dyn/articlesA22650-2005Jan19.html (accessed February 22, 2007).

―――. 2005b. "'American Idol,' Ready for an Unflattering Close-Up?" *Washington Post.* May 3. www.washingtonpost.com/wp-dyn/articles/A32720-2005May3.html (accessed December 11, 2005).

Denhart, Andy. 2008. "Report: 'Idol' to Make Changes in 2009." MSNBC.com. December 11. www.msnbc.msn.com/id/28183600/ (accessed August 14, 2009).

DeVitis, Joseph L., and John Martin Rich 1996. *The Success Ethic, Education, and the American Dream.* Albany: State University of New York Press.

Dictionary.LaborLawTalk.com. "Melisma." n.d. http://encyclopedia.laborlawtalk.com/Melisma (accessed May 26, 2006).

Dixon, Glenn. 2004. "What It Means to Be Hung." *Washington City Paper.* May 7. Copy provided by Glenn Dixon in personal communication, April 18, 2006.

D.M.M. 2003. "Racism in America: Has 'American Idol' Changed the Face of White America?" AfricaHome.com, May 24. www.africahome.com/annews/categories/opinions/EpVFZ1AulVul.RmBZa.shtml (accessed September 5, 2003).

Dobuzinskis, Alex. 2009. "Clouds on Horizon for 'American Idol' Juggernaut?" Reuters.com, May 17. www.reuters.com/article/entertainmentNews/idUS-TRE54G1BP20090517 (August 17, 2009).

Donaldson-Evans, Catherine. "Elton John: 'American Idol' Is Racist." FOXNews.com. April 28, 2004. www.foxnews.com/story/0,2933,118432,00.html (accessed June 17, 2006).

Doorenspleet, Renske. 2005. *Democratic Transitions: Exploring the Structural Sources of the Fourth Wave.* Boulder, Colo.: Rienner.

Drew, Rob. 2001. *Karaoke Nights: An Ethnographic Rhapsody.* Walnut Creek, Calif.: AltaMira.

Drezner, Daniel. 2003. "Democracy by America." *New Republic Online.* March 12. www.tnr.com/doc.mhtml?i=scholar&s=drezner031203 (accessed December 3, 2005).

Dudden, Arthur P. 1961. "Nostalgia and the American." *Journal of the History of Ideas* 22 (4): 515–530.

Dunkley, Christopher. 2002. "It's Not New and It's Not Clever." In *Reality TV: How Real Is Real?* London: Hodder & Stoughton.

Durkheim, Émile. 1997 [1893]. *The Division of Labor in Society.* 2nd ed. Trans. W. D. Halls. New York: Free Press.

―――. 1995 [1912]. *The Elementary Forms of Religious Life.* Trans. Karen Elise Fields. New York: Simon and Schuster.

Dyer, Richard. 1998. *Stars.* Repr. London: BFL.

Eglash, Ron. 2002. "Race, Sex, and Nerds: From Black Geeks to Asian American Hipsters." *Social Text* 20 (2): 49–64.

Ellingson, Ter. 2001. *The Myth of the Noble Savage.* Berkeley: University of California Press.

Elvis Presley Enterprises. 2004. "Robert F. X. Sillerman and Elvis Presley Enterprises Announce Partnership." December 16. www.elvis.com/news/full_story.asp?id=738 (accessed May 7, 2007).

Enck, John J. 1966. "Campop." *Wisconsin Studies in Contemporary Literature* 7 (2): 168–182.

"Entertainment: Millions Vote For Middle East Pop Idol." 2003. From www.jmts fastlink.com/on_news_ details.asp?news_type=3&news_id=146. August 26. Available at www.16ocharacters.org/news.php?action=view&nid=92 (accessed March 13, 2004).

Espiritu, Yen Le. 1992. *Asian American Panethnicity: Bridging Institutions and Identities.* Philadelphia: Temple University Press.

Fairchilds, Kirsten. 2006. "William Hung Will Be King at Artichoke Festival." *Santa Cruz Sentinel.* May 18. www.santacruzsentinel.com/archive/2006/May/18 /local/stories/0710cal.htm (accessed May 18, 2006).

Fales, Cornelia. 2005. "Short-Circuiting Perceptual Systems: Timbre in Ambient and Techno Music." In *Wired for Sound: Engineering and Technologies in Sonic Cultures,* ed. Paul D. Greene and Thomas Porcello, 156–180. Middletown, Conn.: Wesleyan University Press.

Fanon, Frantz. 2004 [1961]. *The Wretched of the Earth.* New York: Grove.

Fantasia. 2005. *Life is Not a Fairy Tale.* New York: Fireside (Simon and Schuster).

Feld, Steven, and Keith H. Basso. 1996. "Introduction." In *Senses of Place,* ed. Steven Feld and Keith H. Basso, 3–11. Santa Fe, N.M.: School of American Research Press.

Fernandez, James W. 1988. "Andalusia on Our Minds: Two Contrasting Places in Spain as Seen in a Vernacular Poetic Duel of the Late 19th Century." *Cultural Anthropology* 3 (1): 21–35.

Filene, Benjamin. 2000. *Romancing the Folk: Public Memory and American Roots Music.* Chapel Hill: University of North Carolina Press.

Fiol-Matta, Licia. 2002. "Pop *Latinidad:* Puerto Ricans in the Latin Explosion, 1999." *CENTRO Journal* 14 (1): 27–51.

Fisher, Luchina. 2009. "Susan Boyle's Talent Revealed Early." ABC News.com . May 4. http://abcnews.go.com/Entertainment/SummerConcert/story?id =7496425&page=1 (accessed November 24, 2009).

Fisher, Walther. 1973. "Reaffirmation and Subversion of the American Dream." *Quarterly Journal of Speech* 47: 160–167.

Fiske, John. 1987. *Television Culture.* London: Methuen.

Forman, Murray. 2000. "'Represent': Race, Space, and Place in Rap Music." *Popular Music* 19 (1): 65–90.

Foster, Derek. 2004. "'Jump in the Pool': The Competitive Culture of *Survivor* Fan Networks." In *Understanding Reality Television,* ed. Su Holmes and Deborah Jermyn, 270–289. London: Routledge.

Fornäs, Johan. 1995. "The Future of Rock: Discourses That Struggle to Define a Genre." *Popular Music* 14 (1): 111–125.

Foucault, Michel. 1995 [1977]. *Discipline and Punish.* Trans. Alan Sheridan. New York: Vintage Books (Random House).

———. 1986. *The Care of the Self: The History of Sexuality.* Vol. 3. Trans. R. Hurley. New York: Pantheon.

Fox, Aaron A. 2004. *Real Country: Music and Language in Working-Class Culture.* Durham, N.C.: Duke University Press.

FOXNews.com, 2006. "'American Idol' Viewers 'Kiss' Paris Bennett Goodbye." May 4. www.foxnews.com/story/0,2933,194190,00.html (accessed August 24, 2006).

———. 2007. "Wednesday's 'American Idol' Draws 36.9 Million Viewers." January 19. www.foxnews.com/story/0,2933,244888,00.html (accessed February 3, 2007).

FoxToledo.com. 2010. "Mama Sox Performs for 10,000." May 14. www.foxtoledo .com/dpp/entertainment/Mama-Sox-performs-for-10-000 (July 5, 2010).

Fraim, John. 2003. *Battle of Symbols: Global Dynamics of Advertising, Entertainment and Media*. Einsiedeln, Switzerland: Daimon.

FremantleMedia.com. 2003. "Idols Compete on the Global Stage to Become World's Favourite Pop Superstar." November 13. www.fremantlemedia.com /page.asp?partid=198 (accessed May 26, 2005).

———. 2005. "American Idol Continues Reign on FOX." November 29. www .fremantlemedia.com/page.asp?partid=441 (accessed March 27, 2006).

Frere-Jones, Sasha. 2003. "When Critics Meet Pop." *Slate*. August 22. www.slate .com/id/2087321/ (accessed July 10, 2009).

Friedman, James, ed. 2002. *Reality Squared: Televisual Discourse on the Real*. New Brunswick, N.J.: Rutgers University Press.

Frith, Simon. 1981a. "'The Magic That Can Set You Free': The Ideology of Folk and the Myth of the Rock Community." *Popular Music* 1: 159–168.

———. 1981b. *Sound Effects: Youth, Leisure, and the Politics of Rock*. London: Constable.

———. 1991. "The Good, the Bad, and the Indifferent: Defending Popular Culture from the Populists." *Diacritics* 21 (4): 101–115.

———. 1999. *Performing Rites: On the value of Popular Music*. 2nd ed. Cambridge, Mass.: Harvard University Press.

———. 2001. "Pop Music." In *The Cambridge Companion to Pop and Rock*. Ed. Simon Frith, Will Straw, and John Street, 93–108. Cambridge: Cambridge University Press.

Fujitani, Takashi. 1992. "Electronic Pageantry and Japan's 'Symbolic Emperor.'" *Journal of Asian Studies* 51 (4): 824–850.

Galician, Mary-Lou. 2004. *Handbook of Product Placement in the Mass Media*. London: Routledge.

Gallo, Phil. 2003. "Motown Trio Still in Groove." Variety.com. May 11. www.variety .com/article/VR1117885947?categoryid=16&cs=1 (accessed June 15, 2006).

Gamson, Joshua. 1994. *Claims to Fame: Celebrity in Contemporary America*. Berkeley: University of California Press.

Gans, Herbert. 2004 [1979]. *Deciding What's News*. Evanston, Ill.: Northwestern University Press.

———. 1979. Symbolic Ethnicity: The Future of Ethnic Groups and Cultures in America. In *Nationalism: Critical Concepts in Political Science*, ed. John Hutchinson and Anthony D. Smith, 1217–1237. London: Taylor and Francis.

———. 1994. "Symbolic Ethnicity and Symbolic Religiosity: Towards a Comparison of Ethnic and Religious Acculturation." *Ethnic and Racial Studies* 17: 577–592.

Garofalo, Reebee. 2002. *Rockin' Out: Popular Music in the USA*. 2nd ed. Needham Heights, Mass.: Allyn & Bacon.

Garrels, Anne. 2004. Analysis: Efforts to Enliven Iraq's New Television Network. All Things Considered, National Public Radio. Broadcast January 28.

Gehrig, Gail. 1981. "The American Civil Religion Debate: A Source for Theory Construction." *Journal for the Scientific Study of Religion* 20 (1): 51–63.

Giddens, Anthony. 1985. "Time, Space and Regionalisation." In *Social Relations and Spatial Structures*, ed. Derek Gregory and John Urry, 265–295. Basingstoke, England: Macmillan.

Gitlin, Todd. 2000. "Prime Time Ideology: The Hegemonic Process in Television Entertainment." In *Television: The Critical View*, ed. Horace Newcomb, 574–594. 6th ed. Oxford: Oxford University Press.

Goddu, Teresa. 1998. "Bloody Daggers and Lonesome Graveyards: The Gothic and Country Music." In *Reading Country Music*, ed. Cecelia Tichi, 45–64. Durham, N.C.: Duke University Press.

Goethals, Gregor T. 1981. *The TV Ritual: Worship at the Video Altar*. Boston: Beacon.

Goffman, Erving. 1959. *The Presentation of the Self in Everyday Life*. New York: Anchor Books.

Gordon, Milton M. 1964. *Assimilation in American Life*. Oxford: Oxford University Press.

Gordy, Berry. 1994. *To Be Loved: The Music, the Magic, the Memories of Motown*. New York: Warner Books.

Gossett, Thomas F. 1997 [1963]. *Race: The History of an Idea in America*. Oxford: Oxford University Press.

Gough, Paul J. 2007. "'Idol' Premiere Draws Second-Highest Ratings Ever." Billboard.com. January 17. www.billboard.com/bbcom/news/article_display .jsp?vnu_content_id=1003534103 (accessed May 4, 2007).

Governor's Newsletter. 2004. Site for Edward G. Rendell, Governor, Commonwealth of Pennsylvania, January 16. www.virtualtours.state.pa.us (accessed April 5, 2007).

Gramsci, Antonio. 1988. *An Antonio Gramsci Reader: Selected Writings, 1916–1935*. Ed. David Forgacs. New York: Schocken Books.

Green, Archie. 1965. "Hillbilly Music: Source and Symbol." *Journal of American Folklore* 78: 204–228.

Gregory, James. 1998. "Southernizing the American Working Class: Post-war Episodes of Regional and Class Transformation." *Labor History* 39 (2): 135–154.

Griffith, Jackson. 2002. "Must Not See TV!" *SN&R (Sacramento News & Review)* newsreview.com. July 18. www.newsreview.com/issues/sacto/2002-07-18/arts .asp (accessed September 22, 2003).

Grigoriadis, Vanessa. "Wild Idol: The Psychedelic Transformation and Sexual Liberation of Adam Lambert." *Rolling Stone*, no. 1078: 52–57.

Grimshaw, M. 2002. "'Redneck Religion and Shitkickin' Saviours?' Gram Parsons, Theology, and Country Music." *Popular Music* 21 (1): 93–105.

Gross, Terry. 2004. Interview with Simon Cowell. Fresh Air, National Public Radio. Broadcast January 15. www.npr.org/lightningcast/index_real.html?audioURL= www.npr.og/dmg/dmg.php?prgCode=FA&showDate=15-Jan2004&segNum=2& mediaPref=RM&getAd=1&ext=.rm (accessed January 22, 2004).

Grossberg, Lawrence. 1988. "'You [Still] have to Fight for Your Right to Party': Music Television as Billboards of Post-Modern Difference." *Popular Music* 7 (3): 315–332.

———. 1993. "The Media Economy of Rock Culture: Cinema, Post Modernity and Authenticity." In *Sound & Vision: The Music Video Reader*, ed. Simon Frith, Andrew Goodwin, and Lawrence Grossberg, 185–209. London: Routledge.

Gubar, Susan. 2006. "Racial Camp in *The Producers* and *Bamboozled.*" *Film Quarterly* 60 (2): 26–37.

Guillermo, Emil. 2004. "William Hung: Racism, or Magic?" SFGate.com. April 6. www.sfgate.com/cgibin/article.cgi?file=gate/archive/2004/04/06/eguillermo .DTL&type=printable (accessed May 7, 2005).

Gupta, Akhil, and James Ferguson. 1992. "Beyond 'Culture': Space, Identity, and the Politics of Difference." *Cultural Anthropology* 7 (1): 6–23.

Gurr, Ted Robert. 1974. "Persistence and Change in Political Systems." *American Political Science Review* 68 (4): 1482–1504.

Gurr, Ted Robert, Keith Jaggers, and Monty G. Marshall. 2005. *Polity IV Data Set.* August 10. www.cidcm.umd.edu/inscr/polity/ (accessed December 11, 2005).

Haas, Michael. 1987. "Comparing Paradigms of Ethnic Politics in the United States: The Case of Hawaii." *Western Political Quarterly* 40 (4): 647–672.

Hackney, Sheldon. 2001. "The Contradictory South." *Southern Cultures* 7 (4): 65–80.

Hadley, Catharine. 2010. "A Record Crowd for Mud Hens, 'Idol' Star." May 15. www.thenews-messenger.com/article/20100515/NEWS01/5150312/A-record-crowd-for-Mud-Hens-Idol-star (accessed July 4, 2010).

Hall, Stuart. 1980. "Encoding/Decoding." In *Culture, Media, Language: Working Papers in Cultural Studies,* ed. Stuart Hall, 128–138. London: Hutchinson.

———. 1992. "New Ethnicities". In *"Race," Culture and Difference,* ed. James Donald and Ali Rattansi, 252–259. London: Sage.

Hallett, Michael T. 2003. "Review: From Civil to Political Religion: The Intersection of Culture, Religion, and Politics." *University of Toronto Quarterly* 72 (1). www.utpjournals.com/product/utq/721/721_review_hallett.html (accessed October 30, 2005).

Halperin, Shirley. 2009. "Adam Lambert Says Censorship of American Music Award Song Would Be 'Discrimination.'" *Rolling Stone.* November 23. www.rollingstone .com (accessed November 23, 2009).

Hangin' with Hung. 2004. DVD by Koch Entertainment, LLC. KOC-DV-9607.

Harada, Wayne. 2004a. "'Idol' Judge Simon Not Counting on Jasmine at All." *Honolulu Advertiser.* HonoluluAdvertiser.com. May 5. http://the.honoluluadvertiser .com/article/2004/May/05/il/il103a.html (accessed February 8, 2005).

———. 2004b. "Weekly Wednesday Wait Is Toughest for Hawai'i's 'Idol.'" *Honolulu Advertiser.* HonoluluAdvertiser.com. May 8. http://the.honoluluadvertiser .com/article/2004/My/09/ln/ln01a.html (accessed May 12, 2004).

Haralovich, Mary Beth, and Michael W. Trosset. 2004. "'Expect the Unexpected': Narrative Pleasure and Uncertainty Due to Chance in Survivor." In *Reality TV: Remaking Television Culture,* ed. Susan Murray and Laurie Ouellette, 75–96. New York: New York University Press.

Harmon, Rod. 2004. "'Idol' Winner Studdard Reaches to the Past to Make a Future." *North County Times.* February 25, 2004. www.nctimes.com/articles/2004/02/26 /entertainment/music/2_25_0414_24_55.txt (accessed June 8, 2004).

Harrington, C. Lee, and Denise D. Bielby. 2001. "Constructing the Popular: Cultural Production and Consumption." In *Popular Culture: Production and Consumption,* ed. C. Lee Harrington and Denise D. Bielby, 1–15. Malden, Mass.: Blackwell.

Harris, Mark. 2009. "Adam Lambert: Shaking Up 'Idol.'" *Entertainment Weekly.* EW.com. www.ew.com/ew/article/0,,20007164_20171835_20277643,00.html (accessed July 29, 2009).

Hartigan, John, Jr. 1999. *Racial Situation: Class Predicaments of Whiteness in Detroit.* Princeton, N.J.: Princeton University Press.

Hartley, John. 1987. "Invisible Fictions: Television Audiences, Paedocracy, Pleasure." *Textual Practice* 1 (2): 121–38.

———. 2004. "Democratainment." In *The Television Studies Reader,* ed. Robert C. Allen and Annette Hill, 524–533. London: Routledge.

Haslam, Gerald W. 1999. *Many Californias: Literature from the Golden State.* Reno: University of Nevada Press.

Hedegaard, Erik. "Cover Story: New Kid on the Block." *Rolling Stone.* July 10, 2003. www.rollingstone.com/news/story/23218342/new_kid_on_the_block/ (accessed July 20, 2009).

Heffernan, Virginia. 2004. "Here Comes the Judge: Take Cover, Would-Be Idols." *New York Times.* May 19. www.nytimes.com/2004/05/19/arts/here-comes-the-judge-take-cover-would-be-idols.html?scp=1&sq=Here%20Comes%20the%20Judge:%20Take%20Cover,%20Would-Be%20Idols&st=cse&pagewanted=1 (accessed May 19, 2004).

Helguera, Pablo P. 2000. "Florence Foster Jenkins: La Diva del Cuarto Tono." *Pauta* 75–76: 96–102.

Hernandez, Greg. 2007. "American Idol's Big Gay Closet." Advocate.com. April 24, 2007. www.advocate.com/issue_story_ektid44063.asp (accessed July 27, 2009).

Herzfeld, Michael. 1982. "Disemia." In *Semiotics 1980: Proceedings of the Fifth Annual Meeting of the Semiotic Society of America,* ed. Michael Herzfeld and Margot D. Lenhart, 205–215. New York: Plenum.

Hesselink, Nathan. 1994. "Kouta and Karaoke in Modern Japan: A Blurring of the Distinction between Umgangsmusik and Darbietungsmusik." *British Journal of Ethnomusicology* 3:49–61.

Hildebrand, Lee. 2004a. "Novato's Hit Factory." SFGate.com. December 26. http://sfgate.com/cgibin/article.cgi?file=/chronicle/archive/2004/12/26/PKG33A-G3AO1.DTL (accessed February 11, 2005)

———. 2004b. "Fantasia is Living Post-'Idol' Dream." SFGate.com. September 19. www.sfgate.com/cgibin/article.cgi?file=/chronicle/a/2004/09/19/PKGPN8MEUP1.DTL (accessed September 19, 2004).

Hine, Christine. 2000. *Virtual Ethnography.* London: Sage.

Hipps, Tim. 2005. "'Military Idol' Competition Begins on Army Installations." August 5. United States Department of Defense. www.defense.gov/news/news article.aspx?id=16956. (accessed March 30, 2010).

Hochschild, Jennifer. 1995. *Facing Up to the American Dream: Race, Class, and the Soul of the Nation.* Princeton, N.J.: Princeton University Press.

Hoit, Jeannette D., Christie L. Jenks, Peter J. Watson, and Thomas F. Cleveland. 1996. "Respiratory Function during Speech and Singing in Professional Country Singers." *Journal of Voice* 10 (1): 39–49.

Holmes, Su. 2004a. "'Reality Goes Pop!' Reality TV, Popular Music, and Narratives of Stardom in *Pop Idol.*" *Television & News Media* 5 (2): 147–172.

———. 2004b. "But This Time *You* Choose! Approaching the 'Interactive' Audience in Reality TV." *International Journal of Cultural Studies* 7 (2): 213–231.

———. 2004c. "'All You've Got to Worry about Is the Task, Having a Cup of Tea, and Doing a Bit of Sunbathing': Approaching Celebrity in *Big Brother.*" In *Understanding Reality Television,* ed. Su Holmes and Deborah Jermyn, 111–135. London: Routledge.

Holmes, Su, and Deborah Jermyn. 2004. "Introduction." In *Understanding Reality Television,* ed. Su Holmes and Deborah Jermyn, 1–32. London: Routledge.

Hoover, Herbert. 1928. "New York City." In *The New Day: Campaign Speeches of Herbert Hoover, 1928,* 149–76. Palo Alto, Calif.: Stanford University Press.

Hoover, Stewart M., and Knut Lundby. 1997. "Introduction: Setting the Agenda." In *Rethinking Media, Religion, and Culture,* ed. Stewart M. Hoover and Knut Lundby, 3–14. Thousand Oaks, Calif.: Sage.

Hoover, Stewart M., and Lynn Schofield-Clark. 1997. "At the Intersection of Media, Culture, and Religion: A Bibliographic Essay." In *Rethinking Media, Religion, and Culture,* ed. Stewart M. Hoover and Knut Lundby, 15–36. Thousand Oaks, Calif.: Sage.

Horsman, Reginald. 1981. *Race and Manifest Destiny: The Origins of American Racial Anglo-Saxonism.* Cambridge, Mass.: Harvard University Press.

Hoskyns, Barney. 2007. *Hotel California: The True-Life Adventures of Crosby, Stills, Nash, Young, Mitchell, Taylor, Browne, Ronstadt, Geffen, the Eagles, and Their Many Friends.* Hoboken, N.J.: Wiley.

Howard, Theresa. 2002. "Real Winner of 'American Idol': Coke." *USAToday.* n.d. www.usatoday.com/money/advertising/2002-09-08-idol_x.htm (accessed August 18, 2009).

Huntington, Samuel P. 1991. *The Third Wave: Democratization in the Late Twentieth Century.* Norman: University of Oklahoma Press.

International Herald Tribune. 2007. "'American Idol' Backup Singers Deliver Every Time." April 4. www.iht.com/articles/ap/2007/04/04/arts/NA-A-E-TV-US-Idol-Angels.php (accessed April 4, 2007).

Isherwood, Christopher. 1966. *Exhumations.* London: Methuen.

Jaafar, Ali. 2005. "'Star' Lights Up Auds in Iraq." *Variety* at Variety.com. August 28. www.variety.com/index.asp?layout=print_story&articleid=VR11179812&categoryid=1445 (accessed December 11, 2005).

Jackson, Peter, and Jan Penrose, editors. 1993. *Constructions of Race, Place, and Nation.* London: UCL.

Jameson, Fredric. 1991. *Postmodernism, or, The Cultural Logic of Late Capitalism.* Durham, N.C.: Duke University Press.

———. 1998. *The Cultural Turn: Selected Writings on the Postmodern, 1983–1998.* London: Verso.

Jasmine Trias Proclamation 5.13.04. 2004. May 13. www.hawaii.gov/ltgov/copy_of_headlines/Jasmine-Trias-proclamation5.15.04/view (accessed May 15, 2004).

Jenkins, Henry. 1992. *Textual Poachers: Television Fans and Participatory Culture.* London: Routledge.

———. 2001. "Convergence? I Diverge." *Technology Review.* June. http://web.mit.edu/21fms/www/faculty/henry3/converge.html (accessed December 4, 2004).

———. 2003. "Convergence Is Reality." *Technology Review.* June 6. www.technology review.com (accessed November 21, 2004).

———. 2006. *Convergence Culture: Where Old and New Media Collide.* New York: New York University Press.

Jermyn, Deborah. 2004. "'This *Is* about Real People!': Video Technologies, Actuality and Affect in the Television Crime Appeal." In *Understanding Reality Television,* ed. Su Holmes and Deborah Jermyn, 71–90. London: Routledge.

Jorge, Rome. 2004. "Jasmine Trias: Everyone's Idol." *Sunday Times (Manila Times Internet Edition).* October 10. www.manilatimes.net/national/2004/oct/10 /yehey/weekend/20041010wek1.htm (accessed November 22, 2004).

Kaplan, Richard. 2009. "Hispanic Viewers again Crown 'American Idol' as Most-Popular Show, Followed by 'CSI', 'The Mentalist.'" *Hispanic Business.* January 22, 2009. www.hispanicbusiness.com/entertainment/2009/1/22/hispanic_viewers _again_crown_american_idol.htm (accessed February 10, 2009).

Katner, Ben. 2004. "Superstar Jamie Squeals!" *TV Guide Online.* June 15. http://144.198.225.50/News/Insider/default.htm?cmsRedir=true&rmDate=061 5004&cmsGuid=%7B4FEF0722-A7F7-4C4C-ABD9-DF1FB5E6F8DA%7D (accessed July 12, 2006).

Kaufman, Gil. 2003. "Ruben Studdard Confronted by Rabid Claymates at Tour Stop." VH1.com. July 14. www.vh1.com/artists/news/1473777/07142003/aiken _clay.jhtml (accessed August 24, 2006).

——— 2009a. "Adam Lambert and Kris Allen Talk 'Ameircan Idol' Finale." MTV .com. May 19. www.mtv.com/news/articles/1611707/20090519/story.jhtml (accessed August 21, 2009).

——— 2009b. "Jennifer Hudson Lip-Synched Super Bowl Performance." MTV .com. February 2. www.mtv.com/news/articles/1604041/20090202/hudson __jennifer.jhtml (accessed July 24, 2009).

———2009c. "American Idol Spotlight on Christian Singers Reels in Religious Viewers." March 13. www.mtv.com/news/articles/1606966/20090313/story.jhtml (accessed March 27, 2010).

——— 2010. "Crystal Bowersox's Hometown: A Tale of Two Bars." May 5. http: //newsroom.mtv.com/2010/05/05/crystal-bowersox-hometown/ (accessed July 5, 2010).

Kavka, Misha, and Amy West. 2004. "Temporalities of the Real: Conceptualising Time in Reality TV." In *Understanding Reality Television,* ed. Su Holmes and Deborah Jermyn, 136–153. London: Routledge.

Keen, Andrew. 2007. *The Cult of the Amateur: How Today's Internet Is Killing Our Culture.* New York: Random House.

Keightley, Keir. 2001. "Reconsidering Rock." In *The Cambridge Companion to Pop and Rock,* ed. Simon Frith, Will Straw, and John Street, 109–142. Cambridge: Cambridge University Press.

Kelly, Kevin. 1995. "Eno: Gossip Is Philosophy." *Wired* (May): 145–158.

Kertzer, David. 1988. *Ritual, Politics, and Power.* New Haven, Conn.: Yale University Press.

Kim, Chuck. 2002. "The Real World Goes Straight." *The Advocate.* October 1. Advocate.com (accessed July 30, 2009).

Kim, L. S., and Gilberto Moisés Blasini. 2001. "The Performance of Multicultural Identity in U.S. Network Television: Shiny, Happy *Popstars* (Holding Hands)." *Emergences* 11 (2): 287–307.

King, Larry. 2006a. Interview with Simon Cowell. *CNN Larry King Live*. CNN, March 17. Transcript accessed at CNN.com. http://transcripts.cnn.com/TRAN SCRIPTS/0603/17/lkl.01.html (accessed March 27, 2006).

———. 2006b. Interview with Paula Abdul. *CNN Larry King Live*. CNN, May 19. Transcript accessed at CNN.com. http://transcripts.cnn.com/TRANSCRIPTS /0605/19/lkl.01.html (accessed May 20, 2006).

Kjus, Yngvar. 2009. "Idolizing and Monetizing the Public: The Production of Celebrities and Fans, Representatives and Citizens in Reality TV." *International Journal of Communication* 3: 277–300.

Korbelik, Jeff. 2004. "'Idol' Chitchat with Kelly Clarkson." JournalStar.com. June 11 . www.journalstar.com/articles/2004/03/19/gz/10046899.txt (accessed June 11, 2004).

Kosman, Joshua. 2004. "'Idol' Hews to Ancient Traditions." *San Francisco Chronicle*. March 27. http://articles.sfgate.com/2004-03-27/entertainment/ 17418205_1_van-cliburn-american-idol-fifth-century-bc (accessed March 27, 2004).

Kourtova, Plamena. 2008. "The Power of Imitation in *Music Idol:* Popular Music, Media Markets, and the Politics of Identity in Post-Communist Bulgaria." Unpublished paper delivered at the National Meeting of the Society for Ethno musicology. October 25.

Kraszewski, Jon. 2004. "Country Hicks and Urban Cliques: Mediating Race, Reality, and Liberalism on MTV's *The Real World*." In *Reality TV: Remaking Television Culture,* ed. Susan Murray and Laurie Ouellette, 179–196. New York: New York University Press.

Kristeva, Julia. 1980. *Desire in Language : A Semiotic Approach to Literature and Art.* Ed. L. S. Roudiez. Trans. T. Gora, A. Jardine, and L. S. Roudiez. New York: Columbia University Press.

Kun, Josh. 2005. *Audiotopia: Music, Race, and America.* Berkeley: University of California Press.

Kupfer, Ruta. 2007. "Its Star Has Fallen." Haaretz.com. January 16. www.haaretz .com/hasen/spages/811361.html (accessed May 4, 2007).

La Monica, Paul R. 2006a. "No False 'Idol' for Fox." CNNMoney.com. May 24. http://money.cnn.com/2006/05/22/news/companies/idol_fox/index.htm (accessed February 22, 2007).

———. 2006b. "American Idol Worship." CNNMoney.com. January 10. http: //money.cnn.com/2006/01/10/news/companies/idol_fox/index.htm (accessed February 22, 2007).

Lang, Amy Schrager. 1998. "Jim Crow and the Pale Maiden: Gender, Color, and Class in Stephen Foster's 'Hard Times.'" In *Reading Country Music: Steel Guitars, Opry Stars, and Honky Tonk Bars,* ed. Cecelia Tichi, 378–387. Durham, N.C.: Duke University Press.

Lanza, Joseph. 2005. *Vanilla Pop: Sweet Sounds from Frankie Avalon to ABBA.* Chicago: Chicago Review Press.

Lee, Jungmin. 2009. "American Idol: Evidence of Same-Race Preferences?" *The B.E. Journal of Economic Analysis and Policy* 9 (1): Article 28. www.bepress.com /bejeap/vol9/iss1/art28/ (accessed August 25, 2009).

Lee, Tong Soon. 1999. "Technology and the Production of Islamic Space: The Call to Prayer in Singapore." *Ethnomusicology* 43 (1): 86–100.

Levine, Ken. 2009. "American Idol: Top 36." *Huffington Post.* July 31, 2009. www .huffingtonpost.com/ken-levine/iamerican-idoli-top-36_b_167630.html (accessed July 30, 2009).

Lewis, Lisa A. 1990. "The Making of a Preferred Address." In *Gender Politics and MTV*, 27–42. Philadelphia: Temple University Press.

———. 2006 [1990]. "Female Address on Music Television: Being Discovered." *Jump Cut: A Review of Contemporary Media* 35 (April): 2–15. www.ejumpcut.org /archive/onlinessays/JC35folder/GirlsMTV.html (accessed May 27, 2007).

———. 1992. *The Adoring Audience: Fan Culture and Popular Media.* London: Routledge.

Lhamon, W. T., Jr. 1996. "Ebery Time I Wheel About I Jump Jim Crow: Cycles of Minstrel Transgression from Cool White to Vanilla Ice." In *Inside the Minstrel Mask: Readings in Nineteenth-Century Blackface Minstrelsy,* ed. Annemarie Bean, James V. Hatch, and Brooks McNamara, 275–284. Hanover, N.H.: Wesleyan University Press, published by University Press of New England.

Lipsitz, George. 1990. *Time Passages: Collective Memory and American Popular Culture.* Minneapolis: University of Minnesota Press.

Livingstone, Sonia, and Peter Lunt. 1994. *Talk on Television: Audience Participation and Public Debate.* London: Routledge.

Lopes, Shawn "Speedy." 2004a. "Wristband Sales Jump After Velasco's Showing on 'Idol.'" *Honolulu Star-Bulletin.* April 6. http://starbulletin.com/2004/04/06 /features/story2.html (accessed April 24, 2004).

———. 2004b. "Simon said Velasco Would See 1 More Week." *Honolulu Star-Bulletin.* 1 April. http://starbulletin.com/2004/04/01/features/story3.html (accessed May 10, 2006).

Lott, Eric. 1993. *Love and Theft: Blackface Minstrelsy and the American Working Class.* Oxford: Oxford University Press.

Lowe, Lisa. 1996. *Immigrant Acts: On Asian American Cultural Politics.* Durham, N.C.: Duke University Press.

Lowenthal, Leo. 1961. *Literature, Popular Culture, and Society.* Englewood Cliffs, N.J.: Prentice Hall.

Lumby, Catharine. 2003. "Real Appeal: The Ethics of Reality TV." In *Remote Control: New Media, New Ethics,* ed. Catharine Lumby and Elspeth Probyn, 11–24. Cambridge: Cambridge University Press.

Lyle, David. 2003. "Idol Worship." Interview with Bob Garfield, *On the Media,* WNYC, October 17, 2003, www.onthemedia.org/yore/transcripts/transcripts _101703_idol.html.

Lynch, Gordon. 2005. *Understanding Theology and Popular Culture.* Oxford: Blackwell.

Lysloff, René T. A. 2003. "Musical Community on the Internet: An On-Line Ethnography." *Cultural Anthropology* 18 (2): 233–263.

Ma, Sheng-Mei. 1993. "Orientalism in the Chinese American Discourse: Body and Pidgin." *Modern Language Studies* 23 (4): 104–117.

Macey, David. 2000. *Dictionary of Critical Theory.* London: Penguin Books.

Machiavelli, Niccolò. 1998 [1532]. *The Prince.* Trans. Harvey C. Mansfield. Chicago: University of Chicago Press.

Malone, Bill C., and David Stricklin. 2003 [1979]. *Southern Music/American Music,* rev. ed. Lexington: University Press of Kentucky.

Malone, Bill C. 2003 [1993]. *Singing Cowboys and Musical Mountaineers: Southern Culture and the Roots of Country Music.* Athens: University of Georgia Press.

———. 2002. *Don't Get Above Your Raisin': Country Music and the Southern Working Class.* Urbana: University of Illinois Press.

Marcus, George E. 1995. "Ethnography in/of the World System: The Emergence of Multi-Sited Ethnography." *Annual Review of Anthropology* 24: 95–117.

Marx, Karl. 1990 [1976]. *Capital: Volume 1: A Critique of Political Economy.* Trans. Ben Fowkes. London: Penguin Books.

Mattos, Jennifer. 1997. "The 1997 Presidential Inauguration: We Are the Solution: Speech Does Not Offend, nor Does It Break New Ground." *Time.* www.time .com/time/inaugural/part5.html (accessed October 30, 2005).

Maultsby, Portia. 1983. "Soul Music: Its Sociological and Political Significance in American Popular Culture." *Journal of Popular Culture* 17 (2): 51–60.

May, Larry. 2000. *The Big Tomorrow: Hollywood and the Politics of the American Way.* Chicago: University of Chicago Press.

Maynor, Dorothy. 1976. "The Spiritual as Soul Music." *Saturday Review.* September 4.

McAlexander, James H., John W. Schouten, and Harold F. Koening. 2002. "Bulding Brand Community." *Journal of Marketing* 66 (1): 38–54.

McBeth, Sally. 1989. "Layered Identity Systems in Western Oklahoma Indian Communities". Paper presented at the Annual Meeting of the American Anthropological Association. Cited in Joane Nagel, "Constructing Ethnicity: Creating and Recreating Ethnic Identity and Culture," *Social Problems* 41, 1 (1994): 152–176.

McCarthy, Anna. 2004. "'Stanley Milgram, Allen Funt, and Me': Postwar Social Science and the 'First Wave' of Reality TV." In *Reality TV: Remaking Television Culture,* ed. Susan Murray and Laurie Ouellette, 19–39. New York: New York University Press.

McClay, Wilfred M. 2004. "The Soul of a Nation." *The Public Interest,* no. 155 (spring). www.thepublicinterest.com/ (accessed September 11, 2005).

McCulloch, Anne Merline, and David E. Wilkins. 1995. "'Constructing' Nations within States: The Quest for Federal Recognition by the Catawba and Lumbee Tribes." *American Indian Quarterly* 19 (3): 361–388.

McFaul, Michael. 2002. "The Fourth Wave of Democracy and Dictatorship: Noncooperative Transitions in the Postcommunist World." *World Politics* 54 (2): 212–244.

McGeveran, William A., ed. 2006. "Nations of the World." In *The World Almanac and Book of Facts 2006,* 750–850. New York: World Almanac Education Group.

McGrath, John. 2004. *Loving Big Brother: Performance, Privacy and Surveillance Space.* London: Routledge.

McLeod, Ken. 2006. "'We Are the Champions': Masculinities, Sports, and Popular Music." *Popular Music and Society* 29 (5): 531–547.

McPherson, Tara. 2003. *Reconstructing Dixie: Race, Gender, and Nostalgia in the Imagined South.* Durham, N.C.: Duke University Press.

Meizel, Katherine. 2006a. "'Be a Fan, Not a Hater': Identity Politics and the Audience in American Idol." *Pacific Review of Ethnomusicology* 12. www.ethnomusic. ucla.edu/pre/Vo112/Vo112html/V12Meizel.html (accessed March 30, 2010).

———. 2006b. "A Singing Citizenry: Popular Music and Civil Religion in America." *Journal for the Scientific Study of Religion* 45 (4): 497–503.

———. 2007a. "Idol Thoughts: Nationalism in the Pan-Arab Vocal Competition *Superstar.*" In *A Song for Europe: Eurovision, Popular Music, and the Politics of Kitsch,* ed. Ivan Raykoff, 159–170. Farnham, Surrey: Ashgate.

———. 2007b. "Idol Loves Idol: Sweater Vests and Presidential Candidates, from Katherine Meizel to Jody Rosen." May 23. www.slate.com/id/2158332/entry /2166866/ (accessed July 30, 2009).

———. 2009a. "Making the Dream a Reality Show: The Celebration of Failure in *American Idol.*" *Popular Music and Society* 32 (4): 475–488.

———. 2010. "Real-politics: *Super Star* and Democracy Promotion in the Middle East." In *Music and Media in the Arab World,* ed. Michael Frishkopf. Cairo: American University in Cairo Press.

Meyrowitz, Joshua. 1985. *No Sense of Place: The Electronic Media of Social Behavior.* Oxford: Oxford University Press.

Miles, Robert. 1989. *Racism.* London: Macmillan.

Mills, Kay, and Marian Wright Edelman. 2007. *This Little Light of Mine: The Life of Fannie Lou Hamer.* Lexington: University Press of Kentucky.

Mitchell, Don. 2000. *Cultural Geography: A Critical Introduction.* Malden, Mass.: Blackwell.

Mizota, Sharon. 2004. "Can the Subaltern Sing? Or, Who's Ashamed of William Hung? *Pop Matters.* May 4. www.popmatters.com/tv/features/040504-william hungmizota.shtml (accessed May 7, 2005).

Moores, Shaun. 1993. *Interpreting Audiences: The Ethnography of Media Consumption.* London: Sage.

Morley, David. 1980. *The "Nationwide" Audience: Structure and Decoding.* London: British Film Institute.

———1993. "Active Audience Theory: Pendulums and Pitfalls." *Journal of Communication* 43 (4): 13–19.

Moss, Corey, with Raquel Hutchinson and Angela Lu. 2006. "The Scourge of *American Idol:* Oversingers." MTV.com. February 6. www.mtv.com/news/articles /1523040/20060202/story.jhtml (accessed July 21, 2009).

Moss, Corey. 2004. "Think You Know Everything about 'American Idol'? Think Again." MTV.com. May 25. www.mtv.com/news/articles/1487448/20040525 /id_1235723.jhtml (accessed May 22, 2006).

———. 2005a. "Can You Still *Rock* if You're on 'American Idol'? Bo Bice and Constantine Maroulis Are Out to Prove You Can." *MTV News: Headlines* at *MTV.com.* March 18, 2005. www.mtv.com/news/articles/1498298/03182005/abdul_paula .jhtml. (March 23, 2005).

———. 2005b. "'Idol' Controversy Starts Early as Singers Argue over Screen Time." VH1.com. February 25. www.vh1.com/news/articles/1497504/20050225/american _idol_12_finalists.jhtml?headlines=true (March 11, 2005).

———. 2006. "Maybe We Should Just Call It 'Southern Idol.'" VH1.com. April 27. www.vh1.com/news/articles/1529538/20060426/index.jhtml?headlines=true (accessed April 5, 2007).

MSNBC.com. 2004a. "Report: Phone Logjams Thwart 'Idol' Voters." May 16. www.msnbc.msn.com/id/4992204/ (accessed December 8, 2004).

———. 2004b. "Simon Fuller: 'American Idol' Svengali—Music Mogul's Earnings at Issue." January 20. www.msnbc.msn.com/id/3943498/ (accessed January 19, 2004).

———. 2004c. "Governors Place Bets on 'Idol' Winner." May 26. http://msnbc .msn.com/id/5060958/ (accessed October 20, 2006).

———. 2004d. "Rise of the South on 'American Idol.'" May 26. www.msnbc.msn .com/id/5053569/ (accessed April 5, 2007).

———. 2004e. "'Idol' Finalist a Huge Hit in Philippines." October 12. www.msnbc .msn.com/id/6233535/ (accessed December 15, 2004).

———. 2005. "Carrie Crowned Latest 'American Idol.'" June 7. www.msnbc.msn .com/id/7980782/ (accessed February 22, 2007).

———. 2006a. "Gay Group Questions 'American Idol' Judges." MSNBC.com. January 25. www.msnbc.msn.com/id/10994783/ (accessed July 29, 2009).

———. 2006b. "Taylor Hicks Is Named 'American Idol.'" June 1. www.msnbc.msn .com/id/12956943/ (accessed May 4, 2007).

MTV.com. 2003. "Booted 'American Idol' Returns to Marines, Corps Will Let Him Tour." May 15. www.mtv.com/news/articles/1471888/20030515/id_1235745.jhtml (accessed August 14, 2006).

Muniz, Albert M., and Thomas C. O'Guinn. 2001. "Brand Community." *Journal of Consumer Research* 27 (4): 412–432.

Murray, Bruce. 2002. "With 'God on Our Side'? How American 'Civil Religion' Permeates Society and Manifests Itself in Public Life." *FACSNET.* March 28, 2005. http://facsnet.org/issues/faith/civil_religion.htm (accessed September 11, 2005).

Nagel, Joane. 1994. "Constructing Ethnicity: Creating and Recreating Ethnic Identity and Culture." *Social Problems* 41 (1): 152–176.

———. 1986. "The Political Construction of Ethnicity." In *Competitive Ethnic Relations,* ed. Susan Olzak and Joane Nagel, 93–112. Orlando, Fla.: Academic.

Najafi, Sina, and David Serlin. 2002. "The Invention of Failure: An Interview with Scott A. Sandage." *Cabinet* 7 (2). www.cabinetmagazine.org/issues/7/invention offailure.php (accessed February 10, 2006).

Neal, Mark Anthony. 1998. *What the Music Said: Black Popular Music and Black Public Culture.* New York: Routledge.

Negus, Keith. 1996. Audiences. In *Popular Music in Theory: An Introduction,* 7–35. Hanover, N.H.: Wesleyan University Press, published by University Press of New England.

Nepo, Mark, ed. 2005. *Deepening the American Dream: Reflections on the Inner Life and Spirit of Democracy.* San Francisco: Jossey-Bass.

Neusner, Jacob. 2003. "The Religion, Judaism, in America: What Has Happened in Three Hundred and Fifty Years?" *American Jewish History* 91 (3–4): 361–369.

Newsome, Melba. 2007. "On 'Idol,' the South Rises Again . . . and Again." *New York Times.* March 25. www.nytimes.com/2007/03/25/arts/television/25news

.html?scp=1&sq=On%20%27Idol,%27%20the%20South%20Rises%20Again%20
.%20.%20.%20and%20Again&st=cse (accessed March 25, 2007).

New York Daily News. 2009. "American Idol Producers Sue Texas Club Over 'Stripper Idol' Competition." January 14. www.nydailynews.com/entertainment/ americanidol/2009/01/14/2009-01-14_american_idol_producers_sue_texas _club_0.html (accessed March 30, 2010).

Ng, David. 2004. "Hung Out to Dry: What We Laugh about When We Laugh about *American Idol*'s Most Famous Reject." *Village Voice.* April 6. www.villagevoice .com/news/0414,ng,52441,1.html (accessed May 7, 2005).

Niebuhr, Gustav. 2000. "The 2000 Campaign: The Religion Issue; Lieberman Is Asked to Stop Invoking Faith in Campaign." *New York Times.* August29. www .nytimes.com/2000/08/29/us/2000-campaign-religion-issue-lieberman-asked-stop-invoking-faith-campaign.html (accessed August 8, 2009).

Nielsen Media Research. 2003a. "The Phenomenon Behind 'American Idol.'" May 19. www.nielsenmedia.com/newsreleases/2003/AmericanIdol_052203.htm (accessed February 22, 2007).

———. 2003b. "Nielsen Highlights 'American Idol' Phenomenon." January 20. www .nielsenmedia.com/newsreleases/2003/AmericanIdol.htm (accessed May 4, 2007).

———. 2005. "Atlanta Ratings Reign for 'American Idol.'" January 18. www. nielsenmedia.com/newsreleases/2005/ AmericanIdol2005.htm (accessed February 22, 2007).

———. 2008. "The Nielsen Company Measures the 'American Idol' Phenom." May 1. www.nielsen.com/media/2008/pr_080515.html (accessed November 28, 2008).

Novak, Michael. 1976. *The Joy of Sports: End Zones, Bases, Baskets, Balls, and the Consecration of the American Spirit.* New York: Basic Books.

NPD.com. 2006. "Does Cingular's Southern Charm Skew 'American Idol' Results?" June 20. www.npd.com/dynamic/releases/press_060620.html (accessed August 12, 2006).

Nye, Joseph S., Jr. 2002a. *The Paradox of American Power.* Oxford: Oxford University Press.

———. 2002b. "The American National Interest and Global Public Goods." *International Affairs* 78 (2): 233–244.

Obama, Barack. 2004. "Reclaiming the Promise to the People." *Vital Speeches of the Day* 70: 623–625.

O'Connor, Ashling. 2007. "Riots as TV Win Splits Communities." *Times Online.* September 29. www.timesonline.co.uk/tol/news/world/asia/article2553740.ece (accessed November 28, 2008).

Oldenburg, Ann. 2004. "Can't Sing or Dance? Give 'Superstar' a Shot." *USA Today.* May 17. www.usatoday.com/life/television/news/2004-05-16-wb-superstar_x .htm (accessed December 20, 2007).

O'Reilly, Daragh, and Kathy Doherty. 2006. "Music B(r)ands Online and Constructing Community: The Case of New Model Army." In *Cybersounds: Essays on Virtual Music Culture,* ed. Michael D. Ayers, 137–159. New York: Peter Lang.

Oster, Andrew. 2006. "Melisma as Malady: Cavalli's *Il Giasone* and Opera's Earliest Stuttering Role." In *Sounding Off: Theorizing Disability in Music,* ed. Neil Lerner and Joseph N. Straus, 157–171. New York: Routledge.

P, Steve. 2006. "Pop News: Top of The Pops." BBC.co.uk. March 23. www.bbc.co
.uk/totp/news/news/2006/03/23/30593.shtml (accessed July 22. 2009).

PBS Kids Go! 2005. "It's My Life: Justin Guarini." http://pbskids.org/itsmylife
/celebs/interviews/justin2.html (accessed June 20, 2006).

People.com. 2004. "Public Complains to FCC over Idol Voting." People. May 20.
www.people.com/people/article/0,,640492,00.html (accessed August 9, 2009).

Peters, Brooks. 2001. "Florence Nightingale." Opera News 65 (12): 20–23.

Peterson, Richard A., and Paul Di Maggio. 1975. "From Region to Class, the Changing Locus of Country Music: A Test of the Massification Hypothesis." Social
Forces 53 (4): 497–506.

———. 1997. Creating Country Music: Fabricating Authenticity. Chicago: University
of Chicago Press.

Pinto, Goel. 2005. "Striking a Note for the Sephardim." Haaretz. August 29. www
.haaretz.com/hasen/spages/618222.html (accessed August 29, 2005).

Plasketes, George. 2005. "Re-flections on the Cover Age: A Collage of Continuous
Coverage in Popular Music." Popular Music and Society 28 (2): 137–161.

Pocock, J. G. A. 2003 [1975]. The Machiavellian Moment: Florentine Political Thought
and the Atlantic Republican Tradition. Princeton, N.J.: Princeton University Press.

Powers, Ann. 2009. "'American Idol's' Bigger Message." Los Angeles Times. May 18.
http://latimesblogs.latimes.com/americanidoltracker/2009/05/american-idols-
bigger-message.html (accessed March 27, 2010).

Pratt, Julius. 1927. "The Origin of 'Manifest Destiny.'" American Historical Review 32
(4): 795–798.

Pressbox.co.uk. 2006. "Former Clay Aiken Fans Respond to Simon Cowell Comments from Larry King Live." March 21. www.pressbox.co.uk/detailed/Enter
tainment/FORMER_CLAY_AIKEN_FANS_RESPOND_TO_SIMON
_COWELL_COMMENTS_FROM_LARRY_KING_LIVE_58613.html
(accessed April 14, 2010).

Punathambekar, Aswin. 2010. "Reality Television and the Making of Mobile Publics: The Case of Indian Idol." In Real Worlds: Global Perspectives on the Politics of Reality Television, ed. Marwan Kraidy and Katherine Sender. New York: Routledge.

Putnam, Robert. 2000. Bowling Alone: The Collapse and Revival of American Democracy. New York: Simon and Schuster.

Raghavan, Sudarsan. 2006. "In Iraq, Singing for a Chance at Hope and Glory."
Washington Post, Page A01, September 1. www.washingtonpost.com/wp-dyn
/content/article/2006/08/31/AR2006083101675_pf.html (Accessed July 10, 2007).

Randel, Don Michael, ed. 1986. The New Harvard Dictionary of Music. Cambridge,
Mass.: Belknap Press of Harvard University Press.

Rapin, Kristen. 2010. "$856 donated to JDRF in May's Name." Toledo Free Press. May
25. www.toledofreepress.com/2010/05/26/856-donated-to-jdrf-in-may's-name
/ (Accessed July 5, 2010).

Reijnders, Stijn L., Gerard Rooijakkers, and Liesbet van Zoonen. 2007. "Community Spirit and Competition in Idols: Ritual Meanings of a TV Talent Quest."
European Journal of Communication 22 (3): 275–292.

Reuters. 2004. "Elton John: 'Idol' Vote is 'Racist.'" CNN.com. April 27. www.cnn
.com/2004/SHOWBIZ/Music/04/27/leisure.john.idol.reut/ (accessed December 4, 2004).

Rice, Timothy. 1997. "Toward a Mediation of Field Methods and Field Experience in Ethnomusicology." In *Shadows in the Field: New Perspectives for Fieldwork in Ethnomusicology,* ed. Gregory F. Barz and Timothy J. Cooley, 101–120. Oxford: Oxford University Press.

Rich, Frank. 1996. "Journal; The 'Too Jewish' Question." *New York Times.* March 16. www.nytimes.com/1996/03/16/opinion/journal-the-too-jewish-question.html (accessed August 16, 2009).

Rischar, Richard Allen. 2000. "One Sweet Day: Vocal Ornamentation and Style in the African American Popular Ballad, 1991–1995." Ph.D. diss., University of North Carolina at Chapel Hill.

Robinson, Michael G. 2004. "The Innocents Abroad: S Club 7's America." *Popular Music and Society* 27 (3): 291–305.

Robinson, William I. 1996. "Globalization, the World System, and 'Democracy Promotion' in U.S. Foreign Policy." *Theory and Society* 25 (5): 615–665.

———. 2004. *A Theory of Global Capitalism: Production, Class, and State in a Transnational World.* Baltimore, Md.: Johns Hopkins University Press.

Rockwell, John. 1976. "Blues, and Other Noises, in the Night." *Saturday Review.* September 4, 32–38.

Rodman, Gilbert B. 1994. "A Hero to Most? Elvis, Myth, and the Politics of Race." *Cultural Studies* 8 (3): 457–483.

Rogin, Michael. 1992. "Blackface, White Noise: The Jewish Jazz Singer Finds His Voice." *Critical Inquiry* 18 (3): 417–453.

———. 1996. *Blackface, White Noise: Jewish Immigrants in the Hollywood Melting Pot.* Berkeley: University of California Press.

Roof, Wade Clark, and William McKinney. 1987. *American Mainline Religion: Its Changing Shape and Future.* New Brunswick, N.J.: Rutgers University Press.

Rosen, Jody. 2003. "The State of American Singing as Heard on 'I-I-I-I-I-I-Idol.'" *New York Times.* May 18. www.nytimes.com/2003/05/18/arts/television/18ROSE .html (accessed May 20, 2003).

———. 2005. "'Yankee Doodle Abie': Tin Pan Alley Sings 'Hebrew.'" Unpublished paper delivered April 15 at theEMP Pop Conference, Seattle, Washington.

———. 2006a. "G-d's Reggae Star: How Matisyahu Became a Pop Phenomenon." *Slate.* March 14. www.slate.com/id/2138032/ (accessed June 15, 2006).

———. 2006b. "The Perils of Poptimism." *Slate.* May 9. www.slate.com/id /2141418/ (accessed July 10, 2009).

Rossman, Gabriel. 2004. "Elites, Masses, and Media Blacklists: The Dixie Chicks Controversy." *Social Forces* 83 (1): 61–79.

Rothenbuhler, Eric W. 1998. *Ritual Communcation: From Everyday Conversation to Mediated Ceremony.* Thousand Oaks, Calif.: Sage.

Rousseau, Jean-Jacques. 1972 [1762]. *Du Contrat Social, ou principes du droit politique.* Ed. Jean-Marie Fataud and Marie-Claude Bartholy, under the direction of Fernand Angué. Repr. Paris: Bordas.

Rowland, Robert C., and John M. Jones. 2007. "Recasting the American Dream and American Politics: Barack Obama's Keynote Address to the 2004 Democratic National Convention." *Quarterly Journal of Speech* 93 (4): 425–448.

RTL Group. 2006. "Director's Report." March 4. www.rtlgroup.com/files/AR2006 _RTLGroup_DIRECTORSREPORT.pdf (accessed May 4, 2007).

Ruprecht, Louis, Jr. 2006. "The South as Tragic Landscape." *Thesis Eleven* (85): 37–63.

Ryan, Joal. 2009. "Update: Another *American Idol* Finale Shocker: Not the Lowest Rated!" E! Online. May 21. www.eonline.com/uberblog/b125186_another_american_idol_finale_shocker.html (accessed August 21, 2009).

Sackett, S. J. 1979. "Prestige Dialect and the Pop Singer." *American Speech* 54 (3): 234–237.

Sandage, Scott A. 2005. *Born Losers: A History of Failure in America.* Cambridge, Mass.: Harvard University Press.

Sanneh, Kelefa. "The Rap Against Rockism." *New York Times.* October 31, 2004. www.nytimes.com/2004/10/31/arts/music/31sann.html?_r=1 (accessed July 10, 2009).

Savadove, Bill. 2006. "CHINA: Brakes Put on TV Talent Programmes." *Asia-Media: Media News Daily.* March 17. www.asiamedia.ucla.edu/article-eastasia.asp?parentid=41120 (accessed March 18, 2006).

Schiller, Gail. 2008. "Idol" Sponsors Now Paying $35 Million Each. Reuters.com. January 16. www.reuters.com/article/sphereNews/idUSN1620948620080116?sp=true&view=sphere (accessed August 18, 2009).

Schneider, Michael. 2009. "Fox Wants Answers from Nielsen." *Variety.* May 18. www.variety.com/article/VR1118003924.html?categoryid=14&cs=1 (accessed August 19, 2009).

Schumpeter, Joseph. 1976 [1942]. *Capitalism, Socialism, and Democracy.* Repr. London: Allen and Unwin.

Serrano, Zenaida. 2004. "Jasmine Overwhelmed by Aloha from Local Fans." *Honolulu Advertiser.* May 14. http://the.honoluluadvertiser.com/article/2004/May/14/il/i1101a.html/ (accessed February 8, 2005).

Setoodeh, Ramin. 2009. "Religion and 'Idol': Could Adam Lambert Be Heading Home?" May 12. http://blog.newsweek.com/blogs/popvox/archive/2009/05/12/religion-and-idol-could-adam-lambert-be-heading-home.aspx (accessed March 27, 2010).

Shain, Michael. 2004. "'Superstar' Producers Lied to Studio Audience." FoxNews.com. May 11. www.foxnews.com/story/0,2933,119593,00.html (accessed July 13, 2006).

Shane, Leo, III. 2005. "Guardsman Is Military Idol Winner." October 24. Military.com. www.military.com/features/0,15240,79208,00.html (accessed March 30, 2010).

Sherwell, Philip. 2006. "Women Fans May Sue over Pop Idol Who 'Wasn't All He Seemed.'" Telegraph.co.uk. March 5. www.telegraph.co.uk/news/main.jhtml?xml=/news/2006/03/05/wido105.xml (accessed March 22, 2006).

Shklar, Judith. 1991. *American Citizenship: The Quest for Inclusion.* Cambridge, Mass.: Harvard University Press.

Shome, Raka. 2001. "White Femininity and the Discourse of the Nation: Re/membering Princess Diana." *Feminist Media Studies* 1 (3): 323–342.

Sider, Gerald. 2003 [1993]. *Living Indian Histories: Lumbee and Tuscarora People in North Carolina.* Chapel Hill: University of North Carolina Press.

Smith, Suzanne E. 1999. *Dancing in the Street: Motown and the Cultural Politics of Detroit.* Cambridge, Mass.: Harvard University Press.

Solomon, Thomas. 2004. "'Every Way That I Can?' Turkey and the Eurovision Song Contest." Unpublished paper presented at the 2004 conference of the Society for Ethnomusicology, Tucson, Arizona. November 5.

Sontag, Susan. 1999 [1964]. "Notes on Camp." In *Camp: Queer Aesthetics and the Performing Subject: A Reader,* ed. Fabio Cleto, 53–65. Repr. Ann Arbor: University of Michigan Press.

Soukhanov, Anne, ed. 1984. *Webster's II New Riverside University Dictionary.* Boston: Houghton Mifflin.

Spivak, Gayatri Chakravorty. 1988. "Can the Subaltern Speak?" In *Marxism and the Interpretation of Culture,* ed. Cary Nelson and Lawrence Grossberg, 271–316. Urbana: University of Illinois Press.

Stahl, Matthew. 2004. "A Moment Like This: *American Idol* and Narratives of Meritocracy." In *Bad Music,* ed. Christopher Washburne and Maiken Derno, 212–232. London: Routledge.

Stanfield, Peter. 2002. *Horse Opera: The Strange History of the 1930s Singing Cowboy.* Chicago: University of Illinois Press.

Starr, Kevin. 1986. "California, A Dream." In *California: A Place, a People, a Dream,* ed. Claudia K. Jurman and James J. Rawls. San Francisco, Calif.: Chronicle Books.

Starr, Michael. 2002. "'Idol' Rich: 26 Million for Show's Ads." October 15. www.foxnews.com/story/0,2933,65664,00.html (accessed August 21 2009).

———. 2008. "'Idol' Takes Back Charity 'Give Back.'" *New York Post.* December 12. www.nypost.com/seven/12122008/tv/idol_takes_back_charity_give_back_143816.htm (accessed August 14, 2009).

Stebbins, Robert. 1992. *Amateurs, Professionals, and Serious Leisure.* Montreal: McGill-Queen's Press.

Steinberg, Stephen. 1989 [1981]. *The Ethnic Myth: Race, Ethnicity, and Class in America.* Boston: Beacon.

Steller, Brian. 2010. "For the Big 'Idol' Finale, a Smaller Audience." *New York Times,* May 27. http://www.nytimes.com/2010/05/28/arts/television/28winner.html (accessed May 28, 2010).

Stephens, Robert W. 1984. "Soul: A Historical Reconstruction of Continuity and Change in Black Popular Music." *The Black Perspective in Music* 12 (1): 21–43.

Stewart, Earl. 1998. *African American Music: An Introduction.* Belmont, Calif.: Schirmer/Thomson Learning.

Stone, R. (Ed), Jr., Thomas F. Cleveland, and Johan Sundberg. 1999. "Formant Frequencies in Country Singers' Speech and Singing." *Journal of Voice* 13 (2): 161–167.

Strenk, Andrew. 1979. "What Price Victory? The World of International Sports and Politics." *Annals of the American Academy of Political and Social Science* 445:128–140.

Sutton, Horace. 1976. "The South as the New America." *Saturday Review.* September 4, 8.

Taylor, Charles. 1989. *Sources of the Self.* Cambridge, Mass.: Harvard University Press.

Taylor, Lindsie. 2004. "'Idol' Finalist Has Been on Exciting Ride." *Deseret News.* July 8. www.deseretnews.com/article/1,5143,595075876,00.html (accessed August 20, 2009).

Telescope Creative Interactive Solutions. 2003a. "Case Studies: American Idol 'Season1' DRTV Viewer Voting." www.telescope.tv/americanIdo11.html (accessed February 22, 2007).

———. 2003b. "Case Studies: American Idol 'Season 2' DRTV Viewer Voting." www.telescope.tv/americanIdo12.html (accessed February 22, 2007).

———. 2004. "American Idol Breaks Its Own Record For Voting . . . Yet Again." June 2. www.telescope.tv/AI3PressRelease_0604.html (accessed February 22, 2004).

———. 2005. "Telescope, Inc. Processes a Record Breaking 500+ Million Votes for FOX's 'American Idol' Season 4." May. www.telescope.tv/ai5_press.html (accessed February 22, 2007).

———. 2006. "Telescope Announces Yet Another Huge Voting Season with FOX's 'American Idol.'" May 30. www.telescope.tv/press_idol_06.html (accessed February 22, 2007).

Thomas, Owen, and Oliver Ryan. 2006. "Did Text Messages Skew 'Idol' Votes?" CNNMoney.com. June 20. http://money.cnn.com/blogs/browser/2006/06/did-text-messages-skew-idol-votes.html (accessed August 12, 2006).

Tincknell, Estella, and Parvati Raghuram. 2004. "*Big Brother:* Reconfiguring the 'Active' Audience of Cultural Studies?" In *Understanding Reality Television,* ed. Su Holmes and Deborah Jermyn, 252–269. London: Routledge.

Tiryakian, Edward A. 1982. "Puritan America in the Modern World: Mission Impossible?" *Sociological Analysis* 43 (4): 351–368.

Titze, Ingo, Christine C. Bergan, Eric J. Hunter, and Brad Story. 2003. "Source and Filter Adjustments Affecting the Perception of the Vocal Qualities Twang and Yawn." *Logopedics, Phoniatrics, Vocology* 28: 147–155.

de Tocqueville, Alexis. 1969 [1840]. *Democracy in America.* Vol. 2. Trans. George Lawrence. Ed. J. P. Mayer. New York: Doubleday, Anchor Books.

Today at MSNBC.com. 2007. "Ratings Down 19 Percent for 'Idol' Finale." May24. http://today.msnbc.msn.com/id/18832703/ (accessed May 31, 2007).

Toff, Benjamin. 2008. "Ratings: 'Idol' Can't Quite Hit the High Note." *New York Times.* January 16. http://tvdecoder.blogs.nytimes.com/tag/american-idol/page/2/ (accessed November 28, 2008).

Toff, Benjamin and Dave Itzkoff. 2010. "ARTS, BRIEFLY: 'Idol' Returns to Winning Ways." *New York Times.* January 14. http://query.nytimes.com/gst/fullpage.html?res=9C00E0DC173AF937A25752C0A9669D8B63&scp=1&sq=ARTS,%20BRIEFLY:%20%27Idol%27%20Returns%20to%20Winning%20Ways&st=cse (accessed January 15, 2010).

Tomkins, Richard. 2004. "Bush, Blair Sound Democracy Refrain." *Washington Times* (Online Edition). November 12. http://washingtontimes.com (accessed May 31, 2005).

Trilling, Lionel. 1972. *Sincerity and Authenticity.* Cambridge, Mass.: Harvard University Press.

Tsai, Michael. 2004. "'Idol' Hooked Hawai'i from Start." *Honolulu Advertiser.* May 23. http://the.honoluluadvertiser.com/article/2004/May/23/ln/ln02a.html (accessed May 10, 2006).

Tsai, Michael, and Wayne Harada. 2004. "Filipino Pride Flows for State's 'Idol' Finalists." *Honolulu Advertiser.* March 23.

Tumposky, Ellen. 2003. "World of 'Idol' Pursuit." *New York Daily News.* December 23. www.nydailynews.com/entertainment/story/148413p-130943c.html (accessed June 6, 2005).

Turner, Victor. 1995 [1969]. *The Ritual Process: Structure and Anti-Structure.* New York: Aldine de Gruyter.

Tyrangiel, Josh. 2006. "Miss Independent." *Time Magazine.* February 4. www.time.com/time/magazine/article/0,9171,1156534,00.html (accessed May 27, 2007).

USAToday.com. 2006. "Who Will Become the Next 'Iraq Star'? Stay Tuned." USAToday.com, July 13. http://www.usatoday.com/news/world/iraq/2006-07-13-iraq-star_x.htm (accessed July 1, 2007).

USPS.com. 2005. "Fans of *American Idol* Finalist and Mail Carrier Vonzell Solomon Can Say 'Congratulations.'" May 10. www.usps.com/communications/news/press/2005/pro5_042.htm (accessed April 29, 2007).

Van Sickel, Robert W. 2005. "A World without Citizenship: On (the Absence of) Politics and Ideology in Country Music Lyrics, 1960–2000." *Popular Music and Society* 28 (3): 313–331.

Vargas, Jose Antonio. 2009. "How a Villager Became the Queen of All Media." *Washington Post.* April 20. www.washingtonpost.com/wp-dyn/content/article/2009/04/19/AR2009041900508.html?nav=hcmodule (accessed November 24, 2009).

Vered, Allie. 2006. "Virginia's Jewish Idol." *Virginia Jewish News.* April 10.

Virilio, Paul. 1986 [1977]. *Speed and Politics.* Trans. Mark Polizzotti. New York: Semiotext (e).

Walch, Tad. 2004. "Utahns Hope to Make It as 'Idols.'" *Deseret News.* January 18. www.deseretnews.com/article/1,5143,590037094,00.html (accessed August 20, 2009).

Walser, Robert. 1992. "Eruptions: Heavy Metal Appropriations of Classical Virtuosity." *Popular Music* 11 (3): 262–308.

Weber, Max. 2004 [1930]. *The Protestant Ethic and the Spirit of Capitalism.* Trans. Talcott Parsons. London: Routledge.

Weber, Sarah. 2010. "Ottawa County Cashes in on Crystal." May 18. www.sanduskyregister.com/oak-harbor/2010/may/18/ottawa-county-cashes-crystal (Accessed July 4, 2010).

Welch, Graham F., and Johan Sundberg. 2002. "Choir." In *The Science and Psychology of Music Performance,* ed. Richard Parncutt and Gary McPherson, 253–268. Oxford: Oxford University Press.

West, Cornel. 2004. *Democracy Matters: Winning the Fight against Imperialism.* New York: Penguin.

Where@Lebanon.com. 2004. "Music: Diana Karazon." January 18. www.lebanon.com/where/entertainment/musicnews230.htm (accessed February 27, 2004).

Whitfield, John. 2006. "Science in the Movies: From Microscope to Multiplex—An MRI Scanner Darkly." *Nature* 441: 922–924. www.nature.com (accessed May 7, 2007).

Whitman, Walt. 2004 [1855]. "I Hear America Singing." In *Leaves of Grass.* New York: Bantam Books.

Wikinfo. 2003. "Melisma." August 27. www.internetencyclopedia.org/wiki.php?title=Melisma (accessed May 26, 2006).

Wilgus, D. K. 1970. "Country-Western Music and the Urban Hillbilly." *Journal of American Folklore* 83:157–179.

Williams, Rhys. 1996. "Religion as Political Resource: Culture or Ideology?" *Journal for the Scientific Study of Religion* 35 (4): 368–378.

Williams, R. H., and N. J. Demerath. 1985. "Civil Religion in an Uncivil Society." *Annals of the American Academy of Political and Social Science* 480:154–166.

———. 1991. "Religion and Political Process in an American City." *American Sociological Review* 56:417–431.

Wilson, Carl. 2007. *Let's Talk About Love: A Journey to the End of Taste.* New York: Continuum International.

Wilson, Pamela. 2004. "Jamming *Big Brother:* Webcasting, Audience Intervention, and Narrative Activism." In *Reality TV: Remaking Television Culture,* ed. Susan Murray and Laurie Ouellette, 323–344. New York: New York University Press.

Winthrop, John. 2001. "A Model of Christian Charity." In *The American Studies Anthology,* ed. Richard P. Horowitz, 12–18. Lanham, Md.: Rowman and Littlefield.

Wireless Week. 2003. "AT&T Wireless Sets Messaging Records." June 4. www.wirelessweek.com (accessed December 4, 2004).

Wittmeyer, Alicia. 2004. "Berkeley Junior Shot Down in American Idol Tryout." *Daily Californian.* February 2. www.dailycal.org (accessed May 17, 2007).

Wolin, Sheldon. 2001. *Tocqueville between Two Worlds: The Making of a Political and Theoretical Life.* Princeton, N.J.: Princeton University Press.

Wolk, Douglas. 2005. "Thinking about Rockism." *Seattle Weekly.* May 4. www.seattleweekly.com/2005-05-04/music/thinking-about-rockism/ (accessed July 10, 2009).

Wong, Deborah Anne. 2004. *Speak It Louder: Asian Americans Making Music.* New York: Routledge.

Wong, Deborah, and Mai Elliot. 1994. "'I Want the Microphone': Mass Mediation and Agency in Asian-American Popular Music." *The Drama Review* 38 (3): 152–167.

Wood, Neal. 1967. "Machiavelli's Concept of Virtù Reconsidered." *Political Studies* 15: 159–172.

Wu, Frank H. 2002. *Yellow: Race in America beyond Black and White.* New York: Basic Books.

Wu, Nina. 2003. "Hawaii Lures Viewers to Spend 'Idol' Time Here." *Pacific Business News.* October 3.http://pacific.bizjournals.com/pacific/stories/2003/10/06/story 4.html (accessed June 26, 2004).

———. 2004. "'American Idol' Brought Hawaii Dollars and Exposure." *Pacific Business News.* May 28. http://pacific.bizjournals.com/pacific/stories/2003/10/06 /story4.html (accessed June 26, 2004).

Wyatt, Edward. 2007. "Howard Stern Tries to Kill 'American Idol' with Kindness for a Weak Link." *New York Times.* March 31. www.nytimes.com/2007/03/31 /arts/television/31idol.html?scp=1&sq=Howard%20Stern%20Tries%20to%20 Kill%20%27American%20Idol%27%20with%20Kindness%20for%20a%20 Weak%20Link&st=cse (accessed April 29, 2007).

———. 2009. "'Idol' Group Numbers: Not So Live After All." *New York Times.* March 25. www.nytimes.com/2009/03/26/arts/television/26idol.html?_r=2 (accessed July 23, 2009).

Yano, Christine R. 2005. "Covering Disclosures: Practices of Intimacy, Hierarchy, and Authenticity in a Japanese Popular Music Genre." *Popular Music and Society* 28 (2): 193–205.

Zeitchik, Steven, and Nicole Laporte. 2006. "The Money Tree: Everyone Seems to Be Joining the 'Idol' Rich." Variety.com. May 7. www.variety.com/article /VR1117942693.html?categoryid=14&cs=1&query=The+Money+Tree%3A+Ever yone+Seems+to+Be+Joining+the+%27Idol%27+Rich (accessed March 19, 2007).

INDEX

Abdul, Paula, 6, 58, 80, 95, 166, 186–87
Academy Awards, 117–18
Aerosmith, 168–69
Afghan Star, 211, 218
African American identity, 63–64, 74–75, 76, 78–79, 129, 155
Aguilera, Christina, 72, 73, 123
Aiken, Clay (contestant), 19–20, 23, 45, 75, 108, 125, 131
Allen, Christopher (fan), 166
Allen, Kris (winner, Season 8), 1, 18, 46, 57, 165
amateurism vs. professionalism, 28–30, 61
"America" as character, 37
American Dream, 15–17, 22, 29, 33, 50, 98, 102, 112; celebration of failure in, 86–87, 89, 95–96, 100; community vs. individualism in, 102, 107–108, 121–22, 144–45; fame as, 118, 122, 143–44; global spread of, 209–211, 215; Hollywood as symbol of, 134–38, 145–47; immigrant experience as, 83–86, 93, 95, 100, 121, 135–36; Jewishness as, 187; as journey, 134–35, 138, 141–42, 148, 183; materialism in, 110–11, 113, 143–44; narratives of, 82–83; and race, 34, 93, 129, 182, 183; and religion, 129; spatial dimension of, 134–38

American identity, 1–4, 7, 9–10, 43, 82–83, 112, 138, 190–91, 218–19; multiculturalism in, 33–34, 136, 139–40; regionalism in, 139, 150–51; in rock music, 52–53. See also *American Idol,* identity formation in

American Idol: advertising revenues of, 7, 28, 230n16; audience demographics, 2, 33–34, 42, 59–60, 160, 179–80; audition process, 4–5, 11–12, 12, 24, 28, 31–32, 35–36, 87, 95, 97–99, 119–120, 119, 135, 143, 145–46, 230nn7–8; award nominations received by, 22, 60, 109, 231n7; backup musicians on, 59, 61, 131–32, 163; charity work of, 105–106, 201–202, 204–206, 231n7, 257n16, 258n28; dancing on, 47, 88, 94–95, 127–28; democratization through, 209–215; as family entertainment, 39, 47, 60, 109–110, 129, 164–65, 171; format of, 4–10, 22–23, 25–26; gender in, 5, 79–80, 144, 153–54, 155; guest stars on, 6, 57, 58–59, 163, 174, 180–81, 202, 238n15, 255n61; identity formation in, 1–4, 17–18, 43–44, 47–48, 159, 177, 190–91, 218–19; interactivity of, 15, 35–37, 40–41, 42–43; intertextuality of, 10–11, 35, 37–41, 44; judges on, 5–6, 33, 42–43, 51–52, 57, 63, 95, 98, 193, 194, 196–97, 219 (*see also*

Photo by Christine Hollinger.

Katherine Meizel is Visiting Assistant Professor at the Oberlin Conservatory of Music. She earned her Ph.D. in ethnomusicology at the University of California, Santa Barbara, where she also completed a doctoral degree in vocal performance. In addition to popular music, her research has included religion and politics, the voice and identity, and Sephardic Jewish music.